GEORGE WASHINGTON AND THE FRENCH REVOLUTION

GEORGE WASHINGTON
& *THE* FRENCH REVOLUTION

LOUIS MARTIN SEARS

WAYNE STATE UNIVERSITY PRESS

DETROIT   1960

Grateful acknowledgment is made to the
Ford Foundation for financial assistance
in the publication of this volume.

This book is dedicated

to three great Presidents

of Purdue University

under whom it was

the author's privilege

to serve from

1920 to 1956:

WINTHROP ELLSWORTH STONE

EDWARD CHARLES ELLIOTT

FREDERICK LAWSON HOVDE

PREFATORY NOTE

George Washington's reaction to the French Revolution is a test extraordinary of his loyalty to revolutionary principles, and thus to his own place in history. Recognizing the obvious connection between the two great revolutions, American and French, would the hero of the former appreciate the essential soundness of the latter, or would he be misled by his emotions, by natural grief for friends among the classes chiefly suffering at the Revolution's hands, into criticism of its acts and mistrust as to its purposes? The peak of Washington's career coincided with the most startling climaxes of a revolution which was the outgrowth in some measure of his own earlier deeds. What would be his responsibility, then, and his action as the head of a new nation toward violent revolution in the country of our late ally? A practical problem, this, of extreme interest, for the French Revolution tested both Washington's theory and practice, and his reaction thereto as political thinker and as statesman constituted an important element in the diplomatic history of the United States.

An inquiry into Washington's reaction to the tremendous scenes being enacted overseas must needs ascertain both the content and the spirit of such reports as came to him and helped to shape his thinking. It carries one naturally to reports from France still reposing in Washington's files, and from thence to other letters and collections which with varying degrees of likelihood came to Washington's attention, including the reports of American agents to the Department of State, and letters in the personal files of Thomas Jefferson, William Short, Gouverneur Morris, and James Monroe.

An inquiry of this sort, proceeding from papers actually directed to George Washington and from others which only possibly he saw easily might wander far afield. The present study had Washington alone in mind, his thinking on the Revolution and at times his action, together with the information which helped to shape that thought and action. At the same time it has seemed advisable to precede each chapter with a summary of what was actually happening in France, whether Washington was informed immediately, long afterward, or possibly not at all. These unpretentious summaries are no more than extended prefaces, so that Washington's reactions may be seen in a clearer perspective; for it is Washington alone who gives our inquiry its purpose. And to Washington himself events were of necessity chronological.

A profession of faith may be in order at this point. Why is the text so strictly chronological and why does it seem to alternate between issues of profound significance and others that are relatively inconsequential? The reply must be that this is life, that life itself is cyclical. Ophthalmologists maintain that even vision comes in waves; otolaryngologists contend the same for sound. The simple pendulum acknowledges that principle. Life is not spent eternally on uplands, tablelands, and high plateaus. The French Revolution itself was a series of alternating currents. Part of Washington's own greatness was his response to natural law.

There are obvious advantages in the topical approach to historical studies. It presents a unity not otherwise obtainable and thereby clarifies and simplifies interpretation. Once the ingredients are assembled, it is easier to write, and for one who likes the encyclopedic method of acquiring information, it is easier to read. Nevertheless it is not life, and therefore in a larger sense it is not history either, for life does not pour in upon us in these nicely docketed and tabulated units. It sweeps along in that vast fourth dimension, Time, and whether we bear readily or not with its dualisms and its multiplicities, we must needs reckon with it, now as a trickling brook moving through unexciting meadows, and then again as a tearing avalanche, but above all never as a unified experience.

So it is with the present study. One could envision an inquiry into Washington's reaction to each of several aspects of the Revolution, all neatly analyzed and separated. But such emphatically was not the way that mighty movement bore in upon his senses. He lived his life, performed his many duties as the first citizen of a new nation, and heard only incidentally, though no doubt often, of movements overseas. He formed his opinions as occasion or necessity arose and developed his philosophy of the French Revolution just as he developed his philosophy of life itself, from the impact of continuous experience, rather than from spasmodic inquiries into dramatic episodes.

In short, to understand George Washington's reaction to the French Revolution, we must credit him with having actually lived in a world that conveyed to him its meaning in much the same fashion that our world today bears in upon the consciousness of those who breathe its air. Hence the frankly chronological development of the present study seems inevitable.

The work owes much to the helpfulness of friends still living and of others gone before. The late Dr. Herbert Putnam, for forty years Librarian of Congress, was ultimately responsible for the constant courtesies to scholars for which his staff was and still is widely noted. To his Chief Assistant Librarian, Martin A. Roberts, also deceased, and to David J. H. Cole, also of the Library of Congress, I owe a special acknowledgment. At the Division of Manuscripts the late Dr. J. Franklin Jameson and his co-workers were generous with time and thought. At the Department of State and subsequently at the Archives of the United States, the late Mrs. Natalia Summers accorded me the benefit, as she has done so many others, of her extraordinary knowledge of the documents. Also her associates, notably Dr. Carl Lokke and Mrs. Kieran Carroll, have been truly helpful. To my former student and research assistant, Mr. John A. Alexander, now of the Indianapolis Bar, I am indebted for the most intelligent cooperation. For recent assistance in checking bibliography, I should thank Mr. Mark A. Lillis, presently of the Library of Congress. To my immediate colleagues, Professor James A. Huston and Professor Charles B. Murphy, I am gratefully indebted for the most helpful criticism. They were especially insistent that a sketch of the French Revolution should precede or at least accompany an inquiry into Washington's more personal reactions. Also to Professor John Moriarty and his staff in the Purdue University Library I am obligated for many courtesies.

Likewise grave injustice would be done did I not mention Dr. Charles Callan Tansill, friend for more than forty years, who in my judgment is the ablest living writer in the field of American diplomatic history and whose brilliance is a constant stimulus and inspiration.

Also, to the Wayne State University Press I am grateful for the gracious yet meticulous editing by Mrs. Georgiana W. Strickland, and her chief, Dr. Harold A. Basilius.

In acknowledgments of this kind, one is tempted to catalogue one's friends; for a chance remark may sometimes lead to unexpected repercussions and to a cerebration unanticipated. To numerous benefactors, no less real because anonymous, I pay my meed of homage.

LOUIS MARTIN SEARS

September 1, 1959

CONTENTS

INTRODUCTION

In a remarkable study entitled *Marie-Antoinette et Fersen,*
Henry Vallotton assembles three quotations from sources most
diverse: "Where no one commands, everyone is master, everyone is slave." (Bossuet) "From the moment that the spirit addresses itself to a goal which seems to be the most desirable, it
is necessary to achieve it. Nothing is more dangerous than feebleness, of whatsoever nature it may be." (Louis XIV, in 1679.)
"No, no! No violence! No blood!" (Louis XVI, to the Vicomte
de Narbonne, October 5, 1789.)[1]

It would be difficult to reduce the French Revolution to a
briefer compass. The great Bishop saw the danger of anarchy;
the great King put firmness first; the weakling was so fearful of
a blood bath that he exposed himself, his family and thousands
of his most loyal adherents to the horrors of civil war, at the end
of which order was finally restored only by the man on horseback.

1

"After us the deluge" was credited to Louis XV; it was the *bon mot* of a weak but clever man. Even as the Foreign Secretary, Choiseul, predicted the American Revolution to the King, the King equally predicted the French Revolution to Choiseul. Indeed, as early as May 1750, a riot in Paris was accompanied by threats of a march on Versailles and the burning of the Château. Everywhere there was discontent and the talk of revolution proceeding from riot to revolt to the overthrow of the régime. Tension was heightened and the treasury was further embarrassed by the disasters of the Seven Years' War and the Austrian alliance. By 1764, Voltaire considered revolution inevitable, destined to break out at the first opportunity.[2] But while the old King lived the opportunity was deferred. It must await his weak and inexperienced grandson.

PART I

From the moment that the spirit addresses itself to a goal which seems to be the most desirable, it is necessary to achieve it. Nothing is more dangerous than feebleness, of whatsoever nature it may be.
—Louis XIV

CHAPTER
ONE

1787

The French Revolution, one of the mightiest movements of all time, influenced the entire civilized world. Its repercussions were and are endless. Unlike the Civil War in England and the American Revolution, which were primarily political whatever their constitutional, legal, social, and even religious consequences may have been, the French Revolution, though it included all these consequences, was aimed at the complete overthrow of a way of life. And the more completely a contemporary movement strives to do the same, the more likely it is to express the ideas, the feelings, and the passions of the French Revolution. Thus the dominance of the Roman Catholic Church in Mexico, the existence of capitalism in the Free World along with lingering traces of colonialism, the survival until recently of monarchy in central Europe and of absolutism in Russia, each in its way represented or still represents, however greatly modified, a way

5

of life. To overthrow them is the very essence of revolution in the present century. The recent revolution in Spain is sometimes spoken of as the belated arrival of the French Revolution south of the Pyrenees.

Hence Marxian Socialism—the most revolutionary force in the world today—is the aspect of modern life which provides the best analogy for the revolutionary process in itself and in its influence on neighboring countries.

The reactions of the modern world to Communism divide perforce into approval, sometimes fanatic and extreme, and disapproval which knows virtually no limits. In this dichotomy they provide a clue to British feeling toward the French Revolution, which among certain persons and classes aroused enthusiasm, while among others it aroused only horror and disgust. Edmund Burke combined the two. His first reaction was approval. But as he came to know more fully the horrors unleashed by revolution, approval gave way to detestation.

America's reaction to the events which stirred Great Britain so profoundly was milder of necessity. Like the rest of the world America divided into elements pro- and anti-French. In party terms the Revolution separated pro-French Jeffersonian Republicans from anti-French Hamiltonian Federalists. But distances were greater, news was less immediate, and the creation of a new America was more absorbing than the more or less routine activities of European society, hitherto conventional and relatively stable. Besides, save for the most nominal traces of feudalism, such as quit-rents, Americans had little or no experience of the *ancien régime*.

Of something like four million contemporary Americans who were affected in some measure by the French Revolution, and whose own reactions influenced in some small degree that volcanic movement, Thomas Jefferson and George Washington were the most significant. Whatever concerns Jefferson's relation to both Washington and the French Revolution is enigmatic and controversial. The personal relation between the two men was somewhat equivocal. Both talked the same language, had common problems on their Virginia farms, and had each a mighty stake in the young republic. But in Washington's first Administration, a two-party system was taking shape in which Washington was drawn to one party, while Jefferson embraced the other. Even so, when Hamilton and Jefferson both quit his cabinet, it is interesting to contrast the formal courtesy with which the President accepted Hamilton's resignation with the genuine warmth bestowed on Jefferson.

In his autobiography, which he dated January 6, 1821, Jefferson devoted fifty-three pages to the French Revolution, the early stages of which he witnessed personally, having succeeded Benjamin Franklin as minister to France from the American Confederation. The French Revolution at its best was his abiding recollection. It is much as if a beholder of Tsar Nicholas in overthrow and the rise of Alexandre Kerensky and Prince Lvov were to form an impression of the Russian Revolution not to be eradicated by the starvation, oppression and forced labor camps resorted to by their successors. One of the happiest evenings in Jefferson's long life was spent in the company of Lafayette and a group of intellectuals and liberals who hung spellbound upon the oracular wisdom of the Framer of the Declaration of Independence and the Elder Brother in Liberty. Such adulation was intoxicating and Jefferson refused to surrender these glowing memories to mere facts as related to him by his successor at the Paris mission, even though that successor might be William Short, who was probably as dear to Jefferson as was Lafayette to Washington. Only the vast ineptitude of Citizen Genêt was able to wean Jefferson partially away from the Revolution he admired. For not only was Jefferson a revolutionary by nature, but he had observed personally the abuses, the chaos, the systematic anarchy which the Revolution strove originally to correct.[1]

With Washington the case was otherwise. He was not a cosmopolite, the brief excursion in his youth as companion to his brother Lawrence scarcely qualifying him as such. A country gentleman of considerable wealth, he had led his fellow citizens in a war against exploitation by a distant power. But an upheaval aimed at overthrowing a society in which by birth, marriage, and association he occupied a privileged position was farthest from his thoughts. Assuredly he was no Tom Paine to be the author of *Common Sense,* nor was the Declaration of Independence his

7

type of composition. His interest in France and her revolution
derived first from those Frenchmen whom he knew, Lafayette,
Rochambeau, and many others; secondly from the fact that his
position as Chief of State coincided with the outbreak of the
Revolution, which thus necessarily became a factor in the diplomacy he was called upon to guide.

A third but probably quite minor influence on Washington
may have been his correspondence along agricultural lines with
Arthur Young, the famous traveller who toured France extensively in 1787 with not the slightest suspicion of the impending
crisis. Also, one may not dismiss entirely Washington's presidency of the Order of the Cincinnati, in which a number of
Frenchmen held membership because of their one-time commissions in the American army.

It is possible to exaggerate the interrelationship of the two
revolutions, American and French. The idea, for example, that
the French encyclopedists and other revolutionary thinkers like
Rousseau, Voltaire, or even Montesquieu greatly influenced
American opinion has been weakened by the revelation that few
of their works were to be found in American libraries. That
they paved the way for revolution in their native land is generally admitted. They removed the intellectual props from an
outmoded social system.

For American influence on France a better case can be presented. French soldiers of fortune could describe on their return
an America in no way subject to feudal dues, taille, gabelle,
tithes, *vingtièmes,* beds of justice or a monarch's arbitrary will.
The story of America was being pretty widely told. More dramatic was the furor created by the unique Franklin—a genius in
homespun, very thrilling to the ladies from duchesses to servant
girls, and the intellectual peer of any man in France. Lafayette,
too, a Frenchman and at the same time by act of Congress an
American, was no mean interpreter to his French countrymen of
his beloved America and his friend and patron Washington.

Unquestionably the richest friendship that George Washington ever enjoyed was with Marie Joseph Paul Yves Roch Gilbert
Motier, Marquis de Lafayette. There was less than sixteen years
difference in their ages, but Lafayette, who lost his own father

at the battle of Minden when he was not quite two, revered Washington as a father, while Washington regarded him as virtually a son. Theirs was the added bond of dangers met and battles shared. Lafayette fought at Brandywine, commanded a division in Virginia, distinguished himself at Monmouth, was instrumental in dispatching Rochambeau's army to America, and participated actively at Yorktown. But it is his subsequent career that interests us here, and that no further than the death of Washington in 1799, although Lafayette survived till 1834—a hero in both his own and his adopted countries.

The great American and the not quite so great Frenchman were in fairly frequent correspondence during the interval between the revolutions. Experience in America and devotion to George Washington naturally stimulated Lafayette's interest in revolution nearer home. There is little doubt that Lafayette hoped to be the George Washington of the French Revolution. He was a leader in its early stages, and from his summons to the Assembly of the Notables in 1787 until his flight from France in 1792, he was a considerable figure in the French Revolution. The American was sure to sympathize with the aspirations of the younger man.

For our present purposes it may be clarifying to outline events in France preceding the Revolution so that Washington's not too frequent comments may have a better reference. To this end it is appropriate to trace the close connection between France and the American Revolution, with a glance at how and why an absolute monarchy was induced to aid distant colonials in their revolt against a lawful ruler. That would take us to the French and Indian War, in which Washington played a most conspicuous role.

The progress of the American Revolution had been followed attentively by a France humiliated by the Peace of Paris in 1763, which surrendered French North America to England. When Britain's troubles with her overseas possessions culminated in the war which the Duc de Choiseul had predicted a dozen years earlier in an attempt to console Louis XV for these enormous losses, authorities in France felt that a unique opportunity was presented to restore national and, what was more important to the King, dynastic prestige. But interference would be dangerous until the Americans should demonstrate a genuine will to win. This they did at Saratoga, which thereby became one of the world's decisive battles.

Between Saratoga in October 1777, and the Franco-American alliance of February 1778, two forces struggled for Louis XVI's decision. Vergennes, the diplomat, favored war; Turgot, the economist, beheld in it the final road to bankruptcy and to consequences too horrible to contemplate. The King had some comprehension of diplomacy, almost none of economics. Diplomacy therefore triumphed, and the American Revolution was saved by French arms and gold.

Both counsellors were right. The sun of monarchy set in unexampled splendor. Bankruptcy precipitated revolution.

American chronology at times presents interesting parallels with European. Thus in 1787, while the Constitutional Convention was assembling at Philadelphia to fashion a new government, the King of France, already sensing in some measure the fulfillment of Turgot's dire predictions and the end of a régime, was convoking an Assembly of the Notables. This was far from equivalent to a meeting of the States General, which had received no royal summons since 1614, but it was an admission that France no longer could be governed by traditional administrative processes. Somehow the finances must be extricated from their terrible dilemma.

The history of this financial crisis is of considerable interest. Jacques Necker, a Genevese banker, had become in October 1776, Controller General of the Royal Treasury, and on June 29, 1777, Director General of Finances, in the expectation that the reforms instituted by Turgot and dissipated by his successor would be restored. Toward such a policy, Necker, who had made an immense fortune in the field of banking, made serious endeavors, but was thwarted by an enormous deficit, and was compelled to additional loans. These were initially successful. To relieve the economic situation, he promoted political reforms with a view to reducing waste and improving the entire economy. He even issued a *Compte Rendu,* or treasurer's report, which became a talisman to a nation wholly unaccustomed to self-government. One might call it a constitutional landmark to concede that the people had some right to understand the national finances. By placing in a separate account expenditures which were incurred for the war in America, which Necker equally with Turgot opposed, the minister contrived to show a modest surplus in the budget. But vested interests, disturbed by these economies and operating on an ignorant King and a frivolous Queen, procured his dismissal on May 19, 1781. Nevertheless, in this preliminary ministry Necker won a deserved popularity.

Necker, freed now from ministerial cares, and from domestic ones also, for he had long since entrusted to his brilliant and loving wife [2] his very large estate along with the paying of all bills, devoted almost four years to a major work in three octavo volumes entitled *De l'Administration des Finances de la France*, published in 1784.

Meanwhile in the French treasury, after Necker, as previously after Turgot, economy was replaced by wild extravagance and gross maladministration. A consequent increase in taxes was imposed by royal will through the instrumentality of incompetent ministers. This orgy culminated in the administration of Charles Alexandre de Calonne, who acted on the supposition that all the credit needed by a bankrupt could be obtained by prodigality. A financial wizard, Calonne seemed able to evoke fresh loans as with a magic wand. He is best remembered as the advocate of waste, extravagance, and splendor as a means to dazzle or wheedle creditors. When these failed, it was Calonne himself, now desperate for funds, who induced the King to call an Assembly of the Notables for February 22, 1787, to extricate the country from its plight.

It can be argued that the French Revolution dated from the King's decision on December 27, 1788, following a disastrous report by Necker, once again the Controller General of Finances, to summon the States General. However, for an inquiry into George Washington's awareness of the movement, it seems preferable to date the Revolution from the Assembly of the Notables in 1787. Certainly the Assembly carried strong overtones of revolution. From Washington's first knowledge of the

Assembly even to his death, his interest in the movement never flagged, though the degree of his approval varied considerably.

To most observers, France in 1787 seemed in stable equilibrium. The argument of Vergennes which had induced Louis XVI to participate in the American War for Independence had been vindicated amply. The Bourbon monarchy had recovered gloriously the prestige it had lost so ingloriously in the Peace of 1763 when Canada and India became the prize of England. Turgot's counter warnings, that war would upset the tottering treasury and bankruptcy would usher in complete disaster, had not as yet been verified. True, an economist might worry over rising deficits, but a glittering court [3] could survey growing prosperity among the industrial and commercial classes and delude itself that all was well. Even wise men might agree. Arthur Young, for example, traversed the length and breadth of France in 1787 and found no hint of an approaching revolution. World famed as an agronomist he could hardly miss the ground swells of agrarian sentiment, but discontent he failed to find. Nor did Adam Smith find it some years before when, as tutor to the young Duke of Buccleuch and Hew Campbell Scott, his brother, he had enjoyed distinguished opportunities to observe conflicting trends.

If further evidence of stability were needed, what better testimony than the willingness of Benjamin Franklin to leave a France that loved him even as he loved the Parisiennes of his accustomed Passy and the gay lords and ladies at Versailles, to participate in the convention at Philadelphia for drafting his country's Federal Constitution. Franklin in 1787 no more realized that Paris would almost immediately be the focal point of the most epochal revolution in all history than had he in 1765, while representing the Colony of Pennsylvania in England, anticipated the furor which the Stamp Act would shortly arouse throughout the American colonies. Had Franklin perceived approaching revolution even dimly he would have retained his box seat at one of the most exciting spectacles of all time.

If these close observers of the contemporary picture saw through a glass so darkly, what must have been Washington's tranquillity toward the European scene? Ever since the An-

12

napolis Convention of 1785, which had been engineered largely by himself and Alexander Hamilton, Washington's attention had been focused mainly on the approaching convention at Philadelphia, subject to minor consideration of his duty to the Order of the Cincinnati which would assemble simultaneously. It is safe to assume that, save for a genuine and fraternal interest in his recent brothers in arms, and possibly for some concern about the fate of his tobacco at the hands of farmers general collecting the King's revenue, Washington's interest in French politics and economics was something less than keen. But from the time the Revolution actually commenced, Washington was to become *au courant* in high degree with the unfolding chapter of events. To assess his attitudes intelligently one must consider not merely his acts and utterances but the influences which bore upon his thinking. As the hero of the American War for Independence he enjoyed an eminence that commanded information from sources numerous and diverse.

Among his principal informants as the great drama overseas unfolded were Thomas Jefferson; William Short, Jefferson's protégé and successor in the Paris mission; Gouverneur Morris, who in turn succeeded Short; and in the later phases of the Revolution, James Monroe, a less fortunate choice as correspondent and informant. Others to enlighten him at various stages as the Revolution progressed were Sir Edward Newenham,[4] representative in Parliament for the County of Dublin; Mrs. Catharine Macaulay Graham,[5] sister of a Lord Mayor of London and herself distinguished as a historian; and from France, Lafayette, of course, pre-eminently; Rochambeau; the Comte de Moustier, minister to the United States when Washington took office; the Marquis de la Rouërie; the Chevalier (later Marquis) de La Luzerne; and various others.

Considering that Washington's chief informant, Gouverneur Morris, is rated by the French historian Taine as one of the four most keen observers the Revolution bred, and that a more recent French historian, A. Esmein, accounts him with Mallet du Pan as one of the first two,[6] it must be admitted that Washington was well served in this department certainly. A calm, judicious mind, fed by incontestable facts, formed intelligent opinions.

That in brief was Washington's reaction to the French Revolution.

Letters addressed to Washington or intended for his eye were not his only source of information, for he constantly received newspapers and pamphlets no longer in his files. As the movement gained momentum, the amount of information sent directly or immediately accessible to Washington was very great. In the opening stages its volume was much smaller. But from the first his information was extensive and authoritative.

Appropriately enough, what was probably the first information to reach Washington of the approaching crisis was a communication from his friend and protégé, the still youthful Marquis de Lafayette. From Paris, on January 13, 1787, the Marquis reported that an Assembly of the Notables had been summoned for the end of the month. It would consist of 144 members, among them archbishops, bishops, nobles, presidents of parliaments, and mayors of towns. Lafayette believed that Washington's only acquaintances in the body were old associates of American Revolutionary days, the Comte d'Estaing, the Duc de Laval, and himself. The chief agenda for the session were to be finances and the reformation of abuses. The end in view was a balanced budget; the means employed were admirable, much credit being due the King and his minister, Calonne. Lafayette hoped it might lead to popular assemblies in the provinces, to the elimination of commercial barriers, to an improvement in the condition of the Protestants, subjects which had long engaged his sympathetic efforts. He mentioned, without offering any explanation—apparently he knew of none—that his name was included on the first list for the Notables, was omitted from the second, and subsequently restored. Politics was at work, with obvious cross-currents. The Marquis promised to keep Washington informed of the Assembly's labors, "not only because nothing that concerns me can be foreign to my general, but also because everything is interesting which affects the well being of twenty-six millions of people." [7]

It is somewhat surprising that Lafayette here spoke so favorably of Calonne. Perhaps this is an advance indication of the poor judgment which was to deprive Lafayette of the leadership

14

he coveted so eagerly in emulation of his great friend Washington. For Calonne was the very embodiment of those unsound fiscal policies which brought the monarchy to ruin. It must be conceded, however, that Lafayette's estimate of Calonne was soon to change.

Three weeks later Lafayette pursued his theme with news that illness of three of the King's ministers was delaying the convocation of the Notables, but reaffirmed his hopes for good results when the Assembly should finally convene. He anticipated the emergence of a sort of House of Representatives in each of the provinces, with power to collect taxes, even if not to assess them, and a sensible reduction in local tariff barriers. The issue of the Protestants would, he thought, probably not be submitted to the Notables after all, due to the reclamations of the clergy and of a bigoted faction. Nothing need prevent the King from settling the issue personally, which would furnish one example of how the benefits of power can offset its inconveniences.[8]

A further communication from Lafayette brought the sequence of events to May 5. Altogether it was the most elaborate account that Washington received of the Assembly of the Notables. It deserves minute analysis.

Lafayette declared that he had been and was too busy to write with the fullness he wished. But Versailles presented an interesting spectacle. Dark secrets were becoming known. Under the present King the expenses of the government had increased by two hundred million francs per annum. The Treasury was now facing such a deficit that Calonne, not knowing how to meet it, persuaded the King to summon the notables of each of the three orders, conceding to them the strongly desired provincial assemblies as a means of obtaining their approval of new taxes, which the government would not otherwise have dared impose. When the Assembly convened, its membership was found to represent a higher civic level than Calonne apparently had at first intended.

Tracing the work of the Assembly to date, Lafayette found that Calonne's project for the provincial assemblies had been amended; his tax schemes had been rejected; a similar fate had overtaken several other plans. Admitting that the Assembly pos-

15

sessed no authority to restrain the Government, it had at least a right to approve only such measures as seemed good. New taxes could not be considered save in the light of a budget of expenses and a list of the reforms projected. The better the finances were understood, Lafayette declared, the more complete appeared the ministry's dependency on the Assembly. Its dissolution would spell collapse of credit.

At the approach of the Easter adjournment, Lafayette demanded an investigation into the millions which had been squandered on the princes and the favorites. His motion was seconded by the Bishop of Langres. To intimidate such troublemakers, the King's brother, the Comte d'Artois, asserted that such proposals should be signed. Whereupon Lafayette did sign. Calonne then demanded that Lafayette be imprisoned in the Bastille. Anticipating a major battle of words at the next session, Lafayette assembled his proofs. But Calonne, by abandoning his portfolio, terminated the controversy. From this tilt with authority, Lafayette believed he had won as much credit with the nation as he had lost at court.

Fifteen days after Calonne's resignation, Loménie de Brienne, Archbishop of Toulouse, became chief minister. His character and attainments met Lafayette's approval. Here again approval was destined to be temporary.

Continuing his account Lafayette declared that the provincial assemblies were to have no power to vote but only to apportion taxes. The King would reduce his expenses by forty million francs per annum, with more publicity in administration. But new taxes and fresh loans must ultimately be approved. Ample room, here, for self-congratulation.

Delicately enough at this point, Lafayette informed his friend and mentor that while the credit of the United States was good with respect to the capital sum of debts held abroad, the uncertainty of interest payments was much decried.[9]

From another old comrade in arms, the Comte de Rochambeau,† Washington was now to receive a slightly different slant on things. The Count was writing from Paris on the twelfth of

† A brief account of his background and subsequent career appears in the Biographical Appendix.

May, 1787. His was the viewpoint of a warrior, an aristocrat, and a liberal, a combination not altogether usual:

> We are here in a terrible crisis of finances which has occasioned an assembly of chief men that last yet. You heard speak of the ministry of M. Necker and of the flourishing *etat* where he had left our finances, a devil of fool, named *Calonne* minister of finances since four years, has believed to be bound to take contrary sense of his predecessor, and has made succeed to an oeconomical administration, a prodigality and a devastation which has no example—being at the end of last year without means, he has imagined an assembly of the chief men in which discovering, in his quality of quack, a part of the wound, he did propose all the remedies of an Empiric. The assembly of chief men at last has unmasked him to our Virtuous King that he had the skill to deceive as well as a part of his council. He has been latily dismissed, and his office is given to the archbishop of Toulouse, the knowledge, probity, order and talents of which give the greatest hopes to the nation. You know enough my-caracter to think that it would not sympathize with that of M. de Calonne, and consequently he did not put me in that assembly, that I have been very glad of. He had also forgot the Marquis de La Fayette. I should have desired he had taken the same course, but his ardour did not permit him to be quiet. We are still in the middle of this crisis which tends to its end.[10]

The end of the Assembly of the Notables arrived early in August, when with some perspective the Marquis assured Washington that it had been a splendid thing for everyone save those who called it into being. Lafayette had benefited personally by his controversy with Calonne. Not in favor with the court as such, he was nevertheless on good terms with the first minister. The Parliament of Paris, though stoutly resisting new taxes, would be compelled to register them, but would probably demand a National Assembly as a logical outgrowth of the provincial assemblies already in process of creation. Prospects for the Protestants likewise continued to improve.[11]

A further estimate of the Notables was contributed by Thomas Jefferson, American minister in Paris. The author of the Declaration of Independence could not fail to sympathize with what seemed at first the happy and well ordered movement of a great nation bent on liberty. The Assembly, he wrote, had accomplished much good. A true reform was under way. Economies were contemplated, though certain fresh extravagances were creating further discontent. This in turn would probably result in a calling of the States General for the first time since 1614. Parliament opposed the King on the registering of fresh taxes. A new ministry augured further improvement.[12]

Jefferson's enthusiasm was only natural. Himself world famous as a liberal, he was regarded by many liberals in France as their elder brother if not their patron saint. A high point in his career—one of many, to be sure—was presently to be an evening spent with Lafayette and others in academic discussion of the principles of politics under a liberalized monarchy. Next morning when the exhilaration had worn off, qualms of conscience drove him to the Foreign Office to report this infraction of diplomatic protocol. Here he was assured by the Comte de Montmorin,† His Most Christian Majesty's principal Secretary of State for Foreign Affairs, that through an intelligence agent at the gathering, the Government was cognizant of all that had been said. Jefferson, the secretary amiably added, was welcome to attend any further seances which he might choose to honor with his presence.

It would be interesting to know whether Jefferson, had he remained in France throughout the Revolution, would have been influenced by its excesses. Certainly in America he retained his faith and was much annoyed by William Short's unfavorable reports, dear though Short was to him, the same Short described by a modern author as "Jefferson's only son."

Had Washington received no other information, the citations already given—from Lafayette, the tenderest of friends; from Rochambeau, the staunch old warrior who was to survive the Terror and become a Marshal of France under Napoleon; from Thomas Jefferson, the acknowledged philosopher of revolution —these would have rendered him fully cognizant of the unfolding drama. His reaction was enthusiastic.

Lafayette was the natural recipient of this enthusiasm, and in thanking his young protégé for news of the Assembly, and more particularly of Lafayette's own protest against the financial methods of Calonne, Washington indulged in very liberal sentiments:

18

The patriotism, by which this motion was dictated, throws a lustre on the action, which cannot fail to dignify the author; and I sincerely hope with you, that much good will result from the diliberations of a respectable council. I am not less ardent in my wish, that you may succeed in your plan of toleration in religious matters. Being no bigot myself to any mode of worship, I am disposed to indulge the professors of Christianity in the church with that road to Heaven, which to them shall seem the most direct, plainest, easiest, and least liable to exception.

The politicians of this country hardly know what to make of the present situation of European affairs.[13]

There is good will toward France in this preliminary estimate of her Revolution. It expressed his attitude for years to come, although in course of time unpleasant incidents were fraught with irritation.

It was early in the Revolution that Lafayette submitted his most illuminating comments. As action grew more hurried and the Marquis was engulfed in the vortex of events, he became perforce the actor and the doer, leaving to others the weighing and recording. Then a third phase entered, that of imprisonment for Lafayette, the cutting off of correspondence at the source, and the nullifying of its importance as coming from a prisoner, the pawn rather than the instigator of great events. Fortunately Lafayette preserved copies of these letters, as the present files of Washington do not contain them.

From Paris on October 9, 1787, the Marquis wrote to Washington in a vein of some discouragement. Not all went to his liking. Affairs were indecisive. The deficit called for taxes which the nation needs must pay without having voted on them. He perceived in French developments a swift consequence of the American Revolution. The Assembly of the Notables had failed to combat the parliaments, which, as mere courts of justice charged only with registering edicts, did not wish to sanction any tax not accepted by the nation. Exile had been meted out to some of their members. A battle of pamphlets was in progress. The Comte d'Artois had been hooted by the populace while executing the orders of his brother, the King, and certain ministers had been burned in effigy. Very foolishly the parliament had consented to an inequitable arrangement, namely, the with-

19

drawal of the two proposed new taxes in return for registering an increase in taxes already existing.

The provincial assemblies had had their preliminary sessions. They were at first required to submit in all respects to the two royal intendants in each province, a provision from which, upon active protest, the King receded. Popular discontent had grown so great that the Queen no longer dared come to Paris for fear of insult. Only a national assembly could now impose a tax.

Next Lafayette launched into a description of his country's politics and morals. The King, he informed Washington, was all powerful. He possessed every means to restrain, to punish, to corrupt. The ministers were drawn alike by disposition and by a sense of duty to preserve despotic institutions. The court was filled with despicable swarms and effeminate courtiers; spirits were enervated by the influence of women and by the love of pleasure. The lower classes were steeped in ignorance. On the other hand, the genius of France was lively, enterprising, and inclined to despise the men who governed. Enlightenment was spread by the writings of philosophers and the example of other nations. Frenchmen were readily motivated by a fine sense of honor, and if they were slaves, they were not precisely willing slaves. The awakened citizens of the provinces were disgusted with despotism and the expenses of the court, with the extraordinary contrast between the Oriental power of the monarch, the care of ministers to preserve it undiminished, and the intrigues and servility of the courtiers on the one hand, and on the other hand the general freedom to think, to speak, to write, notwithstanding the spies of the Bastille and the regulations of the censor.

Other contrasts which Lafayette portrayed were the rising patriotism in the first class of the nation, including the personal servitors of the King, coupled with the fear of losing place and pension; the mocking insolence of townspeople ever ready to flee before the guards; the more serious discontent in country districts; ingredients all of them in a movement toward a general convulsion and the curtailment of royal authority, something which would take time and would encounter opposition from the powerful and privileged.

Great changes, none the less, had been wrought already. The prime minister was honest and enlightened. Granting he had made some mistakes, his talents were distinguished. The political situation held him back. With times more calm he would do great things. The Maréchals de Castries † and Ségur † were no longer ministers, but the former was frequently consulted. Washington would recollect Lafayette's intimate connection with him. The two new ministers were the Comte de Brienne, brother of the Archbishop, for War; and the Comte de La Luzerne, brother of the Chevalier, for the Marine. Luzerne was believed friendly to the interests of Americans. M. de Malesherbes, another whom Washington would remember as a friend of Lafayette, had been recalled to the Council. Taking it all in all, this new administration was made up of honest men, some of them possessing distinguished merit. It was important to have a competent minister who acted for the King. Lafayette wished there were among them some men experienced in war, because it was to be feared that war might come soon.

From the general, Lafayette turned to the particular with a narrative of his more personal experiences to date. He offered no apology for these personalities, fully assured of Washington's strong interest in all that pertained to him. When the sessions of the Notables were terminated, he had turned his attention to the provincial assembly of Auvergne, whose mechanics and politics he described in somewhat tedious detail, but with a natural pride in his own participation and in his local as well as national popularity.

Lafayette conveyed a hint that he was still as in America the soldier of fortune. Indeed, he had been almost on the point of entering the service of Catherine of Russia when the economic crisis and the summons to the Notables detained him on his native soil. More recently a project had been taking shape to enlist him in the service of the United Netherlands, with initial command over 20,000 men and probably more later. The project interested Lafayette. It had, moreover, the sanction of the Maréchal de Castries. Nevertheless, with matters assuming this favorable direction, the Rhinegrave of Salm and the French minister at The Hague had halted the transaction on the score that

21

it would displease the Court of France. The Hollanders now were saying that they had been deceived in this affair as in other instances by the Rhinegrave.

Learning that the Comte de Moustier was sailing for America to assume his duties as French minister to the United States, Lafayette entrusted this lengthy epistle to his hands, as it was very confidential and not suited to the post, especially of his country.[14]

Here indeed was a communication worthy of the touching friendship between the two men, important for the authority with which it speaks of great events, and of interest more personal as a revelation of Lafayette's reaction to the stirring scene in which he played a part. Under Washington he had played most creditably a minor role. Would his genius embrace the present opportunity to lead the French people, even as Washington was leading the American? The tone of this revealing letter raises a doubt concerning the essential greatness of its author. Events would turn that doubt to certainty, but unfortunately in the negative.

As we have noted, Washington's reaction was enthusiastic. He believed that the Assembly of the Notables had accomplished much good. He thought that an intelligent discussion of finances would benefit both King and people. He rejoiced that discussion was so spirited, and attributed this awakened interest in politics to the Revolution in America, which had stimulated political discussion throughout Europe.

To Jefferson he declared:

> I am much obliged to you, my dear Sir, for the Acct. which you gave me of the general state of Affairs in Europe. I am glad to hear that the Assemblée des Notables has been productive of good in France. The abuse of the finances being disclosed to the King, and the nation, must open their eyes, and lead to the adoption of such measures as will prove beneficial to them in future. From the public papers it appears that the Parliaments of the several Provinces, and particularly that of Paris, have acted with great spirit and resolution. Indeed, the rights of Mankind, the priviledges of the people, and the true principles of liberty, seem to have been more generally discussed and better understood throughout Europe since the American revolution, than they were at any former period.[15]

22

Characteristic good sense was displayed in this preliminary comment on France's bid for liberty. It was January 1, 1788, and the States General, with the mighty train of events which their summons would unleash, were not yet met. Washington was setting down his personal reaction to the momentous year now past, calm enough in retrospect but pregnant for the future. In the light of his own record and of the information so far at his command, the verdict could not be other than favorable.

Far heavier tests would shortly tax Washington's judgment and capacity for weighing alien situations. These, too, he would meet with intelligent appraisal.

CHAPTER
TWO

1788

While Washington was penning his approval of the trend of French affairs on New Year's Day of 1788, in Paris his friend the Marquis de Lafayette was bringing down to date his previous relation of events. He informed Washington of his return to Paris after a rather stirring session in Auvergne. Again he displeased the King and again he pleased the people. Auvergne was one of the few provinces that did not contribute to the new taxes. It had taken its position firmly. The condition of France, meanwhile, was certainly extraordinary. There was much ferment, and at the same time much indifference and a fondness for repose. The parliaments were continually exceeding their constitutional limits, trusting to be upheld by the nation; for notwithstanding their numerous unreasonable activities, they had the political sagacity to advocate a national assembly. Perceiving a decline in the royal authority, the Government strove for its recovery, and at the same time practiced a dangerous severity based on the confidence that for the present year at least it would not lack for money.[1] Lafayette's own wish was for a bill of rights and a constitution, and that these might be accomplished as quickly as possible, in a manner calm and satisfactory to everyone.

The Marquis added some reflection on the foreign news, and then comforted his correspondent with assurance of the favorable progress of Franco-American trade negotiations. Jefferson and he had worked together toward this end, and to Jefferson he paid most generous tribute as "the happiest possible choice for minister." [2]

The Marquis must have enjoyed unusual leisure at this time, for on the following day he wrote again, informing Washington that the internal situation of the country constituted a serious problem to the Government. No breakdown was anticipated for the current year, but it was not easy to hold in check the spirit of freedom which pervaded the people, and likewise the spirit of opposition, sometimes quite unreasonable, which distinguished the local parliaments. Indeed, it was the parliaments that would be the focus of attention until the meeting of a national assembly should determine finally the rights of all. Meanwhile, the provincial assemblies were accomplishing much good and Lafayette hoped for great amelioration in the condition of France.[3]

Other news from France in these opening days of the new year was personally poignant. The death of their joint friend, the Comte de Grasse, called forth from Rochambeau an account of the event, and evoked from Washington a sympathetic answer. De Grasse had reached the peak of his career at Yorktown. Subsequent defeat in the West Indies brought upon him the displeasure of the King, and to climax his misfortunes he had married an unworthy woman. Washington and Rochambeau agreed that death was a release.[4] Washington's acknowledgment was unusually prompt, but the case called for condolence.[5]

Before this news came to him, Washington had acknowledged Rochambeau's letter of May 12, 1787, as well as one of 1786. Mostly he confined his comments to events in his own country.

26

But his single reference to French developments was more trenchant than in most of his communications to Lafayette:

> I am very glad to hear that the Assemblée des Notables has been productive of good in France; the State of your finances was really alarming and required a strict investigation and the sanative hand of the nation to restore them to their proper tone.[6]

The times were propitious for that moderate liberalism which would scarce survive the stormier days ahead, and Washington probably derived almost as much pleasure in hearing as was Lafayette's in telling that Civil Rights had been finally bestowed on "the non-Catholic subjects of the King." Washington might imagine the pleasure that recently was Lafayette's when he presented at "une table ministérielle," the first Protestant ecclesiastic to appear at Versailles since the Revocation of 1685.[7] It should be remembered incidentally that this splendid advance in religious toleration was achieved in the ministry of a Roman Catholic ecclesiastical statesman, the so-widely lauded Archbishop of Toulouse.[8]

The more radical Jefferson, whose ideas of reform went far beyond this moderate concession to Protestants, found little to extol in the achievement.[9] For Jefferson, like many another liberal then and since, was none too well aware of the power abiding in history and tradition. A better acquaintance with the past would have shown him that Lafayette was justified in stressing an accomplishment which indeed was largely his.

Lafayette established further title to esteem when more than a year before the event, he forecast a summons of the States General not later than the summer of 1789, instead of the more distant 1792 of which many had been speaking. Admitting that considerable reforms had been effected, a deficit nevertheless remained. Since the parliaments had declared themselves without power to consent to the tax and the provincial assemblies were not yet truly representative of the people, only a States General could cope with the existing situation and, upholding the rights of all, establish the administration of the country on fixed principles.

With similar prescience, Lafayette forecast that the government was preparing an attack on the parliaments. For these, be-

27

ing in their essence simple courts of justice, disliked to register any edicts for new taxes until the States General should convene.

For himself Lafayette expected an important military command. The troops were being divided into four armies, each under the command of a Marshal of France. Lafayette's father-in-law, the Duc d'Ayen, would command one of these, and the Marquis hoped to be the senior major-general under him, in charge of a division.[10] However interesting to Washington this communication may have been, it elicited no immediate reply. Affairs at home were too engrossing. The adoption of the Constitution and the planning for a new government fully occupied the mind of America's first citizen.

One of the most enlightening communications to reach Washington from France in the spring of 1788 was from Thomas Jefferson. The observing foreigner could sense the deeper currents. Jefferson may have been a trifle short on history and its meaning, but no one was more keen on current topics. On May 2 of 1788, a full year from the great days of 1789, he called attention to the fundamental changes already under way. He beheld a nation moving swiftly to a constitution. The monarchy was already limited. The States General would soon assemble and would acquire control of the purse. The structure of the permanent legislative body was still to be determined.[11]

If Jefferson here was brilliant and suggestive, Lafayette was no less analytical in his presentation of the scene as of May 25, 1788. Affairs were at a crisis, with the outcome far from certain. "To die for Liberty" was not a catchword on his side of the Atlantic. The rich liked their repose; the poor were enervated by misery and ignorance. There remained but one resource, namely, to inspire the nation to a passive resistance or disobedience which would exhaust the patience of the Government and defeat its plans. Despite their inadequacies, the parliaments had constituted themselves the advance guard of the struggle. Washington could discover by printed publications, because all of them were sent to him, that the King had set up pretensions and the courts of justice had established principles so contradictory with each other that one could scarce believe that both were the product of the same country and the same century.

Things could not remain like this. The Government had employed armed force against unarmed magistrates. All of this had made Lafayette literally ill. He had been under the care of his physicians.

Lafayette's greatest indignation had been reserved for a bed of justice at which the King created a plenary court made up of judges, peers, and courtiers, without a single genuine representative of the nation, and for the insolence of ministers who dared to say that all the taxes and loans must be registered. A gleam of hope lay in the prospect of a constitution. Magistrates had scorned to sit in the plenary court. Even the peers would disobey, thanks to the courage and sense of a small number of them. Lafayette's friend La Rochefoucauld had been a leader in this move; others had followed more at a distance. The parliaments protested against the new court and appealed to the nation. Malcontents were appearing everywhere, and in several of the provinces were not to be despised. The clergy, just now holding their assembly, were remonstrating. Lawyers refused to plead. The Government was embarrassed and was resorting to apologies. Commandants in certain towns had been stoned. Meanwhile the friends of liberty grew stronger daily, closed their ears to all negotiation, and demanded a national assembly or nothing. In this assembly Lafayette would be a member, or he would join Washington at Mt. Vernon.

Among the various phases of the struggle which Lafayette touched upon in this remarkable letter, none was more vital than this new plenary court and the defiance to the existing parliaments implied by its establishment. At the zenith of the monarchy the several parliaments, particularly the Parliament of Paris, were the sole institutions which interposed between the King and a despotism quite unlimited. Theirs was a right of protest only. This the King could override in a so-called "bed of justice," an occasion when he appeared personally before the parliament and ordered it to register his edicts. At one session of this sort, Louis XVI had appeared with whip in hand to scourge the judges, as it were, into a reluctant obedience.

It is significant that while the contest centered between the King and the parliaments or law courts, Chrétien Guillaume de

Lamoignon de Malesherbes,† friend of Lafayette, eminent jurist and one of the period's most sterling characters, resigned his cabinet portfolio in protest against the position taken by the King. Yet at his sovereign's utmost need, when Louis was on trial for his life, Malesherbes returned to duty as chief counsel for the King's defense. This splendid demonstration of integrity and courage resulted a few months later in his execution at the hands of the Revolutionary Tribunal.[12]

Continuing his very lengthy survey, Lafayette reported that he no longer favored the Archbishop of Toulouse. The more he saw of him and of the Garde des Sceaux,[13] the louder he raised his voice against their "infernal plan." This disillusionment Lafayette shared with many others, yet the minister was too complex a character to dismiss offhand. An ecclesiastic by ambition rather than profession, he had risen rapidly in the Church, though suspect to the orthodox. His election to the French Academy in 1770 was sponsored by Voltaire and d'Alembert, odd backers for a bishop. His tolerance of Protestants was to many in itself a scandal. Undoubtedly he lacked elements essential to greatness but, like most of his contemporaries, he was a victim of disjointed times.

Lafayette was happy to note a relaxing in the tariff before dissension reached its present stage. He still was laboring for commercial freedom along with Thomas Jefferson, whom he admired so greatly. He also paid high tribute to William Short, who had succeeded Jefferson as American Minister to France, and who now became one of Washington's most important sources of information on the French scene. Lafayette described him as "very competent, honorable, and agreeable." [14]

Short was a considerable figure in early American diplomacy who was somehow eclipsed by contemporaries of even greater eminence. He was graduated from William and Mary College in 1779, where three years earlier he had been one of the founders of Phi Beta Kappa and its president, 1778 to 1781. In 1783–84, he was a member of the Executive Council of Virginia. He followed his friend Jefferson to Paris. Next, at the instigation of Jefferson, John Adams and Franklin, he negotiated with the Prussian envoy at The Hague a commercial treaty between

Prussia and the United States. Returning to Paris, he became private secretary to Jefferson and later secretary of legation. Following Jefferson's return to the United States, he was made chargé d'affaires. These upward steps were aided by a rare personal charm that insured his acceptability in the highest circles. As chargé he attempted a commercial treaty with France, in which he had the support of Lafayette. He was later minister to The Hague and in 1793 joined William Carmichael in negotiations at Madrid which bore fruit in the Pinckney Treaty of 1795.[15]

It was Short's misfortune, however, that notwithstanding the fine qualities that attracted Jefferson and Lafayette, he was not personally known to Washington and at critical moments in what seemed a most promising career, he was superseded by men of no greater ability than his own at points where his retention would almost certainly have led to greater eminence. His competence was never adequately recompensed, though he was successful in everything he undertook, including business. Even the recognition of a biography has somehow passed him by.

Lafayette's letter, continuing with a modicum of foreign news, including that of war between the Empire and the Turks, reported a communication from 300 Breton noblemen "declaring it infamous to accept a place in the New administration." [16] This protest was described elsewhere by William Short as manifesting the highest courage on the part of those who signed it.[17]

The part played by the Bretons in the Revolution was one of contrasts. At the outset their province had led in the struggle for traditional privileges against the centralizing tendencies of monarchy. But when the monarchy was overthrown, Bretons were among the leading counter-revolutionists in the uprising of Vendée. A typical case is that of Armand Taffin, Marquis de la Rouërie, who had served in America with Rochambeau and was well known to Washington. He was a delegate from Brittany in 1788 to demand from the King the preservation or, where forfeited, the recovery of provincial privileges. He put his case so bluntly that he was remanded to the Bastille. Later, after the overthrow of the monarchy, he was a Breton leader against the Revolutionists. But campaign rigors impaired his health, and he died in January 1793, in hiding from his pursuers. His papers incriminated the family in whose home he died, twelve of whose members were executed.[18] He was one among many for whom Washington might grieve.

Lafayette entrusted this letter—here quoted with interrupting comments—to M. Brissot de Warville, later an important figure in the Revolution, who hoped at this time to meet Washington and to write a history of the country. He bespoke for the bearer a "glance at your papers," a favor to which love for America merited a claim.

In the contest centering in the courts of law, which represented basically an evolution toward a greater freedom, Washington might compare the views of both his old friends, Lafayette and Rochambeau. Upon what appeared to be a controversy so far-reaching in its implications, Rochambeau was far more matter-of-fact and unimaginative, but his was the directness of the soldier and his viewpoint was respectable. Writing on June 15, 1788, from Rochambeau near Vendôme, he congratulated Washington on the prospects of a federal government in the United States. As for France, he observed that "our constitution tho' monarchical, is in a moment of crisis that has some resemblance with that in which yours has been till now—our twelve parliaments which arrogated the title intermediate between the sovereign and the people, have had always principles of administration entirely dissonant, and grounded upon privileges of place—the King will reduce all that different wills to, an only King, an only law, and an only court for registering, that they shall call, according to an old set form of the monarchy, *cour plénière*, plenary court." Rochambeau approved of such a court provided it was manned by representatives of all three orders, properly elected.[19] He was emphasizing personnel and he could count on Washington's awareness of its importance.

Only a portion of the disclosures, forecasts, and opinions cited in the present chapter, certainly not the interesting conclusions of Lafayette and Rochambeau, had reached Washington when, sensing the oncoming tumult, for experience had taught him that revolutions are not affairs of libraries and cabinets, he offered the youthful Lafayette a word of timely caution:

I like not much the situation of affairs in France. The bold demands of the parliaments, and the decisive tone of the King, show that but little more irritation would be necessary to blow up the spark of discontent into a flame, that might not easily be quenched. If I were to advise, I should say that great moderation should be used on both sides. Let it not, my dear Marquis, be considered as a derogation from the good opinion that I entertain of your prudence, when I caution you, as an individual desirous of signalizing yourself in the cause of your country and freedom, against running into extremes and prejudicing your cause. The King, though, I think from everything I have been able to learn, he is really a good-hearted though a warm-spirited man, if thwarted injudiciously in the execution of prerogatives that belonged to the crown, and in plans which he conceives calculated to promote the national good, may disclose qualities he has been little thought to possess. On the other hand, such a spirit seems to be awakened in the kingdom, as, if managed with extreme prudence, may produce a gradual and tacit revolution much in favor of the subjects, by abolishing *lettres de cachet,* and defining more accurately the powers of government. It is a wonder to me, there should be found a single monarch, who does not realize that his own glory and felicity must depend on the prosperity and happiness of his people. How easily [sic] is it for a sovereign to do that, which shall not only immortalize his name, but attract the blessings of millions.[20]

To Lafayette he indulged only in cautious generalizations. To Jefferson he was more specific. "Should the contest between the King and the Parliaments result in a well constituted National Assembly, it must ultimately be a happy event for the kingdom." [21] This was to a fellow American—a fellow revolutionist. Such comments on the trend of French affairs were kept within the inner circle. Washington was not broadcasting revolutionary principles to subvert the established institutions of allies so recent and so helpful.

Nor, for that matter, was Jefferson himself, if one may judge from an account he had sent recently to Monroe and which in the course of local Virginia friendships came quite probably to Washington's attention. The issue so far, thought Jefferson, lay between the King and parliaments, with good men taking sides with neither but hoping for the ultimate emergence of "a fixed and temperate constitution." For a moment agitation ran so high that an appeal to arms was not unlikely. Jefferson thought that such a crisis might have been disastrous to the

cause of liberty. It was averted, in his opinion, by the moderation of the Government, which in its reforming course was now
yielding up one right after another. Evidences of this extraordinary tractability were the granting of provincial assemblies
not unlike the state assemblies in America, the reformation of
the criminal law, and royal acknowledgment of inability to levy
new taxes save with the consent of the States General, to be
called next year.

> The object of this body when met will be a bill of rights, a civil list, a
> national assembly meeting at certain epochs, & some other matters of
> that kind, so that I think it probable this country will within two or
> three years be in the enjoyment of a tolerable free constitution, & that
> without it's having cost them a drop of blood, for none is yet spilt, tho
> the English papers have set the whole nation to cutting throats.[22]

From this point on until December, the papers of George
Washington yield nothing of great moment regarding the Revolution in progress overseas. His own career was marching toward its most momentous phase, that of the Presidency, and
while his papers must originally have contained important items
of French news, these now are missing. America like all the
world watched French developments most earnestly. And just
as Washington while President was to have all the resources of
the State Department at his command, so it requires but scant
imagination to surmise that the Department of Foreign Affairs
of the Confederation, still functioning under Jay, should have
been a means of information for a chief magistrate so soon to
exercise his functions.

On this hypothesis a letter from Jefferson to Jay from Paris,
August 20, may be considered a portion of George Washington's
current information about the French Revolution. Jefferson
reminded Jay that till the States General should meet, finances
would constitute the most perplexing problem. An *arrêt* of only
two days previously had provided for payments of both principal and interest at twelve sous in the livre, the remainder to be
paid in certificates. This precipitated a crash of values and once
more directed the nation's attention to the necessity of a new
constitution that would substitute collective wisdom for govern-

ment by a single will. "It is a remarkable proof," wrote Jefferson, "of the total incompetency of a single head to govern a nation well, when with a revenue of six hundred millions they are led to a declared bankruptcy, and to stop the wheels of government, even in it's most essential movements, for want of money." [23]

Nor could so notable an event as the return to power of Necker on August 26, 1788, have been unknown to Washington. It is likely that he saw the account transmitted by William Short to Colonel Carrington, a neighbor in Virginia. Money was the explanation. Necker was believed to have the better chance of raising it, so that the wheels might continue to revolve until the States General should have time to meet. The economic crisis would be a means whereby the nation could recover ancient privileges and lay a sure foundation for freedom.[24] Necker, however, enjoyed no genuine or sympathetic backing from the King.

Bankruptcy provided a major theme in Jefferson's despatch to Jay of September 24 and foreshadowed an early calling of the States General, possibly by December.[25] Here Jefferson proved too alarmist, but his theme was interesting. Bankruptcy was obvious. It was in more complex political ramifications and interpretations that Jefferson felt most at home. As the year drew to its close and he could trace its major issues with some slight perspective, Jefferson transmitted to George Washington some views upon the parliaments far surpassing in their subtlety and interest anything which Washington received from sources purely French. He revealed the underlying conflict, not between parliaments and King but between the parliaments themselves and the Frankenstein which they had unleashed in an endeavor to insure their own salvation. The States General, which they held over the King as a trump card for their own protection, might prove the nemesis of King and parliaments alike. Jefferson's letter to Washington of December 4, 1788, is therefore both a narrative and a critical analysis. It is not the least of its author's many titles to intellectual acumen.

Continuing his searching analysis of the constitutional question involved in the contest between the King and the parlia-

ments, Jefferson noted that the royal pledge to summon the
States General had resulted in immediate tranquillity throughout the kingdom. The parliaments resumed their functions but
transferred their fear from the King to the States General, now
soon to meet. For the summons to a body which had met last
in 1614, the Notables were requested to suggest the right procedure. The Court desired that the Third Estate should equal
in numbers the First and Second combined. This the Notables
opposed, insisting upon the tradition of one vote to each order.
On this point Jefferson hoped that the King would disregard the
wishes of the privileged orders. He was confident at all events
that France was entering upon a happier era from which there
would be no retrogression.[26]

In touching upon the rivalry of the three estates, Jefferson
was on quite obvious ground. In sensing the rivalry between
the parliaments and the estates he vindicated his claim to
political discernment. Having diagnosed the existing situation,
he anticipated the results of the forthcoming sessions of the
States General, thus venturing into the domain of prophecy.
Jefferson was satisfied that the States General would encounter
no royal opposition to their periodical convocation, to their exclusive right to levy taxes, and to the right previously enjoyed
by the several parliaments to register and amend the laws. To
demand much more than this would be unwise. Further reforms
would come in due time, subject to some ability, not as yet
demonstrated, to avoid the pernicious influence upon public
affairs exercised by women—a pervasive influence in France
which to Americans would be unbelievable in character and
extent.

A more personal note was struck, and one he knew his reader
would find welcome, when he gave assurance that Lafayette was
safe and a favorite with the nation.

It would thus appear that in these incipient stages of the
Revolution, Washington was abundantly informed of its developments and in a position to analyze its underlying forces
more acutely than many Frenchmen of distinction who were
closer to the events. His reactions had been intelligent, but
intense preoccupation with domestic politics, with the conven-

tion at Philadelphia and the constitution that emerged from it, combined with native caution against interfering needlessly in the politics of other nations to prevent him from frequent or gratuitous expression. The great days of 1789 were likely to elicit more frequent or at least more pungent comments.

CHAPTER
THREE

1789

In various ways 1789 proved to be the great year of the Revolution. In dramatic intensity, in spectacular events, in lasting results, it yields to no other epoch of the movement. A few of the major events, therefore, may serve as pegs for measuring the information that Washington received in that momentous year.

Monday, May 4 witnessed the opening of the States General. For a session the precedents for which had mostly been forgotten in the lapse of almost six generations of men, preparation was needed. What Jacques Necker on January 1 called a "New Year's Gift to France" could not instantly materialize. The drawing up of memorials and petitions and the selection of the delegates took time. The *cahiers* or lists of grievances remain a mine of source material on the *ancien régime*. To most of the delegates the game of politics was new. Absolute monarchy had presented little opportunity. That the game was played with spirit was evident from the history-making names of many of the members. With Barnave † and Lafayette, Sieyès † and Mirabeau † among the delegates, oratory would not be lacking, fiery and inflammatory. Should vestigial traces of the monarchy dare oppose the nation, battle would be joined.

The weakness of the King, and especially his boredom with the entire procedure, which threatened interference with his hunting, the one great passion of his life, were instantly apparent. The sessions were opened with great splendor, to be sure, but the delegates grumbled at a three hours' delay until the King should appear. An opening sermon by the Bishop of Nancy lectured the Court on its sins of omission and commission—a bold tack for the first day. The estates then separated, the Third holding its sessions in the *Salle des Menus Plaisirs* at Versailles, and hopefully anticipating that the nobility and clergy would unite with it. This ambition encountered much hesitation and reluctance but was finally achieved on July 27, when the King "ordered" what he completely disapproved; and that only after the Third Estate had taken the famous Oath of the Tennis Court on June 21 to remain together as a National Assembly until their business was accomplished; and only after the Duc d'Orleans, kinsman of the King, had come over on the twenty-fifth together with the Gardes Françaises. Many other members of the upper orders had anticipated the King's "command" and had joined the Third Estate in abolishing the older forms and constituting a body truly representative of the nation.

It has been noted by French historians that in his desire to perpetuate the nobility as a separate order, the King ignored a basic policy of his predecessors—that of building up the commons to offset the nobles, who in the Middle Ages were the chief counter to royal authority. But times had changed. Louis XIV had transformed the nobility from busy landlords on their estates into gorgeous parasites at court. Weakened and decadent, the nobility were impotent. The Third Estate was taking over. In his own groping way the King apparently was right. He recognized his real opponent.

The National Assembly being legalized, the Court made some

ineffectual plans for counter-revolution. Loyal troops from the frontier, less identified with Paris, were to replace the Gardes Françaises. The arrival at Versailles of the Regiment of Flanders was to set off one of the most violent demonstrations of the Revolution. But that would come in October. Interest shifted meanwhile from the Assembly and the Court to the provinces, where in the breakdown of authority widespread anarchy prevailed, with the burning of châteaux, destruction of the forests, wholesale slaughter of game, and every imaginable form of lawlessness.

Even so, the focal point of revolution lay in Paris, where since April the citizenry had been fearful of the bandits who roamed the Ile de France and threatened to overrun the capital. Confusion provided a field day for the pyrotechnics of Camille Desmoulins,† at the same time that absence of legitimate authority gave rise to the French equivalent of our vigilantes. The "Electors," chosen without legal warrant by bourgeois citizens, proceeded on June 25 to raise a "National Guard" which was to prove a military prop for the brief ascendancy of Lafayette.

At this posture of affairs the city learned on July 12 of Necker's dismissal by the King. The economic reforms Necker had sought, and in some cases instituted, were distasteful to the Court. Further, he had proved unable to resolve the most thorny issue of the day, that involving the seating of the three estates in the States General. Failure to grapple in advance with this issue was to miss real greatness. In the great days of 1789, Necker could not be accounted a central figure. Nevertheless, his removal was clearly a counter-revolutionary measure, for he was popularly held to be the people's man, as distinguished from the Court's. A riot followed. The Gardes Françaises were particularly turbulent. Agitation mounted on the thirteenth and the National Guard proved helpless. Rioters swarmed about the Bastille, a bogey fortress with few prisoners, few guns and few defenders. When the Governor ordered his men to defend this mere shell and symbol of authority, the citadel was stormed and the Governor was slain. The Bastille fell on July 14. A wholly garbled report soon reached the Assembly, which rejoiced as if something really great had happened. And

41

Lafayette, whose function it had been to maintain order and who had failed therein, was able to send his friend Washington a key to the Bastille, still hanging at Mount Vernon.

Three days after the destruction of his fortress the King came cheerfully to Paris, where he was enthusiastically received. The Comte d'Artois, his brother, took the wiser course of exile. Twenty-three years later he fulfilled his promise of a "prompt" return.

One of the great days, or rather nights, of the Revolution was the August 4 session of the National Assembly. Led by the Vicomte de Noailles, impecunious brother-in-law of Lafayette, but supported by a far wealthier peer, the Duc d'Aguillon, a wild enthusiasm was engendered in the Assembly for the abolition of privileges. Here, indeed, was revolution at its most ecstatic. Amidst the most delirious excitement noble after noble surrendered his feudal dues in the interest of a common tax equality, whose only differential should be wealth, not special privilege. This distinction was made clearer when it was established that only personal rights had been thrown into the discard. Rights pertaining to the land as such were to be acquired by the nation, with due compensation to the landlord. However short this fell of the amazing burst of generosity set free by common impulse, it inaugurated a major social change. The *ancien régime* was drawing its last breath.

Meanwhile, trouble in the provinces resulted in poor crops or none at all, with a consequent shortage of bread. To many Frenchmen this spelled actual starvation. Here was a situation ready made for the treasonable designs of the King's kinsman, the Duc d'Orleans, and his friends of the Palais Royale. Of these intrigues, it may be added, Washington was duly informed. Of this more later.

The October 1 banquet to the officers of the Regiment of Flanders in the Orangerie at Versailles produced a spectacular and alarming outcome. Paris learned of it next day, a hunger maddened Paris unprotected against the lords of misrule. On October 5, as soon as they could be assembled, a mob of females marched on Versailles, not led, of course, but followed, by Lafayette, who seems to have been more or less reluctantly compelled to come along with the National Guard. Lacking determined leadership the Guard was a passive spectator of rather than a participant in the humiliation of the Royal Family.

Not least of these astonishing developments was the passivity of the King. A mighty hunter who slew birds and beasts in battues, not to say hecatombs, the King had a horror of human blood. This he would not shed even in the most urgent self-defense. Hence the garrison at Versailles which, though not large, could have withstood a mob armed with one lone cannon, was forbidden to fire. As the King wrote the Comte d'Estaing, Governor of Versailles, "Defend me? It would be necessary for the blood of Frenchmen to flow! My heart cannot conceive such a frightful idea! If I succumb, at least I shall have nothing with which to reproach myself." And he added, "God be willing, my cousin, that public tranquillity be reestablished, but no aggression, no motion which might lead to a belief that I dream of vengeance, even of self-defense." [1]

Finding the Château undefended, the mob worked its will. The private apartments of the King and Queen were penetrated and only Louis' agreement to accompany the viragoes on their return next day to Paris procured some semblance of tranquillity. Never has monarchy been more abased than in the procession of the maenads on October 6, conveying "The Baker, the Baker's Wife, and the Baker's Little Boy" from the proud splendor of Versailles to the ancient palace of the Tuileries, where under the stern eye of their ferocious masters they would present a tattered emblem of times past.

Strange it is that with so appalling an example of mob rule immediately before it, the National Assembly promptly transferred its own sessions to the city. With a political immaturity completely at variance with the ingrained wisdom of the framers of the American Constitution, the men of 1789 in Paris worked constantly under the eyes of the Parisian mob. They, too, brought forth a constitution in the following year, but not until the Assembly had perpetrated two further acts of folly. In November it enacted that no one of its existing membership might sit in the King's cabinet in the government now being constituted. A little later it passed a second self-denying ordi-

nance even more unfortunate. No one of its existing membership might retain a seat in the second National Assembly. By
these two measures the nation was to lose the benefit of whatever wisdom and experience the National Assembly had contrived to glean.

After such monumental folly, a shift in nomenclature from
"provinces" to "departments," though it signified a further break
with history, was a rather minor matter.

From this brief sketch of France in the great days of 1789, it
should be of interest to examine the extent of information available to George Washington and the newly established government of the United States. One finds only a partial answer in
his correspondence, for much information that came to him is
no longer in his files. He had access also through the Department of State to a vast body of information that required no
comment on his part.

A delicate situation in diplomacy confronted the Administration at the very outset, in the possibility of a recall for the French
minister to the United States, the Comte de Moustier. A letter
from Jefferson to Jay on February 4 reveals the care already
taken to remove the minister from any opportunity of harming
relations between the two countries. The good offices of Lafayette were requisitioned. The Comte de Montmorin, Foreign
Minister, was approached, and every effort made to bring about
de Moustier's recall, all of course in greatest secrecy. These efforts were not successful. Montmorin contended that for want
of specific charges against the minister, he could not be recalled
except to another post, nor was there any vacancy at present.[2]

The reason for de Moustier's inacceptability is not entirely
clear. His career had been distinguished. It included missions
to the Elector of Treves and to the Court of Prussia. In 1791 he
refused the ministry of Foreign Affairs, a less desirable office
than in the heyday of the monarchy. Instead, he accepted the
embassy at Constantinople—a dignified escape from Revolutionary France.[3] He seemed indeed a worthy successor to the
Chevalier Anne-César de La Luzerne, whose part in the peace
negotiations of 1783 had been so active and so brilliant. At the
outset of de Moustier's mission, in fact, Jefferson, writing from

Paris, commended him most warmly to Madison as "a great enemy to formality, etiquette, ostentation and luxury," with a disposition "to cultivate society without poisoning it by ill example." [4] When de Moustier found conditions not entirely to his liking, Jefferson regretted that considerations of etiquette were the cause of his annoyance.[5] A later communication from Jefferson to William Short reveals that de Moustier's interest in reviving a French empire in America was responsible for much loss of popularity.[6]

While this intrigue of the slightly subterranean Jefferson was pursuing its rather ineffectual course, it was for Rochambeau once more to give a forthright, soldierly account of early happenings in the new year. His was the viewpoint of a liberal aristocrat, of unquestioning obedience to traditional authority but with a forward look toward social amelioration, including the reform of his own privileged order, the Second Estate. From Paris on the thirty-first of January, he wrote to Washington to the following effect: Events to date were but the preview of greater things to come. He deplored the ingratitude of the privileged orders to the King's benevolence. He and Lafayette were in a minority of the Second Estate in voting for equal representation of the Third. There might be three orders, but there were only two interests, the privileged and the unprivileged. A vote by head, with the Third Estate equal numerically to the first two, would insure the democratic process. To deny this would result in trouble.[7]

If Rochambeau's account lacked some of the subtlety with which Jefferson interpreted events, it was accurate in substance and upheld a point of view that Washington would approve, fellow soldier and cautious liberal that he was.

In another letter, of February 17, Rochambeau expressed surprise that the United States anticipated France in establishing a sound government. The States General would not meet till the end of April. Rochambeau would be detailed with the troops, meanwhile, to supervise elections.[8]

It is not a little curious that this warrior and nobleman of the *ancien régime* saw eye to eye with modern thinkers. He viewed reactionaries as the most dangerous foes, not only to all progress but to the continued existence of the very institutions which they would defend. Rochambeau possessed insight as well as observation.

It was at this point that Washington obtained binoculars, as it were. Henceforth he saw through the keen eyes of Gouverneur Morris. Rochambeau had written, "I have seen with great pleasure, my Dear General, the Governor Morisse, and I have been charmed with the good news he gave me of your health—we hope that you are going to put yourself again at the head of a fine and good government." [9]

Gouverneur Morris, through whose eyes Washington was to observe much of the onrushing Revolution, was a national figure. He it was who lately had whipped the Constitution of the United States into literary form. In his political theories he was akin to Alexander Hamilton and poles apart from Thomas Jefferson. Born to the Hudson River magnates, he was one of the Morrises of Morrisania, New York. As a half brother to Staats Morris, a general in the British service who had married the widowed Duchess of Gordon, he was recognized by his own class overseas as a full-fledged member of the aristocracy.

A French chargé d'affaires was later to say of Morris, "His great talents are recognized, and his extreme quickness in conceiving new schemes and gaining others to them. He is perhaps the most eloquent and ingenious man of his country, but his countrymen themselves distrust his talents. They admire but fear him." [10] In France, he was to become a favorite of Louise de Penthièvre, Duchesse d'Orleans, to be on friendliest terms with the Comtesse de Ségur and others in the highest circles, and was to win as his mistress the intelligent and beautiful Comtesse de Flahaut, whose child had been fathered by Charles Maurice de Talleyrand-Perigord, the unfrocked Bishop of Autun. Morris' vision took in a wide horizon. And this was no less true because he was overseas representing his old business associate, Robert Morris, and for pleasure, not as a diplomat until later.

Morris' first report was brief but to the point. He found that England was the cynosure of every eye. The Mother of Parliaments was the favorite study of those who would embark upon parliamentary careers. Everything English was imitated, from the "cut of a coat" to the "form of a constitution." [11]

Morris was speaking of affairs in general, apparently, for Rochambeau followed with a word on affairs in particular that pointed the exception. We left him bound to supervise elections. His task in large part done, he dutifully reported to his old friend and familiar correspondent that everything proceeded for the most part satisfactorily, saving in Provence and Brittany where the conflict between privileged and unprivileged was exceptionally warm.[12] This as we have seen was precisely the experience of the Marquis de la Rouërie.

Rochambeau tells only what he knows. He philosophizes rarely and his predictions are infrequent. But his reports as man to man are among the most valuable that Washington received. Had Rochambeau been his sole informant, he would not have been served badly.

It was from Paris on April 29 that Gouverneur Morris communicated the first of the elaborate series of pen portraits of the Revolution which justify his reputation as so distinguished an observer. His opening letter may here be reproduced:

Dear Sir

I had the pleasure to write you a short letter on the third of last month. Monsieur de la Fayette is since returned from his political Campaign in Auvergne, crowned with success. He had to contend with the Prejudices and the Interests of his order, and with the Influence of the Queen and Princes (except the Duke of Orleans) but he was too able for his opponents. He played the orator with as much eclat as he ever acted the soldier, and is at this moment as much envied and hated as his Heart could wish. He is also much beloved by the Nation, for he stands forward as one of the principal Champions for her Rights. The elections are finished throughout this Kingdom, except in the Capital, and it appears from the instructions given to the Representatives (called here *les cahiers*) that certain Points are universally demanded which when granted and secured will render France perfectly free as to the Principles of the Constitution. I say the Principles, for one generation at least will be required to render the Practice familiar. We have I think every Reason to wish that the Patriots may be successful. The generous wish which a free People must form to disseminate Freedom, the grateful emotion which rejoices in the Happiness of a Benefactor, and a strong personal Interest as well in the Liberty as in the Power of this Country, all conspire to make us far from indiffer-

47

ent spectators. I say that we have an *Interest* in the *Liberty* of France. The Leaders here are our Friends, many of them have imbibed their Principles in America, and all have been fired by our Example. Their Opponents are by no means rejoiced at the success of our Revolution, and many of them are disposed to form Connections of the strictest kind with Great Britain. The commercial treaty emanated from such Dispositions; and according to the usual course of those events which are shaped by human Wisdom, it will probably produce the exact Reverse of what was intended by the Projectors. The spirit of the nation is at present high, and Mr. Neckar is very popular, but if he continues long in Administration it will be somewhat wonderful. His Enemies are numerous, able and inveterate. His supporters are indifferent to his Fate, and will protect him no longer than while he can aid in establishing a Constitution. But when once that great Business is accomplished, he will be left to stand on his own ground. The Court wish to get rid of him, and unless he shews very strong in the States General they will gratify their wishes. His ability as a minister will be much contested in that assembly, but with what success Time only can determine.

The materials for a Revolution in this Country are very indifferent. Every Body agrees that there is an utter Prostration of Morals but this general Position can never convey to an American mind the degree of Depravity. It is not by any Figure of Rhetoric or Force of Language that the Idea can be communicated. A hundred anecdotes and an hundred thousand examples are required to shew the extreme Rottenness of every Member. There are Men and Women who are greatly and eminently virtuous. I have the Pleasure to number many in my own acquaintance: but they stand forward from a background deeply and darkly shaded. It is however from such crumbling matter that the great Edifice of Freedom is to be erected here. Perhaps like the Stratum of Rock which is spread under the whole surface of their country, it may harden when exposed to the air; but it seems quite as likely that it will fall and crush the Builders. I own to you that I am not without such apprehensions, for there is one fatal Principle which pervades all Ranks: It is a perfect Indifference to the violation of Engagements. Inconstancy is so mingled in the Blood, Marrow, and very essence of this People, that when a man [of] high Rank and Importance laughs to Day at what he seriously asserted yesterday, it is considered as in the natural order of things. Consistency is the Phenomenon. Judge then what would be the value of an association, should such a thing be proposed and even adopted. The great mass of the common People have no religion but their Priests, no law but their Superiors, no Moral but their Interest. These are the Creatures who led by drunken Curates are now in the high Road *a la Liberté*. And the first use they make of it is to form Insurrections every where for the want of Bread. We have had a little Riot here yesterday and the Day before, and I am told that some have been killed, but the affair was so distant from the quarter in which I reside that I know nothing of the Particulars.[13]

Already there is a hint of the skepticism that was to render Morris unpopular in France as the Revolution passed beyond the bounds of respectable, bourgeois control into the hands of violent radicals. But there is a fearlessness of portrayal which etched the picture for the distant reader and at over a century and a half finds confirmation with a later generation. Certainly Washington was not the man to defend the French against Morris' asseverations. His affection for Lafayette, Rochambeau, and numerous other individual Frenchmen never erased entirely his youthful hatred for the victors at Monongahela and the instigators of massacres uncounted along America's wilderness frontier.

A further epistle from the faithful Morris, dated July 31, 1789,[14] more than two weeks after the fall of the Bastille, ignored the revolutionary changes in the States General during May, the organizing of the National Assembly, the play of forces between the rising power of Paris and the only partially loyal army. All of this was news that Washington received in Government despatches from the official minister to France, Thomas Jefferson,[15] who was still on mission and had not yet assumed his duties at the Department of State. Morris, on the other hand, who had a genius for mingling in polite and inner circles, an ear for the most secret gossip, perhaps a penchant for intrigue, gave Washington some news about the King which if not strictly accurate in fact, was surely faithful in spirit.

"The King," reported Morris, "has actually formed the Design of going off to Spain. Whether the measures set on foot to dissuade him will have, as I hope, the desired effect, Time only can discover. His Fears govern him absolutely, and they have of late been most strongly excited. He is a well meaning man, but extremely weak, and probably these Circumstances will in every event secure him from personal Injury. Perhaps an able man would not have fallen into his Situation, but I think that no Ability could now extricate him. He must float along on the Current of Events, being absolutely and entirely a cypher. If however he should fly, it will not be easy to predict the consequences, for this Country is at present as near to anarchy as Society can approach without Dissolution."

From this curiously prophetic picture of the King, the keen American turned to pay his respects to the newly formed National Assembly, Revolutionary successor to the ancient gathering of the States General. He noted the inexperience of even its ablest members and deplored their want of knowledge, judgment and reflection. They were, besides, incurable romanticists. There followed a vignette of Lafayette which Morris knew would interest his correspondent. The two had met while Morris was recently in Paris. Morris had broached the subject of a governorship for the Ile de France, including, of course, Paris. But Lafayette had replied that command over the troops in Paris proper was the limit of his wishes, for he was satiated with power. He had demonstrated his power over the sovereign's person during the late procession from Versailles, and was free to move as he pleased or even to hold the monarch prisoner.

What Morris forbore to mention were the indications of Lafayette's character revealed in the somewhat childish view of his own influence. True, the King was in his power. The thrill of it intoxicated. But there was no hint here of any grasp at genuine authority. Even the Ile de France had no appeal; France itself much less. Circumstances lifted Lafayette to temporary influence. He missed greatness by a mile. This Morris saw, and many others. By 1792, the bubble had burst and all France knew that Lafayette was not the man of destiny. For the moment, though, the calcium light beat round him, and news of Lafayette was news of the French Revolution.

From this little glimpse of Lafayette, its moral obvious but only darkly hinted at by Morris, the enquirer turned to some more general reflections anent the larger scene:

> I do not know whether you will be informed of the critical situation in which things were placed just before the last Ministry was turned out, and the old one restored. My authority is very good, but I will not vouch for the Truth.—It was resolved to reduce Paris to obedience by Famine, to take two hundred of the States General prisoners, to dissolve that Assembly, and to govern in the old fashioned way.[16]

All this you will say was madness and therefore improbable. But was it not equally mad to drive away Neckar, & change the ministry at the Time and in the Manner, which were adopted for that Purpose? The men weak enough for the one were certainly mad enough for the other. Two german Regiments which were to be employed, were regaled by the Queen in the Orangerie at Versailles. They received Promises and Largesses, and were prevailed on to shout vive la Reine! vive le Comte d'artois! vive la Duchesse de Polignac! Afterwards their music played for hours under her Majesty's windows— The Marechal de Broglie endeavored at the same time to conciliate the artillery. But it was at length discovered, that tho the Troops would shout and sing yet they would not fight against their countrymen; all which might have been known long ago. At the moment when this Intrigue was carrying on by the Court, the Gardes du Corps and Gardes françoises combined to defend the members of the national assembly. I pass over those facts which you cannot but know, to mention in one word that the whole army of France have declared for Liberty; and that one reason why his Majesty has not taken the step above mentioned is that he does not know a single Regiment which would obey him.

From these reports and doubtless various others, for in the lapse of times the files are incomplete, and indispensably, of course, from the records of the Department of State, Washington derived a remarkably complete and most illuminating picture of the changing scene.

Jefferson's concluding despatch to Jay, for example, contained a ripened summary of conditions as they appeared on September 23, a despatch which came unerringly to Washington's attention. Jefferson shed further light on the extremity of the finances by his account of the King and his ministry taking their plate to the mint, and women giving up their jewels in the National Assembly. The latter was, in Jefferson's opinion, more a gesture than a remedy for economic ills. He reported that the Assembly moved very slowly in its work of constitution building, owing to diverging wills among the members and to "a tumultuous manner of doing business." He enumerated various questions in controversy, including the all-important issue of the royal veto. The influence of Necker, who had been hastily recalled by the King, was nil. He was likely to resign. Quotations on the Bourse were not encouraging and the populace was exasperated by the dilatory proceedings of the Assembly. It was regrettable, thought Jefferson, that King and aristocracy had interposed such negligible resistance, for otherwise the opposition would have been united, whereas it was now divided. He found four parties in the National Assembly: aristocrats, moderate royalists, republicans, and Orleanists. The second and third of these groups were the most disinterested and patriotic. To a considerable extent they acted together, being bound by a sort of gentleman's agreement. Between these two arms of what was originally the same party, Lafayette was a unifying force. "Should he be obliged to take part against either, it will be against that which shall first pass the Rubicon of reconciliation with the other. His weight should turn the scale. His influence in Paris is overwhelming."

Jefferson's earlier optimism had so far vanished that he now anticipated civil war as a distinct possibility. A shortage of bread, public bankruptcy, the flight of the King, any or all of these might precipitate catastrophe. Here Jefferson asked what the Queen proposed in the present state of things and put his own reply neatly if not quite fairly. "Whatever rage, pride and fear can dictate in a breast which never knew the presence of one moral restraint."

But civil war was, after all, no more than a possibility. Jefferson did not expect it. The patriotic elements would probably avert it. There followed a sharp dig at England. "Without doubt England will give money to produce and to feed the fire which should consume this country, but it is not probable she will engage in open war for that." [17] Jefferson in this estimate of his old enemy was running true to form.

A week later it was William Short who informed John Jay, and only less directly Washington, of what transpired in France. Again there was allusion to the melting of the royal plate. Again the scarcity of bread was viewed with apprehension.[18]

In the meantime, while his ancestral throne was being steadily and swiftly undermined, the elder son of Louis and the Queen departed this life while still Dauphin and heir to the pomp and glory of Versailles. The news came officially to Washington. It demanded personal acknowledgment. Beneath the formal and official condolence there runs a current of personal humanity. He is writing on October 9, 1789:

> Great and beloved Friend and Ally.
>
> By the Change which has taken place in the national government of the United States, the Honor of receiving and answering your Majesty's Letter of the 7th of June, to "The President and Members of Congress" has devolved upon me.
>
> The painful Event communicated in it, could not fail to affect the Sensibility and excite the Regret of the People of the United States, who have so much Reason to feel an Interest in whatever concerns the Happiness of your Majesty, your Family and Nation. They very sincerely condole with you on the Occasion, and are sensible how greatly this Misfortune must have been enhanced by those qualities in the Dauphin which promised to have rendered that Prince a Blessing, not only to his Family, but to his Nation.—
>
> Permit me to assure your Majesty of the unceasing Gratitude and Attachment of the United States, and of our Prayers, that the Almighty will be pleased to keep you, Our great and beloved Friend and Ally, under his constant Guidance and Protection.—
>
> New York the ninth Day of October, 1789.
[Signed] George Washington.[19]

Early in October, Short was presented with a theme for his despatches more thrilling and dramatic than any which the Revolution had previously provided. The mad march of the maenads on Versailles and the return of the King and his family to the capital will arrest forever the imagination of posterity. Short was a keen observer and his report is comprehensive. The story is familiar to all students of the Revolution and needs only to be summarized. Short mentions the banquet at Versailles and the angry reception of this news in Paris. He describes the actions of the women on the following morning in entering by force the Hotel de Ville, where on the whole they behaved quietly. Greater excitement attended their decision to march from Paris to Versailles. Recruits joined them to a number between five and six thousand. He presents Lafayette's dilemma— whether to refuse to march, thus antagonizing not only the mob but army officers as well, bent upon recovering lost assignments at the Court, or whether to lead the troops with all the risks which this implied.

Meanwhile, the women arrived just as the Assembly was rising from its session. The members returned to their hall as to a refuge while the women cried "Bread. Bread." A delegation sought out the King in person, and was assured that measures were being taken to obtain adequate supplies. With the approach of night, scattered firing took place between the mob and the troops on duty at the palace under command of the Comte d'Estaing. The troops were then withdrawn to quarters.

Similar confusion prevailed in the hall of the Assembly till word was brought that the King accepted unconditionally those articles of the Constitution and the Bill of Rights which had been sent him previously.

"In this situation," declared Short,

> The Marquis de la Fayette approached Versailles, about 11 o'clock at night. Although on leaving Paris he was the prisoner of his troops & the mob which followed them, before his arrival he had obtained such a command over them that notwithstanding the impetuosity of the multitude he was able to halt them and make them swear allegiance to the National Assembly & to the King before entering the town.

There followed a paragraph in cipher hinting that much of the disturbance had been inspired by the Orleanists, an insinuation fully warranted but too delicate to entrust to ordinary formulas.

In his interview with Lafayette, the King consented to be guarded by the national troops under Lafayette's command. Order was immediately restored, but hours later, when Lafayette had retired to rest after an entire day and night of exhausting vigilance, the mob got out of bounds, fired on the *gardes du corps* wherever it could find them, and pursued them in some cases to the Queen's antechamber. Hastily summoned in this renewed crisis, Lafayette beheld the mob in gleeful procession, the heads of two of its victims mounted on pikes, while search went on for others. Lafayette's was a work of rescue, but this fresh tumult subsided when the King agreed to accompany the mob to Paris, taking with him his entire family, and accompanied, on its own resolution, by the National Assembly.

The procession quit Versailles at noon on Tuesday, and arrived at the Hotel de Ville about eight in the evening for an orderly reception by the Mayor and Corporation, after which the Royal Family lodged at the Tuileries. "From this moment," Short observed, a "calm reigned through all the streets which seemed to have been the effect of Magic, & the next morning to the astonishment of every body bread became as abundant as ever & has continued so since. This confirms the opinion that the scarcity was not real."

Short was plainly aware of the suspicion thus intensified against the Orleanists, but he spoke cautiously for want of proof. "It is said also that large parcels of bread have been found thrown in the river in order to starve the people of Paris & thus render them ripe for revolt." Artificial or not, should the scarcity return the King and Queen would be more gravely imperilled than before, being now more completely at the mercy of the mob.

Short justified the minuteness of his narrative by the importance of the events described. He declared that the larger implications of the matter lay open to conjecture, the effect upon the provinces being as yet unknown. But his own comment was prophetic: "It being certain that it will be unsafe to deliver any other than the most popular sentiments in the Assembly whilst in Paris, it would seem as if the constituents of the other parts of the Kingdom might have just cause of complaint."

The King meanwhile professed to be satisfied. He had written to the Assembly requesting that it transfer its sessions from Versailles to Paris, where the objects chiefly under consideration by the legislative body would be some remaining articles of the Constitution, a change in criminal procedure, and a restoration of finances.[20]

In transmitting these reports two days later, Short informed the Department of State that inquiries had been instituted to determine the responsibility for the bread shortage and the crisis which it precipitated. A conspiracy was obviously suspected and arrests had been made.[21]

In the light of an account alike so comprehensive and so interpretative, the Government of the United States—and this meant assuredly George Washington—could not be deemed uninformed of major movements in this exciting struggle.

That Washington received rather than gave goes almost without saying. His not to compromise relations with "our good Friends and Very Great and Good Allies." Decorum utterly forbade, and Washington was perfect master of punctilio. Yet now and then he breaks the silence, as in the following to Morris:

> The revolution, which has been effected in France is of so wonderful a nature that the mind can hardly realize the fact. If it ends as our last accounts to the first of August predict that nation will be the most powerful and happy in Europe; but I fear though it has gone triumphantly through the first paroxysm, it is not the last it has to encounter before matters are finally settled. In a word the revolution is of too great magnitude to be effected in so short a space, and with the loss of so little blood. The mortification of the King, the intrigues of the Queen, and the discontent of the Princes and the Noblesse will foment divisions, if possible, in the national assembly; and [they will unquestionably] [22] avail themselves of every faux pas in the formation of the constitution if they do not give a more open, active opposition. To these the licentiousness of the People on one hand and sanguinary punishments on the other will alarm the best disposed friends to the measure, and contribute not a little to the overthrow of their object. Great temperance, firmness, and foresight are necessary in the movements of that Body. To forbear running from one extreme to another is no easy matter and, should this be the case, rocks and shelves, not visible at present may wreck the vessel.[23]

In these observations there is wisdom. On the need and difficulty of moderation he was unassailable. He overestimated, it is true, the power to harm still abiding in the Queen, the princes, and the nobility; correspondingly he ignored the volcanic fires still latent in the proletariat and the classes more submerged. When these lines were penned, he knew, of course, of the fall of the Bastille. The eruptive enthusiasms of the fourth of August and the mad march of the maenads on October 5 and 6, were not yet known in the United States. Considering the data he possessed, his foresight was remarkable.

With these comments, one period not only of the movement but of Washington's own reactions to it terminated. The wings of monarchy were clipped. The National Assembly was indisputably master, and free to fashion at its will the Constitution that it dreamed. The Revolution had completed its first phase, that of clearing away rubbish, the phase of moderate violence.

Other phases there would be, but for the moment veiled. Whatever their import, Washington was certain to be well and promptly notified.

Thus Short informed the Department of State on October 28 that the removal to Paris of the King and of the National Assembly led to a calling of the provincial assemblies to take such action as might be required. That in Dauphiné was feared especially because M. Monnier from that province, hitherto a loyal adherent of the Revolution, had retired from the National Assembly disgusted with developments. Other representatives from Dauphiné did not share Monnier's opinions, and the provincial attitude remained uncertain.

More important was Short's allusion to the confiscation of ecclesiastical property to provide a basis for the assignat currency which was slated for the near future, notwithstanding occasional local opposition.[24]

Less important historically but more immediately interesting to Americans then and now was a motion made by Mirabeau in the National Assembly on November 5, that the United States be asked to pay its debt in commodities, principally flour. The ensuing discussion was not complimentary to the financial integrity of the United States. The motion had been postponed, but Short anticipated its eventual passage. He quoted Montmorin as saying that every facility would be extended for the importation of flour.

Highly interesting was Short's report that the estates of the Church had been nationalized, that the parliaments were superseded by a new judiciary, and that the provincial assemblies, contrary to forebodings, approved enthusiastically the transfer to Paris of the King and the National Assembly.[25] Twelve days later he mentioned renewed discussion of the debt of the United States to France, and a project to negotiate a loan in Holland with this debt as security. Montmorin had no confidence in the plan, but even so American credit in the Netherlands apparently was rising. Mirabeau's motion had not been renewed.[26]

By November 30, Short adjudged the political revolution virtually complete. The finances, however, were threatening further trouble.[27] Short's concern was indeed justifiable, for government in the ordinary sense no longer functioned. Taxes were not collected, loans were not subscribed, gifts were wholly insufficient, and capital daily was in flight.

On the same day, Thomas Jefferson, while weighing the State Department portfolio against return to Paris, wrote Washington that governmental changes seemed to offer important commercial opportunities.[28]

Short's concluding despatches for 1789 contained some technical discussions about meeting or postponing French governmental obligations; some details of a riot at Toulon and the imprisonment and release of the commandant of the port; a preliminary allusion to the extension of the Revolution to the Colonies; a further reference to the new jurisprudence; the arrest of a counter-revolutionist formerly of the guards of Monsieur, with an account of his successful vindication of himself.[29] Somewhat minor issues these appear by contrast with the tragedy and deep significance of the October days. But the Revolution did not move at even tempo, and it was not always at the highest pitch. Human nature could not have endured such pressure. There must be lulls as well as crises.

Nor did the progress of the Revolution elicit further comment for the moment from George Washington. He was far too busy in these opening days of his Administration to volunteer gratuitous comment on the affairs of neighbors, however interesting those affairs might be. Among the many matters that must have demanded his immediate attention were Hamilton's plan for funding the debt, Indian troubles, difficulties with the English on the frontier, and the Nootka Sound Affair.

From his distant coign of observation Washington had already witnessed the brightest of the Revolution's phases. New phases of the Revolution and new personal reactions might lie ahead. Their interpretation would reflect his well established attitudes and principles.

CHAPTER
FOUR

1790

The merging of the States General into the National Assembly, the fall of the Bastille, the march of the maenads on Versailles were but some of the dramatic events which signalized the outgoing year. The oak had crashed in 1789. The new year was a time of planning. To continue the figure, a sapling had been planted. Could it anticipate a normal growth? The National Assembly was erecting a constitution. Could the resulting instrument anticipate the happy fate of its American counterpart? Their roots were far from parallel.

Despite misgivings in some quarters, the Americans had created a powerful executive. The Government rested directly on the citizen. But the Americans had been fighting England. They had not opposed authority as such. They did not cut off the head for fear it was a tyrant. The French, on the other hand, were in arms not against their weak and amiable king, but rather, in the view of a recent and distinguished historian,[1] against Louis XIV, dead since 1715. The philosophy underlying all their deliberations was the theory of compact. The head had violated his compact. Away with him. There was no Darwin to assure them that every organism requires a head. To the men of 1790 a strong executive was unthinkable. Their substitute was a phantom.

What of the Chamber of Deputies in this Constitution of 1790? Would it represent the nation? Yes, if property was the criterion. The citizenry were to be divided into "active" and "passive." The latter would have no votes. To be a citizen of the first degree, one of the 4,298,360 voters, one must pay taxes in the amount of three days' work. These petty tax-payers did not elect the actual deputies. They merely chose a wealthier group of "delegates" who paid taxes to the amount of ten days' work. The actual deputies to be elected finally by these very solvent citizens must themselves pay taxes in the amount of a *marc d'argent,* that is fifty livres, and have landed property besides.[2] Monarchy apparently was giving way to something like plutocracy. The *tiers état,* the bourgeoisie, was coming into its own. Its favored position was to be altered, however, in the Constitution as revised in 1791.

Meanwhile bankruptcy, which had precipitated the Revolution, was intensified rather than alleviated in the ensuing months. Convulsions in Paris and the provinces did not create that atmosphere of confidence in which business prospers. Capitalists were hard hit—not too great a sorrow to the radicals—but artisans by the thousands lost their jobs and became a public charge, doing made work in national factories. As financial problems grew ever more acute, the vast wealth of the Church, accumulating through the centuries, became an increasing temptation to an exhausted treasury. Nor was there sufficient wisdom in ecclesiastical circles to forestall the crisis by large and timely loans. On October 10, 1789, Talleyrand, not yet unfrocked as Bishop of Autun, moved to seize all property of the Church. The motion carried and the resulting seizures created an actual surfeit of wealth resulting in problems not much less acute than deficits. Their solution was the assignats, a currency resting not on the traditional metallic base but on the State-owned land. They were issued in accelerating volume until they became one of the classic jokes of economic history. Another result perhaps equally damaging was to alienate the clergy, lower as well as upper, and thereby to forfeit the support of a power which previously had served the Revolution.

Allowing for the difficulty of expressing economic realities in terms of currency alone, for the price level is always changing and what in one era may seem a modest burden is something other in an economy geared to smaller figures, the French debt in 1790 was formidable. In this second year of the Revolution the public debt stood at 4,242 millions of livres. Of this, 2,339 millions represented interest-bearing certificates, with no call on principal. This vast sum was divided into two classes of *rentes*. The demand debt, with the principal subject to call, totalled 1,902 millions. Included in the latter was the debt of the clergy which the State assumed when the Church property was expropriated. Also, a much larger sum, 1,340 millions of livres, had been assumed when the State undertook to reimburse numerous functionaries whose perquisites it had taken over. Interest at $6\frac{1}{2}$ percent on the various types of debt came to 232 millions. Issuance of the assignats was apparently the only means available for meeting these huge obligations. A fresh issue was decreed on September 29, and by the year's end a total of 1,200 millions was in circulation.[3]

Possibly the worst advised of all the Revolutionary decisions was the division of the Church, not in terms of doctrine or of worship but of loyalty to the civil rulers rather than the Papacy. The National Assembly, to be sure, numbered some Protestants and many others who in their own or their ancestors' persons had suffered from the heavy hand of the Church. But the decision was less vindictive than fanatical—a mad enthusiasm for the new political creation to which all else must bow. It was only after the most painful hesitation that the King, believing that he was consigning his own soul to Hell, finally on December 26 "ordered" the clergy to take an oath to support the Constitution.

Two hundred priests refused the oath. Only four bishops obeyed, two of them being the infamous Talleyrand, and the now not too reputable Cardinal Loménie de Brienne.

For the King himself it was a physical, moral, and political disaster. Bodily it induced a raging fever; morally he came to feel that such an outrage released him from all his former pledges; and politically it turned his thoughts toward foreign aid, in what the nation when it learned of it considered as high treason. There ensued two foreign policies for France. For the King's personal diplomacy was not revealed to the Foreign Office established by the National Assembly. It was then that the Queen's brother, the Emperor of Austria, came into active contact with the Revolution.

Till now the Revolution had encountered few if any foreign obstacles. The neighboring monarchs thought less of the humiliations of a fellow monarch than of the strategic advantages to be gained from the reduction of *la grande nation* to a state of helpless anarchy. Their attitude was understandable. The second year of Revolution brought a steady sundering of military bonds. King and Assembly, Minister of War and Lafayette alike were helpless against the dissolving ties. An outsider might readily conclude that the glory of France had departed. Any lingering doubts should have been dispelled by the formal oath of self-denial taken by the Assembly on May 22, 1790. "The French Nation renounces the thought of undertaking any war with the object of conquest." [4] What unbelievable surprises the near future had in store!

The first breach in the pacifist formula came with the appeal of the Papal city and county of Avignon for incorporation into France. After a display of sophistry and dialectic that it was not a conquest, since Avignon took the initiative, admission was granted in 1791.

When royalty quit Versailles, Royalists fled France in growing numbers. For the most part they were kindly welcomed in the neighboring lands, but they were generally impecunious, their complaints became monotonous, and their influence was rather negligible. The Comtes de Provence † (Monsieur [5]) and Artois,† brothers of the King, Provence as "Regent," were the natural leaders of this unorganized and scattered group. The former, intelligent but plodding, the latter, brilliant but erratic, were not the men to breathe life into a dying cause. Artois soon became obnoxious at Vienna. Elsewhere many émigrés regretted their impulsive action. Meanwhile the Duc d'Orleans, a prince of the blood and father of a future King, remained in France to pursue his dark intrigues and to contribute his modest talents to the Revolution.

The elements were present. Great events were pending. The ensuing year would be dynamic. News thereof would come to Washington from sources now grown customary.

For an understanding of the cross currents, Washington still possessed the perspicuous comments of William Short and of the better known but scarcely more acute observer, Gouverneur Morris. Also his files contain numerous effusions from individual Frenchmen, protesting in disgust the growing breakdown of the social order.

Thus the Marquis de la Rouërie declared that if Washington could behold the general disorder, he would sail immediately for his own much happier land. "Our constitution makers, dispute, slander, fight and kick each other most unmercifully, they reproach each other with being entirely destitute of the parts necessary to the frame of legislators or even administrators; on that point the wise and attentive part of the nation agree pretty well with them." A moderate specimen this is from a letter that rants on for pages more.[6] It is unlikely that it particularly affected George Washington's thinking.

Rather more objective but in a not dissimilar vein was the report of the Comte de Moustier, now at his home in France, written to his erstwhile host at Mount Vernon, and deploring France's failure to emulate the wisdom of the United States in conducting her revolution. Better leadership was the great need. The people now possessed more freedom than capacity to utilize that freedom wisely.[7]

The volatile qualities of his fellow citizens and their individual vanity further roused the Count's mistrust and colored his opinions as a moderate conservative. It is probable that Washington interpreted them readily but accorded them respect.

63

Far more optimistic was the temper of the liberal Lafayette, whose popularity was soon to be increased still further when on February 4 he refused to extend his command to all the national guards of the kingdom. His was not a news letter, he maintained. Short took care of news. It breathed affection only, coupled with an assurance that the new political and constitutional edifice in France would guarantee freedom. Some allusion followed to Lafayette's own achievements and experiences, and to the signs of dawning liberty in other parts of Europe. He proposed to encourage them by all means in his power. Meanwhile, with best regards to his American friends, he wished they might see in person the changes wrought in France.[8]

From another French friend, the Chevalier de La Luzerne, now a Marquis and the French Ambassador at London, Washington received an interpretation which might be construed as midway between those of Rochambeau and Lafayette. Like the others, Luzerne was a liberal aristocrat. He regretted that enthusiasm for liberty had exceeded the bounds of moderation and had been overzealous in diminishing the executive authority. Luzerne concluded with a fine tribute to their joint friend Lafayette. Fortunately for France, but not for him, he was at the Revolution's head. Beset by a thousand difficulties, "he has occasion for all the aid of that wisdom and prudence which he acquired under your tuition, and assuredly he has hitherto proved himself worthy of his master—having supported the most difficult situation with the rarest talents, and most astonishing foresight." [9]

These spirited and gifted French correspondents gave Washington a unique insight into the national temper. It was, nevertheless, to official despatches that he must look for orderly reports. Those of Short lost nothing of their insight. As the year opened he disclosed the extreme embarrassment created by slavery and the slave trade in the West Indies. Large commercial interests were at stake. Loss of the islands was predicted if slavery were abolished.[10] "Liberty, Equality, Fraternity," and the rights of man did not exactly coincide with slavery. But regardless of the economic and moral dilemma presented by the Breton merchants, the Assembly wanted their support.[11] A further complication was free trade, which Revolutionists might favor but which merchants, accustomed to monopoly, could not approve. With true political acumen, Short set forth the contentions of the rival groups:

The mercantile interest in both France and the islands was vociferous in its insistence upon the traditional monopolies. The Assembly hesitated at a frontal attack. To contend with the upper orders was a sufficient assignment without antagonizing the mercantile interests. Altogether it was a rather delicate balance.[12]

On January 23, Short's despatch showed why the National Assembly gripped the nation so unitedly. It had destroyed abuses onerous to most without as yet enforcing new taxes or collecting old ones. Short found materials present for a counter-revolution but did not believe that one immediately threatened. He admitted his own distaste for the new geography which had superseded the old provincial nomenclature, but conceded his error in the premises, for the new system worked. The efforts of the neighboring states, notably Sardinia and Spain, to exclude French ideas and Frenchmen too were persistent, but rather ineffective. Short did not sympathize with such a censorship. Corsica, meanwhile, had been incorporated into France. The trial of M. Favras was in progress.[13] Favras was accused of being a counter-revolutionist who aimed to carry off the King, apparently to Peronne, that old meeting place of Louis XI and Charles the Bold.

Short was after all the protégé of Thomas Jefferson and not of Washington, and it is probable that already the President relied more confidently on his own friend, Gouverneur Morris, an unofficial agent destined soon to be official. Morris' comments on the influence of Breton and other west coast merchants corroborate the views of Short. The idea of foreign war as a means of composing internal difficulties, which he propounded personally to Montmorin, now seems naive. Montmorin listened patiently, but replied that finances simply could not support a venture of the sort, and that he was not himself the minister to "embrace the great whole of the public business." Proceeding next to Lafayette, the observer indulged himself in a satiric tone which the subject perhaps warranted but which could scarcely have pleased Washington. Lafayette, not content with confusion in France, was promoting a revolution in Prussia, and burned with eagerness to lead a French army into Flanders to overthrow the Stadtholder. The part he played was splendid but dangerous. His constitutional views were open to criticism, and it was evident that he had left America before his political education was completed.[14]

The entire communication is in the homely vein of intimacy. But this homely vein is lost in the elaborate communication of January 24, which ranks as one of the most brilliant of Morris' interpretations. He sees the Revolution and sees it whole, its origins, its progress, and its prospects. His description of procedure in the National Assembly is extremely pointed. His analysis of the newly projected currency, the assignats, is profound but not encouraging. His prediction that the Revolution is heading into darker days will all too soon be fulfilled. But the author's style is at its best in vignettes of Louis and his ministers, including an elaborate pen portrait of M. Necker. An excerpt or two may be quoted here:

> The middle Party, who mean well, have unfortunately acquired their Ideas of Government from Books and are admirable Fellows upon Paper; but as it happens somewhat unfortunately that the men who live in the World are very different from those who dwell in the Heads of Philosophers it is not to be wondered at if the Systems taken out of Books are fit for nothing but to be put into Books again.

Clever, is he not? And what of this description of the King?

> If the reigning Prince were not the small-bear Character that he is, there can be but little Doubt that watching Events and making a tolerable Use of them he would regain his authority. But what will you have from a Creature who situated as he is eats and drinks and sleeps well and laughs and is as merry a Grig as lives? The Idea that they will give him some Money which he can oeconomize, and that he will have no trouble in governing contents him entirely. Poor Man! He little thinks how unstable is his Situation. He is beloved; but it is not with the sort of Love which a Monarch should inspire. It is that Kind of good natured Pity which one feels for a led Captain. There is besides no Possibility of serving him, for at the slightest shew of Opposition he gives up every thing, and every Person.[15]

Page after page there is of equally good writing.

Endowed with no such qualities of style, Short's reports were far less pungent, but they depict historic backgrounds with a comprehensive sweep. In February, he was concerned with a well conceived attempt to put the King himself at the head of the Revolution, winning for the Crown a needed popularity and helping stabilize the country through a recognition that the Revolution was a fact accomplished.[16]

The immediate effect of the King's action in going before the National Assembly to sanction all that previously had passed, was immense. A perfect ecstasy of popular acclaim greeted his appearance. But as time passed and the royal approval settled none of the economic problems, which grew continually more pressing, the temperature of the populace turned cooler, as Short was quick enough to note.

With the national debt so widely held and multitudes of people dependent on the public funds, Short considered the growing deficit and the total inability to balance budgets as ominous indeed for the tranquillity of France. Of similar economic import were the persisting troubles in the West Indies, where the issue was tightly drawn between the local planters, intent upon free trade, and the French merchants jealous of their own monopoly, with the National Assembly still disposed to straddle.[17]

With his pronounced leaning toward the economic interpretation of events, Short did not fail to record the action of the market. In these March days of 1790, as for many days preceding, stocks were falling steadily, to the accompaniment of rising anxiety in the public mind. Since his previous despatch, however, another issue had approached solution. The Assembly, contrary to the wishes of Mirabeau and contrary to its own convictions respecting human freedom, had pleased both colonists and merchants by voting to uphold the slave trade to the West Indies. Of more personal import, Favras had been executed in what Short conceived to be a blot upon the Revolution.[18]

Of equal economic import was the next despatch. A further crash in stocks presaged oncoming bankruptcy. Many citizens were leaving Paris, thereby reducing below the bounds of safety a currency inadequate already. An offer by the municipality of

Paris to purchase ecclesiastical property to the amount of two hundred millions was disputed as beyond that body's competence. Over the gabelle or salt tax, also, a division had arisen between the previously taxed and non-taxed districts, and a tendency was evident to abolish the monopoly in tobacco held by the farmers-general.[19] Such a step would interest American planters, who long had chafed under severe restrictions.

To restore order in the Treasury, Necker desired the creation of a Treasury Board, with representatives from the Assembly in its personnel. The Assembly operated under rules forbidding executive appointments to any of its members. Nevertheless, the royal influence was enlisted on behalf of Necker's proposal, a political manoeuvre rightly esteemed by Short to be distinctly prejudicial to the monarchy.[20]

Short's despatches for March concluded with further comments on West Indian discussions in the Assembly, and with information that a new judicial system had reached the forum of debate, the system adopted in the United States being much admired.[21]

Despatches like these from Short lacked the intimate note afforded by Lafayette's famous letter of the seventeenth of March, favoring Washington with a sketch of the Bastille as it was a few days after the order for its demolition had been issued, and presenting him with the principal key to the fortress. No mean recognition, this was, of Washington's position as a world revolutionist, and possibly the most valued gift that he ever received. "It is a tribute which I owe to you, as son to my adopted father, as aide-de-camp to my general, as a missionary of liberty to its patriarch." [22]

Brilliant and valued as the Marquis might be as an occasional correspondent, it was upon Short that Washington and the American Government naturally relied for a consistent record of events. Short performed his duties steadily and earnestly. Only a very active gatherer of news, only a man received in influential circles, could have maintained so high a frequency and standard in his despatches. They are frequent, lengthy, and rich, worthy it would seem of separate study.

From Paris on the fourth of April 1790, Short, with a sort of genial irony, revealed once more the influence of the coast towns upon the most far-reaching economic and commercial decisions of the Assembly, winning their case this time by a promise to support the assignats which were soon to be emitted. Short believed they would be substantially a paper money issue, with slight regard to theoretical land values pledged to their support. In this he proved correct.

Turning to the plans for a judiciary and to certain prejudices which would need to be forgotten, Short coined a memorable epigram: "The opinions of many men like a pendulum, frequently fix at the true point only after vibration."

Plans for reorganizing the army were contradictory. A counter-revolutionist had been unearthed, or one reputed to be such. An occasional émigré returned to Paris, notably the Prince de Conti. Of more significance, the inquiry into the march upon Versailles began to yield results, though these were so compromising that they might be suppressed for the sake of certain leading men, including several members of the National Assembly. "No body doubts," asserted Short, "that the expedition to Versailles was effected by a faction who had views of a very criminal nature—they failed in their object as well on account of the King's refusing to quit Versailles & retire to Metz, as the conduct of the French grenadiers, who entirely devoted to the Marquis de la fayette, became the protectors of the Royal family as soon as the posts which they desired, were put into their possession." [23]

Short had made a point of forwarding the Leyden *Gazette,* but copies apparently were not arriving, for Jefferson, now Secretary of State, requested his special attention to the matter. "The English Papers," reminded Jefferson, "bring their Lies very fresh; and it is very desirable to be provided with an authentic Contradiction in the first Moment." [24]

Much acrimony was stirred at this time by the publication of the *Livre Rouge,* a list of former pensioners of the King, citing names and amounts but omitting reasons for the pensions, which were of course legitimate in many cases. Short thought this procedure needlessly provocative. At the same time, with the growing derangement of finances, Necker's position was deteriorating. Lafayette, on the other hand, continued in the heyday of his influence. The King sought his opinion about the degree of power that should be vested in the monarch under the Constitution. Lafayette replied in writing, adding that should the King accept the terms suggested, he would uphold him against all parties. Favorable action by the King would unite all moderate men for the suppression of anarchy and the restoration of the State.[25]

Eleven days later, Short reported that the King had accepted Lafayette's proposals, some of them half-heartedly, and that a new ministry was to be formed, with the Marquis naming the incumbents. The despatch contained much fiscal information. The assignats were to be issued on favorable terms. At least the momentary action marketwise was beneficial, though depreciation might come later. An extended parliamentary discussion of religion, deeply interesting to the nation, and described in detail by Short, resulted in such a way that France was now almost as advanced as the United States in attaining complete freedom of conscience. In all of this Lafayette played a conspicuous role, to the still further enhancement of his enormous popularity, a popularity which Short contemplated with obvious pleasure. As Lafayette's star was rising to even greater heights, Necker's was sinking to an eclipse which Short described dispassionately, his emotions no more enlisted than in the practical suggestions for commercial intercourse with which the despatch concluded.[26]

From this summary of state papers, it is agreeable to turn to the robust soldier who had led the French at Yorktown and whose career was far from ended. The Count was writing from his estate of Rochambeau, near Vendôme, on the eleventh of April 1790:

> Do you remember, my Dear général, of the first repast that we have made together at shad-island. I did you remark from the soup the difference of the character of our two nations, the french in burning their throat, and all the americans waiting wisely of the time that it was cooled.—I believed, my dear general, you have seen since a year that our nation has not change of character. we go very fast—God will that we come at our aims. I have had my part of troubles of that revolution. I have passed half of the last year in my department of Picardy, they made me passed in the month of July in that of the province of alsace—

I did find there Strasbourg and all the province in a terrible insurrec-tion—I have employed there six months to retrieve good order. I came back here afterwards to rest myself and make some remedies for my health which has been altered of.—the natal air made me well, and the King has named me yet here commissary to have an eye to the organisa-tions of the assemblies of department—you are you, my dear general, in a full enjoyment of a work of fourteen years, and we will in a year of time complete a work that cannot be but the fruit of the patience that I have known to you and of a complete regeneration of the man-ners—God make us arrive to it and make forget to the univers some wicked strokes that have not fouled the revolution of america—Let us hear of you my Dear General and be well persuaded of the inviolable attachment with which I have the honour to be

my Dear General
Your most obedient
and very humble servant
le Cte de Rochambeau

a thousand kindness and compliments to M. Jefferson, to M. Knox and to all my ancien camarades and friends which are near you.[27]

Rochambeau was not dull. He possessed capacity for thought and feeling. But his range of interest and experience contrasted sharply with the omniscient perspective of even a rather minor diplomat like Short. To such an one the student turns for stead-ier guidance. In despatches of May 1, 1790, Short continued his account of the religious changes which, though liberal, were far from universally approved. He gave a searching interpreta-tion of the politics behind the balloting for President of the As-sembly, in which the Duc d'Aguillon, a violent opponent of the Royal Family and among those implicated in the riots of Oc-tober 5 and 6 preceding, was defeated by a M. de Vivieu, who in turn resigned his new position next day. The account is too detailed for repetition but does credit to Short's insight. Further insight was manifested in his account of the intricate political manoeuvre designed to speed the Assembly to its tasks and bring about its early dissolution. Numerous details completed a large canvas.[28]

On the ninth, Short set forth the contrary arguments and opinions of the Assembly respecting the new judiciary system, as well as the present status of the assignats. Here he demon-strated the power of clerical influence to develop Catholic opposition, particularly in the southern provinces where the Huguenots were strongest. The clergy assured their followers that the sequestration of Church lands and the issuing of assignats against them was the device of a Protestant majority in the National Assembly to wreck the Catholic Church. Considerable fanaticism was thereby aroused.

Here and there, reported Short, members of the Noblesse had suffered violence. But of far greater interest was the continued investigation into the causes of the October riots. Apparently the Government intended to unearth the situation, whoever might be inconvenienced. Always in the hinterland of suspicion were the Duc d'Orleans and his faction. Some evidence of comparative tranquillity was afforded by the return of several émigrés, notably the Cardinal de Loménie, a character obnoxious to many of his compatriots.[29]

A week later, Short presented the debate on the royal prerogative respecting war and peace. He summarized the discussion regarding the authors of the October 5 and 6 outrages. It was generally believed that large sums of money had been employed to incite the people to the massacre of the Garde du corps and the forcible entry into the Château of Versailles.[30]

In his next despatch Short summarized the decision of the Assembly on the King's prerogative respecting war and peace—a decision acceptable to the right wing and approved by the left to save face with its constituents, as Short very cleverly demonstrated. The victory lay with Mirabeau and Lafayette. The Jacobins for the moment knew defeat. Their time was not yet come. Short described it all in a memorable report, a credit to himself and to American officialdom.[31]

On the more personal side of correspondence, on May 1 Thomas Paine expressed to Washington confidence in the outcome of the Revolution. "I have not the least doubt of the final and compleat success of the French Revolution—little ebbings and flowings, for and against, the natural companions of revolution, sometimes appear, but the full current of it, is, in my opinion, as fixed as the Gulph Stream." [32] A month later Paine was still of the same mind. "The french Revolution is not only compleat but triumphant & the envious disposition of this nation [he wrote from London] is compelled to own the magnanimity with which it has been conducted." [33]

Like the contrary reports of bulls and bears in a broker's office, Washington might set against the optimism of Tom Paine the gloom of Moustier. Though still French minister to the United States, he had been at home in France for some time. The Count saw in the two revolutions, American and French, the contrast between the erection of a strong government in the one case, its destruction in the other. Not only had the French monarchy been deeply wounded, but the remedies now advocated on its behalf might readily prove fatal. Too many of the physicians, moreover, were incompetent or insincere.[34]

George Washington was a world figure. One measure of such eminence is the pleasure shown by people everywhere in contributing their mite of information and respect, with no expectation of replies. Voluminous as was the great man's correspondence, outgo by no means equalled intake. Nevertheless, such old friends as Luzerne and Lafayette were entitled to the courtesies of correspondence. To Luzerne's letter of the preceding January, Washington replied on April 29:

> You are right in conceiving, that nothing can be indifferent to me, which regards the welfare of the French Nation. So far removed from that great Theatre of political action, and so little acquainted with many of the minute circumstances, which may induce important decisions, as I am, it would be imprudent for me to hazard opinions, which might possibly be unfounded. Indeed, the whole business is so extraordinary in its commencement, so wonderful in its progress and may be so stupendous in its consequences, that I am almost lost in the contemplation. Of one thing, however, you may rest perfectly assured, that nobody is more anxious for the happy issue of that business than I am; as nobody can wish more sincerely for the prosperity of the French Nation, than I do. Nor is it without the most sensible pleasure I learn, that our friend the Marquis de la Fayette, has, in acting the arduous part which has fallen to his share, conducted himself with so much wisdom and apparently to such general satisfaction.[35]

To Lafayette he was similarly vague but cordial:

> How much, how sincerely am I rejoiced, My dear Marquis, to find that things are assuming so favorable an aspect in France! Be assured that you always have my best and most ardent wishes for your success; and that, if I have not troubled you with letters of late, it was because

73

I had nothing, which it was very essential to communicate, and because I knew how much better your time was employed, than in answering letters merely of a private nature.[36]

Washington could not have known as yet what Short wrote privately to Jefferson, that while Lafayette's popularity was still increasing, a combination of his enemies was taking place which might soon give serious trouble.[37]

A rather technical despatch from Short on June 14 included an item or so of permanent historic interest, one describing the grief displayed by the Assembly on news of Franklin's death; the other reporting the King's insistence that aristocratic and other disaffected elements must accept the Revolution.[38]

Other despatches of this period mentioned a renewed interest in abolition of feudal privileges and titles, reminiscent of the fourth of August in the year preceding. They indicated that abolition of these dues would tend to further alienate any possible good will on the part of German princes and of the Pope. A proposal greatly to reduce the salaries of even high ecclesiastics would be certain to antagonize the numerous creditors of these functionaries.[39]

With the fall of the Bastille an event of less than one year previous, fears were already entertained that Bastille Day might become an anniversary of turbulence. There was fear, moreover, lest the Duc d'Orleans should contrive to stir up violence, a fear considerably lessened because of "his known unwillingness to undertake what is evidently dangerous." [40]

Considering its theme, it is not improbable that Washington was informed of the contents of a private letter from Short to Jefferson on July 7, 1790. His subject was their joint friend Lafayette. Short believed the Marquis was exhausting his personal fortune. He would accept no salary, yet frequently he set a hundred plates at table. Madame de Lafayette had been desperately ill but was now recovering.[41]

Short was for the present both officially and unofficially the chief purveyor of French news. A despatch of July 7 reported the debates relative to the proposed return of the Duc d'Orleans. Lafayette, it seemed, urged against it strongly, though admit-

tedly the nearer drew the Bastille anniversary the less there was
to fear from His Royal Highness' presence. The King was known
also to oppose his relative's return. Deputies had been arriving
from the provinces, and crowds were massed in huge numbers
at the Champ de Mars in anticipation of the July fête. So far
all was gay, but mob action under the impact of foreign gold
was quite unpredictable.[42]

The Duc d'Orleans did return, powerful opposition to the
contrary, and Short unofficially described his reception at court.
This was glacial on the part of all except the Queen, who treated
him cordially enough but kept him waiting quite unconscion-
ably. At the Assembly he met with a welcome far more genial,
due no doubt to his own strong partisans among the members.
Details were appended in a private letter to Jefferson concerning
the approaching festivities of the fourteenth of July. Nothing
could reveal more fully the extent to which social revolution
had progressed than the plans for hospitality to civilian delegates and soldiers appointed to take part:

> The deputies are lodged in private houses, that is such as chose to receive
> them—the private soldiers are treated with the greatest marks of civility
> & attention, even by the Marechals of France who lodge them. In short
> it is impossible to concieve [sic] a more equalising system than that
> which prevails at present.[43]

The Revolution interested Short so intensely that on July 14,
he wrote Jefferson privately of his hope to be retained at his
present post in preference to any other possible appointment.
To leave Paris in the midst of such absorbing drama would be
like quitting a play at the end of the third act.[44]

The festivities of the fourteenth went off with great éclat.
Short described it all to Jefferson, but unofficially, perhaps for
greater freedom. The taking of the oath by the King evoked a
marvelous enthusiasm. Short had never seen its equal. And the
entire spectacle was so magnificently staged as to be genuinely
impressive. The Duc d'Orleans played an inconspicuous role
and apparently nothing occurred beyond the perfectly auspicious.[45] Perfect harmony was maintained between the temporary
delegates and the National Assembly until the visitors returned

75

to their respective provinces, a harmony which Short rather dryly intimated was "contrary to the fears or hopes of every party." [46]

Trustworthy information came also from the Comte de Moustier, unknowing victim, as we saw, of Jefferson's determination to be rid of him just as the Federal Government commenced to function. In July he wrote, somewhat incoherently, that we in France "plunge deeper and deeper into a dangerous labyrinth; a mixture of the love of celebrity, of taste for novelty, of irreflexion, of cupidity, has bewildered many minds; France is at this day in complete anarchy." And, with a patriot's alarm, "There are very few men worthy of true liberty, which cannot exist without virtue and respect for the laws, especially those which respect property. Philosophy supplies at this day new masks to ambition and intrigue." Again, "It is bitter for a good citizen to behold his country serving as a lesson to nations, while she might have furnished them with an example." [47] Thus pessimism had the ear of Washington.

In August the wheels of Revolution turned anew. A furious debate argued the propriety of allowing Austrian troops to cross French territory en route to the Low Countries.[48] Proceedings were nearing their conclusion in the Chatelet's investigation of the October troubles at Versailles. Rumor had it that the Duc d'Orleans and Mirabeau were both involved. Short thought under such conditions it was politically unwise to keep the question open.[49] Short here was writing Paine, and it is unlikely that Washington ever saw this letter, but the sentiment was current.

Meanwhile Washington himself was thanking Lafayette for his letter of March 17 and the key to the Bastille which had been forwarded through Thomas Paine. His gratitude was expressed felicitously. The sentiments were genuine but cautious:

> Happy am I, my good friend, that, amidst all the tremendous tempests,[50] which have assailed your political ship, you have had address and fortitude enough to steer her hitherto safely through the quicksands and rocks which threatened instant destruction on every side, and that your young King in all things seems so well disposed to conform to the wishes of the Nation. In such an important, such a hazardous voyage, when every thing dear and sacred is embarked, you know full well my best wishes have never left you for a moment. Yet I will avow

that the accounts we received through the English papers (which were sometimes our only channels for information) caused our fears of a failure almost to exceed our expectations of success.[51]

While Washington expressed a guarded optimism, Short was penning privately to Jefferson a picture of social dissolution which boded ominously to any friend of Lafayette or France. Complete breakdown of finances was the keynote. The absence of central authority and the corresponding rise of municipal sovereignties, each intent on self-defense and the ferreting out of counter-revolutionists, resulted in a burden of expense out of all proportion to the revenues.[52]

Also there was increased acerbity in the discipline meted by the Assembly to its own offending members. Short related a case involving the president himself, who was sentenced to eight days in prison, later commuted to eight days under guard at home, for printing an address which the Assembly had refused to listen to and declined entirely to endorse.[53]

Other letters of this period from Short to friends not immediately in Washington's circle were darkly pessimistic. The American liberal detected a growing turn toward most illiberal practices, which boded ill for the happier progress of the Revolution. Perhaps he caught the turning point. If so his official report of August 27, that certain regiments having disbanded had declined to renew their obligations, revealed a growing cancer. A government so incapable of even rudimentary discipline was not in a good way.[54] Morris agreed. As he reported, "Their Assemblée is losing ground daily in the public opinion. The army, long encouraged in licentious Conduct, is now in Revolt. All the Bands of Society are loosened, and authority is gone." [55] Alexander Hamilton accepted this same opinion and reinforced it in a cabinet memorandum to his chief concerning proper American reaction to the Nootka Sound Affair and its possible demands upon the Bourbon Family Compact.[56] There was confirmation, too, from a French source. The Marquis de la Rouërie lamented that a once powerful empire had been brought so low that history either ancient or modern could afford no parallel.

The Marquis had apparently forgotten Spain. But he at least remembered one circumstance which is most illuminating. No

matter how universal is disaster, there seem always to be some
who go prosperously ahead. La Rouërie was one of these in
France, and his testimony supports the argument that general
rules ignore specific cases:

> While castles were Burning on every parts of France & in my neigh-
> bourhood, I was adding considerable Buildings to mine; in a word,
> all what has pass'd has not occasion'd me to take a step less or more
> than I was accustomed. My ancient vassals have continued to act with
> that friendship & respect which they testified to me Before; and except
> those who have a seat in our national assembly, every one of which
> I despite with profession, no matter which side they have taken, for they
> have all betray'd their charges, I have the same friends I had Before.[57]

Lafayette added his testimony to a growing belief that the
Revolution faced a turning point between the right and left.
He did not say this in so many words, and perhaps he did not
fully recognize the wider implications, but his description of
the change in his own situation was a case in point. Constantly
attacked by aristocrats on the one hand and by Revolutionary
factions on the other, he could not say with certainty which was
the more responsible for insurrection. The National Guard remained the best hope of safety. More ominous than Lafayette
could yet perceive was the rising power of the Jacobins, to which
he testified. He anticipated that the following week would see the
report to the Assembly on the affair of October 5 and 6. He
thought evidence was insufficient against either Orleans or Mirabeau. Their system was obscure but they did not appear to be
acting in collusion. Lafayette noted an unmistakable boredom
among the populace with the dilatory tactics of the National
Assembly and perhaps with the Revolution as a whole.

If the reader of these comments has come to appreciate the
perspicuity of William Short, he will enjoy this tribute from
Lafayette:

> I rely on my friend Short to give you the political news. His talents,
> zeal, and the esteem which he enjoys enable him to provide you with
> the best information. Mr. Jefferson knows his merit as well as I do and
> can assure you that he is the most suitable person to represent here the
> interests of America.[58]

Short justified this generous encomium by a despatch of September 5, unusually rich in content and interpretation. A mutinous guard regiment at Nancy was vigorously punished by an army under the command of M. de Bouillé. The news of this in Paris pleased the National Assembly but alarmed the city mob, who professed to see therein the finger of the counter-revolution, and even went so far as to demand removal of the ministry and the hanging of certain ministers. Inflammatory journalists made the most of their opportunity for mischief. Futher news concerned the resignation of M. Necker after a strong protest against issuing two billions in paper money. Here Short made some sane observations upon economics, to which he added a comment on the Revolutionary press, with special reference to *L'ami des peuple* and the even more sensational *c'en est fait de nous,* where the suggestion was lately made to kill the Queen, imprison the Dauphin, and hang between 700 and 800 members of the National Assembly, with Mirabeau at their head.[59]

Despatches of this period mentioned with alarm the waning power of Lafayette. In Short's opinion, his influence with the National Guard and the more solid citizens was the best and virtually the only insurance against mob violence. Short put the case something like an epigram. "The Marquis de la fayette has sworn enemies in all the parties, owing to his having endeavoured to conciliate them all." He was pointing the finger at a fatal flaw of leadership. Too big for Lafayette already, the task was growing daily bigger. Indeed, Marat, the extremist, now dared to attack him and even to call him traitor. But such an attack was premature, for there were honors still in store for Lafayette.

Finances also occupied much space in Short's despatches—a chronic theme but just then more acute with Necker's resignation uppermost and fiat money shortly to be issued.[60]

A year after the event, almost to a day, Short reported that the inquiry into responsibility for the mob violence in October 1789, failed to impeach Orleans and Mirabeau.[61] It had been a long drawn-out investigation. Probably neither contemporaries nor posterity were satisfied. But there was nothing more to do about it.

A further despatch on the twenty-first treated of Santo Domingo, once more defining the conflict between the doctrinaire Assembly and hard-headed planters wholly committed to the slave trade. The despatch contained a lengthy summary of politics in the Assembly and described perceptively the position of Montmorin and other ministers. Futher references occur to the assignats and to diplomatic representation in the United States, where Moustier had yielded place as minister to another not yet announced, but undoubtedly to be Ternant,† a friend of Lafayette and well qualified.[62]

Short's common sense told him that a plan of Lafayette's to place in the ministry men hitherto unknown for rank or wealth or achievement, but newcomers, as a tribute to democracy, might not work so well. It might be all well enough to level down the aristocracy, but there were dangers in elevating their inferiors.[63]

From Amsterdam whither he had gone earlier in November, Short reported the attack by a Paris mob upon the Hotel de Castries, to punish its owner for a duel he had fought with M. de Lameth, a demagogue high in favor with Parisians—just one more sign of growing violence and disorder. The sale of Church lands, on the other hand, was proceeding well and promised a satisfactory solution of the debt, provided it did not lead to economic excesses.[64] For, as Gouverneur Morris remarked about this time, France was an eternal variable. A system that might serve to extricate her in adversity might fail her in prosperity.[65]

If Short had been a trifle blinded to the true inwardness of things by his friendship for Lafayette, Gouverneur Morris had no such inhibitions. In his survey of French leaders of the period, he was iconoclastic in removing the Marquis from his pedestal. He described Lafayette as one

who has hitherto acted a splendid Part. Unfortunately both for himself and his Country he has not the Talents which his Situation requires. This important Truth known to the few from the very Beginning is now but too well understood by the People in general. His authority depends on Incidents and sinks to Nothing in a Moment of Calm, so that if his Enemies would let him alone his twinkling Light would expire. He would then perhaps raise Commotions in order to quell them. This his Enemies have long charged him with unjustly I believe but I would not answer for the future. The King obeys but detests him. He obeys because he fears. Whoever possesses the royal Person may do what he pleases with the royal Character and authority. Hence it happens that the Ministers are of la Fayette's appointment. A short Description of their use was given the other Day by Mirabeau—"We make ministers (says he) as we used formerly to send servants to keep our Boxes at the Play House." Lafayette thinks that these his creatures will worship their Creator [quite a different explanation, this, from Short's], but he is mightily mistaken. You know du portail the Minister of War. He is said to be violent in favor of the Revolution.

Sketches followed of Du Portail and of other, perhaps lesser, lights, not one of whom could meet the test the times imposed.[66]

Concluding despatches for 1790 from William Short, still at Amsterdam, presented no great novelty. Reasons why members of the National Assembly desired the more or less indefinite continuation of its sessions were exhaustively, if perhaps cynically, analyzed. Lafayette was complimented, but his increasing difficulties were admitted. The moral and economic dilemma respecting the West Indies, Short further noted. Counterrevolutionary forces were recognized, their danger apparently perceived by those who superficially might profit from them. "It was cause of much uneasiness at court & particularly to the King & Queen—the latter would in such a case be in very real danger, as she is still very obnoxious to the people & their leaders, & considered by them though unjustly, as the soul of all the efforts made against the revolution." [67]

Thus with the close of 1790, it should have been clear to informed circles in the United States, to George Washington most of all, that the French Revolution was entering upon a new and dangerous phase which might burst the bubble of inflated reputations and which might undo besides much of the good that already was accomplished.

CHAPTER
FIVE

1791

1791 was in various ways the year of decision. The Emperor Leopold, for example, who had steadfastly refused to intervene until his brother-in-law should quit Paris, received strong inducement for a more vigorous policy in the abortive attempt which Louis actually made. Artois, whom his brother's representative considered a mischief maker, received his *congé* in January. Farther east the Empress Catherine, sometimes called a "Machiavelli in petticoats," hoping to secure a free hand in Poland, was prodding her neighbors at Vienna and Berlin to intervene in French affairs. Equivocal conditions in eastern France, where the Holy Roman Empire still claimed feudal rights notwithstanding the Abolition of Privileges, afforded some excuse for intervention whenever it was so desired. In France, Mirabeau and Lafayette, both of whom had stability at heart, could find no common basis of agreement. And the Court, to its supreme misfortune, could not agree with either.

More momentous than the plots of Catherine, than the ill-co-ordinated efforts of feeble princes without, or the rivalries of politicians within France's borders, was the loss of the (im)moral giant Mirabeau, whose death on April 2 removed the last prop of monarchy. In his well justified self-estimate, "I carry the last rags of the Monarchy away with me." [1] With almost his last breath he warned the King to remain in France. Attempted flight would precipitate the gravest consequences.

Three events marked April as an historic month. Mirabeau died, the Pope condemned the Civil Constitution, and the King was denied permission to spend Easter at Saint Cloud. As Louis saw it, nothing now remained save exile. But preparations needed time. The flight would come in June.

As the skies for royalty were darkening, it is fair to say that the intrigues of *ci-devant* princes and nobles, not to mention the schemes of foreign potentates, ran afoul of both Louis' and Marie-Antoinette's sense of duty to France. The Queen beheld in the bad deeds and bad intentions of the émigrés self-interest only, with no consideration for herself or the King. She regarded her brothers-in-law, the Counts of Artois and Provence, as chiefly to blame for the dangers menacing the Royal Family. Writing on May 14, 1791, to her sister-in-law, Madame Elisabeth, she denounced the movements of the émigrés as nothing short of a calamity. Artois especially was contemptuous of her views and his brother's. She noted that her own brother, the Emperor, despised these émigrés.[2]

Such was the posture of affairs, actual and emotional, when on the morning of June 21 the *premier valet de chambre,* Lemoine, entering the bed chamber of the King, found it unoccupied. The Queen was missing, too. They were already well on their ill-starred journey to the frontier. When almost there the Royal Family was halted at Varennes and on the orders of Lafayette was returned to Paris, in terrific heat and dust amid the jeers and curses of a gathering mob. Lafayette maintained some order in the city, and silence reigned as the King returned to the palace. But the monarchy had plumbed fresh depths. The Royal

Family had lost any semblance of free movement. Thereafter its confinement would be narrower even than the Tuileries.

Beyond a natural interest in such a lowering of the curtain on monarchy, it was of concern to Americans that Count Axel Fersen, the young Swedish nobleman who had accompanied French forces in the American Revolution, and Gouverneur Morris, by then our minister to France, both played conspicuous roles in the plot to succor the King. Morris was specifically violating instructions which forbade any participation in the Revolution.

On June 26, the King was cross-examined by the Deputies and shortly afterward was suspended from his functions, though in the excessive weakness of the executive under the new Constitution, that probably did not greatly matter. Meanwhile, at least one brilliant man found his loyalty shifting away from the Revolution. Barnave had been one of the commissioners sent to Varennes to return the King to Paris. Riding in the berlin with the Queen, he had become captive to her charm. Though not originally a friend of monarchy, he was now convinced that the Revolution had moved too fast and too far, and resigned his seat in the Jacobin Club, which increasingly was supplanting the National Assembly as the real legislature of France. Barnave could not know it but he was taking a long step toward the guillotine, though it would bide its time till 1793.

Sieyès, too, now declared that monarchy was a better guaranty of liberty than a republic, this in reply to Thomas Paine. Others, notably Alexandre Lameth and DuPort, also found their sympathies shifting.

Reminiscent of the rioting that culminated in the fall of the Bastille just two years earlier, was the incident of the Champ de Mars on July 17, when a mob, drunk with the blood of two wretches about whose misdeeds, if any, stories varied, hurled rocks at the National Guard. With more patience than might have been expected from men who had been under arms all through a hot and tiring day, the Guard fired their muskets in the air. As the next move in this meaningless but hectic drama, a mobster fired point blank at Lafayette. This was too much for the Guard. It then fired on the mob, killing or wounding many rioters. Lafayette's popularity could not long survive events like this.

The early months of 1791 had been difficult ones for Lafayette. On February 28, he had driven from the Tuileries the "knights of the poniard." On April 18, in the rioting to prevent the King's departure for Easter at Saint Cloud, he had resigned his command, but resumed it on strong urging. And the decision to order the King's arrest at Varennes had not been an easy one to make. To offset these difficulties, he was promoted to the rank of Lieutenant General on June 30. Far more than in his earlier and not too valorous part in the rioting at Versailles, Lafayette had now become the symbol of law and order. As Commander of the National Guard he became the protector of the bourgeoisie by whom it was established. The cleavage between this moderate right of center group and the clubs on the extreme left had now become unbridgeable. Lafayette's subsequent incarceration in an Austrian prison unquestionably saved him from the guillotine.

The third year of the Revolution saw no improvement in the economic situation. Harvests were a quarter below those of the preceding year, and artisans were being dropped from the national workshops. They were destined to make future trouble. Political wisdom reached a new low when the Assembly decreed that its present members were ineligible for re-election. On September 13, the King formally accepted the Constitution, though he regretted the weakness it imposed upon the executive. Its work accomplished, the Assembly shortly afterward adjourned in a mood, strange to say, of enthusiastic loyalty to the King—a loyalty in which even the Queen enjoyed a modest share.

But fresh storms were gathering. The designs of Monsieur and the Comte d'Artois were bearing fruit. The foreign monarchs still were hesitating. They favored Louis' acceptance of and loyal adherence to the Constitution. They drew up the innocuous Pillnitz Declaration. But they permitted the émigrés to add the Coblentz Manifesto which breathed direst threats of extermination and decapitation against the Parisians. Even Marie Antoinette, not too clever a politician, understood the threat to her family in such a treasonable move by the King's brothers. To her it spelled "Cain." [3]

The King was equally dismayed. That he perceived the menace to his throne and his life from the armies gathering on the frontier is evident from a letter of August 15, 1791, to Condé, military leader of the émigrés, who as a prince of the blood might properly take an interest in the survival of the monarchy:

> My Cousin! In vain have I testified to my brothers how contrary to wise politics, to the interest of Frenchmen in exile, to my own cause, were these armed gatherings on the Rhine frontier. These gatherings which never will have my approval multiply a hundred fold the strength of my enemies. These enemies regard me as the soul of your preparations. They suppose me to be a secret council under the name of the Austrian Committee which guides the spirit of the Queen, which is sustained by my will, and which retains you on the borders of the Rhine. If it is necessary for me to descend from the throne, to mount the scaffold where Charles I was immolated, to abandon all that I hold dearest on earth, I am ready. *But no war, no war!* [4]

As government under the new Constitution came into being, great importance would attach to the personnel of the Assembly. Many of its figures were to write their names on some of history's bloodiest pages. Significant from its earliest sessions was the superior zeal of the left wing—a phenomenon as true of the Twentieth as of the Eighteenth Century. In a conciliatory gesture to the new leadership, the King demanded the return to France of his brother, the Comte de Provence, the self-styled "Regent." He was not obeyed. Louis XVIII waited for Napoleon to leave. Again on the constructive side, Louis named his putative kinsman, the Vicomte de Narbonne, as Minister of War—a capable official.[5]

On the ominous side, the new Assembly, constituted largely of atheists—page once more the Twentieth Century—renewed the attacks upon "refractory" priests. Failure to accept the Constitution spelled arrest and imprisonment. This the King could and would not accept. He might have stood his ground successfully had it not been for fresh frontier alarms. The great wars of the French Revolution were soon to break.

That they did break out was due in part to the fatuity of Louis, who, under the reckless urging of the Queen, on December 3,

1791, addressed top secret letters to his fellow monarchs urging the calling of a European congress which should employ at least the threat of armed force for restoring order in France.

Of these, the chief events of 1791, to what extent was Washington informed? In much detail, we may suppose, considering the increased volume of his correspondence. Throughout the year preceding, the despatches of William Short to the Department of State afforded Washington the most reliable and continuous information concerning French affairs. Surely he must have recognized Short's competence, nor can one believe that he would have dispensed with so well qualified a guide had he not perceived in Gouverneur Morris even greater talent. The change did not occur immediately, and Short's despatches continued to bring fresh news of France to Washington's attention.

In January reports were current in Amsterdam, where Short was sojourning, that the National Assembly might soon terminate its labors. Short doubted this. A further item of good news was the quiescence, on the whole, of the clergy under the changes in their property and status. Fresh disturbances were reported from the sugar islands, but there were few details. Short either had not learned them or he supposed that they were more quickly known in the United States than in the Netherlands.[6] Privately, Short informed Jefferson that Lafayette's stock was rising. His party strengthened in proportion as divisions marked the Jacobins. The Marquis had himself been ill, however, for the first time since the Revolution started.[7]

Short was premature in the bill of health he gave the clergy. Their refusal to subscribe to the Civil Constitution of the Clergy was general. An exception was the curate of St. Eustache, the King's confessor, who took the oath in obedience to the King's desire to avert disorder. Recusants were with difficulty protected from mob violence. The National Guard was once more indispensable.

As yet the emission of the assignats was proving beneficial. They were properly employed in the purchase of the nation's obligations and the funds were rising. Depreciation was less than might have been anticipated. Affairs would assume a rather smiling countenance if only the Assembly should complete its business and go home.[8]

Not long afterwards, Short officially reported two remarkable occurrences. One was a petition from 2,000 citizens of Strasburg for the re-establishment of the nobility and clergy, a petition which aroused in Paris, as in the case of the Penguins of a far earlier day, neither joy nor sorrow, possibly, but a very great surprise.[9] The other was the delayed transmission to the National Assembly of a letter to the King from his brother-in-law, the Emperor, dated from Vienna on the fourteenth of December last. Short would not vouch for the letter's authenticity. He thought it well might be a forgery. He transmitted, however, a French translation of the original in Latin.

Short was unduly skeptical. The communication bore internal evidence of validity. It was an emphatic protest by the Holy Roman Emperor against the injuries which his feudal vassals, ecclesiastical and lay, encountered in the abolition of privileges traditionally theirs in eastern France, and guaranteed to them by the Treaty of Münster. It was the inevitable conflict between feudalism surviving in central Europe and feudalism abolished in France, a conflict which would not be resolved until the armies of Napoleon should sweep away the debris of the past.[10]

On the more personal side and directed immediately to Washington, was a note from Lafayette on January 25, evidently hurried and with little news beyond the status of commercial relations between his own and his adopted country.[11] Also, an enthusiastic admirer in the British Parliament transmitted the verdict of a moderate conservative "viewing with alarm" from across the Channel. Sir Edward Newenham feared that too much had been attempted too suddenly. Projected changes in the Church were especially disturbing to conservatives; and neighboring Princes could not be expcted to view the Revolution with indifference.[12]

Sir Edward at this time represented the county of Dublin. He was rich and highly placed, a strong opponent of Catholicism, much interested in the reform of the British Constitution.[13] His letter scarcely contributed to Washington's information, but it was a sound analysis and may easily have had some imperceptible but real effect upon the thinking of its recipient.

Short's were apparently the only communications on the French Revolution to be received, or at all events to be preserved, for February. Short hastened on the seventh to correct his error about the Emperor's letter. The country had the word of Montmorin that it was genuine, also the assurance that it was only a form letter which the Emperor was obligated to compose. The disturbances behind the Strasburg petition, it could now be stated, were subsiding. The position of the clergy was less favorable. Nonjurors were being rapidly replaced by clergy more subservient, with some prospects of disturbance in the provinces.[14]

Short's stay at Amsterdam was considerably prolonged, but as he informed the Department on the eighteenth, the legation was in the hands of a good secretary—a tribute well deserved, else how could Short have remained so minutely informed of the Revolution's movements as his despatches indicate?[15] For the synopses here transcribed present only a partial picture of the wealth of Short's material.

Interesting was his account of the King's aunts. Few more amiable or harmless personages[16] could have been found in Europe at this time than the somewhat elderly, wholly nonpolitical aunts of the King. These daughters of Louis XV, symbols to their own and later times of elegant simplicity and the refinement which sometimes subsists in palace walls, were overwhelmed by events which lay outside their ken. Possibly they felt the Pope alone could give them comfort and assurance. At any rate, they desired to go to Rome, and the King upheld them in their wishes. The municipality of Paris, on the contrary, was violently opposed, and needed to be reminded by the King that the Declaration of Rights allowed every citizen to go and come as he saw fit. Which caused Short to observe rather dryly, "It is remarkable that for some time past those who are considered as the greatest enemies to liberty have been obliged most often to invoke the declaration of rights & the principles of the Constitution—They in general however invoke them in vain.—The acts of tyranny exercised by the people assembled or by their municipal or legislative representatives are considered for the most part as legitimate, by a kind of subversion of all the ideas of true liberty." [17]

Short expected no improvement in this distorted picture until the National Assembly had quit its labors and been replaced by an authority better constituted. Indeed, the imbecility of the parliamentary methods employed in the Assembly inspired Short's frequent comment. He felt that its attitude toward American commerce, none too friendly at the moment, might be imputed to his disadvantage; just as a saner attitude, certain to develop some day, would be credited to his successor of that date [18] —good political reasoning, no doubt, for parties as for individuals.

Meanwhile, the journey of the King's aunts to Rome caused serious rioting in Paris, armed men even entering the royal presence for the purpose, as many believed, not of attacking or even of defending the King's person, but of taking advantage of confusion to remove him to some other part of France, or even beyond the frontier. Report had it also that the Bishop of Speier was contumacious in the defense of his feudal rights, suggesting confidence in firm support. "This however will probably depend on circumstances," remarked Short, "—the disorders of France may in time beget so much internal discontent as to invite foreign interference, but I cannot think they would have anything of that sort to fear if their Government were properly organised & order restored." [19] Decidedly a pregnant utterance.

As part of a despatch devoted chiefly to oils, tobacco, and general commerce, Short included on March 12, 1791, excerpts from a letter of his secretary of legation as of March 7. Reminding Jefferson that the secretary was a friend of Lafayette, extremely well informed and most reliable, but temperamentally excitable, he quoted with occasional comments of his own a passage illustrating the pitch of passion to which approaching hostilities from beyond the Rhine were driving the Parisians. Days of unprecedented violence were come, the secretary said. The aristocrats were making no attempt to hide their fury. The Jacobins and the '89ers [20] were set for mortal combat, while

91

terror loomed along the Rhine. Recruiting was in progress in
Baden. At Carlsruhe and Worms there was talk of nothing save
invasion. The same was true at Coburg. Factionalism reared its
head. Domestic insurrection threatened. In the event of invasion, it would be impossible to estimate how many heads would
fall. For the moment Lafayette was favorably situated, but as-
sassination threatened him from many quarters. Twice recently
he was believed to have been slain.[21]

Before the month was past, Short returned to Paris, from
whence his Revolutionary letters derived increased authority.
He found things quieter than he had anticipated, but noted
that the Revolution had been marked throughout by just such
alternations between veritable frenzy and entire tranquillity.
He quoted the Marquis de Lafayette, the Duc de la Rochefoucauld, and the Comte de Montmorin as sharing the opinion that
the Assembly would soon adjourn. Short disagreed. He believed
that with these moderates the wish was father to the thought;
also that they were deceived by the eclipse in popularity of radicals like the Lameths and Barnave, an eclipse which Short believed was temporary.

Viewing the Civil Constitution of the Clergy already in some
slight perspective, Short thought it the most ill-advised measure
which the Assembly as yet had passed. He felt that it imposed
a needless test of loyalty upon the less enlightened portions of
the population as between their devotion to Church and State,
a distinction which might operate to the disadvantage of the
latter. Symptom of the strong feeling which the taking of
the oath involved was the controversy between the Pope and the
Cardinal Loménie de Brienne, who had taken the oath out-
wardly as a prudential measure, but had rejected it inwardly.
The Pope reproved the Cardinal, not only for the act but for
the motives and the subterfuge. The Cardinal then returned
his red hat to Rome, refusing to retain it longer. This action had
political significance, for in the event the Pope should declare
the kingdom in a state of schism, there was a possibility that
Loménie would be declared Patriarch in a new national church.
Short believed the Pope intended to work the maximum of mischief.

Further gossip asserted that a recent invasion of the King's apartments had brought on an alarming indisposition. He was recovered for the moment, but it was unlikely that he could long support such mental agitation and bodily inactivity as was now his lot. Short attached high importance to the monarch's health, as upon his health and more especially his life, hung the issue of civil war, which would immediately follow any personal disaster to the King.

Short had special grounds for believing this, because while in the Netherlands, he had heard much wild talk of émigrés who were convinced that Europe was arming in their cause. Maintaining that three fourths of all Frenchmen opposed the Revolution, they believed a handful of foreign troops could turn the balance in favor of conservatism. They were likely to attempt this dangerous experiment. That Short was right, the massacres of 1792 would soon reveal.[22]

From Lafayette there came a letter of March 7, of perhaps greater historical interest than could attach to Short's communications, however penetrating their insight. For Lafayette was still a key man in the Revolution and his position, so splendid yet so dangerous, lent high importance to his words. His account reflected deep anxiety and a doubt as to his living long. With such bitter enemies among both aristocrats and radicals the worst might happen. But whatever dangers might surround him personally the success of the Revolution, thank Heaven, was assured in France and, if order could be maintained at home, would extend to the rest of the world. Unfortunately to date the populace had shown greater aptitude for overthrowing despotism than for respecting laws.

Following some comments on the tobacco trade, Lafayette paid tribute to his friend Jean de Ternant, the new minister to the United States. He praised particularly his love of liberty, his time-tested devotion to the American cause, his veneration for Washington personally. Ternant was beloved by patriots in the Assembly. The King, too, held him in high regard. It was in all respects, affirmed Lafayette, an admirable appointment.[23]

With his capacity for keen analysis, epigram, and sweeping generalization, Morris wrote Washington two days after the

93

above from Lafayette and to somewhat similar effect. He sapiently observed,

> . . . in the present Effervescence very few Acts of the Assembly can be considered as deliberate Movements of the national Will. There still continue to be three Parties here. The *Enragées,* long since known by the name of Jacobins, have lost much in the public opinion, so that they are less powerful in the Assembly than they were, but their Committees of Correspondence, called *Sociétés patriotiques,* spread all over the Kingdom have given them a deep strong hold of the People. On the other hand the numerous Reforms, some of them unnecessary, and all either harsh precipitate or extreme, have thrown into the aristocratic Party a great number of the discontented. The Military, who *as such* look up to the Sovereign, are somewhat less factious than they were; but yet they are rather a Mob than an Army, and must I think fall either to the aristocratic or Jacobin side of the question. The middle men are in a whimsical situation. In the Senate they follow the Jacobine Counsels rather than appear Connected with the other Party. The same principle of Shamefacedness operates on great occasions out of Doors, but as the Aristocrats have been forced down by a torrent of opinion from the *Heighth* of their absurd Pretensions, and as the middle men begin to be alarmed at the Extremities to which they have been hurried, these two Parties might come together if it were not for the personal animosities among the Leaders. This middle Party would be the strongest if the Nation were virtuous, but alas! this is not the case, and therefore I think it will only serve as a Stepping Stone for those who may find it convenient to change sides. In the midst however of all their Confusions, what with confiscating the Church Property selling the Domains curtailing Pensions, and destroying Offices, but especially by that great Liquidation of public Debts a paper Currency, the Nation is working its way to a new State of active Energy which will I think be displayed as soon as a vigorous Government shall establish itself. The intervening Confusions will probably call forth Men of Talents to form such Government and to exert its Powers.[24]

With searching insight both Short and Morris had separately forecast some of the essential developments of the Revolution, not merely for 1792 but for a more distant future. With similar intelligence, if possibly less comprehension of futurity, Sir Edward Newenham also favored Washington with an historical comparison which was decidedly arresting. He found a striking analogy between affairs in France since October 1789, and those in the last ten years of Charles I. The similarity extended to the resolution for the redress of grievances, the appointment of committees for the several departments, the seizure of Church revenues, the annihilation of Episcopal authority, and control of the armies.[25]

With a military forthrightness worthy of Rochambeau but decidedly more severe, General Armand, Marquis de la Rouërie, presented Washington with a most distracting picture of his country and with a generalization or two, pathetic by contrast with the incisive comments of American observers previously quoted. Politics to the worthy nobleman was in a wretched state, with France an example to all future times of the risks inherent in over-hasty reforms entrusted to the conflicting interests of selfish men.[26]

It would seem that such a wealth of comment should have elicited from Washington some expression of opinion. It did so, both officially and unofficially. In the former, the Department of State expressed its gratitude to the National Assembly for taking official notice of the death of Benjamin Franklin.[27] This homage of one nation to a private citizen of another was unique and was deeply felt by his compatriots. Yet even in his unofficial capacity, and to so close a friend as Lafayette, Washington did not divest himself of caution:

> The distance, which separates us, joined to the delicacy of the subject, has always suspended my opinion on your national affairs. I am well aware, that it is impossible to judge with precision of measures, the motives of which are sometimes unknown, and the necessity of them not always understood. But there is one circumstance, on which I find it difficult to suppress an anxious wish; that the present National Assembly may not protract their own existence so long, as to beget any uneasiness on that score. The confirmation of their decrees will be best made by a second representation of the People, and that representation, to act efficiently, as a legislative body, may possibly be required to be reorganized. My affection for the French nation, my sincere wish that their government may be respectable, and the people happy, will excuse the disclosure of this sentiment, the only one, I believe, that I have ventured to offer on the subject of the revolution.[28]

There is an evident connection between this opinion of the President's and the almost constant disparagement of the National Assembly which he received from Short and others. Yet the advice was bad, for the self-denying ordinance of the National Assembly when it eventually laid aside its duties was to mean the introduction into Revolutionary politics of new and untried men and still further demoralization in society and government.

The death of Mirabeau afforded Short the text for an excellent homily on April 8. His views on this great man have remained the views of history. Mirabeau's final and complete ascendancy over the King and over everyone else save a few aristocrats and a few demagogues; perhaps most of all his mastery over himself after so turbulent a youth and middle age; his extraordinary insight into men and measures; the clarity with which he comprehended and the eloquence with which he expounded; yes, even his state funeral and the declaration by the Assembly that the Church of Ste Genevieve, the place of his interment, should be a national sepulchre (the *Panthéon*) into which only the greatest of mankind should be privileged to follow him, electrified contemporaries and captured the imagination of posterity.[29]

Short had shown rare comprehension in his criticisms of the Civil Constitution of the Clergy, and the oath imposed on members certain to be conscientious objectors. Events confirmed his view. The oath provoked needless confusion of conscience and was responsible for a great loss of popularity for the King himself, who blew now hot now cold to a law which he was forced to sanction. At the King's request one of his confessors had reluctantly taken the oath. Later the King insisted upon hearing the mass read by priests nonjurors. News of this spread through Paris and resulted in much rioting; in a refusal to allow the King to spend Holy Week at Saint Cloud; in open defiance of Lafayette, who sought to maintain order and to guard the royal person; in the resignation of the Marquis from his command of the National Guard; and in his reacceptance of command upon the almost prayerful request of the municipal authorities of Paris. Taught by such upheavals, the King consented to be served by priests who had taken the oath. But the mischief had been done. Thereafter, Short perceived a definite waning of attachment to the King and a corresponding movement toward the left.[30]

Less informative than the remarkable despatch describing these events, but interesting as coming from a man of wide experience in both America and Europe, was a communication from Berlin, of April 26, written by the Comte de Moustier. He struck pretty hard at the "chief of a Revolution." Was Lafayette in mind?

Boasting of his love of country, Moustier lamented the abuses of the past, and regretted that the present was no improvement, going about with its head too far in the clouds. Still speaking apparently of Lafayette, he complained, "The tissue of a false glory —the enthusiasm of the perfection of Government—cupidity— vengeance & hatred are not good ingredients for forming the chief of a Revolution." [31]

De Moustier was worth reading, but Short was more consistently available. A long despatch from Short on May 3, continued on May 4, presented little that was new but rather a continuation of old issues in fresh developments. The Church was still the major theme. French politics and the repercussion of the island colonies, abolition of the tariff barriers for Paris, a burning of the Pope in effigy, a decision whether Avignon and the Comtat should be considered part of France, were continuous problems.[32]

Five days later, these issues seemed to Short in better equilibrium. First and foremost, the National Assembly, with scarcely a dissenting voice, had pronounced in favor of the utmost freedom in religion, "whether by worship or otherwise." It remained to be seen, however, in what manner the Paris mob would accept the renting of churches to nonjuring Catholics. Yet even the profession seemed remarkable to Short. By philosophers it would not have been surprising, but in this case, toleration was applauded by conservatives.

Once more, reported Short, attacks were launched against Lafayette, this time "by a demagogue of the party of the Lameths," on the score that having surrendered his commission in the National Guard, Lafayette could not resume command until elected by the several sections of Paris. Meanwhile, his acts were those of a tyrant and usurper. The American observer felt that petty persecution of this sort would only prolong the popularity of Lafayette.

Between the Papacy and France, a severance of diplomatic relations seemed in prospect. The Pope refused to accept M. de Ségur as ambassador, on the score that he had sworn to uphold the Civil Constitution of the Clergy. For its own dignity the Court of France felt obliged to ignore the Papal Nuncio.[33]

Amid these generalities, there was one outstanding personality. Lafayette remained so spectacular a figure of the Revolution that Washington must have been deeply interested in the Marquis' own estimate of recent happenings, including his resignation from the National Guard. Declaring that the rage of parties had barely stopped short of shedding blood, Lafayette naively but truthfully went on to say that he himself was attacked by all parties because they saw in him an insurmountable obstacle to their evil designs. Extraordinarily enough, however, his popularity was undiminished. Here followed the National Guard episode from the viewpoint of the central figure, saving possibly the King alone.

With equal authority as an insider, if not as a prime mover, Lafayette proceeded to a discussion of the Assembly and its prospects, not more illuminating, perhaps, than the despatches of William Short, but a trifle more authoritative. There was about it all a rather sweet simplicity. Lafayette considered himself a great man. The error was pardonable. And he was writing with the candor of his nation and his native frankness to a friend who most assuredly would sympathize.[34]

More from the periphery than from the center, the Marquis de La Luzerne wrote on the fifteenth that the great error of the Revolution had been a determination to accomplish everything at once. A good King and an intelligent Assembly could have brought the nation happiness, "but the mania to be creators, the desire to go beyond all other people, the ignorance of political principles, united with abstracted ideas of philosophy, have plunged us into an abyss from which it is perhaps impossible we should ever recover, at least for a long time." What followed must have been familiar to Washington, for it is unlikely that Luzerne in London was as minutely informed of the Revolution as was Washington in Philadelphia. His comment upon Lafayette, however, could not fail to interest:

> The Marquis de la Fayette has been placed at the head of the national militia of Paris, and to a certain point has maintained order, and notwithstanding what Detractors say, who are very numerous, he has done much good, and prevented still more harm— His courage, his personal virtues always assure him a great number of suffrages, but his popularity is lost—he has already several times desired to resign—it is only his patriotism which continues him in a place impossible to fill. If, like the Americans we had possessed a man sufficiently elevated by his reputation and his virtues to command all the nation, and to know exactly the length we ought to have gone, we should have been like the Americans, one of the happiest of the nations of the world, having the best laws, and I may say at present without fear of being thought to flatter, we should have been governed by a prince the best qualified by the dispositions of his heart to make subjects happy. Pardon, Sir, this long discussion of the misfortunes of my country—but I am so much affected by them, and I am so sensible of the interest which you take in them that I could not avoid pouring them out into your breast.[35]

The waning influence of Lafayette was mentioned in Short's despatch of June 6, 1791, so that with predictions so frequent, Washington cannot have been surprised when disaster finally overtook his friend. More surprising was its long delay. His original ascendancy was powerful.

In a budget often brimming with complaints at the general ineptitude of Frenchmen, Short now and then admitted some striking sign of progress, as for example the new status of the Post Office. He informed the American Secretary of State that letters were no longer opened and censored at the Post Office. The National Assembly was anxious to uproot this ancient custom.[36]

The Assembly was likewise expressing itself most earnestly of late on the subject of commerce with America, in a manner unsatisfactory to the latter; [37] and, on what must have been far more interesting to Frenchmen, the prospects of invasion by the émigrés, and the probable degree of loyalty to the Revolution among officers of the army.[38] Short thought the danger of invasion was exaggerated.

In this he was proved wrong. Indeed, his very next despatch, June 22, 1791, related the escape two nights previously of the King and Queen and the Royal Family from Paris, to the amazement and the consternation of the Revolutionary leaders. When the King's departure became known next morning, orders to intercept him were sent to all parts of the kingdom. His speedy capture at Varennes and the excitement it aroused led Short to anticipate that "the Assembly will conduct themselves with moderation but it is impossible to answer for the excesses of the people & particularly with respect to the queen.—The crisis is really tremendous & may have a disastrous issue." [39]

Four days later, details of the King's escape and capture being now well known in Paris, Short contributed a detailed account. The story is familiar, one of the classics of the Revolution. It was conveyed immediately to the Department of State and consequently to George Washington. In Short's version, the Assembly acted with much dignity and efficiency. The episode, however, was certain to delay the elections for the legislature previously ordered. It added also to the difficulties and dangers of Lafayette, who was delegated to watch over the safety and to be responsible for the person of the King, to be in short his jailer. Meanwhile, the fate of the King and Queen would be determined by the Assembly. He might be retained in nominal authority, or at the behest of mob elements in Paris, he might be totally discarded.

Some commentary on the character and intelligence of the royal captives may be gleaned from a paragraph of Short's describing the abuse and vituperation indulged in by the King and Queen against Lafayette's aide-de-camp who arrived at Varennes for their arrest. The Queen was especially venomous, the King somewhat less so, notwithstanding that to him they owed their lives, while for them Lafayette had sacrificed his popularity. [40]

With some slight perspective on the Varennes affair, Short felt that the results for Lafayette might be disastrous. As guardian of the King's person, he could please neither King nor populace and his authority would further wane. Even before the King's escape, reports from the provinces indicated a striking growth in republicanism. Any new body of representatives would voice this sentiment. The National Assembly as presently constituted was monarchical at heart. Hence its increased reluctance to order elections in the provinces, which were well nigh certain to go contrary to its principles. So low had sunk the prestige of the King that he was now frequently denominated as *Louis le faux* or *Louis le parjure*. In her explanation of how they managed to escape, the Queen seemed determined to incriminate Lafayette; whereas Bouillé was in reality responsible.[41]

From so great a crisis as Varennes and an aftermath which appeared to be portentous, it is anticlimactic to contemplate a routine and pedestrian epistle from Lafayette on June 6, well before this new phase in the drama was enacted. Washington was presented with a synopsis of France's daily troubles. The émigrés assembled on the frontiers were intriguing with all the despotic governments. The French army was officered by aristocrats, and manned by undisciplined troops. The capital was a prey to partisanship. The Assembly was exhausted by protracted labors. The oath demanded of the clergy presented additional difficulties. But progress was evident. Neighboring governments might detest the Revolution but they hesitated to intervene for fear of the contagion.

In view of the large part which William Short has occupied in these present pages, a further tribute to his merit may not be amiss. The love and esteem in which Short is held in France, says Lafayette, is as beneficial to the public as it is honorable to himself.[42]

It was inevitable that the flight to Varennes should long color the minister's despatches, representing as it did so enormous a loss of prestige to the monarchy. On July 8, *inter alia,* Short discussed the voting on a governor for the Dauphin. There were ninety candidates, many of them obscure and unsuitable. The election was suspended till candidates could be investigated. In transmitting various newspapers and pamphlets, Short apologized for their disgusting contents, unworthy in ordinary times to be read at all, but now submitted for their illustrative value as to the state of public sentiment. The abolition of monarchy was a favorite theme, and Paris was deluged with placards and leaflets of this tenor. Of personal liberty there was none. The émigrés were more active. Necker, having been some time in private life, was now engaged in writing. Short recommended his account of the Revolution to date as "not the most flattering," but certainly the truest that had been presented.[43]

As a result of the flight the King was suspended from his duties as executive. He would be restored only when the Constitution should have been completed and accepted. Short thought this a most unwise procedure if the Assembly really desired to preserve the institution of monarchy, which he believed it did. In the extreme tension of affairs a new orator had arisen in the person of Brissot † de Warville, reputedly the ablest and most eloquent since Mirabeau. Also with pen, rather than voice, M. de Condorcet † was coming into prominence as an advocate of republicanism.

Under the circumstances much rioting might be anticipated. This proved to be the case, and required energetic suppression by the Assembly and the military. Even more significant was the growing menace of foreign intervention, under pretext either of injury to the feudal rights of the Holy Roman Empire, or of safeguarding the Royal Family. Economically, matters were improving. The assignats maintained their value, and ecclesiastical property found ready purchasers. Indeed, prosperity was cited by republicans to prove that the people were ready for self-government. As for foes beyond the border, the émigrés were divided and would be formidable only in the event of grave disunity at home.

An atmosphere of mystery surrounded the arrest, polite detention, and release at this time of the Jew Ephraim, reputed to be an agent of the King of Prussia. Whatever underlay his arrest and prompt release, such consideration was remarkable in a land where *habeas corpus* was so utterly suspended.[44]

It will be recalled that Short considered republican sentiments to be more widespread in the country as a whole than in the National Assembly. Thomas Paine, who undoubtedly possessed "grape-vine" information on anything so dear to his heart as republicanism, reinforced this opinion, writing from London on July 21. "I arrived here from France about ten days ago. M. de la Fayette was well. The affairs of that Country are verging to a new crisis, whether the Government shall be monarchical and hereditary or wholly representative? I think the latter opinion will very generally prevail in the end. On this question the people are much forwarder than the national assembly." [45]

The Department of State was favored by its minister in Paris on July 24, 1791, with estimates of troops available in the event the country was invaded. As a probable defender, Rochambeau, commanding on the northern frontier, received honorable mention for "the open & decided part he has taken in the revolution," while in the event of an allied attack, Lafayette would assume command of the mobile forces. It was the misfortune of the Revolution, however, that the violent and arbitrary actions of the National Assembly so antagonized good men.[46] For genuine enthusiasm and loyalty would be needed when prospects pointed—and here Short was decidedly prophetic—to foreign war in 1792. Some opposition to the Revolution was inevitable. The crowned heads of Europe were becoming its avowed and personal enemies as they beheld the humiliation of their brother monarch.[47]

With the Revolution overseas so obviously pressing toward fresh crises, it would have been strange and even heartless had Washington expressed no interest at this time. He did express it, and warmly so, though one would hardly glean as much from the Ford edition of his writings which "edits" away the heart of his communication as respects affairs in France, leaving only a rather formal and chilling pronouncement.

Washington wrote to Lafayette from Philadelphia on July 28, 1791, expressing his deep anxiety at the personal danger enveloping the Marquis, an anxiety by no means alleviated by the letters which Lafayette had sent him. Nevertheless, Washington was ready to admit that for a man engaged in bold enterprises for the welfare of his country, for a man who was animated by pure and lofty views like Lafayette's, personal safety was a consideration wholly secondary. A warm heart, said Washington, could never be indifferent to the welfare of four and twenty million human beings. Above all an American, indebted for such great help from France at a time of deep distress ought to deplore the disorders in that country and the uncertainty prevailing there. One must trust in Providence which governs great events, believing that It can, by Its will, produce order out of chaos notwithstanding present clouds.

The populace in great cities is always turbulent and redoubtable. Its violence for a time overthrows all public authority, with consequences sometimes extended and terrible. At Paris presumably tumults are especially disastrous with the public mind in so high a state of fermentation and so great a number of malignant and intriguing persons fomenting trouble and upsetting public tranquillity in order to attain their ends, something which never fails to happen in similar circumstances. Tranquillity can hardly be restored, until the Constitution has been completed and a government established and the body of the national representation has been renewed, for until such time the enemies of the Revolution will not abandon the hope of re-establishing everything in its former status.[48]

Supplementing the above, one may include a brief paragraph of tender warning for the Marquis: "I readily perceive, my dear Sir, the critical situation in which you stand, and never can you have greater occasion to show your prudence, judgment, and magnanimity." [49]

That same day, apologizing for his infrequent letters, Washington wrote Morris:

> The communications in your several letters, relative to the state of affairs in Europe, are very gratefully received; and I should be glad if it were in my power to reply to them more in detail than I am able to do. But my public duties, which are at all times, sufficiently numerous, being now much accumulated by an absence of more than three months from the seat of Government, make the present a very busy moment for me.
>
> The change of systems, which have so long prevailed in Europe, will, undoubtedly, affect us in a degree proportioned to our political or commercial connexions with the several nations of it. But I trust we shall never so far lose sight of our own interest and happiness as to become, unnecessarily, a party in their political disputes. Our local situation enables us to maintain that state with respect to them, which otherwise could not, perhaps, be preserved by human wisdom.[50]

Early in August it became evident to Short that the Constitution, slowly wrought and long deferred, at last was nearly ready. Hence the fresh importance of what would happen once the King accepted it and its regulations took effect. The King's position was anomalous. As a prisoner he could not possibly exercise authority. As a freeman he would probably quit the kingdom at the first opportunity. Facing a dilemma of this sort, no government could operate with energy or confidence. Confusion would continue. Nevertheless, in the field of foreign policy an encouraging factor was evident. The Queen had almost certainly urged the Emperor, her brother, not to intervene in France. It would be too dangerous for herself and family.[51]

By the twenty-fourth of August, it was expected that the Constitution would be ready in another week, and that it would be accepted by the King, possibly with intent to overthrow it at the earliest opportunity. Some uncertainty still existed as to the prospective status of princes of the blood. It was believed they might be permitted to retain their titles, while denied the rights of citizens on the score of being dangerous to society.[52]

As usual Short was well informed. The Constitution actually was near completion, and the status of the Royal Family proved to be what he conjectured. The Duc d'Orleans seized the opportunity to declare that he valued far more highly his rights as a citizen than his privileges as a prince, which, as Short declared, merely made him further ridiculous to his enemies.

With an eye to shifting politics, the American minister now ventured the opinion that the outstanding demagogues in the Assembly, Alexandre Lameth,† DuPort,† and Barnave, were in collusion with the King, that their change of front was suspected by their constituents, and that their popularity was on the wane. What they wished was to be members of the Cabinet. A decree of the Assembly prohibited executive appointments to its members. The triumvirs wanted a repeal of the decree. In this they encountered violent opposition. The King, his suspension from office still continuing, no longer received the ambassadors of foreign powers, but he did not lack the society of Frenchmen and maintained, in fact, a veritable court. There was cause to fear, in view of the elections now in progress, that the membership of the next Assembly would include "many violent exaggerated & bad men." News from Santo Domingo was disturbing, also, with the color issue sharply to the fore. On the immediate frontiers, the hatred of the upper classes throughout Europe for everything connected with the Revolution aroused apprehension.[53]

Some final preliminaries remained before the acceptance of the Constitution, questions chiefly as to the ritual involved. But in due time, a delegation from the Assembly headed by M. Thouret formally presented the Constitution to the King and was graciously assured that His Majesty would examine the document promptly and render his decision without delay. Despite these amenities, Short thought that the nation reposed but little confidence in the King. Election results revealed, however, a more moderate choice for the new legislature than had been expected.[54] An immediate result of the interchange of civilities between the Assembly and the King was the removal of his guards and the restoration of his liberty.[55]

The next step in reconciling the legislative and the executive was the appearance of the King before the bar of the Assembly, the Queen accompanying him, to take the oath. The King on this occasion requested an amnesty for those under prosecution because of the Revolution. On motion of Lafayette the amnesty was granted amid general approbation. But this temporary appearance of good will could not conceal the anxious posture of affairs. "Much will depend on the conduct of the King & the future Legislature—I fear however that events will occur either at home or abroad which they will not be able to controul by the force of the constitution as it remains at present."

With the adoption of the Constitution, the National Guard was to be reorganized, thereby giving Lafayette a long awaited opportunity to quit the service.[56]

The occasion called for Short's keenest efforts at interpretation. He noted the earnest purpose of the King to make his acceptance of the Constitution appear genuine and hearty, even to the extent of antagonizing those aristocrats who still remained in France. He believed that for the present the King was sincere in his complaisant attitude, under a conviction that the restoration of tranquillity would spell security for himself and family. Besides, the opposite course, namely of antagonism to the Constitution and reliance upon foreign aid, would play into his brother's hands, something he would resort to only in a dire emergency. Much would depend upon the attitude of the incoming Assembly. Further encroachments upon the royal prerogative and continuation of the state of anarchy might drive the King to "the alternative however disagreeable of putting himself under the protection of his brother & foreign aid." [57]

The minister here manifested his usual keenness. The King's position was certainly ambiguous and would become increasingly embarrassing should his brothers bring their preparations to the point of actual invasion. The King would then be compelled to make war upon his brothers and the émigrés in defense of a Constitution which he surely could not favor, but to which he was bound by solemn oath.[58]

With his customary shrewdness of interpretation and vigor of presentation, Gouverneur Morris confirmed privately these official communications of the minister. He, too, noted the obvious eagerness of the King for popularity, adding sagely, "indeed his Life and Crown depend upon it." Democratic principles would pervade the new Assembly. Sectionalism, Morris found, was sharply drawn, with democratic radicalism in the south, marked ecclesiasticism in the north; an attachment to Germany and the Empire in the east, and a survival of aristocracy in Normandy and a part of Britanny. One of the curiosities of the times lay in the financial workings of the outgoing National Assembly. Called for the purpose of averting bankruptcy, it had seized Church property to the amount of one hundred millions sterling and yet was quitting its deliberations with the economic crisis worse than ever and bankruptcy inevitable. The increasing exodus of aristocracy need not blind the world to the impossibility of restoring old abuses. It was very doubtful just what aid the foreign powers would give them. Strategically, Flanders was the most exposed to invasion by the foreigners, with Artois and Alsace-Lorraine only slightly more secure. But notwithstanding considerable paper strength in the armies now gathering, Morris had no fear of action in the present year.

Montmorin had quit the ministry; Moustier was rumored as his possible successor—an unlikely choice, thought Morris, the position under Constitutional limitations having become quite meaningless. Colonial affairs were still precarious.[59]

On the tenth of September, Washington, whose information throughout the year had been more than usually extensive, wrote to two of his French friends, Luzerne and Lafayette. Both epistles were of similar tenor. Luzerne died before receiving his. It will suffice to quote from that to Lafayette:

> The lively interest which I take in your welfare, my dear Sir, [titles had been abolished, it will be recalled] keeps my mind in constant anxiety for your personal safety amidst the scenes in which you are perpetually engaged. Your letter of the 6th of June by Monsieur de Ternant gave me that pleasure which I receive from all your letters, which tell me you are well. But, from the account you there gave it did not appear that you would be soon relieved from your arduous labors and from the information we have received of an important event which has taken place since that time it does not appear likely that the clouds which have long obscured your political horizon will be soon dispersed. As yet we are in suspense as to what may have been the consequences of this event; and feeling, as we do in this country, a sincere regard for the french Nation, we are not a little anxious about them. Opinions we are not able to form here therefore none can be given on the subject. But at any rate, you may be assured, my dear Sir, that we do not view with indifference the happiness of so many millions.[60]

It would not appear that the leading editors of Washington's writings who published the previous paragraph took a very lively interest in the question of his relation to the French Revolution, for they omitted a postscript of September 21 in which Washington, having meanwhile learned of the adoption of the Constitution, felicitated Lafayette upon the event, anticipating advantages would flow from its adoption not to France alone but to the world. The prayers and blessings of every friend of the human race were following France in her great movement, nor would mankind be satisfied until the affairs of France were fully regulated under law, with equality respected. No one would more rejoice in the happiness of France and in the part which Lafayette personally had played by conduct as noble as it was unselfish, than his sincere friend Washington.[61]

It is regrettable that expressions so warm and human should be deleted in the more available editions of the writings of George Washington. The public needs to know his sympathetic nature.

A type of information to which Washington quite logically had access was the reports of French ministers in the United States. A hint of this appeared in a communication from Tobias Lear, personal secretary to the President, written on October 2, 1791. Lear reported the Minister as somewhat perturbed and very busy over affairs in Santo Domingo. In France he felt certain that the Assembly would recognize the King's inviolability and that the nation as a whole, the Parisian mob excepted, would approve. The nation was in full readiness to repel foreign invasion. Confronting such an emergency, partisan divisions would be forgotten.[62] In fine, good order and tranquillity might be anticipated soon.

From Paris, meanwhile, William Short wrote on the same day, his information still weeks distant from his native shores, that the National Assembly had been prorogued on September 30, and that the King had received extraordinary demonstrations of affection from the floor and from the galleries. A more solemn note added that the time was approaching when the King must take action against his brothers and the émigrés [63]—a major test of his sincerity.

That the King was capable of playing politics in a minor way, even though he made mistakes on serious issues, appeared from his success in balancing the people of Paris against the Assembly on the mighty question of whether his chair in the Assembly should or should not be emblazoned with the fleurs de lis. Short thought his manoeuvres advantageous in limiting the overweening power of the Assembly.[64]

The King's emergence from his suspension of authority was signalized at Vienna by permission for the French ambassador to appear once more at Court. At Paris, the ambassador from Sweden, obedient to orders from his King, had refused to conduct business with the Assembly. He, too, appeared at Court once more. These were the outward and visible signs of restoration of the royal dignity. Perhaps a further sign was the return of Lafayette to his estates, followed by the good wishes of the National Guard and the citizens of Paris, who proposed a petition to the Assembly to reimburse him for expenses he had incurred in support of the Revolution.[65] An even more delicate attention, characteristic of the national courtesy at its best, was a gift from the municipality of Paris of a marble bust of Washington, to be executed by Houdon and set up at whichever of his estates Lafayette might designate, "in order that he may have always before his eyes his friend whom he has imitated so gloriously." [66] Not being in direct communication with Washington, Short asked Jefferson to convey this information.

With the coming of November, pessimism replaced this modest cheer. The American Government was informed of Montmorin's resignation and the difficulty of finding a successor; of extreme insubordination in the fleet; of continued dissatisfaction in religious minds over taking the oath for the Civil Constitution of the Clergy; of a budget no nearer than ever to a state of balance; of the eagerness to join the émigrés manifested not only by the nobles and the clergy but recently by commoners as well; and finally of continued discontent in the West Indies and among the merchants in that trade.[67]

The aggressive tactics of the émigrés finally called forth the written disapproval of the King. His brothers, ordered to return to France, openly disobeyed him on the assumption that Louis did not act as a free agent. It was with the idea of disproving such an allegation that the Assembly submitted to a test case of the prerogative, and lodged no protest when the King vetoed a law passed against the émigrés in general but most severe against the Princes. Fear still reigned in the minds of some that the King meant to quit Paris at his earliest opportunity. It led to an awkward incident when a sentinel on duty held him under virtual arrest for several hours.[68]

Unaware, of course, of these most recent changes, but still under the profound impressions aroused by the adoption of the Constitution, Washington on November 22 renewed his felicitations to Lafayette:

> I cannot conclude this letter without congratulating you most sincerely on the King's acceptance of the Constitution, presented to him

by the National Assembly, and upon the happy consequences which promise to flow upon your Country as well as to mankind in general, from that event. The prayers and wishes of the friends to the human race have attended the exertions of your Nation, and when your affairs are completely settled under an energetic and equal government the hearts of good men will be gratified, and no one will rejoice in your felicity, and for the noble and disinterested part you have acted more than your sincere friend and truly Affectionate, etc.[69]

Such optimism should have been considerably tempered by reports in December from the somewhat disillusioned Newenham, and the seldom sanguine Morris. Said Newenham, "The affairs of France for this last Month do not please me—Internal Tumults & Divisions, encreasing Imigrations—no Military *Subordination*—Scarcity of Money—& the peaceable Manner in which the ce Devant Princes allowed to Array their Troops in several of the German States, & the vast supplies of Money they get from Different Powers—it astonishes me, that the French Government does not immediately send an Army across the Rhine & disperse the Enemy at Coblentz & Worms." [70]

Discoursing at far greater length, Morris used as a text "every Day proves more clearly that their new Constitution is good for Nothing." Want of confidence was general both in the Constitution and in the body of the citizenry. The Assembly proceeded daily to fresh follies, one of the more recent of these being a threat to carry "Liberté" beyond the Rhine, armies for that purpose having been already designated. It would not be so bad if there were any organization, but Washington could not conceive of such a lack of it. America at its worst could afford no comparable example, for there the criminal law at least was executed, "not to mention the mildness of our manners." As for the French soldiers, they represented "that corrupted Scum of overgrown Population of which large Cities purge themselves, and which without Constitution to support the Fatigues, or courage to encounter the Perils of War, have every Vice and every Disease which can render them the Scourge of their Friends and the Scoff of their Foes." Nor had Morris any better word for the economic situation. "The Finances are so deplorably bad that the Bankruptcy which already exists by the Depreciation of the Paper Money, must soon be declared by stopping Payment in some quarter or other, unless those effectual Remedies be applied which seem to be beyond the Power of the Government and beyond the Talents of those who administer it." [71]

Information of similar import, but in more guarded language than this familiar letter of a friend, reached the Department of State from William Short, as of December 30, 1791.[72] Thus George Washington and the Government which he presided over should have been pretty well prepared for war and great events in 1792. If the Revolution began as we have been considering in 1787, it is a striking circumstance that the great wars of the French Revolution were not precipitated till five years afterward. Yet on so magnificent a scale were events now taking place that five years was a mere gestation period for the monster seeking birth.

PART II

"No, no! No violence! No blood!"

—Louis XVI

CHAPTER SIX

1792

If one regards the expiring monarchy as the focus of interest from 1787 or 1789 until the King's execution in January 1793, the amazingly bad judgment shown by the Court at every turn in its tragedy of errors dominates the scene. Posterity still marvels at such misguided choices. There were men in France devoted to the throne even if not to the anarchic abuses of the *ancien régime* who, if their abilities and purposes had been even partially understood by a muddled King and his meddlesome mate, might have saved King and country—the one from destruction of the monarchy; the other from the overthrow of everything for which the Revolution struggled.

Mirabeau had been such a man; but the Court judged his morals rather than his intellect. It gave him a subsidy but ignored his advice. Lafayette was another potential prop for the shaking throne, but here again the Court could not forget his early vacillations and was imperfectly aware of his actual services.

Personalities, however, hung on the event of war. Disasters or victories alike would result in violent repercussions. The Girondists in temporary power, the Jacobins seeking to replace them, the King quite willing to adorn his throne with military laurels, the neighboring princes subordinating rescue of a brother sovereign to more material gains—all wanted war. The excuse for war could be manufactured readily.

War was in the air from the year's opening. On the twenty-fifth of January the National Assembly requested the King to put the question of war or peace directly to the Emperor Leopold. The Austrian reply on the nineteenth of February was haughty and uncompromising. But on March 1, the not wholly unreasonable Leopold died suddenly, to be succeeded by his son Francis II, whose long reign was a continuous struggle against the Revolution in all its manifestations.

Meanwhile, the economic crisis in France was worsening, with assignats at a 40 percent discount, an augury of their eventual worthlessness. The military situation likewise apparently was weakened by the dismissal of Narbonne. This was engineered by the Court, which never could distinguish between the competent and the incompetent, between loyal men and traitors. Nevertheless, the Girondist Party, whose real leader in the Assembly was the eloquent if shallow Brissot de Warville, found in Charles François Dumouriez † an aggressive Minister of Foreign Affairs and later a general in the first great victories of the war. The party was enjoying a brief tenure of power before its overthrow by the Mountain—the fiercer Jacobins.

Not unlike the French boasts of 1870, so appallingly refuted by the Franco-Prussian War, Narbonne while at the War Office had boasted of France's complete readiness for all eventualities. This confidence was almost equally unwarranted. Out of 9,000 officers, 6,000 unfriendly to the Revolution had quit the army. Of a total force of 150,000 men, the infantry numbered 110,000; the cavalry, 30,000; and the artillery, 10,000. When the test came, the artillery proved stronger than the enemy's; but what could not be anticipated, let alone measured, was that Revolutionary fervor would prove the factor of decision.

But this is anticipating. On March 27, Dumouriez sent an ultimatum to Austria. And on April 20, with the royal assent, war was declared by almost unanimous vote, with commensurate opportunity for oratorical outbursts. Words eclipsed deeds, for the first battle of the war was a disaster for the French. On April 28, an attack by Generals Dillon and Biron on the Belgian frontier was utterly routed by the Austrians and their allies. Had their victory been followed up the war might have ended then and there. But sloth and caution and the more congenial investing of fortresses lost an opportunity which was not to be repeated for another twenty years and more.

A domestic repercussion of the recent defeat was an order of May 27 for the deportation of nonjuring clergy and a parallel order of the same date for disbanding the King's guard of 6,000 troops. Thus the King was deprived of all protection against a rising tide of violence. A few days later the Assembly, with the royal sanction readily procured, permitted an army of 20,000 "Federates" to be stationed near Paris. This was in furtherance of Revolutionary principles, whatever these might mean to the Jacobins, for ere many months the Girondists would lose control.

Indeed, a rift in power soon became apparent, for on June 13 the King, in one of his last official acts and with a surprising burst of energy, dismissed Roland as Minister of the Interior, Clavières as Minister of Posts, and Colonel Servan who had been now in, now out, of the War Office.

Stirred to counteraction by Madame Roland, far more of a man than her husband, and by other members of her salon, a crowd of 8,000 assembled on June 20 to celebrate the anniversary of the Oath of the Tennis Court. The crowd, intoxicated with alcohol and a maudlin enthusiasm, marched first to the Assembly, which received it with much loss of dignity. Next it advanced upon the virtually unguarded Tuileries, where it forced the King to don the *bonnet rouge,* but where further mischief was averted by the arrival of the National Guard. This

117

was just one more step in the constant harassment and humiliation of the monarchy.

Meanwhile Lafayette, who was no Girondist but merely a great noble, loyal to the Revolution but personally loyal to the King, fell between two fires. At the Jacobin Club, Camille Desmoulins denounced him as "a villain and an idiot." [1] On the other hand when Lafayette learned that the King proposed to review the National Guard on June 29, he begged to be allowed to show himself before his former troops and to lead them against the Jacobins. His offer, which conceivably might have averted the September massacres and the whole infamy of the Terror, was instantly rejected. Not only rejected but compounded with treachery, for the Court informed the ignoble Pétion, mayor of Paris, of Lafayette's intentions and the review was called off. What could one do in the face of stupidity so monumental and at the same time so infamous? A vindictive Queen fancied she was getting her revenge.

On July 2, the "Federates" were permitted to enter Paris proper, but as events soon showed they afforded no defense for life and property. On the contrary they proposed to complete the Revolution. Old institutions must fall. Monarchy in particular had outlived its usefulness. Even so, Brissot de Warville, Girondist chief, tried to bargain with the King. If Louis would restore his ministers, the party in its turn would uphold the throne. The King refused. He was rushing headlong to the guillotine.

On August 9, Brissot concluded that the King's obstinacy placed him beyond the pale. That same night special elections, inspired by Danton in what amounted to a *coup d'état,* replaced the Council-General of the Paris Commune, consisting mostly of Royalist constitutionalists, with more violent Revolutionists who hurried to the Hôtel-de-Ville as a preliminary to the famous assault of August 10 upon the Tuileries.

This murderous attack struck down a number of men in the immediate defense of the King, who in his own desperate haste to find refuge for himself and his family in the Manège or Hall of the Assembly, forgot to tell his faithful Swiss to lay down their arms. The Swiss died to a man in one of the Revolution's bloodiest atrocities. The Lion of Luzerne is their monument. Their memory lives in the hearts of all who find in duty a categorical imperative.

The increasing tempo of the Revolution bore witness to the transfer of power from the Gironde to the Mountain. Names commonly asociated with the most violent phases of the conflict were coming into focus. The greatest of these were Robespierre,† originally a moderate, for he had some regard for priests and property; Danton,† half monster, half lion, capable of "drinking blood," but a pillar of the national defense; and Marat,† the incarnation of personal savagery—some such scum as National Socialism spewed to power in the camps at Buchenwald and Dachau.

The King, who had entrusted himself on August 10 to the Assembly, was "confided" by it on the twelfth to the Commune of Paris, which promptly incarcerated him in the Temple, a prison from which he would emerge only for his execution. Executive power passed from the deposed King to the rising Danton, who was promoted from leadership in the Cordelier Club of Revolutionary extremists to the post of Minister of Justice. His was the supreme authority before and during the September massacres, which are an eternal blot upon his name. His was the responsibility for driving the Allies from the sacred soil of France.

In some extenuation of the frenzy that gripped France at this time, the Pillnitz and the Brunswick (or Coblentz) Manifestoes may be cited. The former was more moderate. It was issued in the previous year by the Emperor and the King of Prussia at the insistence of the Comte d'Artois, but its effect was cumulative. The Brunswick Manifesto was bloodcurdling. It threatened the very terrors which the September massacres imposed. Both reflected mid-summer madness: Pillnitz, August 21, 1791; Coblentz, late July 1792. The Allies hurled the atrocious menaces; the Paris mob perpetrated the abominable deeds.[2]

Meanwhile, approaching Paris by the old historic route, the Duke of Brunswick's † army on September 2 took Verdun. The way was open to the Argonne. The major crisis of the Revolution had arrived. Its repercussions in the capital were terrific.

Goaded on by wild rumors that the King had planned a massacre of the citizens, one of the most bloodthirsty mobs that history records proceeded to the various prisons, bent upon the slaughter of their inmates whether nonjuring priests, aristocrats, or the miscellaneous objects of civil justice who had no connection whatever with the Revolution.

From September 2 to 6 inclusive, the massacres raged on, with a total of 1,176 known and 438 probable murders, the victims in each case being captives, helpless and unarmed. Some boasted of these deeds of blood; others turned their heads in shame, pretending ignorance of what was happening. The Jacobin Club voted its approval of the people's "justice." There was a hint in all this that the extremes might yet destroy each other, with the moderates as their survivors.

If Danton shared in these atrocities, of which he would eventually be a victim, his glory was the courage he inspired in a land that sprang to arms with unexampled fervor to expel the foe. Others led the armies; he aroused their spirit.

The turn from defeat to victory came on September 20, when the French army, led by General François Christophe de Kellermann defeated the Duke of Brunswick and the King of Prussia at Valmy, the "Thermopylae" of France. Dumouriez as reorganizer of the armies deserved much credit, but the victory was Kellermann's. The army of the monarchy, sometimes victorious but frequently defeated, had been succeeded by the army of the Revolution, eager to carry the spirit of *Liberté, Égalité,* and *Fraternité* to all the rest of Europe. The Revolution was on the march. Its next great victory, won by Dumouriez on November 6, 1792, at Jemappes, near Mons, Belgium, would be on foreign soil. And foreign soil would continue to be the scene of French battles almost without exception until 1814, when the Napoleonic empire was entering its eclipse.

During the autumn both Nice and Savoy were overrun. The new Government of France, the National Convention, which met in Paris on September 21, could raise its sights. That there remained some conscience in France was demonstrated by the indictment (by no means the conviction) of Danton for his part in the September massacres. Perhaps it is too generous to call it conscience. Politics is a more likely word, for the Girondists wanted to make capital of the crimes of the extremists.

A gravely troubled year soon would yield to a terror to which the September massacres were little more than preface.

Upon American awareness of these momentous issues the correspondence of George Washington sheds light. The great wars of the French Revolution were to render Paris the key post of American diplomacy. It was natural, therefore, that Washington should transfer William Short, the friend of Jefferson, to a somewhat lesser mission at The Hague (much to Short's regret [3] though not at all to his discredit) and should replace him by a close personal friend whose communications would have the pungency and vitality never to be attained in impersonal communications, however capably composed.

The obvious choice was Gouverneur Morris—a brilliant choice if measured by the incumbent's intellectual capacities; a questionable adventure if appointments to key positions in the diplomatic service should be determined by the personal acceptability of the minister to the country to which he is accredited.

In the communications from Morris previously cited, an anti-Revolutionary bias is readily detected. Times of turbulence and the endless talking they call forth provide the loudest voices and the shallowest minds an open sesame to prominence. Demagogues spring up like mushrooms to the amusement or the indignation of the more sophisticated, of whom Morris assuredly was one. He never failed to see the littleness and the self-seeking of the flotsam and jetsam cast up by Revolutionary forces. What he may have missed at times was the deeper tides that underlay the foam. Or, to change the figure somewhat, the picture he might paint would have the detail of a miniature or the accuracy of a photograph, while somehow lacking the imaginative sympathy of a true portrait. Washington himself, out of his own far greater depths, would be called upon to make the necessary discounts and to provide the fuller comprehension.

The nomination of so bold a critic of the Revolution proved most distasteful to the more pronounced Republicans in the United States Senate.[4] Confirmation hung fire between December 22, 1791, and January 12, 1792. The final vote was 16 to 11, by no means flattering to a candidate upheld by all of Washington's prestige. So pronounced an opposition was responsible, no doubt, for an extraordinarily tactful but forceful letter from the President, reciting to the new envoy the criticisms raised against him. These, reduced to their essentials, spelled the general deficiencies of many witty persons, namely, their seemingly incorrigible willingness to sacrifice a friendship to an epigram.[5]

While this political manoeuvre was in process, Sir Edward Newenham was venturing one of those enlightened comments respecting France which could not fail to stimulate the thinking of his illustrious correspondent. The picture was encouraging. Affairs were at the crisis, with a favorable outcome likely. Credit was improving and trade was brisk. Emigrants were returning. A few refractory priests were the chief sign of faction.[6]

From General Headquarters at Metz, as of January 22, 1792, Lafayette described his brief sojourn at home on his farm, no longer a "seigneurie," among neighbors, no longer vassals, in an atmosphere of rare good will. It was a happy interlude all too quickly terminated by the "senseless preparations of the émigrés and especially the support which they encounter at the hands of neighboring powers."

To oppose these gathering forces, the King and the Assembly were forced to adopt a more vigorous system. Three armies were assembled, each having a paper strength of 50,000 men, the army of the right under Marshal Luckner; that of the left under Marshal Rochambeau; the center being under Lafayette's own leadership. It was all contrary to his hopes. He preferred retirement. But no other course was open when liberty and the Constitution alike were threatened than "to fight for our old cause." Washington would be pleased to know that his journey from Auvergne to Paris and then Metz was filled the whole way with evidence of affection.

These preparations apparently were not without effect, for the German Princes receded from their threatening position, to the great discouragement of the émigré conspirators. The leaders of the movement, Monsieur and the Comte d'Artois, had been deprived constitutionally of their rights in the succession and were both to be adjudged as "contumacious" by the supreme court of the nation.[7]

The great question, continued Lafayette, was the intention of the major powers. Detesting utterly the Revolution, they would like to tear it to pieces, but dared not touch it lest it prove contagious. This applied especially to the Emperor, from whom a categorical statement of intentions was demanded not later than the tenth of February. The King of France meanwhile declared as traitor anyone who sought to change French institutions or who entered into negotiations looking toward a modification of either the letter or the spirit of the Constitution.

Lafayette's command would need 30,000 men for garrison duty and another 30,000 for a mobile army—a figure which he would not immediately attain. In due course he would send Washington a table of his strength, as a continuing evidence that he was Washington's lieutenant, employed in their common cause. In the rather skeletonized regiments already in the field, the soldiers and non-commissioned officers were patriotic but badly disciplined. Among commissioned officers, one third were loyal, one third had quit the service, the other third would soon depart, or so Lafayette hoped. There was a special deficiency of generals, a majority of whom were Tories. Lafayette alone among them, by virtue of his popularity, could hope to establish a firm discipline in spite of the clamors of the Jacobins. He trusted the army would do well.[8]

In the slow communication of the period, neither Short nor Morris knew at once of the change in their assignments. So that it remained for Short to keep his superiors informed of happenings in France. In doing so he somewhat alienated Thomas Jefferson. A comparison of the elaborate reports of Short with the brief replies of his friend and patron sheds an interesting sidelight on the mental processes of that great man. Brilliant Jefferson was, but not always open-minded. He had an a priori faith in the soundness of the Revolution. That faith was not to be disturbed by accounts of the futility and incapacity of leaders. Originally Short doubtless shared these Jeffersonian hypotheses, but prolonged residence and observation had their inevitable effect. Jefferson remained the doctrinaire; Short became the realist. Intellectually they drifted far apart, though their fundamental basis of good will was apparently unshaken.

On January 25 particularly, the elaborate despatch of Short's could not have sat well with the Secretary. "If any thing had been wanting," reported Short, "to establish the real state of insanity in which many of the influential members of the Assembly are, it would have been furnished by the late debates." Such a wholesale condemnation of the people's representatives was hardly Jeffersonian, but that it was justified Short promptly demonstrated. Their most alarming weakness was their inconsistency, now challenging their most powerful neighbors to immediate war, and then refusing to bring the army to a state of minimum defense either in numbers or discipline, a quality which patriots were not supposed to need. That France had not been attacked long ago was due, in Short's opinion, almost entirely to their neighbors' fear of contact with Revolutionary notions sure to prove contagious. The Emperor was adding to his forces chiefly in the Low Countries, but his measures were defensive. The effect of war, if, when, and as it finally should come, might be wholesome rather than otherwise for France, compelling her in the interest of self-preservation to abandon present anarchy. Meanwhile, the conflict of the have's with the have-not's was becoming critical, the immediate issue being a sharp rise in sugar prices to a point outside the pockets of the poor—to the accompaniment of rioting. To this might be traced a project for the change of the French diplomatic system, just one idea, said Short, of the innumerable nonsensical ideas which might be apprehended from the "seven or eight hundred members of the Assembly, or some one of the thousands of members of the different clubs employed in governing the Country." [9]

If Jefferson found these frank communications distasteful, it was fortunate that not he but Washington must peruse the brilliant analysis of French politics which Gouverneur Morris expounded from London on February 4, 1792. Morris traced the origins and early history of the Jacobins and of the *Quatre Vingt Neufs,* or 89's, whom Short had mentioned not infrequently. To

Mirabeau as a pillar of the 89's, Morris paid his respects, *en passant,* as "beyond all Controversy one of the most unprincipled Scoundrels that ever lived." [10] Nevertheless, his passing left a chasm in his party. The Jacobins for a time hoped that the two factions might unite. Failing this, to secure their own authority they were driven to make concessions to the populace beyond their own ideas of wisdom. For the Jacobins, said Morris, had more extended views than the associates of Mirabeau had ever dreamed of. The 89's sought only personal advantage; the Jacobins envisioned a constitution genuinely liberal.

It was the stalemate of these parties, the aristocrats being politically negligible, that caused the self-denying ordinance in the National Assembly, against accepting office from the Crown or standing for election to the next Assembly. The Constitution was itself stultified and emasculated by these divisions. This led in turn to a curious oscillation wherein the two parties were obliged to enter some sort of alliance to uphold the instrument which their own divisions had so considerably weakened. It was an alliance which involved the royal authority as well, for as Morris put the case, "the Plan of the Allies was to induce a Beleif [sic] in the Court that they alone had sufficient Popularity in the Nation to preserve the monarchical Authority against the Republican Party, and on the other Hand to convince the Assembly that (having in their Hands the royal authority) all favors offices and grants must come thro them." Thereby they became what Morris termed "Government-Brokers of the Nation."

So far Morris was interpreting the 89's and the leaders of the Jacobins. He found that the Republican Party was built largely on the foundations of the rank and file of earlier Jacobins who had refused to follow their leaders into this moderate combination.

Up to this point, and his letter was hardly more than started, Morris had directed Washington's attention to a political lineup which might readily have escaped his notice had he depended solely on the despatches of William Short or on other means of information at his own disposal. Morris now continued with a very searching comment:

It was this Coalition [of Jacobins and 89's] which prevented the King from accepting the Constitution in a *Manly* Manner; pointing out its capital Faults marking the probable Consequences calling them to reconsider it and declaring that his Submission to its Decisions arose from his Belief that it was the only means to avoid the Horrors of civil War. They saw that this Conduct would render them responsible and altho it was the most likely means of obtaining a good Constitution at a future Day, and would have bound the King down to the Principles he should then advance, yet they opposed because such good Constitution would be established not only without, but even against them & would of Course deprive them of those objects which they were in Pursuit of. The King contended strongly for that kind of acceptance which I have just mentioned, but he was borne down, being threatened with popular Commotions fatal to himself and his Family, and with that civil War which he most wished to avoid as the necessary Result of such fatal Commotions.

Turning from these generalized reflections to the immediate personal and political scene, Morris next favored Washington with thumbnail sketches of the ministry: DuPort, the Keeper of the Seals; de Lessart, Minister of the Interior; Du Portail, the Minister of War; Bertrand, Minister of Marine; and de Moustier, to whom the King had offered the portfolio of Foreign Affairs but who was opposed by the coalition as an aristocrat, with the result that there was a prolonged vacancy in the office following Montmorin's departure until it went finally to the Comte de Ségur.

Following a brief incumbency, Ségur too resigned. The place had been seeking the man. It was now the man's turn to seek the place, the man being Monsieur de Narbonne, reputed to be a son of Louis XV by his own daughter. Morris joined the names of Narbonne, Choiseul and Talleyrand, the Bishop of Autun, as all three "young men [of] high family, men of Wit, and Men of Pleasure." Talleyrand's long connection with American affairs renders highly pertinent this early mention of him to George Washington:

On the Score of Morals neither of them is exemplary. The bishop is particularly blamed on that Head not so much for adultery, because that was common enough among the Clergy of high Rank, but for the Variety and Publicity of his Amours; [11] for Gambling; and above all for Stock Jobbing during the ministry of Monsieur de Calonne with whom he was on the best of Terms, and therefore had opportunities which his Enemies say he made no small use of. However I do not believe in this, and I think that except his Galantries and a Mode of thinking rather too liberal for a Churchman, the Charges are unduly aggravated.

Carrying gossip somewhat further, Morris represented Narbonne as a lover of Mme de Staël, illustrious daughter of the illustrious Necker, and correspondingly displeased to find that his friend Talleyrand, as all the world believed, enjoyed some small share, at least, of her affections. Morris himself enjoyed the friendship of the lady, who assured him there was nothing to her attachment to the dear Bishop. The rift was healed, at any rate, when Talleyrand actively supported Narbonne for the ministry of Foreign Affairs, an appointment which the King opposed because of the supposed indiscretions of Mme de Staël. But after certain shifts, Narbonne did receive a less conspicuous portfolio, M. de Lessart being transferred to the Ministry of Foreign Affairs.

Not impossibly it was his intimate acquaintance with this intrigue that disgusted Morris with the influence of women upon French politics.

The ministry as finally assembled under the new Constitution was, in the opinion of Morris, a pretty disjointed affair, and not too talented, at that. Narbonne was witty, and "a very pleasant lively fellow," but not a man of business; Bertrand possessed the necessary talents, but "one Swallow never makes a Summer." Worse yet, the ministry had no faith in the Constitution which it was sworn to execute; while among the members of the Assembly, some were unquestionably in the pay of England, among them, to judge from his pro-English attitude and anti-patriotic measures, being almost certainly the orator, Brissot de Warville.

The finances continued very ominous. A change of system was imperative but a change itself was dangerous after so many pompous protestations of perfection. War might be the means to cloak the necessary changes, a consideration which led Morris to a profound survey of current attitudes on the subject. For all sorts of reasons, some of them the complete antithesis of one

127

another, Morris found the several political parties and factions virtually unanimous in their eagerness for war. These embraced Republicans, aristocrats, moderate monarchists, people of every shade of political opinion, all convinced that war would further their own special programs. The King alone opposed, from what Morris conceived to be a true appreciation of the royal interest. For war would necessitate the centralization of authority. Enemies of monarchy would not tolerate this. Hence the very existence of monarchy might be put in jeopardy.

It was with this idea of destroying root and branch the ancient system, that the radicals contemplated a reversal of alliances. The diplomatic revolution of 1756, which had linked the fortunes of France with those of the Empire, was to be overthrown by what might be termed a counter-revolution, with Great Britain and Prussia as the new allies. With this end in view Talleyrand was gone to London, "authorized," so rumor had it, "to propose the Cession of the Islands of France and Bourbon and the Island of Tobago as the Price of an Alliance against the Emperor." Not content with such concessions, "Mr. de Warville proposed in the diplomatick Committee the Cession of Dunkirk and Calais to England [shades of Mary Tudor!] as Pledges of the Fidelity of France to the Engagements which she might undertake. You will judge from this Specimen of the Wisdom and Virtue of the Faction to which he belongs; and I am sure the Integrity of your Heart will frown with indignant Contempt when I tell you, that among the Chiefs of that Faction are Men who owe their all to the personal Bounty of the King."

The mission of Talleyrand, so drastic in its implications, had produced somewhat of a schism in the coalition then controlling the Assembly. And the Emperor was accordingly assured that no harm to him was contemplated. Rather the nation would work out a scheme for good relations with his nation. All this nonsense was of course distressing, continued Morris, to men of common sense, and intensely so to the King and Queen. Which in turn led Morris to a most confidential communication, in which he proved that in these last weeks before the European War broke out, the King was pursuing independently a course of policy quite contrary to that of the Assembly—a policy of independence which was to lead, when war did come, to what the nation called high treason and was to cost the King his life. .

This letter represents an American contribution to the question of the guilt or innocence of Louis XVI, on trial as a traitor to those Constitutional principles which he was sworn to defend but which he never understood:

> The King and Queen are wounded to the Soul by these rash Measures. They have I beleive [sic] given all needful Assurances to the Emperor & King of Spain; a confidential Person has desired me to assure you on their Behalf that they are very far from wishing to change the System of french Politics and abandon their old Allies, and therefore if any advantage is taken of the present advances to Britain that you will consider them as originating meerly [sic] in the madness of the Moment, and not as proceeding from *them* or as meeting with *their* approbation, *but the contrary.* I shall send this Letter in such Way as promises the greatest Safety and I must entreat you my dear Sir to destroy it for fear of accidents: you will feel how important it is to them that this Communication be not disclosed. It is meerly personal from them to you and expressive of Sentiments which can have no action until they have some authority.[12]

After a communication of such far-reaching import the more superficial comments of Sir Edward Newenham represent an anticlimax. But they fill in their bit of detail, with hopeful prospects unless French border troops should attack German territories. In southern France signs of returning prosperity were numerous, with credit rising and trade improving, according to the first-hand observations of Newenham's son.[13]

Morris, it will be recalled, outlined the project of an alliance with Prussia and Great Britain to supersede the Austrian connection. Short officially alluded to the same plan on February 8, informing the Department that at London Talleyrand was well received, whereas at Berlin the Comte de Ségur was very badly treated, rumor insisting that he was even driven to an unsuccessful attempt at suicide. Politically, a natural conclusion was the determination at Berlin to act in concert with Vienna.

Illness prevented Short from additional despatches until three weeks later, when he reported that the Emperor was minded to keep the peace so long as his sister and her family appeared safe. Foreign affairs might be improving, but in the domestic situation, "all the sources of public & private calamity are increasing every day"; [14] a conviction not reversed a fortnight later, with every day bringing a new quota of alarms with which the Government, certainly the King, was not prepared to cope. Moments of anger were the King's substitute for energy of character. In one of these moments he had dismissed Narbonne, which when known would assuredly displease the generals of the army, Lafayette, Rochambeau and Luckner. In the world of foreign affairs the recent death of the pacific Emperor boded ill for France. Short thought it a calamity.[15]

By mid-March, Morris had heard the gratifying news of his appointment to the Paris mission. In a personal letter to Washington, he acknowledged his new honor gratefully and graciously, with a considerable volume of more or less disjointed news. Summarizing the failure of Talleyrand's London mission, he indulged in quiet mirth: "Now you will observe that no Court could prudently treat with France in her present Situation, seeing that no body can promise in her name otherwise than as Godfathers and Godmothers do at a Christening, and how such Promises are kept every Body knows."

Interesting if true was Morris' further news. The French ministry held documentary proof that the Government of William Pitt was fomenting disturbances in France and intrigues in the French sugar islands. Morris had not seen the evidence. But gossip of this sort awakened some interesting reminiscences. Morris thought the development, if true, opened profitable possibilities for American commerce with the West Indies.

Morris may well have broadened Washington's perception of world reaction to the Revolution when he accounted for Britain's unfriendliness to the movement on the following rather complex line of reasoning:

Now putting aside the personal Feelings which naturally agitate the Sovereign of this [England] as well as of other Kingdoms [Prussia] in Regard to the french Revolution, it is notorious that, from the very Dawn of it, agents were employed to foment a Spirit of Revolt in other States, particularly in Prussia. The King of Prussia therefore feels for the french Revolution all the Enmity of a proud passionate and offended German Prince. Add to this that the Elector of Hanover, as such cannot wish for a Change in the Government of Germany. If therefore it had been the Interest of Great Britain to establish a free Constitution in France (which it certainly is not) I am perfectly convinced that this Court would never have made a single Effort for the Purpose.

The free play of a mind like Morris' on the vast chessboard of contemporary Europe produced interesting points of view. Short undoubtedly possessed ability; Morris was endowed with genius. The public service would not suffer by the change in contemplation.

Further interest attaches to Morris' cool description of the venality of M. de Narbonne, impeached for gross malfeasance and dismissed under a cloud.[16]

As yet, Morris knew only of the President's nomination for the mission. On hearing of his confirmation by the Senate, he expressed his satisfaction more on party than personal grounds, for rejection would have signified disunion in Federalist counsels. Turning more particularly to his projected mission but writing still from London, he made a precautionary analysis of the new French Minister of Foreign Affairs:

> I find that the King of France has appointed to the Office of Foreign Affairs a Monsieur Demouriez and that it is considered as a Sacrifice to the Jacobins. He is a bold determined man. I am not acquainted with him personally, but I know that he has long been seeking a Place in the Administration and was about six months ago, determin'd if appointed one of the Ministers to destroy at the Peril of his Life the *jacobin* and all other Clubs, and to effect a change in the government. How far he may have changed his opinions since, I really cannot tell, but I mention this to you *now* because when I know more I can refer to this Letter and say that *by coming into Office he has not changed his Sentiments* if he persists in those antient Determinations. If not, I will tell you that *he is more prudent than was supposed*. And these words will in either case mean nothing more than is here set down for them.
>
> The King consulted him (as I was told by *his* confidential friend in the middle of last October) on the State of Affairs when Monsr. de Montmorin went out, but the high toned measures he proposed were not adopted.[17]

Surely the change in agents was bringing Washington into closer touch with French affairs. No little scheme like the above could have been arranged with Short, who had not the honor of the President's acquaintance and whose nearest approach to familiarity was a private letter to the Secretary of State for informal transmission to the President. Not yet replaced at Paris, it fell to him to announce on March 25 what must be viewed as the alarum bell of war—namely an almost complete shift in the ministry till all portfolios save that of war were held by advanced radicals, leaders in the Jacobin Club, "whose exaggerated & dangerous principles have been long known wherever the French revolution has been heard of." The King did not conceal his regret at losing his former ministers. It was to be expected, though, said Short, that executive responsibility would drive a wedge between the ministers and their partisan associates, with a possibly resultant schism. For the moment assignats were rising sharply, coinciding with vast speculations in the currency.[18]

Amid these darkening perils for the country of his friend, Washington could not fail to welcome an epistle in Lafayette's familiar hand. The General was at Paris (March 15, 1792) whither he had been called in conference, presumably because of the Emperor's death on March 1. He thought war a possibility, though the powers would hesitate to press it; but a greater peril lurked in widespread anarchy, which was bad enough in all conscience, but not so bad as English stories pictured. "Liberty and equality will be preserved in France, that is certain; but if they should succumb, you know well that I shall not survive them."

As for the Constitution, as yet not fully tested, it established the people in its rights, destroyed nearly all abuses, converted vassalage into national dignity, and restored to man the enjoyment of those faculties which nature granted and society was obligated to assure.

At this point Lafayette, the friend of Short and far from pleased at Short's approaching transfer to The Hague, launched into an attack upon the aristocratic and counter-revolutionary principles of Morris as totally unfitting him for his new post. He pulled no punches. "I hate everything that savors of despotism and aristocracy, and I cannot refrain from wishing that principles both American and French be in the heart and on the lips of the ambassador of the United States in France." To make his point still clearer, Lafayette paid homage to the departing envoy: "Let me add here the tribute of respect which I owe Mr. Short for the sentiments which he has professed and for all the approbation which he has inspired in this country. I could wish that you knew him personally."

Pretty close this was to a serious rebuke for Washington, and from his bosom friend. Time would determine its full justice.

The remainder of this most outspoken brief confirmed what Short was soon to say concerning the radical character of the new ministry in France. But its members were pledged to the re-establishment of order, and, "After all, the affair will go on, and the success of the Revolution cannot be doubted."

As for Lafayette, his army had reached its full quota of 60,000 men, with recruits still pouring in. The armies of Luckner and Rochambeau were inferior to his, but in emergency could be increased. He concluded with a bit of moralizing. "Licence under a mask of patriotism is our worst evil, for it threatens property, tranquillity, and liberty itself." [19] Always interesting, Lafayette here surpassed himself. With perfect friendship and respect, he rebuked his friend in language unmistakable. This letter marked the high point in a rich correspondence.

April seemed a dull month, to judge by correspondence only. Yet in some ways it was the very crisis of the Revolution, for it was then that the movement was converted to a general European war, destined to continue with only the briefest interruptions until the Congress of Vienna in 1815.

With the future thus portentous, a communication from Gouverneur Morris was of greater personal than general interest. He expressed gratitude for Washington's frank and friendly statement of the objections raised in Congress to his appointment. Morris proposed to turn criticism to a good account by reforming on the points at issue, adding a specific promise, so that "my Sense of Integrity may enforce what my sense of Propriety dictates."

The King of Sweden had been assassinated, rumor having it by the agency of the Jacobins. Morris disbelieved the rumor. "Such sudden Deaths in so critical a Moment are extraordinary but I do not usually believe in Enormities and I cannot see how a Club can pursue a Path of Terrors in which Secrecy is essential to Success." [20]

On the twenty-second, Short, who was still in Paris, announced that a declaration of war had been made against Hungary, a declaration very popular in the Assembly though opposed by the King and two smaller factions in the legislative body. The first of these factions consisted of genuine friends to the Constitution, who mistrusted the effects of war upon that instrument, preferring to see it gradually and peaceably reformed. The second represented a portion of the Jacobin Club who feared the increased power of the executive and of military leaders certain to occur in war.

It was a favorable time, in Short's opinion, for Morris to assume his duties. Prospects for a commercial improvement were more encouraging than they had been for some time, and, he generously added, the intelligence and zeal of his successor would take full advantage of them.[21]

The war got off, in Short's estimation, to a bad start. Certainly there was nothing in his two concluding despatches from Paris to indicate appreciation of the volcanic forces pent up within the Revolution and now to be released upon a world which they would change forever. Rather was he obsessed with the immediate view, which appeared most discouraging for France:

> Hope seems to have abandoned the most sanguine—the most bold dare not look forward to a prospect which presents this unhappy Country torn by faction & groaning under anarchy, ready to yield without resistance from the present state of its Army, to the Ennemies [sic] they have provoked, & what may perhaps be worse than all abandoned for some time to the efforts of private vengeances armed with the sword of Justice & clothed in the robes of law.[22]

Short was so perturbed over the difficulties which the French seemed certain to experience that he professed a positive satisfaction in leaving the report of them to Morris—doubtless a bit of rationalization. Be that as it may, Morris did embark upon his mission in very stirring times. From Paris on June 10, he wrote separately to Washington in person, and more at length to the Department. To Washington, he gave the answer to his previous code arrangement:

134

Although I have been above a Month in this City I have not been able untill within a Day or two to make up my Mind as to the Sentiments of the Person mentioned to you in mine of the twenty-first of March, or rather I could not obtain that Certainty which was needful before I could properly mention them to you. I can now venture to assure you that *by coming into Office he has not changed his Sentiments.*

We may pass by allusions to discipline in the French armies and a vast increase in assignats, to a comment on the French reception of the letter of condolence from Washington to the King, conveying the grief of his countrymen and himself at the premature death of the Dauphin:

Your Letter to the King has produced a very good Effect. It is not relished by the Democrats who particularly dislike the Term *your People* but it suits well the prevailing Temper which is monarchic. The jacobine Faction approaches to its Dissolution, as you may perceive by its agonies. In Fact the Deliberations are so absurd & so extravagantly wild that they daily furnish new Arms to their Enemies.[23]

How fallible is wisdom! Here was a singularly acute observer who could not sense that the Jacobins possessed the future not the past. No doubt the wish was father to the thought.

In his first despatch to Jefferson, the new minister outlined at far greater length the general European situation as it affected France. He thought that war had never been declared more frankly, its inner reasons more openly avowed. The attack upon Hungary was merely an excuse to invade the Flemish territories of the Emperor, an invasion not likely to be popular among those who were invaded. Surveying the military strength of the belligerents, Morris believed the French to be decidedly outnumbered. The Allies could muster 180,000 men, exclusive of French émigrés, whom they probably would not employ, for an army of gentlemen volunteers would inevitably lack discipline. Besides, this particular army was the storm center for too many hatreds. The Allied monarchs themselves were enemies to aristocracy as the nucleus of opposition to their own authority. And they would have no wish to restore in France a system they despised. They would sympathize more readily with a military dictatorship. England alone would be likely to oppose one, from a desire to keep her neighbor weak.

135

Morris here was treading if not on sacred ground, at any rate on prophetic. The Napoleonic dictatorship came soon enough to vindicate his prophecy, even if the details were not precisely as he envisioned them.

On the other hand, thought Morris, the Allies would hold no brief for orderly progress under a constitution. That would involve the deep contagiousness of freedom which in the first place made them fear the war. The conclusion then must be that the Powers proposed to vest all authority within the King—a course for which the ground had been prepared by overzealous friends of liberty. "In their eagerness to abolish ancient institutions they forget that a *Monarchy* without intermediate ranks is but another name for anarchy and despotism." The former was already everywhere in evidence; the latter would be generally welcomed if it restored security of person and of property. Bankruptcy was another means of establishing despotism according to this American observer, who had apparently forgotten that it was despotism that brought on the case originally. Whatever the causes and results of bankruptcy, it was increasingly a fact. The Church lands had been confiscated, but debts were even greater than before.

It seemed to Morris—and here his wonted keenness was in evidence—that the Parisian populace was thoroughly aware that the safety of their city and themselves was intimately involved in retaining the person of the King as hostage. With him in their possession, they would not be attacked.

Turning next to political divisions within the Assembly, the deputies from Bordeaux were reported to be highly influential —a circumstance which boded ill for commercial intercourse with the United States, the merchants being jealous of their own advantage.

In this turmoil and welter of confusion the chief minister, Dumouriez, was eager for French armies to strike first before the Allies could mass their strength. Hastening to the frontier, he urged Luckner and Lafayette to take the aggressive. Each of them emphatically declined, "the situation of their respective armies not permitting any well grounded expectations." In the event of their junction, Luckner was to have chief command, a reversal of previous arrangements and boding ill for Lafayette's relations with the new governors of France.

From all of which Morris accurately deduced, and he trusted Jefferson to see his point, that the times were not propitious for pressing a commercial treaty.[24]

In so unstable a situation, ministries could not be very permanent—something they have never been in France since constitutional government began. Accordingly, the Department of State had early news of the ministerial upset which deprived M. Roland and several others of portfolio. The party in power had been that of the Gironde. The Jacobins were dormant, but their future was assured. "On the whole Sir we stand on a vast volcano we feel it tremble and we hear it roar but how and when and where it will burst and who may be destroy'd by its eruption is beyond the ken of mortal foresight to discern."

It is doubtful whether Jefferson, to whom this lament was inscribed, could comprehend its tone. When he left France, the Revolution was at its most auspicious turn. The memories he retained were hopeful. Such gloomy pictures as were lately drawn by Short and now by Morris could convey but little meaning, though Morris surely did his best as the following suggests: "I cannot go on with the picture for my heart bleeds when I reflect that the finest opportunity which ever presented itself for establishing the rights of mankind throughout the civilized world is perhaps lost forever." [25]

Naturally enough after his long observation of and contact with the Revolution, William Short maintained his lively interest. Indeed, a compensation for his transfer to The Hague was the nearness of his new post to his former, and his despatches from the Netherlands are chiefly interesting for their sidelights on the Revolution. On June 29, he expressed himself quite frankly on the probable ability of Lafayette to stem the rising tide of radicalism. Success would depend upon "a conduct as vigorous & as firm as his intentions are pure & patriotic." But at best his task was heavy. Foreign war and internal disorganization made no simple combination.[26]

That Washington was watching the Revolution's course most attentively appears from a letter acknowledging Morris' assurance that Louis XVI was not in sympathy with the changes the Revolution had brought in France's system of alliances—a most significant and confidential note to which Washington alluded in properly ambiguous terms:

> Since writing to you on the 28th. of January I have received your several favors of the 27th. of Decr. from Paris; 4th. of February, 17th. and 21st. of March, and 6th and 10th of April from London. I thank you very much for the interesting and important information contained in several of these letters particularly that of the 4th. of February. If the last article of which it is comprised, should in your judgment require an acknowledgment I shall rely on your goodness to make it in suitable and respectful terms. You can be at no loss to discover the paragraph to which I allude.

The President then proceeded to an explanation of his silence on issues that were certain to arouse in him the liveliest response. What follows is his own explanation for what long ago must have impressed the reader as a paucity of comment:

> The plot thickens, and development must have begun; but what the final issue will be, lyes too deep for human ken. I will hope for the best, without allowing myself to wander in the field of conjecture for the result. Your letters, though extremely interesting in point of information, require but little to be said in the way of reply. The accts. given therein will be treasured up, to be acted upon as circumstances will warrant, and as occasions may present.[27]

One looks to private letters for the more pointed, pungent, and brilliant analyses of passing men and measures. The steady sequence of despatches to the Department of State provided, however, the more coherent picture. It was while rounding out this picture that Morris informed Jefferson, July 10, of another of the frequent and rather meaningless reconciliations between the King and the Assembly. He added with prophetic insight that while the King's course was clearly charted, namely to safeguard the Constitution and the liberty of France, his success in hewing to his course would be highly problematical. "Whether he will live thro the storm is also uncertain. It will blow hard."

Here was genuine prophecy as contrasted with mere advance information. This too, Morris seemingly possessed, for fifteen days in advance he forecast in astonishing detail the Brunswick

Manifesto which so importantly contributed to the downfall of King Louis. He anticipated that the pronunciamento of the Allies would disavow the Constitution, demanding for the King his "rights," and for the clergy their possessions; that it would hold the city of Paris responsible for the safety of the Royal Family; and that it would deny military status to the National Guard, thereby depriving them of the protection of the laws of war. "The allied monarchs are to declare themselves in arms not against France, but against the *revoltés*. You will easily see that these broad terms will mean whatever power may chuse to explain them to."

Altogether, appended Morris, the times were unpropitious for negotiating a commercial treaty.[28]

Poor Jefferson faced some uneasy hours if he took seriously the assurance of his agents in the field. Morris was on the whole more temperate these days than Short. The latter maintained that the most serviceable men a foreign foe could ask for

> have been those mad & corrupted people in France who under the name of liberty have destroyed their own Government & disgusted all the real supporters of the constitution; men of honesty & property, with an order of things where all the rights of humanity & those of society & property are daily violated with impunity, where universal anarchy prevails & where of course there is no succour from the protecting arm of the law against mobs & factions which have assumed despotic power.[29]

On the twenty-seventh, Prussia having meanwhile formally declared war on France and invasion being imminent, Short described the King as a bone of partisan dispute; one faction desiring to move him southward, setting up a new capital; the other insisting upon his detention in Paris. Naturally the enemy would also seek possession of his person. "I cannot be without my fears for his personal safety in this contention." [30]

The Brunswick Manifesto having been proclaimed to an expectant world, it might be anticipated that the National Assembly would turn from its incessant speech-making against Lafayette to something more constructive. Short thought the form in which the manifesto was published "the most humiliating possible." At the same time, he thought that many Frenchmen, from sheer revolt against the prevailing anarchy, would give at least a tacit support to the invaders. Lafayette himself, disgusted as he could not fail to be by the madness of his countrymen, would be compelled by the logic of his career to resist the enemy.

The émigrés, continued Short, were none too pleased with a manifesto which failed utterly to champion their special interests, though they probably continued in the hope that once the King was captive he would restore the *ancien régime* as a symbol of good order, later modifying it as necessity or opportunity arose. All this presupposing that "the poor unhappy Monarch" should survive the storm. Already the sections of Paris were assembling so as to render their opinion on the question of declaring him dethroned.[31]

How serious were the diatribes against Lafayette may be appreciated from the passing comment of Gouverneur Morris. "I only believe that if Mr. de la fayette were to appear just now in Paris unattended by an army he would be torn to pieces. Thank God we have no populace in America and I hope the education and manners will long prevent that evil." [32]

It is improbable that either Morris or Jefferson or their leading French contemporaries had a true perception of this vast unpopularity of Lafayette's, so completely the reverse of his former popularity. The key has been advanced, however, by an eminent modern French student of the Revolution, Monsieur A. Aulard, who finds that Lafayette was never a "republican" in the sense the Revolution presupposed. Rather he was the champion of a constitutional monarchy in the world of politics, and of a bourgeois scheme of property in the world of economics. In its extreme radicalism the Revolution had utterly outstripped his views. Lafayette and the newer leaders possessed no common meeting point.

Even granting that Lafayette might have consciously wished to be the Washington of France—something which Aulard considered very far from proved—his whole philosophy pointed not to a federal republic as in America, but to a crowned republic, in which he would be the first citizen. "To be a Washington under Louis XVI," remarks Aulard, "there is the dream which resolves the acts, words, and authentic writings of La Fayette," and in it he was in agreement with Washington himself who saw with displeasure as did a majority of Americans, the overthrow of royalty in France. "In any case, notwithstanding the evidence indirect and tardy of Durand-Meillane, I do not believe that a single authentic proposal of Lafayette can be cited wherein he has expressed the intention of establishing in fact and *at once* a republic in France." [33]

At the beginning of August 1792, everything that Lafayette esteemed hung in the balance. His country and he himself were at the crossroads. The Girondists were scarcely proving equal to their tasks, while the tasks of Lafayette as leader were nearly done.[34] Before the month was over, he would be an exile and a prisoner—victim to his own principles of moderation in an age that wanted none of them.

The predominating spirit of the times, the extreme recoil to the violent manifesto of the Duke of Brunswick, found its expression in the horrors of the night of August 10, in the massacre of the Swiss Guards at the palace, and the complete humiliation of the King. Strangely enough, Short's account of these events is far more vivid, Morris' more philosophical. Let Short speak first:

> Accounts by the express say that the whole Regiment of Swiss guards have been massacred by the people & that the streets literally are red with blood, the King & his family who had taken refuge in the assembly were present during the debates of that execrable day & night & heard all the insulting denunciations brought against themselves & countenanced by the Assembly—they are still alive, but suffer a thousand deaths daily.—The constitution being thus destroyed by the destruction of one of its essential parts, it remains to be seen what will be the conduct of the Army. Those who have taken so many oaths to support it. . . .[35]

Perhaps it was shrewdness, a preference not to trouble the Secretary of State with bloody details which he would scarcely credit; or possibly it was a greater preoccupation with the underlying aspects of the situation; at all events the despatch from Morris was in a vein distinctly quieter. Since his last, "another revolution has been effected in this city. It was bloody." So much for the Swiss Guards. More followed of the interplay of politics, in which the minister forecast a disappearance of the moderates and their absorption into aristocrats and radicals. It was a situation that boded ill for monarchy. Left to itself the country would go republican. An incalculable element, of course, was foreign intervention. Here prompt action would determine the result. If the Duke of Brunswick counted on support in France, he must act before public opinion had time to crystallize in favor of the new republic. Jefferson would conclude, and correctly so, that the decision lay at last between absolute monarchy and a republic. A middle ground was quite untenable.

In transmitting the usual gazettes, the minister warned Jefferson of new and necessary discounts to be made in accepting their opinions, so rigid was the censorship. Also he informed the Secretary of his own intervention in the choice of a French minister to the United States. Notorious immorality made Bon Carère, the intended choice, unsuitable. Morris intervened effectively. With affairs so swiftly moving, he begged for additional guidance from the President and the Department.[36]

Three days after Morris penned these comments, Lafayette crossed the frontier and thereby became a mere cipher amid events which he had erstwhile hoped to shape. His action was the inevitable result of his growing disgust with the course of the Revolution. He had never liked the Jacobins, whose power was increasing at this time, and their invasion of the Tuileries on June 20 put a climax to his discontent. He even quit his post to go before the Assembly on June 28 in a demand for a requisition against the authors of the insurrection. Over violent opposition he won his point.

Two days later he left Paris to return to his post, but denunciations continued to multiply. He was outraged by the massacre of the Swiss Guards on August 10, and the suspension of the King. He wished to use the army to deliver the King and restore the Constitution. On August 14, he ordered the town of Sedan to arrest commissioners sent by the Assembly. Retaliation was swift. On the seventeenth, the Executive Council summoned him to Paris to explain his conduct and his military command was forfeited. Realizing that he could no longer rely upon his troops, Lafayette crossed the frontier near Mouzon on the nineteenth, accompanied by twenty-two officers of his staff. That eve-

ning at eight, all were arrested at Rochefort. Incarceration followed, drastic as befitted a major Revolutionary now fallen into
the hands of hostile monarchs.[37]

Just one week later, he wrote to William Short from his prison
at Neville, requesting intervention on the score that he was "an
American citizen, an American officer." It was a dual citizenship
that Lafayette took pleasure in. If he regained his freedom while
there was still a hope for liberty in France, he would retire
quietly to an English village, to be as near his native scenes as
possible. If, however, the French case continued hopeless, he
"would become again solely American, and finding in that happy
land a people enlightened and friendly to liberty, law abiding
and grateful for the services I was happy enough to render them,
I would tell my respectable friend Washington and all my other
companions how in spite of all my efforts the French Revolution
has been polluted by crimes." [38]

Lafayette's exile and imprisonment was news of world-wide
interest. Morris heard it promptly and passed it on to Jefferson
with the remark that he had anticipated it, and that Lafayette
had lasted beyond his expectations.

On the larger scene of war, it was Morris' conviction that the
Duke of Brunswick was advancing much too slowly to achieve
success. Time was not on his side. Meanwhile the ambassador
from Great Britain had asked for passports. He was accredited
to the King of France. With no King reigning, his mission had
lost point. In departing, he subjoined the hope that nothing
would happen to the King or the Royal Family, for any injury
to them *"would excite the indignation of all Europe."* Morris
interpreted this as an open threat of war. As for himself, he proposed to remain in France, as his departure would look like taking sides against the Revolution, something his instructions did
not warrant. Perhaps he stayed more readily because it was
hinted very broadly in certain quarters of Paris that he would
better go. He concluded with a courageous sentiment:

> It is true that the position is not without danger; but I presume that
> when the President did me the honor of naming me to this embassy,
> it was not for my personal pleasure or safety, but to promote the inter-

ests of my country. These therefore I shall continue to pursue to the best of my judgment and as to consequences they are in the hand of God.[39]

Morris had from the first been critical of Lafayette, whereas Short had been consistently his admirer. Correspondingly, Short's account of Lafayette's passage into the enemy lines is more detailed and sympathetic. He saw in it the General's only remaining protest against the overthrow of the Constitution effected August 10, and the determination of the Revolutionists at Paris to control the army. Short's long despatch of August 24 was a defense of Lafayette against possible misunderstanding by his friends in America. But from the point of view of general history, the Marquis had written his finis. The future lay with radicals, not with constitutional moderates, and Short's preliminary comment on Robespierre has more significance than any valedictory for Lafayette. "Robertspierre [sic] and others of that atrocious & cruel cast compose the tribunal [i.e. the judiciary],— named by a popular election—we may expect therefore to hear of such proceedings, under the cloak of liberty, egalite, & patriotism as would disgrace any *chambre ardente* that has ever existed—humanity shudders at the idea." [40]

Lafayette from his imprisonment placed his friend Short and thereby the Government of the United States in a most painful situation. A captive and desperate, he called upon Short to visit him and to use his diplomatic influence for intervention, on the score that Lafayette was *bona fide* a citizen of the United States. Citizen by courtesy no doubt he was, but not a government in Europe would seriously regard such citizenship as valid. To call it into service on his own behalf was the action of a thoroughly self-centered egotist. No good could come of it, as Short well knew, and the best that he could do was to place substantial sums of money at Lafayette's disposal in the assured conviction that such action would be pleasing to our Government.

While thus performing the offices of friendship, personal and national, Short was alert to the menace which the present scene suggested. As for the Royal Family, he wrote,

I see no possibility of the Kings being saved; & it is possible the invaders or a part of them may be more indifferent about it, than has been gen-

144

erally imagined. So long as the present Monarch is alive the allied powers can march but in one line, but suppose him & the Queen out of the way & a variety of new combinations present themselves, one particularly which seems to me the most alarming for the rest of Europe I have not heard hinted by any body, & therefore I endeavour to treat it with myself as visionary.

Nevertheless, despite the vagueness of his fears and the modesty restraining him from prophecy direct, he outlined darkly the climax of the Revolution and perhaps the Napoleonic Wars when he added, "I own it seems to me these things may bring on a torrent of circumstances the force of which is perhaps not yet calculated by the parties themselves." [41]

If for the moment their places seem reversed, with Morris, generally rated as the keener of the two, writing despatches of far less interest than Short's, an explanation may be found in the immediate peril of Morris' own situation. In the new, mad phase of Terror, which had no respect for the amenities of an outworn diplomacy, an aristocratic suspect like the American minister found scant protection in the immunities of office. His home was actually invaded in a search for weapons. With great dignity and courage, he resisted the intrusion and won his point. Reporting the case to Jefferson he used some noble words:

> You will see by all this my dear sir that I have sufficient cause to take offence and depart if I were so inclin'd. I will stay if possible so as to preserve to you the most perfect liberty of action. I do not indeed feel offended at what is done by the people, because they cannot be suppos'd to understand the law of nations, and because they are in a state of fury which is inconceivable and which leaves them liable to all impressions & renders them capable of all excesses. I shall endeavor nevertheless to preserve the proper firmness and let what will happen. I hope that tho my friends should have reason to lament my fate, they will never be oblig'd to blush for my conduct.[42]

Morris here established a high standard for ministerial conduct in the midst of grave emergencies. He had previously established a high standard for ministerial reporting, which he now abundantly sustained in his account of the September massacres. The indignities which were perpetrated upon the body of the Princesse de Lamballe, beheaded, disembowelled, her head and entrails paraded on pikes and her body dragged behind were

145

vividly portrayed. The murder of the Duc de la Rochefoucauld in the presence of his wife and aged mother was poignantly set forth. The execution at the Abbaye of M. de Montmorin, long the kindly disposed friend of Jefferson and numerous other statesmen in America, was briefly noted. The minister was sufficiently the artist to perceive that here was stark and vivid tragedy, best unadorned. His despatch gained by simplicity.[43] Here were the facts; let others moralize.

As if by studied contrast Short wrote from his distant coign of vantage the most elaborate of all his reports, and on a visionary line. Dismissing facts, or at any rate reducing them to their minimum, he launched upon a discussion of the probable future of France, granting as a virtual certainty the execution of her King. With a tediousness almost incredible, which must have taxed the patience of his reader, the minister at The Hague discussed the possible domestic and foreign combinations which might result. As an exercise in sheer hypothesis it was an *opus magnum*. For our present purpose, divorced as this despatch was by its very length from any likelihood of Washington's perusal and from influence therefore upon his thought and action, it suffices that Short's argument pursued the following general plan: First, the destruction of the King was well nigh certain. Secondly, the French might prefer a republic but they could not flaunt this wish in the face of Allied Europe. Thirdly, a monarch would certainly be imposed.

Would that monarch be Monsieur, next brother to the King? Hardly so. Too many interests would oppose. More likely—and here Short was quite original—the Duke of York would be the successful candidate. Considerable ingenuity and an appalling weight of words were mustered to support this view. Analyzed with some such brevity as this, it may have come to Washington's attention. Life was certainly too short for perusal of the entire despatch.[44]

On the nineteenth Morris sent to Jefferson, with only a brief comment of his own, the interpellation of M. Masuyer in the Assembly regarding the desolation wrought by the September massacres, and the feeble reply of M. Roland, admitting he was unable to fix responsibility. If Jefferson had doubts concerning

146

the Terror into which France had fallen, these should have been dissipated by the evidence.[45]

Again, on the twenty-seventh, and this time more elaborately, the American minister set forth the fate of Lafayette and its connection with the larger course of politics in France and Europe generally.[46] The imprisonment of Lafayette, it should be said, had been a subject of the most active correspondence among all the ministers of the United States in Europe. All had felt the deepest sympathy, personally and on behalf of the United States. Yet none had seen the slightest ground for intervention. The case was most embarrassing from every aspect viewed.

News of Lafayette's misfortune encountered the usual delays in reaching the United States. Tobias Lear had evidently just learned of it on October 7, the news being thirty-five days from Ostend. Apparently the account was pretty accurate, with the further information that the army which the Marquis had recently commanded was so mutinous and distracted as to be in danger of being captured by the enemy or of turning upon its friends.[47]

Doubtless the most affecting account to reach Washington personally at any rate was from Madame de Lafayette. On order of Roland, she too had been arrested on September 11, but was permitted to remain on parole at Chavaniac after October 2.[48] Like her husband's, her plea could only embarrass further the country he had served. Omitting the details of her narrative, one may quote her plea for aid, leaving to imagination the difficulty in which it placed Washington:

> In this abyss of grief, the idea of owing to the U. S. and to M. Washington—the life & liberty of M. Lafayette re-animated my heart with some hope.—I hope every thing from the goodness of a people with whom he has set an example of that liberty of which he is now the victim—and shall I dare speak what I hope?—I would ask of them, through you, an envoy who shall go to reclaim him in the name of the Republic of the U. S. wheresoever he may be retained, and who may make, in their name, with whatsoever power he may be, the necessary engagements to emancipate him from his captivity, & carry him to their bosoms.—If his wife & his children could be comprised in this happy mission, it is easy to judge how sweet it would be to her and to them; but if this would retard or embarrass, in any degree, the progress or his

147

success—we will defer the happiness of a reunion yet longer, and when he shall be near you, we will bear the grief of separation with more courage.

May heaven deign to bless the confidence with which it has inspired me.—I hope my request is not rash.—Accept the homage of the sentiments which have dictated this letter to me, as well as that of attachment & tender respect with which I am—Noailles Lafayette.[49]

How wholly feminine, how moving, how impractical! Not the type of letter to render Washington's position easy. Officially he was powerless to help, save in the most general requests to the captors of Lafayette. His aid could be but personal, but here it was most generous, both in the first emergency and for years to follow.[50]

But the fate of Lafayette, painful as it was to the President of the United States and to many others on this side of the Atlantic, was only one among the countless personal tragedies of the French Revolution. Its significance being only personal, once the General had relinquished his command, one should not emphasize it at the expense of broader movements. For these were swiftly shaping.

Short had these movements in mind when from The Hague, on October 12, he continued his allusions to the Royal Family and their approaching fate. Concluding that the Duke of Brunswick had far other ends in view than to rescue the Royal Family, if one might judge by his movements from the Manifesto up to date, Short ventured some interesting predictions that despotism might be the outcome of all this Revolutionary tumult. But his more specific account of the immediate situation of the Royal Family was even more illuminating:

The first intelligence of the combined Armies retiring, will I apprehend induce some member of the convention to urge the trial of the King, & if once proposed, I fear no body would be found to oppose it. —The manner in which the Royal family is confined renders it difficult to be certain of their personal situation—but it seems not to be doubted that the Queen's health has much suffered—one of the circumstances with respect to her which seems to be relied on, & which may serve as a guide to the others, is that she is so absolutely without attendance as to be obliged to wash the Dauphin's linen.[51]

With the executive in prison and soon awaiting trial for treason, there was no responsible authority with which the United
States might negotiate the service of its debt. Under the circumstances Jefferson instructed Morris to suspend interest payments,
not from any wish to defer just obligations; above all, not to
oppose the settlement of the Government in any way the nation
might see fit, "but," as Jefferson expressed it, "from our anxiety
to pay this debt justly and honorably, and to the persons really
authorized by the Nation (to whom we owe it) to receive it for
their use, nor shall this suspension be continued one moment
after we can see our way clear out of the difficulty into which
their situation has thrown us." [52]

The retreat of Brunswick's army, which Short had predicted as
the signal for Louis' trial, was the chief item in his despatch of
October 19. Certain he was, whatever betided, that the King
could never be restored. His previous humiliation was too
drastic.[53]

Short felt a genuine solicitude for the King and his family.
Morris shared the sentiment and in a private letter to George
Washington, given over in large part to the affairs of Lafayette,
the minister outlined the preliminary accusations in the trial of
Louis. "You will have seen," he wrote,

> that the King is accus'd of high Crimes and Misdemeanors, but I
> verily believe that he wish'd sincerely for this Nation the Enjoyment
> of the utmost Degree of Liberty which their Situation and Circum-
> stances will permit. He wish'd for a good Constitution, but unfor-
> tunately he had not the means to obtain it, or if he had he was thwarted
> by those about him. What may be his Fate God only knows, but History
> informs us that the passage of dethroned Monarchs is short from the
> Prison to the Grave.

The ominous plight of the King led Morris to reflections on its
causes. These he found to be chiefly in the mistakes of the Duke
of Brunswick. It was a capital error to issue so insulting a manifesto. It could only serve to unite France against him. It was
error number two not to advance immediately upon Paris after
the events of August 10. A rapid move at that crisis would have
enlisted many friends. A third error, equally disastrous, was to

149

advance at all, the proper moment having passed. Of all these capital mistakes King Louis was chief victim. Far better would his case have been had the Duke entrenched himself, leaving more aggressive tactics to an enemy but ill prepared and likely to be soon discouraged. Then in the following spring, the country would have been well nigh defenseless.

There was doubtless a connection between the incompetence of generals and the fatuity of monarchs. Morris, at any rate, subjoined an *obiter dictum* to the effect that "there is but one Sovereign in Europe, the Empress of Russia, who is not in the Scale of Talents considerably below Par." [54]

Brilliant observer and reporter that he was, Morris was capable of divergent types of composition. In the preceding private letter he was pointed in his style, analytical but brief. In a state paper of identical date to Thomas Jefferson, he was broadly philosophical, concluding his despatch with a memorable summary:

> With respect to the present temper of the people of this country I am clearly of opinion that the great decided effective majority is now for the republic. Whatever may be the temper and opinion six months hence no prudent sensible man would I think take upon him to declare. Much must depend on the form of government which shall be presented by the convention. If vigorous it is very problematical whether the departments will adopt it unless compelled by a sense of impending exterior danger. If feeble it is humanly speaking impossible that it can control the effervescent temper of their people and that appears sufficiently by the facts of the late constitution. Whether they will be able to strike out that happy mean which secures all the liberty which circumstances will admit of combin'd with all the energy which the same circumstances require; whether they can establish an authority which does not exist as a substitute (and always a dangerous substitute) for that respect which cannot be restor'd after so much has been done to destroy it; whether in crying down and even ridiculing religion they will be able on the tottering and uncertain base of metaphysic philosophy to establish a solid edifice of morals, these are questions which time must solve.[55]

It would be interesting to record the immediate reaction of George Washington to these mighty movements and events, but distance and the slow communication of the times, together with his extreme preoccupation with American affairs, rendered his opinions of no immediate chronological significance. They were significant chicfly as reflections of a general attitude and in some instances of a policy already fixed or forming. On October 20, he made some general comments of this sort to Morris:

> Although your letter of the 10th of June, which I have received, did not paint the prospects of France in the most pleasing colors, yet the events which have since taken place give a more gloomy aspect to the public affairs of that kingdom, than your letter gave reason to apprehend.
>
> A thousand circumstances, besides our distance from the Theatre of Action, made it improbable that we should have, in this Country, a fair statement of facts and causes through the medium of the public prints; and I have received no other accounts than what have come in that channel. But taking up the most favorable of these, and gloomy indeed appears the situation of France at this juncture, it is hardly probable that even you, who are on the spot, can say with any precision how these things will terminate; much less can we, at this distance, pretend to augur the event. We can only repeat the sincere wish that much happiness may arise to the French Nation and to Mankind in general out of the severe evils which are inseparable from so important a Revolution.[56]

In a private communication of this sort, Washington naturally was speaking for himself. In important instructions from the Department of State, he shared responsibility with Thomas Jefferson, who spoke equally the opinion of his chief, for such instructions could not be fashioned independently. Washington was speaking indirectly, therefore, in the instructions of November 7, 1792, which admitted the delicacy of Morris' recent situation; approved his action up to date, notably his intervention against the sending of M. de Bon Carère as minister to the United States; and left free scope to his own judgment regarding situations personally dangerous:

> Whenever the scene became personally dangerous to you, it was proper you should leave it, as well from personal, as public motives. But what degree of danger, should be attended, to what distance or place you should retire, are circumstances which must rest with your own discretion, it being impossible to prescribe them from hence.

Morris was instructed further that the will of the people must determine the government with which he dealt. Any government so grounded was both *de facto* and *de jure*.[57]

Almost from the outset of the Revolution, it had been observed by Short and others that its progress was in alternating cycles, intense activity followed by deceptive calm. A lull of this sort seemed to follow the massacres of September and the military hazards of October. It was correspondingly reflected in the files of Washington and the archives of the Department of State. Communications in November were less voluminous, though they did not flag in interest. For example, Short described the differing opinions among the émigrés. Calonne was spokesman for the extremists, who would restore *in toto* the *ancien régime* with all its intolerable features. Breteuil † was exponent of the moderate reform which met approval at Vienna—the Emperor himself according to unimpeachable report being in favor of the English form of government as well suited to the French.[58]

In his following despatch, Short detailed his scruples against paying out American money to a Government as seemingly illusory as that assuming power in the *coup d'état* of August 10:

> I wait with anxiety & impatience however to know the will of the President as to the monies in the hands of the Commissioners at Amsterdam, having written repeatedly to the Secretary of the Treasury on the subject since the King's suspension. I hope ere long to receive orders.[59]

On the sixteenth, Short transmitted to the Department its first knowledge of the citizen Genêt, soon destined to create a mighty stir in Franco-American relations. Morris was to follow with a more elaborate account of the gentleman, but neither of our ministers found much about him to commend. In 1792 Genêt's appointment was to the Netherlands. As Short describes it,

> M. de Genet, late chargé des affaires at Petersburg is to be sent here [i.e., The Hague]. It is not yet known whether he has a public character & when he will arrive. Should he present letters of credence it will bring this country to the test & perhaps it may be the wish of the French government to have a pretext for complaint.[60]

It would be easy to read into this passage more than Short intended. Allusion was rather to existing difficulties between the Netherlands and France and the strained relations of diplomacy, than to any personal inadequacy in the prospective minister.

Meanwhile the armies of France were heading toward that amazing course which astonished all Europe and culminated in the rise of Napoleon. Short sagaciously observed of these early triumphs that "it does not appear to me that a conquering Army of such immense numbers returning elated with conquest from all their neighbours around them will be a very useful or manageable ingredient in the composition of a commonwealth." Nor would their maintenance be simple, with assignats embarking on a wild inflation.[61] But Short was learning to doubt his own conjectures, the Revolution invariably taking such surprising turns. He modestly admitted that Morris would be more immediately informed but justified his own contributions on the score that all of Europe thought of little else, and that few events of special interest were occurring at his post.[62]

Morris more than fulfilled these expectations. His despatches proved minute or generally interpretative as occasion demanded. His final for the year presented Jefferson, and therefore Washington, with an analysis of the conflict in the Convention (which had replaced the Assembly) between the Brissotines or Girondists, as they more commonly were called, and the Jacobins. Victory lay with the former for the moment, and by a handsome margin. Their enemies might bide their day. The bone of chief contention was the King. It was dangerous to let him live. On the other hand, his death would precipitate dangers of another sort. With rare insight Morris showed that the King was really without friends, even so-called monarchists being willing to let him die in order to shock the nation into a new loyalty. It was all pathetic, for Louis was the mildest of his line. To portray him, as his enemies were doing, as a bloodthirsty tyrant was a very travesty on truth.[63] Yet these slanders carried weight, for his enemies, in full possession of his papers, garbled their contents to place him with the populace in an abhorrent light.

Morris had little confidence in the integrity or popularity of the Duc d'Orleans, who had been stirring in very muddied waters hoping to benefit his own house by the downfall of his kinsman. So far, thought Morris, his principal victory had been over his own conscience, which now was never bothered.[64] Political victories of the kind he sought would never be attained.

This concluding despatch for 1792 is memorable further for the earliest mention, outside of the gazettes which were regularly forwarded, of the coming leader, Danton. "Shortly after the tenth of August," remarked Morris, "I had information, on which you may rely, that the plan of Danton was to obtain the resignation of the King, and get himself appointed chief of a Council of Regency (composed of his creatures) during the minority of the Dauphin. This idea has never, I believe, been wholly abandon'd. The *Cordeliers* (or Privy Council which directs the Jacobine movements) know well the danger of interverting the order of succession." No danger, therefore, that Orleans would profit by their action.[65]

Before the year quite ended, Morris wrote personally once more to Washington. For any who may have doubted, though, that official despatches have little relevance to a study of George Washington and the French Revolution, it may be observed that Morris himself thought otherwise. Thus on the twenty-eighth, he wrote, "My Letter of the twenty-first Instant to Mr. Jefferson will communicate my View of Things, to which I could add but little at this Day."

A bit of news was reserved for Washington himself. It concerned Genêt, whose mission to the United States was not yet officially announced, the new authorities in France being neglectful of diplomatic courtesies, but which was so certain to take place that Morris thought it wise to investigate his antecedents. In the light of what was soon to happen, this report and others following are significant:

> I have not yet seen Mr. Genest, but Mr. Paine is to introduce him to me; in the mean Time I have enquir'd a little what kind of Person it is: and I find that he is a man of good Parts, very good Education, Brother to the Queen's first Woman; from whence his fortune originates. He was, thro the Queen's Influence, appointed as Chargé d'affaires at Petersburgh, and (when there) in Consequence of Dispatches from Mr de Montmorin, written in the Sense of the Revolution and which he interpreted too litterally, he made some Representations in a much higher Tone than was wish'd or expected. It was not convenient either to approve or disapprove of his Conduct, under the then Circumstances, and his Dispatches lay unnoticed. This to a young Man of ardent Temper, and who feeling Genius and Talents may perhaps have rated himself a little too high, was mortifying in the extreme. He felt himself insulted, and wrote in a Style of petulance to his Chief, believing always that, if the royal Party prevail'd, his Sister would easily make fair

Weather for him at Court: which I doubt not. At the overturn of the Monarchy, these Letters were so many Credentials in his Favor to the new Government, & their Dearth of Men has opened his Way to whatever he might wish. He chose America, *as being the best Harbor during the Storm,* and if my Informant be right, *he will not put to Sea again untill it is fair Weather,* let what will happen.[66]

Washington was soon to have experience with the young upstart. This description and one or two that followed it helped him to understand the new type of French minister. Washington was further interested, no doubt, in Morris' report of a plan, sponsored by Thomas Paine, to send the King and his family to the United States—a humane solution of a vexing problem.

Thus ended, as far as the files of Washington and of the Department of State record it, one of the most stirring years of the French Revolution. Constitutional, bourgeois reform had given way to violence best symbolized by the overthrow of monarchy, the slaughter of the Swiss Guards in August, the September massacres, the imprisonment of Lafayette, and the impending fate of Louis XVI. Ominous for the future was the declaration of war and its success, exceeding expectation and pointing to the bloody years ahead. For better or for worse, the year had been momentous.

CHAPTER SEVEN

1793

For a brief time in 1792 it had appeared that the Girondist leaders might save the King. That promise proved illusory. But to these comparative moderates the King did owe his trial. This the Mountain, the Jacobins, would have denied. The King was granted defense attorneys, the elderly and distinguished Malesherbes, the younger and very clever Desèze. The chief argument for the defense was the "irresponsibility of the monarch" under the Constitution of 1791. This was sound law considering the impotence to which the King had been condemned. But what was law among friends? The Mountain worked its will. On January 15, the verdict "guilty" was unanimous.

There ensued twenty-four hours of voting on the punishment. The verdict on January 16 was 387 for death, 334 opposed to death or for it under certain conditions. Many of the yeas, the Duc d'Orleans, Robespierre, and Danton among them, would be guillotined within the next two years. Strangely enough, Sieyès, without explaining why, voted for the King's death. Condorcet was one who voted for the most severe punishment short of death. To his everlasting credit, Tom Paine, the permanent revolutionist, first American then French, voted no,[1] and in this he was joined by DuPort, and others, who considered the death penalty uncivilized. The execution was a giant show. It took place January 21 on the Place Louis XV, now the Place de la Concorde. On the scaffold the King was a far nobler figure than he ever had been on the throne.

The European coalition meanwhile was causing great alarm, the more since England with her great wealth and her incomparable sea power was disturbed by a French occupation of Belgium which touched her interest closely. On February 17, Dumouriez, disgusted with the regicide convention and already plotting treason, was called to the defense of Brussels. On March 3, his colleague Miranda abandoned the siege of Maastricht and fell back on Liége. The military picture was not propitious.

In the constant interaction between war and politics, the loss of Liége and the defeat of Dumouriez on March 20 at Neerwinden drove the National Convention to two of its most momentous actions. First, the Revolutionary Tribunal was created as a foundation for the oncoming Terror. Secondly, the Committee of Public Safety was destined to drive a more or less reluctant country to a rising tide of victory which still astonishes the world.

Of even greater weight with a conservative peasantry than the execution of the King, was the persecution of the priests and the dragooning of young men into a distasteful military service. Mounting indignation drove three western provinces, La Vendée, LaManche, and Normandy, to armed revolt, and nearby Brittany was in ferment.

Defeat on the frontier and domestic insurrection, capped with the defection of Dumouriez, their hero, were cumulative threats to the Girondists, who for some time had dominated politics. True, they delivered counterblows. They impeached the savage genius Marat, but he was acquitted. They set up a Commission of Twelve, but it fell speedily under Jacobin control. By May

30, the Paris "sections," so called, sought to terrify the Girondists, who were rallying provincial support to offset the city's dominance of the Revolution.

The crisis came on June 2 when a mob crying "To the guillotine with the Girondins" besieged the Convention. Death was voted promptly for twenty-two of the Convention's leading members, all of whom had made important contributions to the Revolution. They were to be arrested in their own houses. Many fled, only to be hunted down in frenzied fashion. Popular excitement reached a new pitch when much of the south and southwest joined the revolt of the western provinces. Unfortunately for the Girondists, the issue was clouded by the presence of many Royalists, thus affording the Mountain some excuse for suppressing the entire movement—that of so-called "Federalism."

In the midst of widespread tragedy, an almost humorous note was struck when on June 24 a new Constitution was declared by a vote of 1,801,918 to 11,600. In such tumultuous circumstances, the dissidents obviously were heroes. But the Constitution, a creation of disordered dreamers, was deemed too unrealistic for the times. It was never put into effect.

Amid counter-revolutionary perils on the fringe of France, the very heart of the Revolution was endangered by the growing rivalry between Robespierre and Danton. As president of the Jacobin Club, Danton was at the height of his power between September 1792 and September 1793. But his failure to comprehend the subtle tactics of Robespierre insured his downfall. The defeat in the west of Westermann was not dissimilar in its effect upon his patron, Danton, to the defeat and defection of Dumouriez in its effects upon his friends of the Gironde. On July 10, membership in the Committee of Public Safety was reduced from sixteen to nine, with the name of Danton omitted. He took it philosophically. That was hardly wise.

As Danton's star was declining, Robespierre's was clearly rising when he was appointed to the very committee from which his rival was excluded. He and his colleagues were the real rulers of France in the critical summer of 1793, when unity between Austria and Prussia might conceivably have led to their early victory. But once more, as in the previous summer, the dilatory

159

tactics of the Allies gave France her opportunity. In the armies newly forged, illustrious names were coming to the fore—Hoche, Jourdan, Moreau, all young in 1793 but destined for great deeds. For the moment the name to conjure with was Lazare Carnot, "the organizer of victory," "the organizer of discipline."

The parallel between the first and second years of war unhappily extended further. Uncertainties and fears bred terror. Massacres, like those which rendered 1792 forever infamous, began earlier in 1793 and ended later. Madame Roland was condemned on July 1. At thirty-nine she met her fate with dignity. Indeed among the long roster of victims most knew how to die—melancholy exceptions being the aging Madame du Barry and the horrible Hébert, atheist editor of the *Père Duchesne*. Who more dissimilar in personality than Madame Elisabeth, sister of the late King, and Charlotte Corday in 1793, Camille Desmoulins and Hébert in the following year? On October 16, after a trial that shamed her jailers, the Queen followed Louis to the place of execution, her bearing noble as a Hapsburg Princess and a Queen of France.

On September 5, the Paris "sections" demanded terror as the order of the day. They so far had their way that a member of the Convention could say, "Let us go to the foot of the great altar and attend the celebration of the red Mass." [2] The cautious Robespierre did not commend wholesale murder as a Revolutionary instrument until much of the worst had passed, not only in Paris but in the provinces, where Carrier † was to engrave his name with permanent infamy for his massacres at Nantes and along the Loire; where Tallien, with "Death to the Liberticides," was to win comparable disgrace in the southwest; and Fréron was to wreak his will in Provence. There is little profit in tallying the victims. They were numbered by the thousands—a mark to stand until the present century when Germany and Russia both counted their victims by the millions.

Partly due, one may suppose, to Robespierre's belief in the sacredness of private property was the infrequency of socialist or communist propaganda in these turbulent days. On September 30, however, the Socialists did move to nationalize the factories. Ardent advocate of this radical scheme was Fou-

160

ché, a future millionaire and Minister of Police for Napoleon.

But whatever conservatism might survive in economics did not extend to religion, for 1793 beheld the enthronement of Reason as a goddess whose temple was the former Cathedral of Notre Dame. The most revolting orgies attended her worship, to the equal disgust of Danton and Robespierre. Indeed, 1793 did not present a convincing demonstration of reason, whether horse sense or goddess.

Strangely enough, or perhaps logically, the absurdities and cruelties of the Terror did weld the nation into an instrument, a virtual machine for victory. Early fruits of the strength thus grimly forged were the defeat of the Duke of Brunswick by Hoche at Kaiserslautern, and the joint victory of Hoche and Pichegru at Landau. The King of France was dead but his brother sovereigns were in no position to inherit.

It was a France convulsed by these maddening excitements that Washington confronted as a head of state in 1793. What would he make of the Franco-American alliance of 1778, which still had five years in force, though its purpose, as well understood at the time of its agreement, was long ago fulfilled? What did wisdom dictate in such a maelstrom of events? Neutrality proved to be the answer.

That Washington in a year certain to be difficult did not enjoy the full cooperation of his pro-French Secretary of State is apparent in several of Jefferson's communications highly critical of neutrality,[3] and in Jefferson's concluding instructions to his disillusioned friend Short.

Indeed, a good example of the conflict between affection for Short and enthusiasm for the French Revolution is Jefferson's last instruction to him while Secretary of State, penned on January 3, 1793. Jefferson believed that most Frenchmen were Jacobins. Their excesses, if one called them such, reflected the national will. "In the struggle which was necessary many guilty persons fell without the forms of trial, and with them some innocent. These I deplore as much as any body, & shall deplore some of them to the day of my death. But I deplore them as I should have done had they fallen in battle." In this comparison Jefferson went on with great fanaticism to add,

> It was necessary to use the arm of the people, a machine not quite so blind as balls and bombs, but blind to a certain degree. A few of their cordial friends met at their hands the fate of their enemies. But time and truth will rescue & embalm their memories, while their posterity will be enjoying that very liberty for which they would never have hesitated to offer up their lives. The liberty of the whole earth was depending on the issue of the contest, and was ever such a prize won with so little blood?

Jefferson should have heard by January of the September massacres! But these vicarious sacrifices were not too distressing, for he went on to express sentiments more suited to a Marat or a Stalin than to a moderate liberal. "My own affections," he conceded,

> have been deeply wounded by some of the martyrs to this cause, but rather than it should have failed I would have seen half the earth desolated. Were there but an Adam & an Eve left in every country, & left free, it would be better than it now is. I have expressed to you my sentiments, because they are really those of 99. in an hundred of our citizens. The universal feasts and rejoicings which have lately been had on account of the successes of the French shew the genuine effusions of their hearts.

Having let off steam as it were, at this point Jefferson turned to the serious business of the instruction. Short had been grieved by the sorrows of his friends, but he had expressed himself too freely, not only in his despatches but even more so in conversations which had not failed to be reported. The President had been induced

> to break silence and to notice the extreme acrimony of your expressions. He added that he had been informed the sentiments you expressed *in your conversations* were equally offensive to our allies, & that you should consider yourself as the representative of your country and that what you say might be attributed to your constituents. He desired me therefore to write you on this subject. He added that he considered *France as the sheet anchor of* this country and its friendship as a first object.[4]

In the light of such opinions, which one must assume perforce were quoted accurately by Jefferson, it is passing strange that William Short, gentle liberal that he was, should be replaced by Gouverneur Morris, fiery aristocrat, personal associate of many of the Revolution's victims.

162

A continental war of the dimensions already taking shape could not be inconsequential to Great Britain and when she joined the Allies in 1793, the diplomacy of the United States was further tested as between the mistress of the seas and the arrogant successors to our friends of 1778. Neutrality was the necessary keynote to American diplomacy, but its preservation was a task of utmost magnitude, a task intensified by the maladroit Genêt, whose presence in America bore living witness to the mad ways of the new era and gave Washington first hand experience with the type of men whom Short and Morris had repeatedly described.

Thus Washington in 1793 was driven into positive action rather than philosophical reflection regarding the French Revolution. The climax of this action was his Proclamation of Neutrality, of April 22, which ever since has been regarded as one of the great state papers of American history, and a decided step forward in the whole field of neutrality as a portion of the Law of Nations.

Also, the passions engendered by the Revolution came to dominate American domestic politics, which in 1793 and for some years afterward were unduly influenced by local prejudices against and enthusiasms for the leading characters and events in France. This sharpening of party controversy in America was extremely painful to George Washington, but thenceforth until his death, the French Revolution was a vital factor in his political, and for a brief period, his military life. France gave, in fact, a species of unity to a career that opened in 1753 on a frontier in dispute with France, and terminated in the abortive war of 1798 to 1800.

The year began in a more optimistic fashion than events soon justified, with Morris calling attention to friendly overtures from France to Great Britain and explanations elsewhere that were apparently pacific. The army, too, had entered winter quarters.[5] The domestic picture was less hopeful. The Jacobins were determined to rule or perish, and the time seemed drawing nearer for a test of their pretensions. The Girondists, still nominally in power, showed very little spirit. In the midst of such uncertainties and with war against Great Britain still a possibility,

163

Morris felt he should remain in Paris through the holidays.[6]

This was to the Department. For the President's own eye, of the same date, Morris presented a most amusing and revealing sketch of the much inflated Citizen Genêt. It is too good for partial excerpts and is given here in full:

Paris   6 January 1793

My dear Sir

Since I had the Pleasure of writing to you on the twenty eighth of last Month I have seen Mr Genest and he has din'd with me. He has I think more of Genius than of Ability and you will see in him at the first Blush the Manner and Look of an Upstart. My friend the Marechal de Segur had told me that Mr Genest was a Clerk at £50 p^r an: in his office while Secretary at War. I turn'd the Conversation therefore on the Marechal and Mr Genest told me that he knew him very well having been in the *Ministry* with him. After Dinner he entered into Dispute on Commerce with a Merchant who came in and as the Question turn'd chiefly on Facts the Merchant was rather an overmatch for the Minister. I think that in the Business he is charg'd with he will talk so much as to furnish sufficient matter for putting him on one side of his Object should that be convenient. If he writes he will I believe do better—

I have endeavour'd to shew him that this is the worst possible Season to put to Sea for America. If he delays there is some Room to suppose that Events may happen to prevent the Mission perhaps a british Ship may intercept that which takes him out. And I incline to think that untill Matters are more steady here you would be as well content with some Delay as with remarkable Dispatch.

I am always yours

Gouv^r Morris.

George Washington Esqre [7]

It is unfortunate that this critical estimate of Genêt did not reach Washington until May 3, nearly two months after Genêt's arrival at Charleston. An earlier receipt might have been useful, although Washington was already in some degree prepared and his own perceptions were not dull.

For the time being the communications of the minister were more frequent to Washington directly than to Jefferson and the Department. Only four days after his thumbnail sketch of Citizen Genêt, he presented his friend and chief with a most informative account of friction and disloyalty to one another among French generals, notably Westermann and Dumouriez, both of whom he characterized in terms that should distress their descendants, if they have such. Above these bickerings the destiny of Louis hung in the balance:

> The King's Fate is to be decided next Monday the fourteenth. That unhappy Man conversing with one of his Counsel on his own Fate, calmly summed up the Motives of every Kind and concluded that a majority of the Convention would vote for referring his Case to the People and that in Consequence he should be Massacred—I think he must die or reign.[8]

The execution inevitably came and on the twenty-fifth Morris reported it to the Department. He gave but few details, among them the drowning of the King's voice by drum beats, and the mangling of his head by an ill-aimed axe. Rightly he gave more space to the probable effect of the atrocity upon Europe generally and Great Britain in particular. His personal opinion was that the treatment of the King would be more powerful against the existing rulers of France than an army of a hundred thousand men. Great Britain especially would be goaded to a pitch of horror. War was certain and in no distant future.[9]

Perhaps the misfortunes of the late King deepened American sympathy for a living victim of the Revolution—the ill-fated Lafayette. At any rate the month that sealed the fate of Louis found Morris requesting the bankers of the United States in the Netherlands to have their correspondent in Magdeburg establish a credit for Lafayette of 10,000 florins, drawn on funds of the United States. The object was to furnish him with creature comforts while a prisoner. Also Washington wrote in his own hand to Mme de Lafayette a letter of great tenderness and kindness that one must hope she appreciated, although her previous communication to him had indicated a total inability to distinguish between public duty and private friendship. The letter with its pretended repayment of a loan is a masterpiece of delicacy:

> Philadelphia, Jan. 31, 1793
>
> Madam,
>
> If I had words that could convey to you an adequate idea of my feelings on the present situation of M^r. de la Fayette, this letter would appear to you in a different garb. The sole object in writing to you now is to inform you, that I have deposited in the hands of Mr. Nicholas Van Staphorst of Amsterdam, Two thousand three hundred and ten

165

guilders holland currency, equal to two hundred guineas subject to your orders.

This sum is, I am certain, the least I am indebted for services rendered me by Mr. de la Fayette, of which I never yet have received the account. I could add much, but it is best perhaps that I should say little on this subject. Your goodness will supply my deficiency.

The uncertainty of your situation (after the enquiries I have made) has occasioned a delay in this address and remittance; and even now, the measure adopted is more the effect of a desire to find where you are, than from any knowledge I have obtained of your residence.

At all times, and under all circumstances, you, and yours will possess the affectionate regards of him, who has the honor to be,

Your most obt. and most
humble sert.
G^{o.} Washington

Madam de la Fayette.[10]

The present kindness was one of many to the lady and her family culminating in the prolonged entertainment at Mount Vernon of her son and his tutor.

As winter neared its end, the keen mind of Morris scanned the skies for possible developments. On February 13, he entertained his superiors in America with a survey of the immediate future that was a credit to his intellectual acumen, though the facts as they later developed proved him wrong. He was correct, however, in sensing a new wrath in Europe resulting from the King's execution. And he was acute in prognosticating immediate bankruptcy; a cancellation of debts by further issues of assignats, based this time on the property confiscated from the laity rather than the Church; and a corresponding release of energy on the part of a people newly emancipated from the bonds of debt. It would seem that this insight into economics, both theoretical and practical, was one of Morris' many claims to intellectual penetration.

That the minister was impressed with the dangerous possibilities of his situation would appear from his purchase of a house between twenty and thirty miles from Paris, and outside the prospective march of armies. Here he would be near enough to transact business in the capital, yet remote from tumults certain to arise should the enemy blockade the city and impose a famine.

166

Nor could his distance from the threatening scene be a source of discontent among the French, in view of his actual purchase of a home site in such troubled times. No doubt he was sincere in saying, "In all this my judgment may err but I can truly say that the interest of the United States is my sole object. Time alone can tell whether the conduct be as right as I know the intention to be." [11]

Privately to Washington on the following day the minister presented a gloomy picture of French prospects. Worse than the great force which the enemy could muster, worse than financial troubles and the exhaustion of resources, was the total want of organization in the Government, and the almost universal venality and corruption. The enemy would be dull indeed if he could not locate traitors. Many honest men felt that their loyalty belonged to the former Government. Everything was resting on a quagmire. Nor was Morris' personal situation altogether pleasant. He could be popular, if he chose, but popularity dared not be risked. "The different Parties pass away like the Shadows in a Magic Lanthorn, & to be well with any one of them would in a short Period become Cause of unquenchable Hatred with the others."

The contrast with what he saw and what he left at home moved Morris to a patriotic outburst not unlike the emotion expressed by Henry V at Agincourt in Shakespeare's matchless version:

Happy Happy America Governed by Reason, by Law, by the Man whom she loves, whom she almost adores. It is the Pride of my Life to consider that Man as my Friend and I hope long to be honor'd with that Title. God bless you my dear Sir and keep and preserve you. Your cool and steady Temper is now of infinite Consequence to our Country.[12]

Morris' frank devotion to his chief lent vitality to all their correspondence. Toward Jefferson, somehow, far more self-consciousness entered. Jefferson was a philosopher of world-wide reputation. He must accordingly be addressed in broad and sweeping generalizations. Morris rose to the occasion in a slightly stilted fashion. With Jefferson he was often somewhat gauche. Thus news that Genêt had departed for the United States with three hundred blank commissions for the fitting out of priva-

167

teers induced Morris to some moralizing on the wickedness of chartered murder, the national degradation attending upon riches dishonestly acquired, and the greater wisdom of employing the European crisis in building honestly an American mercantile marine. The idea was sound enough but it needed no embellishments. Jefferson was abundantly equipped to form his own conclusions.

As concerned the war in Europe, Morris was naturally able to add genuine information. His comments on the unexpectedly slow progress of recruiting were doubtless news, and his views upon the necessity and wisdom of a draft possess a rather permanent interest. For the present, he deemed it "an experiment of very doubtful and dangerous complection," with slight prospect of immediate utility.

The party of the Gironde was likely to be punished soon for the execution of the King. The Jacobins would then replace them. Another vindication this was of the accuracy of Morris' information. Much of the remainder of his long despatch covered military probabilities. The sum total of his budget entitled him to say, "On the whole my dear sir, the hour is big with important events." [13]

The coolness attributed to Washington by Morris, perhaps his most essential quality, did not desert him even in this crucial year. But there was nothing in Washington's nature to approve the sanguinary developments toward which the Revolution had been heading. Nor could he feel any permanent bond of sympathy with a firebrand like Thomas Paine. With due recognition of Paine's service to the American Revolution, and with a determination not to part with him in anger—though this broke down at last—Washington and Paine were as far apart as Common Sense and Nonsense. It is quite possible that Washington's instinctive thinking was reinforced by a word from Sir Edward Newenham:

> Mr. Pain's writings occasioned the Murder of Lewis, though he voted against it, but his principles were too deeply rooted in the minds of the People; that Idea of Equality stimulated the Dregs of the People to all the Massacres; I hope in God, he will never revisit America, for he might distract your now happy Government.[14]

Newenham was a faithful correspondent, but it was Morris who bore the brunt of gathering news. It was Morris who gave the first report, next day confirmed, of a French defeat in Flanders, and who concluded that the safety of Paris was more assured by distance than by military force.[15] Defeat further endangered the waning power of the Gironde, though Dumouriez might still retrieve the recent setback. At all events the ship of state was not quite ready for new officers.[16] Before the month was past, however, Morris was convinced that the days of the "Brissotines," as the Girondists were sometimes called, were few.[17] There was no regret in the announcement.

In a world profoundly moved by sentiment, the misfortunes of Lafayette were to his American friends a continually recurring theme. The generosity of Washington has already been noted. On the eleventh of March, he further instructed Jefferson to do the utmost that propriety permitted in the way of diplomatic pressure for Lafayette's release. Jefferson more than cheerfully obeyed, with instructions to Morris, later transmitted to the other ministers as well, and with a personal letter to Mme de Lafayette which Washington accepted verbatim and sent her as his own.[18]

In the regular course of business, Jefferson wrote Morris on the twelfth of March approving his action to date in an emergency which had demanded considerable independence and initiative, at the same time reasserting the legitimacy of any government France might set up, as the only body with which our government might deal. *De facto* must quickly become *de jure* would be a fair condensation of Jefferson's somewhat involved remarks. Meanwhile, for the minister's enlightenment, he reported the pleasure it had given the government at Philadelphia to grant timely aid in Santo Domingo, all in payment of our Revolutionary debt.[19]

Three days later he transmitted with Washington's approval special instructions concerning Lafayette. A state paper of unusual interest, it illustrates the personal equation as an influence in diplomacy. Only genuine affection could have prompted Washington and his advisers to a course of action so remote from the immediate concerns of the United States.

169

Phila. Mar. 15, 1793

Dear Sir,

The President has seen with satisfaction that the Ministers of the United States in Europe, while they have avoided an useless commitment of their Nation to the subject of M. de la Fayette, have nevertheless shown themselves attentive to his situation. The interest which the President himself and our citizens in general take in the welfare of this Gentleman is great and sincere, and will entirely justify all prudent efforts to serve him. I am therefore to desire that you will avail yourself of every opportunity of sounding the way towards his liberation, of finding out whether those in whose power he is are very tenacious of him, of insinuating through such channels as you shall think suitable, the attentions of the government and people of the United States to this object, and the interest they take in it, and of procuring his liberation by informal solicitations, if possible. But if formal ones be necessary, and the moment should arrive, when you shall find that they will be effectual, you are authorized to signify, through such channel as you shall find suitable, that our government and nation, faithful in their attachments to this Gentleman for the services he has rendered them, feel a lively interest in his welfare; and will view his liberation as a mark of consideration and friendship for the United States, and as a new motive for esteem and a reciprocation of kind offices towards the power to whom they shall be indebted for this act.

A like letter being written to Mr. Pinckney, you will of course take care that however you may act, through different channels, there be still a sufficient degree of concert in your proceedings. I am with great and sincere esteem, Dear Sir, etc.

Th: Jefferson.[20]

On the same day that the above instruction went forth to our ministers abroad, Washington, utilizing, as Mr. Gilbert Chinard has noted, the letter form suggested by Thomas Jefferson, wrote what almost amounted to a state paper to Mme de Lafayette, once more expressing his deep sympathy but reminding her of the limits imposed by sheer necessity upon diplomatic representations.[21] It was a most difficult letter to compose, and taxed the tact and wisdom, not to say the humanity of both Jefferson and Washington. Every attendant circumstance seemed to increase the delicacy of such a composition, not least among embarrassments being the inability of Mme de Lafayette to view the case from any other point than her own. Intensely feminine, she was utterly devoid of objectivity. What could have been more troubling to the spirit than her letter of this very time, March 12, inquiring, with slight consideration of the postal delays of the period, why there had been no reply as yet to hers of October 1 preceding.

> Has this letter reached you? —was it necessary to excite your interest? —I cannot believe it!—But I confess to you, Sir, that your silence— and the abandonment of M. Lft. & his family is perhaps of all our evils the most inexplicable to me.—I hope it will not continue forever, and if I am ever to see his face again & to be reunited to him—the hope of accomplishing it still rests upon your goodness—and upon that of the U. S. . . . I shall add no more at present, but to repeat my confidence in M. Washington, in whom my whole hope is founded.[22]

One can only regret that Washington's sensitive spirit should have been exposed to so bitter an insinuation by the wife of the one man for whom he felt the tenderest affection.

Washington may have turned with some relief, although this particular letter could not yet have reached him, to the composition of one of his own necessarily infrequent letters to the faithful, yes, the affectionate, Morris. It is withal a noble letter:

> It was not till the middle of February that I had the pleasure to receive your letter of the 23d of October. If you, who are at the fountain head of those great and important transactions which have lately engrossed the attention of Europe and America, cannot pretend to say what will be their event, surely we, in this distant quarter, should be presumptuous indeed in venturing to predict it. And unwise should we be in the extreme, to involve ourselves in the contests of European nations, where our weight could be but small, though the loss to ourselves would be certain. I can, however, with truth, aver, that this country is not guided by such a narrow and mistaken policy as will lead it to wish the destruction of any nation, under an idea that our importance will be increased in proportion as that of others is lessened. We should rejoice to see every nation enjoying all the advantages that nature and its circumstances would admit, consistent with civil liberty and the rights of other nations. Upon this ground the prosperity of this country would unfold itself every day, and every day it would be growing in political importance.[23]

On April 4, Morris informed his Government of fresh disaster to Dumouriez; of the quarrel between the defeated general and the Convention; and of the resultant menace to a capital which seemed largely unaware of it. Of Dumouriez he wrote, "Perhaps he may experience a similar fate to that of Lafayette, but he is in much better circumstances for a high game and much abler to play it." It was all confusing and required the presence of the minister at Paris to safeguard the interests of Americans.[24]

The minister wrote again next day, so swift were military movements. The army of Custine in the Vosges Mountains seemed cut off entirely from retreat. That of Dumouriez was loyal to its chief and could be depended upon to attack the Convention if he so desired.[25]

Considering Morris' well known dislike for the Jacobins and all their ways, indeed for whatever savored of the radical, his despatches registered a studied caution. The warning sent by Washington at the outset of his mission, his own awareness of the liberalism not to say the (quasi-) radicalism of Thomas Jefferson, curbed his pen effectively. It will be recalled as well that William Short, firm friend of Jefferson and reputed sharer of his principles, on witnessing the violence of the Revolution, adopted a tone of disapproval far more extreme than anything which Morris now indulged in. The results at Philadelphia were precisely what might have been anticipated. Morris won repeated approbation for his conduct; Short, on orders from the President, was strongly censured by his chief. The case was ironical, considering the underlying sentiments of the two men, and elicited from Short a sharp reply to Jefferson.

The Secretary was reminded, and inferentially the President, that Short's despatches were strictly confidential, for the Department's information solely, and that the acrimonious style objected to was limited to the despatches and not purveyed in conversation. Otherwise, hating the Jacobins as he had learned to do, he would not be designated as one by the society in which he moved at The Hague. Short would probably share Jefferson's approval of the Jacobins if he had never seen them, but the difference was, he had. It was the ancient controversy between theory and practice. Morris, on the contrary, who wrote so cautiously in his despatches, was remarkably outspoken among associates. A sentence or two will disclose the bitterness which Short had nursed since quitting Paris—a bitterness quite natural in the circumstances:

172

I have some right I think to know from whence he [the President] got this officious information—& it seems to me a little odd that he should so soon know my conversation from the Hague and blame them, from the supposition of censuring the French Jacobins, whilst he remained ignorant of M. Morris's words at Paris not only against the Jacobins but against the principles of the revolution—& his deeds against the constitution itself—or if he was not ignorant of them thought proper to reward them by giving him his confidence & making him the representative of the U.S.—with the King of that constitution he always ridiculed & went further in intriguing to destroy—those things were public in Paris & published in their gazettes. Still they were unknown to the Prest. it seems. I suspect how & why he got the information as to me—I shd have supposed his caution & sagacity wd have made him suspicious of the chanel—but it seems that things which come through a favorite chanel are recieved [sic] with too much favor to be examined by the most cautious.[26]

No comment is needed on this letter. Some discount might be warranted for the effusion of a very angry man. But anger sometimes directs a searchlight upon a situation. From his own viewpoint, certainly, Short spoke the truth. Which is, nevertheless, in no sense a reflection upon the ability or usefulness of Morris. Both were very able men, but unfortunately they were rivals and Morris held the advantage.

The opinion of Morris, for example, respecting Dumouriez, so accurate and quickly formed, was confirmed to the Department from Dutch sources, and that promptly. A certain Mr. Rodolph Vall-Travers, writing to the Secretary of State from Rotterdam on April 9, 1793, affirmed the rift between the General and the Convention, adding that Dumouriez now wore the white cockade of the Royalists and was ready to make war on the Convention:

He has offered to join the combined antigallican armies, to restore the Crown to Louis XVII; & the antient Form of Government; with what Alterations he may be able to obtain in Favor of the Bulk of the People groaning under all kinds of oppressions and miseries.[27]

It appeared from a subsequent despatch of Morris' that Dumouriez had enlisted for this venture not more than 12,000 men, and that the public was disposed to await events before yielding to undue excitement. "There seems to be more of treason in this

GEORGE WASHINGTON & THE FRENCH REVOLUTION

country than was imagined, and every day increases suspicion, which whether well or ill founded has always the effect of distracting the public councils."

Treason was difficult to define in such a kaleidoscope of governments, and it was Morris' opinion that there was latent, even in the ranks of the Convention, a considerable loyalty to the former Constitution and to the principle of monarchy. Treason this might be if one were too meticulous in chronology. But definitions would altogether differ. Amid such aberrations, suspense was general. Some decisive action was awaited:

> The attempts made to excite disturbances in Paris have hitherto proved ineffectual but that stroke seems to be reserved for the moment when the deputies now in commission in the departments return. It is possible, merely possible, that all may go off smoothly, but the chances are greatly the other way.[28]

On the twentieth of April, Jefferson, anticipating briefly the Proclamation of Neutrality which was the reply of the American Government to the unfolding war in Europe, reminded Morris of the deep antipathy of Americans toward war and their firm resolve to maintain a fair neutrality. Neutrality, if properly interpreted, would be more useful to our French allies than an open declaration on their behalf. So, at any rate, the minister might reassure his hosts. For only in this way could the American flag protect provisions needed in the islands.[29]

Six days later the Secretary of State officially transmitted to all American ministers abroad, Morris, Pinckney, and Short, a copy of the famous Proclamation of April 22, 1793. The commanding place which this document has won in the entire field of International Law and its application to neutrality justifies its reproduction here. It was one of the most notable of Washington's reactions to the French Revolution:

> Whereas it appears that a state of war exists between Austria, Prussia, Sardinia, Great Britain, and the United Netherlands, on the one part, and France on the other; and the duty and interest of the United States require that they should with sincerity and good faith adopt and pursue a conduct friendly and impartial towards the belligerent powers:
>
> I have therefore thought fit by these presents, to declare the disposition of the United States to observe the conduct aforesaid towards those

174

powers respectively; and to exhort and warn the citizens of the United States carefully to avoid all acts and proceedings whatsoever, which may in any manner tend to contravene such disposition.

And I do hereby also make known, that whosoever of the citizens of the United States shall render himself liable to punishment or forfeiture under the law of nations, by committing, aiding or abetting hostilities against any of the said powers, or by carrying to any of them, those articles which are deemed contraband by the modern usage of nations, will not receive the protection of the United States against such punishment or forfeiture; and further, that I have given instructions to those officers to whom it belongs, to cause prosecutions to be instituted against all persons, who shall, within the cognizance of the courts of the United States, violate the law of nations, with respect to the powers at war, or any of them.

In testimony whereof I have caused the seal of the United States of America to be affixed to these presents, and signed the same with my hand. Done at the city of Philadelphia, the 22nd day of April, 1793, and of the independence of the United States of America the seventeenth.[30]

The proclamation did not spring from the head of Zeus, full grown. It was the outcome of profound deliberation, and submission to the Cabinet of a questionnaire on the extent and present validity of America's obligations to France under the Treaty of 1778. Hamilton, as is well known, was for nullifying the treaty, on the ground that it was made originally with a government no longer functioning. Jefferson, on the contrary, held that the treaty was between living nations, not their temporary agents, and that it could not be invalidated by caprice. Hamilton appealed to an isolated passage in Vattel to the effect that when a nation found an alliance *"useless,* dangerous or *disagreeable"* it might renounce it. Jefferson appealed to Grotius, Puffendorf, and Wolf for the contention that "treaties remain obligatory notwithstanding any change in the form of government, except in the single case where the preservation of that form was the object of the treaty." He too appealed to Vattel on the ground that *"useless,* dangerous or *disagreeable"* was an isolated passage in utter contravention of Vattel's entire conception of the Law of Nations.[31]

By all the cabinet the subject was elaborately explored.[32] The Proclamation was the outcome.

175

That Washington felt responsible for the preservation of neutrality even in personal matters would appear from an inquiry to Alexander Hamilton on May 5, 1793. The occasion was the reception of the Vicomte de Noailles, a brother of Mme de Lafayette and a known friend of the United States, having served with distinction in our Revolution. The question involved was the precise degree of courtesy to extend a proscribed character, a refugee from the French Revolution. As Washington defined the case to Hamilton,

> In the conversation you may have with a certain Gentleman [Noailles] to-day, I pray you to intimate to him gently, and delicately, that, if the letters or papers, wch. he has to present, are (knowingly to him) of a nature which relates to public matters, and not particularly addressed to me; or if he has any verbal communications to make of a similar kind, I had rather they should come through the proper channel. And thereto, generally that the peculiar situation of European Affairs at this moment my good wishes for his Nation agregately, my regard for those of it in particular with whom I have had the honor of an acquaintance; My anxious desire to keep this Country in Peace; and the delicacy of my situation renders a circumspect conduct indispensably necessary on my part. I do not, however, mean by this that I am to withhold from him such civilities as are *common* to others. Those *more marked,* notwithstanding our former acquaintance, would excite speculations which had better be avoided. And if the characters (similarly circumstanced with his own) could be introduced by any other than *himself;* especially on tuesday next in the public room when, it is presumed, the Officers of the French Frigate will be presented it would, unquestionably be better. But how this can be brot. about, as they are strangers without embarrassment, as the F.[rench] M.[inister] is shy on the occasion I do not at this moment see, for it may not escape observation (as every movement is watched) if the head of any department should appear prompt in this business in the existing state of things.[33]

On the same date as the foregoing, Washington was secretly and confidentially addressed from Lisbon by David Humphreys, a valued officer in the American Revolution, who later won distinction in both diplomacy and business. Humphreys was a shrewd observer, although the passage cited here added little to what Washington could learn through more immediate channels:

By all accounts from France, it appears that the situation of that new Republic is very alarming indeed. Although we have no authentic details to be absolutely relied upon, yet there is little doubt that discord & treachery greatly prevail. The reports of the treasons of Dumourier & other Generals are too monstrous almost for credibility. God only knows how the confusions will end. Still I cannot believe that the antient order of things will be restored.[34]

Ominous as the case might look in Lisbon, Morris, far nearer to the scenes involved, took a rather more cheerful view. Dumouriez had fewer followers than at first supposed; the Allies were awaiting their full strength before indulging in rash moves; French territory was not at any point invaded. On the other hand, national unity was conspicuously lacking and there were important counter-revolutionary movements south of the Loire. Morris was alluding here to the uprising in the Vendée, soon to be so horribly suppressed.[35]

The Revolution had now exhibited most of its chief phases. A lofty zeal for the eradication of abuses, a patient determination to erect a constitutional and bourgeois monarchy, the abandonment of more constructive efforts in the face of European war, social explosions of tremendous violence and the complete overthrow of monarchy, increasing radicalism on the one hand, and on the other increasing tendencies toward dictatorship as the Girondists gave way before the Jacobins and before the need for more energetic prosecution of the war—these marked the outline from 1787 to date of a Revolution which all the world, and Washington not least, had watched with eager interest.

The "coolness" which Morris had esteemed the most essential quality of his President had never been more evident. The Proclamation of Neutrality bore witness to this ability of Washington's "to think without confusion, clearly." Yet for a full appreciation of this dominant characteristic, one needs a foil or contrast, in this case, Newenham. The Irish baronet had been according to his light a liberal. But the Revolution was providing him with too severe a test. Let him speak for himself:

Your Excellency knows my zeal for real & Constitutional Liberty; it is a Principle derived from my Ancestors & which will attend my last moments: I was a warm & zealous Advocate for the First Revolution

177

in France, nay I was for a Monarchy in the most Limited manner, but I was convinced, that such a Kingdom as France could never form itself into a Republic calculated for the General Happiness of the Whole.[36]

Here was a fair specimen of enlightened European sentiment. Washington would have been justified in a similar outlook and opinion. Perhaps at heart he may have felt somewhat as Newenham. But there is no evidence to that effect. Indeed the very want of evidence is a constructive indication of that "coolness" of George Washington's which was so important in the estimation of contemporaries.

Meanwhile the closing days of May, by the overthrow of the Girondists, had marched a step further along the road of violence so congenitally disagreeable to the temperate President. Morris foresaw in the event a fresh revolution, though its nomenclature was not as yet determined.[37]

On the western side of the Atlantic, Citizen Genêt had delivered his credentials and taken up his work as minister, confronting to his considerable chagrin the Proclamation of Neutrality on the one hand; and countering it on the other with a demand for the immediate payment of the entire debt to France, something by no means contemplated in the bond. Morris was accordingly instructed to explain at Paris the impracticability of Genêt's proposal, and if possible to forestall similar demands in future.[38]

This instruction to Morris was followed by one concerning "the lost million," supposedly paid secretly to Beaumarchais in June of 1776, by a Government not yet prepared to recognize the United States but willing to finance it with supplies. Considerable portions of the million had been repaid and the balance was now due. Jefferson, speaking officially for Washington and the Government, thought that sufficient time had elapsed to remove all need for secrecy and to bring the transaction into the open. Morris was accordingly directed to take the necessary steps for clearing the mystery.[39]

What would have passed for Morris' reply to this, had communication been more speedy, but which in the circumstances could not possibly have been such, was addressed to Jefferson on

June 25, 1793. In it the Government was notified of certain violations of the American flag in French ports and the efforts of the minister to secure apologies. Morris appreciated Jefferson's approval of his attitude and conduct, though from a private letter to Washington of the same date, it appears that he still had doubts upon this score. The previous criticism by Short had inevitably influenced Jefferson's opinion, and Morris had been made to realize once more the necessity for tactful conduct on his mission. Again he reminded the Secretary of his loyalty and courage in remaining in France after the events of August 10, 1792, in spite of French advice to consult his personal safety by withdrawing.

A shift of politics in France was next appraised by Morris. The counter-revolution, centering along the Loire, was assuming wide proportions. Monarchy survived as an active principle in France and might eventually reverse much that had been done.

At this point, Morris referred to a speculation in drafts upon the United States. Nothing could be done without his sanction and participation, and, as he informed the Department, he would have made large sums as a reward for acquiescence. His refusal to sanction such a scheme offended its promoters, and he believed them capable of attempting his recall. He was consistent in not entangling himself with any transient group of leaders. Their power was too ephemeral, as witness the exaltation of the Girondists after August 1792, and their abasement in May 1793. Experience in France made him rejoice that neutrality had been adopted as his country's policy. As for France, her fate hung in the balance.[40]

To Washington directly, Morris predicted that the overthrow of the Girondists would mean the recall of Citizen Genêt and his replacement by a Jacobin. As a political observer, Morris had no faith in third parties. The democrats being divided, his theory presupposed that one of their two factions would join the Royalists. Incidentally, the latter were displaying splendid leadership and courage in their insurrection in the west. If they once gained possession of Nantes, they would have thrust a wedge into the fertile heart of France.

One passage in this letter may serve as an interesting example

179

of going over the head of a superior directly to one's chief—an advantage possible in a relation that was both official and personal:

> In my Letter to Mr. Jefferson of this Day I tell him that I shall implicitly obey his orders; but this is in Reply to the broad Hint, that my Embarrassments may have arisen from Inattention to the Principles of free Government. You may rely Sir that I shall be cautious to commit the United States as little as possible to future Contingencies. In my last Letter I gave you my Idea of *Popularity*.[41]

For July 1793, the fourth anniversary of the fall of the Bastille, Washington's records reveal nothing of special interest from France. One may infer, however, that a letter addressed to Charles Cotesworth Pinckney, American minister at London, from Lafayette pining drearily at Magdeburg, came in due course to Washington's attention—the sentiment at least if not the words.

As though to move a heart of stone, scarcely needful in the case of hearts already deeply touched, Lafayette selected the Fourth of July for his lugubrious epistle:

> My dear sir, whilst, on this anniversary, my American fellow-citizens are toasting their joy, I join in a solitary bumper with the happy remembrances, the patriotic wishes which are crowding upon us. Encircled as I am with ditches, ramparts, guards, double sentries and palissades; shut up in a quadruple gated, barred, chained, locked, grated, narrow, moisty, subterranean dungeon; and doomed to the moral and bodily hardship which revengeful tyranny is heaping on me, let it be to-day my frolic, so far to cheat the crowned gang and their vile agents as to be enabled first to scribble, then to convey this homage of a sympathizing heart.
>
> Although a letter I had begun for general Washington was seized from me, I don't doubt but what the French transactions of August have been fully known in America. How differently circumstanced both countries have been! In France, political ignorance, slavish habits, unequality of wealth made the people, even after they had nobly asserted their rights, jealous of every lawful restraint, yet ready for any fashionable oppression, and tossed them up with factions and mobs. Happy it was, though I have been blamed for [it], that the revolution be prefaced with a declaration of rights, which amidst darkness and storms kept up, if not always the practice at least the knowledge of liberty! And that the mass of the citizens be regularly armed, which at the same time it made it inconquerable from abroad, could oppose internal usurpa-

tion, a chance against which, when looking down upon it, I have often warned my countrymen.

Next, in somewhat rambling fashion, Lafayette discoursed upon the progress and accomplishments of the Revolution, and condemned the Jacobins as undoers of much good. But he ended in a key of rather unexpected optimism:

> Let me only observe that a resistance had been well prepared, which so many dilapidations, treasons, follies and disgusts have not yet spent out and that the patriotism and gallantry of the French in fighting for those rights which at home are tramped upon, show that they want civic habits rather than a spirit to assert them.

Following more to similar effect, the captive thanked Pinckney for an intercession which after eight months had resulted in the knowledge that his wife and children were alive. Also, he expressed becomingly his gratitude for the "ten thousand very welcome florins which have been lodged for me in this bank." [42]

A graceful letter, all in all, it was, with ample stress upon the writer's citizenship as an American.

If there was little news from France, there was much action at home. Genêt was busy with his *Sans Culotte,* his *Little Sarah,* now become *The Little Democrat,* and with his own *Le Citoyen Genet.* Jefferson was cooperating very poorly in a neutrality which privately he labeled "pusillanimous," and which he never favored.[43] The British were making frequent representations against the inequality with which they felt neutrality was administered. Altogether, Washington confronted one of the most troubled periods of his Administration. Concerning the belligerent powers, he wrote Henry Lee, the Governor of Virginia, that he was "more than ever overwhelmed with their complaints. In a word, the trouble they give is hardly to be described." [44]

The high-handed conduct of Citizen Genêt and his flagrant defiance of American neutrality rendered perfectly inevitable a demand for his recall. The Cabinet discussions leading to this end, and the eventual "deflation" of the minister, are a portion of the history of the times. A brief account of his career is accordingly appropriate:

The Citizen Genêt, of whom Morris spoke so disparagingly, was of upper bourgeois antecedents. His sister, Madame Campan, was first lady-in-waiting to the Queen, a situation which would not have been open to her in the heyday of the monarchy, when the position would have gone to a duchess. Even so, she was a person of importance, on whose influence Genêt relied to win his pardon should monarchy endure. In the unlikelihood of that event, Genêt counted on his Revolutionary connections with the Girondists in the National Convention. For had he not spoken out as a true patriot and citizen at the court of Catherine the Great, winning thereby her cordial disapproval and speedy ejection from his diplomatic post within her empire? Unfortunately, French politics shifted too rapidly for his Girondist friends to be of help when his mission to America failed even more signally. The Jacobins were a different breed and they sought his scalp to add to those of other and more eminent Girondists.

Arriving in April 1793, more by accident than design at Charleston instead of his destined Philadelphia, he received a huge ovation which expelled what little judgment was his natural endowment. From Charleston, he proceeded northward through a series of demonstrations from a populace which was overwhelmingly pro-French, so that by the time he reached the capital he had convinced himself that he was an emissary of the French nation to the American people. If the United States Government disapproved, it could lump it, for was not he, Genêt, enthroned in the hearts of true Americans? And was not the American executive as feeble as the expiring French?

Moreover, the cold reception awaiting him by Washington was not too disconcerting, for was not Jefferson in the French camp? And with so powerful a protector could he not achieve his ends? Here was another misconception, for much as Jefferson approved of France and her Revolution, as a distinguished official of our Government he must uphold its dignity. And the irresponsible French minister soon found his projects thwarted.

There were, however, some initial successes. Mangourit, French consul at Charleston, enrolled recruits for an expedition into Georgia to subdue the Creeks. And from Jefferson himself Genêt secured permission to send the botanist Michaux to Kentucky as a secret agent. But the arming of French privateers was the rock of stumbling. Disregarding the Proclamation of Neutrality, issued in the very month of his arrival, Genêt insisted that the Treaty of 1778 granted to France privileges in American ports not accorded England. Several ships, as we have noted, captured by French privateers, were interned in American ports. And it was when Genêt, notwithstanding a pledge to the contrary, permitted the *Little Sarah* to put to sea, that the patience of our Government reached a breaking point. Genêt's recall was demanded, to be sure, but humanity reinforced justice in preventing a vindictive course. He was permitted to remain as a private citizen. He married successively daughters of two influential Americans and became a prominent citizen, surviving into the Administration of Andrew Jackson. Our original demand for his recall precipitated a similar demand by France for the recall of Gouverneur Morris.

The unpleasant episode precipitated by Genêt's immature and reckless conduct represented a definite projection of the French Revolution upon American affairs. For Washington it marked a personal contact with the Revolution, unfortunately not his last, and in a temperament less "cool" might have forfeited much of his earlier good will.

Meanwhile, the story of the assignats from their date of issue provided the theme for an important and lengthy despatch from Morris, which an economist would find of special interest. After tracing numerous ups and downs, Morris deduced that "from all this I conclude that the paper must go on perishing day by day and like other consumptive patients be alike weakened by the doctor and the disease." [45] This opinion proved to be unimpeachable!

It is probable that Morris derived some satisfaction from a veiled dig at Jefferson's ideological conceptions of the French Revolution, when, in explaining the damage to American commerce which it was Jefferson's sworn duty to protest, he innocently remarked that "in the present situation the laws are but little respected and it would seem as if pompous declarations of the rights of man were reiterated only to render the daily violation of them more shocking.[46]

If Morris thus enjoyed a little harmless fun at Jefferson's expense, he had the added satisfaction of "I told you so" when his superior informed him, in due course, of the Government's decision in the case of Citizen Genêt. Morris had taken his measure before the Citizen set forth upon his mission. His recall occasioned no surprise. As Jefferson, no doubt reluctantly, explained,

> . . . Mr. Genet had been then but a little time with us, and but a little more was necessary to develope in him a character and conduct, so unexpected, and so extraordinary, as to place us in the most distressing dilemma between our regard for his nation which is constant and sincere, and a regard for our laws the authority of which must be maintained; for the peace of our country which the Executive magistrate is charged to preserve; for it's honor offended in the person of that Magistrate; and for it's character grossly traduced in the conversations and letters of this Gentleman. In the course of these transactions, it has been a great comfort to us to believe that none of them were within the intentions or expectations of his employers. These had been too recently expressed in acts which nothing could discolour, in the letters of the Executive council, in the letter and decrees of the National assembly, and in the general demeanor of the nation towards us, to ascribe to them things of so contrary a character. Our first duty therefore was to draw a strong line between their intentions, and the proceedings of their minister; our second to lay those proceedings faithfully before them.[47]

An obvious case of hedging, this! The actions of the agent had not been disavowed by the superior. The Citizen was typical enough of the Frenchman of the Revolution, whether in or out of power.

Letters in mid-September to Washington direct afforded him pleasure in the one case, interest in the other; or perhaps in each a blend. From Dublin, on the twelfth, Newenham paid tribute to the imprisoned Lafayette:

> —In my humble opinion Fayette was a true Friend to a proper & Free Constitution his confidential Letters to me in 1790 prove it— they are a record of his most Virtuous Principles—had ill-fated France adopted his Measures & Plan, she would have reigned the *Arbitrer* of Europe, & her People been the best Governed—he wished to Adopt the British Constitution, with a few Alterations; these Alterations would have made a Perfect System of Happiness for Governor & Governed; —I cannot presume to Dive into the Secrets of Courts—but *I will say,* that the Prussians Keeping La Fayette in Prison, is contrary to the rules of War—Justice—Generosity or Policy.[48]

It seems not to have occurred to Newenham or other friends that it was precisely to his imprisonment that Lafayette owed his life.

From David Humphreys next came an important news item, destined soon to affect the career of Napoleon Bonaparte, as yet unknown in the United States. The headline was Toulon. Let Humphreys tell it:

> We have at this moment one article of News of very great importance, which you can hardly receive from any other quarter so soon as from this. On the 28th of last Month the Royalists of Toulon gave up the Town & fleet to cooperate with the English & Spanish fleets before it, commanded by Lord Hood & Admiral Langara, in the establishment (as they term it) of Louis the 17th King of France. The Toulon fleet consisted of upwards of 30 Sail, of which 17 were manned & fit for Sea, and several more in great forwardness. This intelligence came in so short a space of time as to render it suspicious, if it were not official to the Spanish Ambassador & the Portuguese Secretary of State for Foreign Affairs, from whom I have it myself. Deputies from Marseilles were likewise said to be on board the combined fleet for the purpose of making the same cession of that City.—An article which is more certain, is, that the advanced Corps of the French Army on the frontiers of Spain has been defeated by General Ricardos with the loss of 15 Cannon & a considerable number of men.[49]

The continued decline of the assignats, or, to put it another way, the continued rise in prices, elicited from Morris an economic disquisition creditable to his judgment. He appended some comments on the Girondists, then in prison and not likely to emerge save for a journey to the guillotine. But accurate as he was on these important issues, he was guilty of one capital error in overestimating the influence of the Royalists—a not unnatural mistake in the light of their exploits along the Loire and at Toulon. Also, he was unduly pessimistic concerning French resources for a protracted conflict.[50]

A minister is, of course, not merely an observer and reporter. He is primarily an agent. It was in this latter capacity that Morris was instructed on October 3 to explain to the French Government the revoking by the United States of the exequatur of M. Duplaine, French vice-consul at Boston. Duplaine, much of a piece with Citizen Genêt, had offended against American neutrality. He had ceased to be of use to either country. But Morris was required, as in the case of Citizen Genêt, to distinguish sharply between the agent and the employer, and to assure the French of our continued affection and esteem. He was to represent our action as inspired by friendship; and to emphasize our trust that the French would do as much for us if the occasion should present itself.[51] The hand was the hand of Washington; the voice was the voice of Jefferson.

Morris carefully obeyed instructions in these matters, conscientiously laboring to make drastic action as palatable as might be.[52]

A participant as well as an observer in contemporary movements, Morris carried the dual responsibilities of minister and consul. It was enough for any man that he be minister to France of the Revolution. Nevertheless, economy or inattention in the United States had neglected to provide him with a full corps of consular assistants, far less to set up an independent jurisdiction for that office. As a result the minister was constantly plagued with protests over losses to our shipping. These in turn conflicted with his primary function, that of maintaining cordial international relations and developing general treaties.[53] It was a heavy handicap to American diplomacy that consular and diplomatic issues were not immediately distinguished from each other.

In this dichotomy the diplomatic function fared better than the consular. Certainly with respect to the moot case of Citizen Genêt, French politics played into the hands of American desires. Not only were the Jacobins prepared to recall the Girondist emissary; they even threatened to recall him by commission, sending over a deputation of four men to bring him home a prisoner, with the guillotine at journey's end. The project came to naught, but on its face it surely represented all the cooperation that America could wish.

The despatch conveying this report to Philadelphia bore added news of brutalities in the Vendée, where the victorious armies of the Convention were reducing all before them to a desert. It depicted a scene of economic ruin, political ineptitude and military danger that must have saddened any friend of France.[54] Military news, of course, might easily improve with the

186

ebb and flow of battle. And even in the midst of gloom fresh hope was entering. Next day reports arrived that a French army had compelled the Prince of Coburg to raise the siege of Maubeuge. In Alsace, on the other hand, affairs were growing steadily more threatening.[55]

Lest Washington derive his views of French affairs solely through the formal channels of diplomacy; worse still, through somewhat emasculated reports tempered to the special prejudices and predilections of a Secretary of State who was himself no enemy of Jacobins, Morris chose times of crisis for personal communications. Witness the following concerning the recall of Citizen Genêt and the execution of the Queen:

Paris   18 October 1793

My dear Sir

You will see by the Official Correspondence that your orders are complied with, and that your Intentions are fulfilled. Permit me on this occasion to remark that had the People of America been well informed of the State of Things on this Side of the Atlantic no one would have dar'd to adopt the Conduct which Mr. Genest has pursued. In reading the few Gazettes which have reach'd me I am surprized to see so little sound Intelligence.

The present Government is evidently a Despotism both in Principle and Practice. The Convention now consists of only a Part of those who were chosen to frame a Constitution. These after putting under arrest their Fellows, claim all Power and have delegated the greater Part of it to a Committee of Safety. You will observe that one of the ordinary Measures of Government is to send out Commissioners with unlimited Authority. They are invested with Power to remove Officers chosen by the People and put others in their Place. This Power as well as that of imprisoning on Suspicion is liberally exercis'd. The revolutionary Tribunal establish'd here to judge on general Principles gives unlimited Scope to Will. It is an emphatical Phrase in fashion among the Patriots that *Terror is the order of the Day.* Some years have elapsed since Montesquieu wrote that the Principle of arbitrary Government is *Fear.* The Queen was executed the Day before yesterday. Insulted during her Trial and reviled in her last Moments, she behav'd with Dignity throughout. This Execution will I think give to future Hostilities a deeper Dye and unite more intimately the allied Powers. It will silence the opposition of those who would not listen to the Dismemberment of this Country, and therefore it may be concluded that the Blow by which she died was directed from a Distance. But whatever may be the Lot of France in remote Futurity, and putting

187

aside the military Events, it seems evident that she must soon be governd by a single Despot. Whether she will pass to that Point thro the medium of a Triumvirate or other small Body of Men seems as yet undetermind. I think it most probable that she will. A great and awful Crisis seems to be near at Hand. A Blow is I am told meditated which will shroud in grief and Horror a guilty Land. Already the Prisons are surcharg'd with Persons who consider themselves as Victims. Nature and I yet Hope that these Ideas are circulated only to inspire Fear.

I am my dear Sir
Very truly yours
Gouv^r Morris.

George Washington Esqr.
President of the United States.[56]

With clairvoyant insight, Gouverneur Morris was predicting the *coup d'état* of 18 Brumaire; the rise of the Consulship, with three consuls, of whom Napoleon was First; and finally the emergence of Napoleon as dictator of the French and thereby of Europe. From this prophetic vision he drafted one of the most remarkable epistles which Washington received during the French Revolution.

These sweeping generalizations, uncanny in their vision, were followed by an epistle of approximately equal length devoted to the question of Genêt's recall and punishment. The American minister favored making him an extreme example, a warning to others who might in future be tempted to offend. Humanitarian considerations had little weight. Morris was vindictive. He was willing that the deputation should not only seek Genêt, but that it should bring him home, whatever might betide him there. On the legalistic aspects of the case, his stand was seemingly incontrovertible. "It may be an important *judicial* Question how far a minister is protected by the Law of Nations after the arrival of his Successor. In my Opinion the same Principles which exempt him from the municipal Law subject him to the will of his Sovereign." [57]

While Washington was being favored with these intimate revelations, he was himself being subjected to the censorious criticism of Madame de Lafayette. In a letter to her imprisoned husband, she indulged her spleen—his reply is evidence to that effect—politely, no doubt, as became so great a lady, but no less pointedly. To which Lafayette not too loyally replied, "You complain to me, my dear heart, that General Washington does not comprehend certain European manners; but that is on points concerning which men of virtue are not instinctively aware. I love to think that in that good land of liberty news of me comes through your correspondence with him." [58]

Although neither could know it, Mme de Lafayette was shortly to be arrested for a second time, on November 12, under the terms of the law of suspects of September 17, 1793. She was interned first at Brionde, later transferred to La Force at Paris on June 7, 1794.[59]

The writer of these pages must confess that the present study has not taught him to like the Lafayettes, particularly Madame. If he is prejudiced, the reader will doubtless make the needful discount.

Reverting to the broader sweep of Revolutionary currents, it will be remembered that Morris had done useful work in transmitting so accurate and suggestive a pen portrait of Genêt. He rendered similar service for the commission sent to supersede him. He committed these free comments not to the official record but to the President for his immediate perusal:

> . . . A Commission is named (the Appointment not yet gone through the Forms) to consist of four Persons. The Minister is a Mr Fauchiet Secretary of the Executive Council a young man of about three and thirty whom I have not yet seen but he is said to possess Genius and Information. The Secretary of Legation is a Mr Leblanc a Man of about fifty and who was lately at the Head of the Police Department in this City. Him also I am as yet unacquainted with but he is mention'd to me as a prudent sensible man. Mr. de la forét goes out as Consul General and Mr. Petrie his friend and Companion as Consul in the Port of Philadelphia. These two will undoubtedly draw together and will probably sway the Conduct of the Commission for the Minister is to take no important Steps without being previously authoriz'd by the Board. I understand that a Kind of Etiquette has been establish'd by which the Consuls as not being properly diplomatic Characters are not receivd or invited with the Minister and I perceive that there is a strong wish to enjoy the exterior Respect of Office as well as the solid authority. I cannot pretend to judge nor even to guess how far any Thing of this Sort consists with the general Rules which you may have found it proper to establish but I think I can perceive that the

189

two Consuls expect to govern the Commission by two Means One their great Knowledge of our Country and Laws and Inhabitants The other a Perswasion to be inculcated on the Minister and Secretary that they enjoy the Confidence of our Government. Perhaps a little Vanity may also be for Something in the Business, but your Judgment will well discern Motives and therefore I only give Hints. I think that Mr. de la forét and his friend being men of understanding will endeavor to keep Things in a Line of Prudence and Propriety therefore being uncertain (at present) as to the personal Character of the other two it seems to be well that the Board be kept steady by the anchors we are acquainted with and as the others unfold themselves it will appear what Reliance can be plac'd on them. The Minister, in the Conference I had with him just now, has again reiterated the Assurance that he and other Members of this Government have the most sincere Desire to be on the most cordial Terms with us and I am the more disposed to believe in these Assurances because America is the only Source from whence Supplies of Provisions can be drawn to feed this City on which so much depends. The coming Winter will be I believe dreadful and the Spring (should the War continue) must open with partial Scarcities if not general want. To the Sufferings unavoidable from many other Causes no small addition will be made by the Laws limiting Prices which must endure till they shall be shattered to Pieces by the iron Hand of Necessity.[60]

For once the private letter to the President was less interesting than the official despatch to the Secretary. For on November 16, 1793, Morris could report not only the rising value of the assignats in a period of increased currency emissions—in appearance contrary to the rule of reason—but he could describe with penetrating irony the worship of Reason wherein an abandoned, dissolute, and mentally subnormal danseuse of the opera was selected for the role of Goddess, and received in solemn state, in the sanctuary of Notre Dame Cathedral, the worship of the President of the Convention and other leaders of the nation. Strong medicine, thought Morris, for those who still retained their former sentiments, and a deliberate insult to revealed religion. Notwithstanding these absurdities, the fate of France would be decided not by her enemies but by herself.[61]

It is likely that Morris enjoyed presenting in all apparent innocence the Revolution as it was in fact, not in a liberal's imagination, as a planned shocker to the startled Jefferson. One dare not miss a word:

190

I must, by the way, drop one word as to the overthrow of the Catholic religion. It is now expiring under wounds from the true French weapon; ridicule. The people who, five years since, fell down in the dirt as the consecrated matter passed by, now dance the *carmagnole* in holy vestments, and perform other mummeries, which it might seem profane to mention. The late Feast of Reason is a very striking feature in the countenance of the revolution. You know the opera girl, Saunier, who is, though very beautiful, next door to an ideot [sic] as to her intellectual gifts. It is said, also, that she is anything except what the French call *sage*. It is she, who lately asked the painter, David, to invent for her (to appear in the Ballet of Paris) some dress which should be more indecent than nakedness. And the painter, it seems, had genius enough to comply with her wish. But I speak only from hearsay, not having been at any of the theatres for nearly two years.

Well, sir, it so happened that this actress, remarkable for fine attitudes in dancing, was pitched upon to represent Reason in a kind of opera performed at Notre Dame. In the course of it, she stood in the place *ci-devant* most holy, and was there adored on bended knees by the President of the Convention, and other principal characters. At this spectacle, the devout will unquestionably be scandalized, and it seems, in effect, to be a strong experiment on the national feelings. The burning of legs, and arms, and grinders of saints, male and female, with relics from the wood of the original cross, must have the good effect of undeceiving those who imagined there were miraculous qualities inherent in those crumbling materials. But the dismission of all the bishops and curates is a matter of more serious import. A national economy of four millions sterling will be thereby effected; but what degree of ferment may be excited by the disbanding of those ecclesiastical regiments, is yet a problem.[62]

Matters reserved for the following despatch were narrower as history now views them, but more immediately related to the duties of a minister. Commerce of the United States with France was on the point of ceasing altogether, with ninety-two vessels tied up at Bordeaux and with the Convention betraying a fatuous inability or unwillingness to grant redress. The most persistent inquiries were answered courteously, but there the matter ended. Want of coordination in the Government suspended the most essential functions. Bordeaux had too much influence at Paris.

Morris was too engrossed with these commercial problems to give more than passing heed to the final fate of the Girondists and of *Son Altesse Royale,* the Duc d'Orleans.[63]

191

In the paucity of reports for December from French or European sources, one may recur to Lafayette's imprisonment, which was of undiminished interest to Americans. Among those feeling a special concern for the unfortunate man was Mrs. Church, a major London hostess, and sister-in-law of Alexander Hamilton. To her Jefferson wrote on November 27, renewing his assurance of the continued zeal of the Administration on Lafayette's behalf although "the distance & difference of principle give little hold to Genl Washington on the jailors of La Fayette." [64]

On the tenth of December, the prisoner gave direction to his former aide-de-camp and friend, Monsieur La Colombe, that copies or extracts of all matters relative to his captivity be forwarded to Washington, to Jefferson through the American ministers, and by the agency of Mrs. Church to Colonel Hamilton. He further hoped that his own letters *"et tout ce qui y a rapport,"* should be submitted to Mr. Pinckney or to his secretary of legation; or to Smith, Lafayette's adjutant general; and that his friends should look upon the American ministers as his natural confidants and defenders. Carmichael would be certain to do everything in his power and "you know to what degree Short is my friend." Lafayette wished that Short would act in concert with Pinckney, whose interest in his fate had touched him deeply and whose position at London made him logically *"le chef du conseil de mes amis."* Another friend on whom La Colombe could count was M. Paulus at Rotterdam, minister of the department of the Meuse, but care must be taken not to compromise him, and Short would know the means of safe communication.[65]

This letter was followed shortly by a graceful acknowledgment to Pinckney of his important services. To them Lafayette owed the first news of his family. To them he owed pecuniary aid, an hour daily in the open air, and more than that his life, which without American intervention he was certain would already have been forfeited, by methods either lingering or swift. "I am informed that after many negociations with the combined powers, to obtain my delivery, you are preparing a formal, public, spirited demand, a measure I am the better pleased with, as it appears to me the most likely to succeed and will, at all events, be most agreeable to my feelings." Finally there was the usual emphasis on the writer's claim to citizenship as an American. "Wa'n't I an American citizen long before there could be such things as citizens in France?" [66]

December being, as previously noted, not rich in Revolutionary news, there was little novelty in Morris' renewed complaints about commercial restrictions at Bordeaux, continued trouble in the Vendée, further struggle for possession of Toulon, and the outrageous powers of representatives on mission for the Committee of Public Safety. Their actions frequently nullified even the decrees of the Convention, thereby depriving agreements with that body of value. "I need not," reiterated Morris, "dwell on such a state of things for you will readily draw all the perplexing and vexatious consequences. Happy they who contemplate them at a distance. A view of what our countrymen suffer in this respect so torments me that it is very difficult to be patient." [67]

In retrospect, this bloody year of 1793, so disastrous for the King and Queen and their old enemy and kinsman, Orleans; so marked by counter-revolution at Toulon and along the Loire; so offensive to Americans through the mistaken zeal of Citizen Genêt; so valiant in defense of French frontiers; and so absurd in the methods utilized against religion—this most confusing whirl of war and politics, of economics and of atheism running rampant—was nevertheless inherently less interesting than the earlier years of Revolution. In the earlier phases, despotism was on the defensive if not actually on the run. The world, both European and American, thrilled to the prospect of a new freedom succeeding an ancient monarchy. But beginning in 1792 and continuing through the melancholy year just traced, the new freedom was fatally in jeopardy and the ground was fertilized by blood for the erection of a tyranny more odious than the Benevolent Despots of the *ancien régime* had ever dreamed of.

So far as it was possible for an informed contemporary to recognize these trends, they should have been perceptible to Washington.

CHAPTER
EIGHT

1794

The incoming year was to behold a Terror self-consuming, its leading rascals devouring one another. Before his own execution, Robespierre had erased so many of his fellows as to become *de facto* dictator. On March 24, Hébert, a cringing and grovelling wretch, met his Maker. Less than two weeks later, on April 6, Danton, a far nobler rival of the "Sea-green Incorruptible," as Carlyle has dubbed him, mounted the same scaffold, proclaiming "Vile Robespierre! The scaffold claims you too. *You will follow me!*" With no major rivals left, Robespierre had personally devoured the Revolution. The easy-going monarchy, oppressive only locally because of surviving feudal dues and vexing obligations, had been replaced by the bloody apotheosis of virtue as exemplified by Robespierre, the woman hater, the coldly chaste and unsullied, the man who dreaded money and who at his death left only a few hundred francs of depreciating assignats.

Strange compound, timorous but thirsting blood, less typical of France than almost any other man in her history, Robespierre during his brief reign was to intensify the Terror to the point of boredom even for the crowd that gathered daily round the scaffold.[1]

A legal framework for these fresh hecatombs was provided by the "Law of Prairial," passed in June 1794, under which the calling of witnesses was suppressed as no longer needed. The Committee of Public Safety henceforth might send the accused directly to the Revolutionary Tribunal. Thus facilitated, the roll of victims between June 10 and July 28, when Robespierre himself was executed, totalled 2,085. By natural law such extremes begat their antibodies. For Robespierre the nemesis proved to be Fouché, who spent weeks in quietly demonstrating to members of the Convention that no one was safe while such a monster was at large. Fouché's garments were no cleaner than those of the men he approached, but his arguments were persuasive.

Some credit is due Robespierre for abolishing the worship of Reason and restoring the worship of God. This was accomplished in one of the Revolution's greatest spectacles. Robespierre was its priest and prophet. Some think he may have confused himself with the God whom he restored. It was Robespierre's high moment. In his delirium he lost contact with reality and was slow to recognize the conspiracy that compassed his undoing. Even when he knew the danger, he was hesitant and dilatory and overcautious in his measures for suppressing it. His death was unusually painful. He had been shot through the jaw. Some repair work had been done. Just before the knife dropped, the executioner withdrew the bandage. He yelled with pain, then joined the thousands of his victims. Posterity shudders but does not grieve.

The death of Robespierre removed a frightful incubus. The revulsion was complete. Then and there the Terror ended. The way was paved for counter-revolution. Had the émigrés displayed a modicum of wisdom, a constitutional monarchy might have emerged. But their princes, Provence, Artois, and Condé, seemed resolved to superimpose terror upon terror. The clock must be turned back to 1789. Victims were demanded by the hundreds of thousands, possibly the millions. To a people tired of murder this prospect was disturbing. The émigrés might cool their heels in foreign courts. France wanted none of them. Counter-revolution assumed a milder form, leading not to restoration but to the Directory and to Napoleon.

A preliminary step toward moderation was abolition of the Commune of Paris on July 27, the day before Robespierre was guillotined. In an even more drastic step, the Convention on November 12 closed the Jacobin Club. Conclusive proof of a new spirit was the recall of the Girondists to the Convention, and the execution on November 16 of their old enemy Carrier, terror of Vendée and "Butcher of Nantes." On the twenty-fourth, the law of "maximum" was repealed, the law that set a maximum price on every type of goods, and which at various times and places had contributed to widespread starvation in the natural reluctance of peasants and others to sell below the cost of production.

But the Terror, whose ugly side predominates, had nevertheless its offsetting grandeur. It galvanized a faltering nation and forced its armies to ever greater deeds. Some of Danton's own spirit of dare and dare and dare the utmost had been infused into the armies. The results confounded Europe and mankind.

In the spring campaign, Pichegru with 160,000 men joined Jourdan with a somewhat smaller force, who then advanced against the Austrians to a decisive victory at Tourcoing, May 18. This was repeated on June 26 at Fleurus, one of the major victories of the Revolutionary armies. On July 6 the Austrians and their Prussian allies evacuated Brussels, which five days later was entered by Jourdan. On the twenty-third, Pichegru defeated the British. Antwerp was his prize. By autumn the Convention heard of "eight pitched battles gained, 116 towns and 230 forts taken, 90,000 prisoners and 3,800 cannons captured." [2] By year's end other victories were recorded. Pichegru and Macdonald, aided by severe weather, occupied Dutch fortresses which had withstood Louis XIV, and subdued most of Holland.[3] Europe was in retreat before an all conquering urge, a continent-convulsing rage which was driven on by something of the mystic and the transcendental.

In the realm of the economic and material, harvests were only fair and the assignat had dropped in December to 20 francs on the 100.[4] Its barometer was falling. Prices rose appallingly and inflation was acute. But France had survived. Terror ended, the worst was over. The future offered less of cruelty and despair, more of hope.

For Washington, the French Revolution of 1794 was something to view with detachment and that "coolness" for which he consistently was noted. Contemporary leaders were inferior to the men of 1789 and pygmies by contrast with the colossus who succeeded them. Too much blood had been already spilled in the name of a liberty that forever was receding to justify enthusiasm for a cause so travestied. Genuine freedom would be best conserved by close attention to the interests of the United States.

These were served brilliantly, as we have seen, by Gouverneur Morris, but perhaps more brilliantly than effectively, owing to the mistrust which Frenchmen not unjustly felt of his sympathy with their Revolution. It might readily be forecast that Morris would not long retain his post following the disgrace of Citizen Genêt. Etiquette prescribed a *quid pro quo* and Morris was slated for the *quid*. His mission terminated in the late summer of 1794.

Meanwhile, his difficulties were increased by failure to receive instructions. These were sent with reasonable frequency, according to the records, but with almost equal regularity they failed to reach him, due largely to the neglect to send each in triplicate. But notwithstanding many difficulties, it was a mission from which Morris, like his predecessor, retired reluctantly, France in Revolution being far too interesting a scene to quit.

On January 15, 1794, not Morris as minister, nor Edmund Randolph, who had succeeded Jefferson upon his resignation as Secretary of State, but Washington himself in his own hand wrote a personal intercession to the King of Prussia for the captive Lafayette. Feeling triumphed over prudence. The letter is a richly human document:

Philadelphia Jany 15th 1794

To His Majesty the
     King of Prussia.

Sire:

However unusual it may be for your Majesty to receive an address from a person, who, at the very moment of making it, disclaims the exercise of any public function, and acts as a private individual yet it is believed from your illustrious character, that the motives which lead me to the measure will serve as an ample apology.

I cannot longer resist the impulse of friendship, to lay before you, who know so well, how to appreciate its force, my personal and affectionate anxiety for the welfare of M. de la Fayette. Report informs me that he is under confinement in the dominions of Prussia, and therefore at your disposal.

At an early period of his life—at a season, and on an occasion far remote from the time and causes, which have subjected him to his present condition, he pursued his military career, with so much benefit to my country, and honor to himself, that he acquired a most endearing place in my affections.

A sincere attachment then commenced was strengthened by an intercourse which continued after the return of peace had separated us until more active and interesting scenes served to interrupt it.—Upon the events, which succeeded, I shall be silent; only entreating your Majesty to be persuaded, that as I separate myself, in this letter, from my official station, to render a tribute to your liberality; so I beg to be understood as intending to observe that delicacy, which becomes every man, whose country has, with perfect sincerity cherished peace and impartiality towards the whole world.

Permit me then to ask and obtain from your Majesty, a favor, in which the most lively sensibility of my fellow-citizens is engaged—the release of M. de la Fayette on his parole. If his word should not be deemed a sufficient pledge, I shall regret that your Majesty does not entertain the same conviction of his fidelity as a full experience has impressed upon myself.—But I can never be persuaded of the possibility of his departing from that innocence of conduct, which is always to be expected of a prisoner of war.

This request, unsolicited by, and unknown to him asks the patronage of your Majesty's sensibility; and is dictated by a confidence that he could not be in the power of any sovereign, who would more delight in indulging a friendship, which cannot acquit itself, without thus endeavoring to deliver him, under your benevolent auspices.

I pray God to preserve your Majesty in his holy keeping.

G°. .Washington.[5]

The depth of friendship manifested by Washington in writing a letter of this sort can be appreciated only in the light of his constant endeavor not to compromise in any way the official relations of the United States with foreign powers. It was a distinct departure from his strict principles.

Still at his post in Paris, Morris favored the Department on January 21 with a communication interesting chiefly for its reference to Danton and his followers, among them Robespierre, as milder men than some, and for an elaborate exposition of contemporary politics. Also the minister falsely reported Thomas Paine to be a prisoner, whose amusement in confinement was an attack upon Jesus Christ. "I do not recollect whether I mentioned to you that he would have been executed along with the rest of the Brissotines if the adverse party had not viewed him with contempt." Paine was disposed, like Lafayette, to emphasize his citizenship as an American. But Morris thought the claim impossible in view of Paine's English birth and his naturalization in France.

Morris was disposed to view the existing governors of France with more respect than the crew which they supplanted. They were more likely, though, to bring things to a crisis, and the explosion when it should arrive might readily blow up the Dantonists. Whatever was to come, Morris doubted that the Revolutionary committees would survive much longer. Complaint against them was too universal.

Viewed in the large, thought Morris, the unity of France was due to the plans of the Allies for dismembering the country. Men of the most opposite opinions united for national defense. Alsace was an exception, but it was alien in any case. The Vendée was a further exception, French at that. The measures of suppression were proportionately violent and the casualties appalling, running possibly to half a million, with some estimates doubling even that.

In the special objects of his mission, Morris could report slight success. The shipping at Bordeaux was still tied up. The Convention and the Committees were too preoccupied for successful intervention. Well they might be, with 15,000 prisoners in Paris, ten times as many in the provinces, and an immensely complicated economic situation, together with threats upon the frontier. Amid these vast complexities, Morris found his own case complicated by the failure of the United States to distinguish his duties as a consul from his functions as a minister. In his dual role Morris encountered numerous irritations which he viewed with commendable detachment, "because the conduct of men in the midst of a revolution is not to be judged so severely as under a regular government." [6]

There was much in Morris' temperament and situation to intensify his expectation of disaster. A more cheerful note might with equal truth be sounded by one more optimistically inclined; and this it was, from London, by Tobias Lear, the confidential friend and secretary of George Washington:

> The eyes of the people here are beginning to open with respect to France. It is openly said here & in almost every part of the Kingdom that it is folly to contend longer with that nation—which is now considered as the most powerful & energetic at this moment in Europe. The great successes of France can no longer be hid from the people—and the reports of their internal dissensions are no longer believed—as all operations & the accounts of impartial men coming from that Country give the lie thereto.[7]

Similar recognition of the amazing success of the Revolution in defying all its foes enlivened the only record for February to be found either in the personal files of Washington or in the archives of the Department of State. Newenham was writing, with unaffected admiration:

> According to present appearances, the French are every where Victorious—Toulon evacuated—Alsace relieved—Fort Louis blown up— The Toulon & Lyannois armies gone to the Eastern Pyreneans must subdue the small force of the Spanish Dons—the Western Pyreneans they seem Victorious, & the Convention announces that Joudains Army is 3 Times as Strong as Yorke's & Cobourgh—the Invasion of England is announced in all the Jacobin speeches—the Plunder of Proud London's Bank is beheld, as a matter of course by the Sans Culottes—they announce 170 Sail of Transports ready to Bring over their Troopes; they declare that their fleet at Brest is 34 & our Channel Fleet, but 26 sail of the Line; that their fleet will, at least, prevent ours from disturbing the Invasion—.[8]

To this there should possibly be added a letter to Thomas Jefferson (supposed by the author to be still Secretary of State) from the Baron de La Morre de Villaubois, describing his experiences in the Revolution as a refugee noble.[9] It was very lengthy, in a fine handwriting, and Washington could not read French. Even so it may have been reported to him. He was unquestionably familiar with narratives of similar type.

Far less could be learned from the self-pitying declamations of ruined noblemen than from the forthright representations of America's accomplished minister. In March, Morris noted some slight tendency toward lenient measures and a rule of law in place of violence. Happy omen if proved true! Fear only fertilized the soil for future despotism. Also he admitted, not too joyfully, that he had yielded to Paine's demand to the extent of claiming him as an American—not one to be proud of. He had warned Paine that too urgent pleas on his part might simply draw the lightning, with the result that he would prematurely join the other Brissotines. There was no telling, though, what Paine would do, "for in the best of times he had a larger share of every other sense than of common sense and lately the intemperate use of ardent spirits has (I am told) considerably impaired the small stock which he originally possessed."

With his usual attention to economics, the minister reported total failure of a scheme to compel all persons with capital deposited abroad to exchange their bills of claim for assignats. Food supplies were low and difficult to procure even for the larders of the well-to-do, an ominous condition. The Vendée was a case in point. A district formerly supplying Paris with six hundred large beef cattle weekly now needed to import provisions. Further outbreaks would mean a war of extirpation on both sides.

Morris' pet troubles at Bordeaux showed few signs of lifting. Nor was he aided by the premature and tactless efforts of the injured shippers. No demands that Morris could make, short of a declaration of war, ever seemed to satisfy them. His personal situation was difficult. And it was further complicated by the shelter he afforded in the American legation to a victim sought by French authorities. The issue was still pending.[10]

Amid so many annoyances, some of them petty, Morris lost interest in those sweeping generalities and pungent personalities that distinguished his earlier letters and despatches. Thus the rather melancholy keynote of a letter of the twelfth:

> The probable Events of the Campaign about to open are not favorable to the french Republic. It will be extremely difficult for them to subsist the Armies needful for their Defence and the extreme Severity exercised by the present Government will in Case of adverse Events excite an universal Insurrection. At present the People are restrained by Fear from shewing any Sentiment unfavorable to the existent Authorities, but, as is usual in like Circumstances, should that Fear be remov'd it will be succeeded by sharp resentment. If however the Armies of the Republic should prove successful they would in my opinion be the first to overturn the Convention for such is the usual course of Things.[11]

It would seem that Morris was aware of some decline in brilliancy, possibly a sort of ennui, for in his first despatch to Randolph after learning that Jefferson no longer headed the Department, he blamed the former Secretary for a decided toning down in his despatches,

> because judging in my lamentable dearth of intelligence from such feeble lights as I could collect in scattered rays from different quarters, it seemed to me that my letters would have been more acceptable had I been deceived as to facts and probabilities, or capable of communicating sentiments and opinions I did not entertain.

Morris was here indulging in what for him was a restrained expression of pent-up feelings. No two Americans could have been more antithetical than Jefferson the democrat and Morris the aristocrat. Their correspondence was formally correct. But Morris found it inexpedient to tell Jefferson the situation as he saw it, for Jefferson would never have credited it, any more than he credited the accounts of William Short.

If Morris had indeed declined, he was now bent upon amends. For he indulged in a most illuminating survey of the fall of the Dantonists and then the Hébertists, accompanied by the rise of Robespierre. Of the two factions, the Dantonists were patriotic, with some leanings toward the monarchy; the Hébertists conceivably had some connection with the Allied Powers. Warming to his theme, he added,

> . . . Danton always believed and what is worse as to himself always maintained, that a popular system of government for this country was

203

absurd. That the people were too ignorant, too inconstant, and too corrupt, to support a legal administration. That habituated to obey, it required a master. And that even had it been educated in the principles of freedom, and joined to the energy of sentiment the force of habit, yet like ancient Rome it had reached the period in which Cato was a madman and Caesar a necessary evil. His conduct was in perfect unison with those principles, when he acted; but he was too voluptuous for his ambition, too indolent to acquire supreme power. Moreover his object seems rather to have been great wealth than great fame. He has fallen at the feet of Robespierre. As to the Hebertists, whatever may have been the ultimate view of some, I presume that the greater number had nothing more in view than a second edition of the 31st of last May. The destruction of all these chiefs has given great power to the Committee de Salut public whose monthly renewal is so much a thing of course that they may be considered as a permanent body. Hence it follows that the next considerable party ought to arise there. The Hebertists believed the Convention to be so low in public opinion that they could overturn it without the aid of its own members. They were deceived, or at least they were anticipated. The Dantonists supposed that in the want of respect for their rulers the people would readily turn on the little Prisoner of the Temple that enthusiastic sentiment so congenial to the heart of man, so essential to that which beats in a French bosom. They also were anticipated: but if they judged rightly they have unwielded a dreadful mystery.

Here Morris moralized a bit upon the fate of them that draw the sword. Westermann inspired the revolution of the tenth of August; Westermann had perished by the guillotine. Danton was the force behind the September massacres; Danton also perished by the guillotine.[12] The thought was susceptible of considerable development.

Three days later, Morris told how Danton, when informed of his sentence of execution, declared that he was glad to quit a state of society so abominable as that which then prevailed.[13]

But Danton after all was dead. More interesting it was to speculate on what manner of man had succeeded to his power. For Washington himself was reserved the thumbnail sketch of Robespierre:

> . . . It is a wonderful thing Sir that four years of Convulsion among four and twenty Millions of People has brought forth no one either in civil or military Life whose Head could fit the Cap which Fortune has woven. Robespierre has been the most consistent, if not the only

consistent. He is one of those of whom Shakespeare's Caesar speaks to his frolicksome Companion. "He loves no Sports as thou dost Anthony." There is no Imputation against him for Corruption. He is far from rich, and still farther from appearing so. It is said that his Idol is Ambition; but I think that the Establishment of the Republic would (all Things considered) be most suitable to him. Whether he thinks so is another question which I shall not pretend to answer, nor how far such Establishm^t. may appear to him practicable. If it be supposed that a man in his Situation should absolutely despair of the Republic, and have so much Diffidence either in his abilities or his Influence, as to despair also of obtaining, much less of preserving the Supreme Power, then it might be supposed that Danton's Plan would be by such Person carried into Execution. Yet all this Supposition is conjectural Foundation of new Conjecture.[14]

Here was the supreme evidence of competence. These estimates of Danton, Hébert, Robespierre withstand the lapse of time. Surely their author was a brilliant representative of his country. He was one of the very able pioneers in American diplomacy who erected a standard never since surpassed. But forces far beyond the abilities of any man were urging his removal. And upon a plain demand from Fauchet, successor to Genêt at Philadelphia, Morris was recalled. The explanation given him by Randolph was tactful and evidently sincere.[15] Washington added his own appreciation of his conspicuous services.[16] He was the atonement for Genêt's recall.

Needless to say, the notice of recall did not reach him instantly, nor did advance warning of this sort mean that Morris should immediately quit his post. For some time yet, he honorably fulfilled his mission. Military movements and some statistics as to the size of armies were his theme on May 6, together with some observations on the enormous powers entrusted to committees and the supposed intention of Robespierre to retire to private life as soon as might be.[17]

Nothing more there was until the thirty-first, when he reported, not as giving it any credence but on the authority of a friend who was usually well informed, that Thomas Jefferson had been recently in Paris on his way to Switzerland to attend a congress of the neutral powers. The circumstance was utterly incredible; even its invention was surprising, for the citizens of

Paris were presumably too busy with the guillotine to fabricate such yarns.

Lest his readers miss the significance of the power lodged in the central committees, Morris declared that such tremendous power would knit together those who held it, lest divisions cause their overthrow and utter ruin. Pressure from the foe without would further strengthen their united front. Correspondingly, a yielding to divisions from within, or a subsidence of pressure from without, would be attended by the breakdown of a system founded upon terror and maintained by executions.[18]

On the same date, but in a separate despatch, Morris drew a clear-cut distinction between the two kinds of depredation upon American commerce: that of the British on the one hand, proceeding "from cool meditation of regular government"; that of the French, on the other, arising from the spontaneous ferments of the Revolution.[19] Here was decided magnanimity in face of much annoyance. Or perhaps it was plain wisdom, for in the circumstances there seemed little that could be done about abuses to our commerce. No more, it seemed, than could be done for Lafayette, who now was urging that the United States officially demand his liberation as an acknowledged citizen—the one thing his friend Washington could not do.[20] In writing unofficially but personally to the King of Prussia, Washington had done the very utmost that propriety permitted. To ask for more was a serious breach of delicacy, but Lafayette had been spoiled by wealth and popularity and now he was a prisoner. Due allowance should be made for such a state of mind.

Propriety was equally involved in the question as to what degree of courtesy to extend to M. de Talleyrand Périgord, who came as an émigré from France, bearing a letter of the warmest recommendation from the Marquess of Lansdowne.[21] The former bishop and the future statesman was already a man of note under the *ancien régime* and in the early stages of its breakup. His case was not unlike that of the Vicomte de Noailles which Washington had previously confronted. In the present instance, civility to the individual was certain to offend the minister and nation. Washington placed the issue on a broad and general basis:

My wish is, and it is not less my duty, as an officer of the Republic, to avoid offence to powers with which we are in friendship, by conduct towards their proscribed citizens which would be disagreeable to them; whilst, at the same time, these emigrants, if people of a good character, ought to understand that they will be protected in their persons and property, and will be entitled to all the benefits of our laws. For the rest, they must depend upon their own behavior and the civilities of the citizens at large, who are less restrained by political considerations, than the officers of government must be.[22]

Fauchet, the minister in question, who had shone originally by contrast with Genêt, developed an increasing intransigence in keeping with the increasing violence in his homeland. Some light upon this spirit and upon the reaction it aroused at Philadelphia can be gleaned from an instruction of Edmund Randolph to James Monroe, soon setting out for Paris to assume his duties as American minister, and thus inducted early into the responsibilities of his mission. The issue was a fund of fifteen thousand dollars advanced by the United States to the refugees of Santo Domingo. The Government desired that this advance be credited to the national indebtedness to France. That might have been all right, but unfortunately many of those aided were aristocrats. Fauchet stubbornly insisted that aid to democrats alone should be thus counted, and no impression could be made upon him. With Fauchet so obdurate, the only recourse left to the United States was to press the issue through their minister at Paris, and Monroe was accordingly instructed. The new minister would naturally inherit the unfinished business of his predecessor and was commanded to be especially diligent in safeguarding the rights of individual citizens, prisoners included, and in prosecuting the shipping cases which had so vexed the days of Morris.[23]

The missions of Monroe to France and of Jay to Great Britain were parallel in time, if in little else. Each is relevant to a study of George Washington and the French Revolution. But each has been the theme of special studies drawn to a scale not contemplated here. Both missions reflected in some part the attitude of Washington and his Administration to the French Revolution. This was obviously more true of Monroe's mission than it was of Jay's, for the latter's purposes were only indirectly influenced by the war between Great Britain and France and by French considerations generally, whereas Monroe was America's immediate emissary to France in Revolution. But it suffices to regard both these European missions as special studies, to be recognized but not pursued.

After such an *apologia* may one venture to submit a private letter to Washington from Jay, discussing French conditions?

> The observations I have hitherto made induce me to believe that the war with France is popular; and that a War with us would be unpopular. The word Jacobins is here a Term of Reproach, & used as such among the common people. They who wish the Reform of their Government do I apprehend wish a certain Degree of Success to the present French cause, not because they like it, but because they think such success would promote their favorite objects. I often hear Gentlemen converse on these subjects, but think it prudent to be reserved—as to their internal Parties and Divisions I make it a Rule to remain silent.[24]

I have spoken of Monroe's mission perhaps prematurely. Monroe had his instructions and his course was charted, but Morris was still the incumbent. His were the reports to the Department. His powers of observation were not dimmed. On July 22, he submitted a routine message on the assignats and their price range,[25] which he followed with an account of victories of French arms against the King of Prussia, so important as probably to influence Jay's mission. Faced with a foe so formidable as France now proved to be, Britain would retire behind her walls of wood in no mood to add America to her enemies. Here was more than a touch of Morris' penetration.

Nor did Morris fail to see the relationship of war and agriculture. It was providential, though he did not use the word, that crops ripened earlier than usual this year and in a uniform and remarkable abundance. Nature seemed determined to restore an exhausted granary. And she timed the process just to the line for the avoidance of a famine. It seemed a veritable conspiracy for the benefit of France and her armies.

Politically the scene was little changed. The central committees retained their immense power. Catastrophe, if coming, was yet distant and dependent upon military issues veiled in futurity.[26]

Privately to Washington on the twenty-fifth, Morris described the fresh calamity to his protégés in the imprisonment of Mme de Lafayette, and of the efforts of the American legation to accomplish her release. Morris employed his most ingenious casuistry to convince the French Government that her connections in America and elsewhere made the lady an unsatisfactory captive —one not safe to hold. Undoubtedly he did his best. Meanwhile she, as usual, displayed a total want of sense, demanding in this grave emergency 150,000 livres from the United States in addition to the 100,000 that Morris personally had already advanced, chiefly for improvements on the Chavaniac estate. The security thus offered to a foreign Government was to be this property and her own and husband's honor. Morris endeavored to persuade her—doubtless with but slight success—that Governmental funds could not be so employed.[27]

Two more communications completed the sum of Morris' official observations on France in Revolution. That of August 18 was a graceful acknowledgment of the courteous tone adopted by the Government in asking his recall. "To be recalled on the application of the Committee de Salut public and to preserve at the same time the confidence of government is getting out of a wretched position on better terms than I ever hoped for." There was news of the harvest, now seen to be less abundant than at first supposed. Also the coalition against France, which might vary in its make-up, was not likely to dissolve even in the face of the Republic's now triumphant armies.[28]

A second and final despatch of August 31 made one recommendation as to his successor or those who should come later, namely, that undue emphasis should not be placed on personal acceptability. It was true that in normal times this quality was important. When times were wholly out of joint, however, more would be gained by "a firm and decisive tone and conduct" that would keep uppermost in mind the country's dignity. "Switzerland will not be insulted and yet there is no extended waste of waters to separate her from France." [29]

In his first despatch to the Department, comparable for length and interest with the best his predecessor had transmitted, Monroe described the fall of Robespierre. Indeed, the universal rejoicing over this event was the first thing that he noticed at Havre on his landing, and all the way to Paris he saw signs of general joy. That the fate of Robespierre and his associates was merited, no one seemed to doubt. Their death occasioned an inexpressible relief. The riddle was worth investigating. Monroe believed he knew the answer. His solution ran to the following effect:

The fall of Danton had vested in his rival a power that knew no limits. It was a power certain to attract jealousy in any case; and from the bloody way in which it was administered, was certain to drive multitudes to fear and hate—a combination very dangerous to its possessor.

Yet the cruelties of Robespierre were inherent in his situation. The fall of Danton had attracted multitudes to the scene of execution, in hopes apparently of some adequate explanation of the act. It was done under prevailing forms, admittedly, but the populace expected a real interpretation of the case. With none forthcoming, it broke up in a sullen mood, and from that moment, Robespierre, suspecting here and there and everywhere an enemy, was goaded into a system of espionage and revenge which converted the guillotine from a toy that had at first amused the populace into a grim symbol of annihilation threatening everyone, obscure or powerful.

With each execution multiplying enemies, the towering height of cruelty must ultimately topple under its own weight. The crisis came when Robespierre uttered threats against Tallien and others in the Convention. This meant either swift death for Tallien or a complete turn of the tables. For a time the issue hung suspended as to whether Robespierre or the Convention controlled the troops in Paris. With this decided, the tyrant was bound over to execution and France breathed freely once again.

As for the unlamented victim, Monroe doubted that he had ever aimed consciously to overthrow the Republic or to erect a despotism. He was urged on by his particular daemon and by the attending circumstances. Finally he stood athwart the Revolution's deeper purposes, and thus inevitably perished, like all the others who in their time and manner had set themselves in op-

210

position. This relentless characteristic of the Revolution led Monroe to one of his best passages:

> . . . It will be observed by those who wish to form a just estimate of the future course and fortune of this revolution, that from its commencement to the present time, no person ever raised himself to power, but by the proof he had furnished of his attachment to the cause, by his efforts to promote it; and that from the moment doubts were entertained of the solidity and purity of his principles, did his influence begin to decline in equal degree. This was seen in the instances of La Fayette, Dumourier, Brissot, Danton, and finally of Robespierre himself; two of whom, tho' popular generals, were abandoned by the armies they commanded, the former compelled to seek refuge in a foreign country, and the latter in the camp of the enemy; and the others tho' eminent in the civil department, were upon like charges condemned by the public voice to the same fate. In fact the current of principle and sentiment has been such that no character or circumstance has been able to obstruct its course: on the contrary it has swept every thing before it.

This being true, no frankly selfish tyrant could enlist the popular support indispensable to an anti-revolutionary dictatorship. Even Robespierre had no such purpose, at any rate in the beginning. His was a personal rivalry with Danton, not a scheme to wreck the Revolution by his own supremacy. When logic forced him finally into this originally unsought position, his fate was sealed. He must join those others who had sought to stem the tide. Meanwhile, in the general happiness over Robespierre's execution, the Revolution gave promise of new life. An emancipated people assured it new support. Such, in brief, was the essential meaning of Monroe's first despatch. It augured well for the future of his mission.[30]

All too soon, however, such augury was dissipated by Monroe's folly in acting as the ambassador of the American people to the French nation instead of what he actually was, the minister of the American Government to the Government of the French Republic. This fatal misconception of his office was to vitiate his efforts and finally to terminate his mission in disaster. It first appeared in his haste to be recognized and in the want of dignity with which he went before the Convention, engaged in osculations with its President, and pledged the affections of his countrymen to their younger brothers in Liberty. It was a thoroughly hurrah! occasion. His hosts were in transports. But it was a false start and led to false conclusions. That he was unaware of his mistake would appear from his own description of his welcome and its accompanying festivities.[31] The Government at home, long tried by these *enfants terribles* of the Convention, might be less agreeably impressed with Monroe's achievement and his "favorable press."

Jay, at any rate, instantly perceived the impropriety of his co-worker's conduct. His comment in the premises was dry: "The Secretaries Letter by Mr. Munro, and the speech of the latter to the Convention, are printed; and have caused a disagreable [sic] Sensation in the *public* mind here, and probably in that of the Government." [32]

So long as Morris remained in Paris, Monroe and he could be relied upon to paint opposing pictures of the passing scene. Monroe, for example, on September 15, depicted the essential moderation of French character, its well known love of peace, and the new serenity following the death of Robespierre which had restored its norm of quiet dignity.[33] The glow of his reception lingered and nothing was too good to say of Frenchmen. Whereas Morris, who had probably forgotten more about the French than Monroe would ever learn, concentrated on the peace efforts now in progress and dictated by dire necessity. Advances were in train toward Spain after a recent contemptuous rejection of her overtures. And plans were in the making to detach Savoy and Italy from the Allies. Should these efforts fail, the south of France would starve. Apparently the phenomenal crops of 1794 were no longer counted on.[34]

That Randolph's sympathies were with Monroe rather than Jay appears from his instructions of September 25, minimizing any possibility of Jay's success and emphasizing the increased importance of maintaining good relations with the French Republic.[35]

Supposing a Secretary of State to be the official spokesman of an Administration, Randolph might be presumed to speak for Washington. To some extent, of course, he did so. Certainly a breach with France formed no portion of the policy of the first President. Neutrality was, on the contrary, the keynote of that policy. And undue friendliness toward Paris would endanger this essential. Washington perceived this clearly. It is not evident that Monroe or Randolph grasped this view. Certainly the Administration during Monroe's mission conspicuously lacked teamwork. The result was serious confusion.

One dare not say, however, that Washington at any time lost control of fundamental policy. It coincided with a deep-thought game to play both ends against the middle. Viewed thus, Monroe was the victim of his own sympathies and was used as such by his superiors. When at last he realized the case, all friendship terminated between the two Virginians. But the country had been saved. Jay's Treaty averted war with Britain; Monroe's mission did as much for France. Between the two, and towering above them both, Washington had maintained neutrality. His statesmanship prevailed.

There is a certain incongruity in alternating questions of deep statecraft with ordinary communications from persons having no claim to a place in history. Yet in a work so frankly chronological as this, one that insists moreover that the reaction of George Washington to the French Revolution, like the reaction of any other man to any great event, was the result of a sum total of impressions, such alternations in the plane of thought inevitably occur. Washington must often turn from deep currents of diplomacy to the individual sorrows of a friend. Such a transition was implicit in a communication from the Comte de la Belinaye from London on September 30.

Belinaye was an uncle to Washington's old friend and correspondent, Armand, Marquis de la Rouërie. After serving his King in America, the Marquis had served once more in Brittany —apparently in the counter-revolution, though Belinaye did not particularize. Here he died. On rumor that he had been a Royalist, his body was exhumed, three weeks after death; whereupon he was beheaded, and his head sent to the Convention. The immediate object of the Comte was not, however, to retail to Washington this news of an old friend, but to inquire whether the President would advise his coming to America. He would plan, if he came, to live very modestly on the six or seven thousand pounds remaining from what was once a fortune.[36]

213

For October, the only communication from the scene of Revolution—either to Washington personally or to the Government of the United States—was a lengthy despatch from Monroe devoted chiefly to the rise and fall and the existing status of the Jacobins. The story was doubtless sufficiently familiar to Washington and his colleagues. Monroe added little to their knowledge or to ours by his narrative of facts. He did throw light, however, on how so monstrous a society was able to enroll among its members so many of the wise and good. The reason was two-fold. Taking August 10, 1792, with its overthrow of monarchy, as the dividing line in the history of the party, many good men had sought to join it in its early phase as the best means of erecting the republic of their dreams. And republican idealism was, of course, a perfectly respectable emotion. To become a Jacobin for the furthering of such a cause was in no wise reprehensible.

The second phase, however, of the party's history, from August 10, 1792, until the fall of Robespierre, revealed a growing and devouring monster. How reconcile good men with such a nauseous institution? Monroe did it very simply. No good man was safe outside the party. To join it was a kind of life insurance. Thus the lives of many individuals were saved; but these men never won the party dominance. It remained in bloody hands.

With the fall of Robespierre, the Jacobins entered their third and current phase. With their party in eclipse and their leader guillotined, they must walk softly if they wished to walk at all. But so weary was the nation with the recent sanguinary orgies, that there was little violence against even the bloodiest survivors of the unholy crew. Monroe anticipated that some few of them would even yet be punished, but the monstrous era of the guillotine was past.[37] In this he was correct.

Monroe might list as an immediate success in his French mission and an outgrowth of his enthusiastic appearance before the bar of the Convention, the release of Thomas Paine. Monroe was a good lawyer, for he noted instantly that which Morris had missed altogether, that Paine was imprisoned as a "foreigner." By speedy logic Monroe convinced himself and apparently the French that notwithstanding English birth, Paine became an American citizen by the act of independence. His presence in

France was by invitation only, and he had never forfeited his claims upon America. Confronted with such reasoning and in a mood of high good will, the Convention speedily granted his release. Morris might have knocked in vain; for Monroe the door was opened.

Of those in whom America was interested still languishing in French prisons, Mme de Lafayette was unquestionably the chief. Monroe thought her case more difficult than Paine's, nor did he anticipate immediate release. In interviews with her counsellor —communication was indirect—he assured her of the solicitude of his countrymen and the utmost will to aid her.[38]

Privately to Washington on the nineteenth, Monroe related his embarrassments over passports for Gouverneur Morris to Switzerland and return. The Convention thought it bad enough that he should be in such unseemly haste to join his friends the émigrés and quite indecent that after such a visit he should contemplate return. The affair was settled by agreement on the part of Morris to remain abroad.

This news was only incidental in a communication rich in detail. The successes of French arms were general and startling, and peace prospects were excellent with all save England. The time was ripe, in Monroe's opinion, for a close union between America and France, "and believe me I have done all in my power to promote this object. But I have had to contend with many difficulties of a serious nature & which still embarrass me to a certain degree."

No account of public affairs at this period would have been complete without some further mention of the Jacobins. They were too vividly remembered. Their most recent calamity had been the closing of their hall by the Convention.[39] Similar news was relayed to Edmund Randolph, with the added comment that Carrier, notorious for his cruelties at Nantes, was remanded for trial before the Revolutionary Tribunal.

But this was incidental only to an epistle of extraordinary interest in illustrating Monroe's early thinking on Spain's New World colonies. For the moment he said little about French concerns, beyond a reassurance that French arms were everywhere triumphant.[40]

As an observer, Monroe was acquitting himself well; as a conciliator, also, he achieved considerable success. It was in this second capacity, however, that he met his first reproof. The Department did not act in haste. It waited for official confirmation of the general news reports describing Monroe's hysterical appearance before the Convention. Even then the subject was cautiously approached. Randolph made some slight allusion to the incident in his instructions of November 17,[41] but it was not until December 2 that he administered a severe rebuke:

> With the frankness of my friendship, I must discharge the obligation of my office, by communicating to you the opinions which we entertain here concerning the speech, which you made on your introduction into the National Convention.
>
> When you left us, we all supposed, that your reception, as the Minister of the United States, would take place in the private chamber of some Committee. Your Letter of Credence contained the degree of profession, which the government was desirous of making; and tho' the language of it would not have been cooled, even if subsequent publicity had been foreseen; still it was natural to expect, that the remarks, with which you might accompany its delivery, would be merely oral, and therefore not exposed to the rancorous criticisms of nations, at war with France.
>
> It seems, that upon your arrival, the downfal [sic] of Robespierre, and the suspension of the usual routine of business, combined perhaps with an anxiety to demonstrate an affection for the United States, had shut up for a time the diplomatic Cabinet, and rendered the hall of the National Convention the theatre of diplomatic civilities. We should have supposed, that an introduction there would have brought to mind these ideas—"The United States are neutral: The allied powers jealous: with England we are now in treaty: by England we have been impeached for breaches of faith in favor of France: Our citizens are notoriously Gallican in their hearts: it will be wise to hazard as little as possible on the score of good-humour: and therefore in the disclosure of my feelings something is due to the possibility of fostering new suspicions." Under the influence of these sentiments we should have hoped, that your address to the National Convention would have been so framed, as to leave heart-burning no-where. If private affection and opinions had been the only points to be consulted, it would have been immaterial, where or how they were delivered. But the range of a Public Minister's mind will go to all the relations of our country with the whole world.—We do not perceive that your instructions have imposed upon you the extreme glow of some parts of your address; and my letter in behalf of the House of Representatives, which has been

considered by some gentlemen as too strong, was not to be viewed in any other light, than as executing the task assigned by that Body.

After these remarks, which are never to be interpreted into any dereliction of the French cause, I must observe to you, that they are made principally to recommend caution; lest we should be obliged at some time or other to explain away or disavow an excess of fervor, so as to reduce it down to the cool system of neutrality. You have it still in charge to cultivate the French Republic with zeal; but without any unnecessary eclat; because the dictates of sincerity do not demand, that we should render notorious all our feelings in favor of that nation.

Monroe was next enjoined to a more vigorous defense of America's commercial rights.[42]

Not a comfortable instruction, this! Monroe may well have smarted. He could not fail to see in it the hand of Washington. Yet so important was the larger policy of playing each belligerent against the other that the Administration only three days later guarded against too sudden a reversal of Monroe's attitude by an instruction in almost utter contradiction to the reprimand at first administered. "We are fully sensible," wrote the Secretary of State,

of the importance of the friendship of the French Republic. Cultivate it with a zeal, proportioned to the value, which we set upon it. Remember to remove every suspicion of our preferring a connection with Great Britain, or in any manner weakening our old attachment to France. The caution suggested in my letter of the 30th ultimo [evidently Dec. 2] arises solely from an honorable wish to sustain our character of neutrality, in a style which may be a pattern for the neutrality of nations. The Republic, while they approve the purity of our conduct, cannot but be persuaded of the purity of our affection.[43]

Here again the voice was Washington's. No other comprehended quite so perfectly his purpose of neutrality.

Before he learned of the consternation which his introduction had caused at Philadelphia, Monroe obtained from his French hosts a substantial object of his mission, namely compensation for the losses of American shippers detained by the embargo of the port of Bordeaux. Truly there were benefits to be derived from popularity.[44] Or, on the other hand, a part of such success might be due—as Gouverneur Morris hinted to George Washington on December 30—less to generous inclination or to the minister's accomplishments, than to French desire to retain an old ally, now drifting, if Jay's negotiations were an augury, into close relations with Great Britain. If Morris was correct, the benefits were accruing early from the seemingly opposing missions of Monroe and Jay.[45]

In any retrospect of the year as it concerned the United States and France, Monroe's mission possesses prime significance. The year 1793 had been distinguished by the adoption of neutrality as a fundamental policy. The year now closing beheld its further application. Recognizing neutrality as the lodestar of Washington's diplomacy, one may believe that he viewed the rise and fall of men and parties overseas chiefly as they might affect this policy. Human sympathy, and Washington had much of it, might respond to the miseries of Lafayette, or General Armand, or even Thomas Paine. But over and above the person rose the statesman. The recent currents of the Revolution impinged on Washington the statesman. Until his Proclamation of Neutrality in 1793, he was chiefly the observer. Thereafter, and his task was not yet done, he was the statesman and administrator, facing problems accentuated by the Revolution. All his steadiness, all that "coolness" for which he was admired, were now required to maintain, in the midst of general European war, neutrality as the first goal of American diplomacy.

PART III

Where no one commands, everyone is master, everyone is slave.

—Bossuet

CHAPTER
NINE

1795

In a reaction from the Terror, many terrorists were executed, among them the blood crazed Fouquier-Tinville who, unlike his many victims, received a fair trial by a Revolutionary Tribunal soon to be abolished. Able to escape the fate they had imposed upon so many were Carnot, Tallien, and Fouché. Carnot was spared because of his great services to the state. His fellows trusted to chicanery and their native wit. In what may be termed a counter-counter-revolution, hunger-inspired riots were directed against the Convention on April 1 and again on May 20. On the latter occasion the National Guard freed the imperilled Deputies after one of them had been slain and his head paraded on a pike for all the Deputies to see.

In August, the Convention roused much of the country to wrath by its decree that two thirds of the next legislature should be picked from its existing membership. This time 60,000 of the

National Guard, previously so reliable, menaced the Convention. The Convention's President Barras summoned the promising young Napoleon, who had already displayed his prowess at Toulon in 1793, to its defense. Napoleon acted instantly. He dispatched a dashing young cavalryman destined one day to be King of Naples, Joachim Murat, to seize the cannon at the nearby camp of Sablons. These cannon came into use on October 5 in street fighting which saved the Convention and gave Napoleon tremendous impetus to power.

The fashioning of a new constitution was still the business of the Convention. The Constitution of 1791 was inoperative. That of 1793 was immobilized. Louis XVII, unhappy child, was dead this very year. All possibility of monarchical restoration was blocked by the intransigence of his uncle, Louis XVIII, who had no conception of compromise, or for that matter, of reality. But there was the Revolution to be saved. Its chief economic gain, the shift in landed property and its more equitable distribution, must be hedged with proper safeguards. To that end an elaborate system of voting was erected, not unlike the passive and the active citizenry of 1791.

Citizens possessing a certain amount of property might vote for Electors, who in turn might vote for 750 Deputies: men still young but thirty years or over constituted the Five Hundred; their elders were the 250 "Ancients." The Five Hundred could propose decrees which would be given final consideration by the "Ancients." Executive power, inadequate since the collapse of the monarchy, was vested in a Directory of five. These Directors had no veto over any law passed by the two Councils. The temptation to usurp authority was not always resisted.

Further preparation for a reign of order was to be found in the extension of religious toleration on February 21, wherein "the exercise of any religion may not be disturbed," [1] the State meanwhile to keep hands off and to contribute nothing to religious upkeep. Likewise by a decree of May 3, private property was to be restored, saving a few exceptions. The Bourbons might not regain theirs; nor the estate of Mme du Barry. Others excluded were the heirs of those who had been outlawed on 9

Thermidor, that is, July 27, 1794, the fall of Robespierre. These exceptions were relatively unimportant.

Having drafted the Constitution, the Convention's work was done. Let Louis Madelin, distinguished interpreter of the period, summarize its accomplishments:

A certain solemnity was imparted to the moment [of adjournment] by the thought of the tremendous career of the expiring Assembly. In the space of three years it had lived a hundred, amidst unheard of perils: it had proclaimed the Republic in the France of Louis XIV, and it had organized, in the name of Liberty the most formidable tyranny any country had ever known; it had sent a king to the scaffold, and raised armies that had driven back the Powers of Europe; by its decrees it had shielded the Terror which had ploughed bloody furrows even through its own ranks; it had put down civil war, and in spite of tragic vicissitudes, it had carried France towards her natural frontiers; it had voted two Constitutions, driven God out of the temple, and then recalled the Deity, the God of *Sans-culottes,* under a new name; it had separated Church from State, it had proposed every kind of problem, and till its very last moment it had crushed out "factions." It would be unjust not to remind our readers that by the law of the 3rd Brumaire —its political last will and testament—it finally set before its successors the great problem of Public Instruction, remembering the words of the most remarkable of its members and the most illustrious of its victims, that "next to bread, the most urgent need of the people is education." So convinced was the Assembly of the truth of these words, that in spite of the innumerable dangers that hemmed it in, it founded (on the 7th Ventôse of the year III) the *lycées* of the future, the *Écoles Centrales;* on the 7th Vendémiaire of the same year the *École Polytechnique;* and on October 30, 1793, the *École Normale;* it reorganized the *Conservatoire des Artes et Métiers,* and, finally, proceeded to that "great and majestic creation," as Daunou called it, the Institute of France. Thus it had destroyed and built up; it had terrorized and it had pacified, it had touched the nadir of crime in some men's eyes, and the zenith of virtue in those of others.

Yet so discredited was it at last, that it seemed as if the president did not dare to enumerate its services.

"I declare the session closed. Union, friendship, concord between all Frenchmen: these are the true means of *saving the Republic!"* [2]

Meanwhile the armies of the Revolution were scoring victory on victory along the road of *la belle gloire.* Pichegru occupied Amsterdam in January,[3] the Stadtholder fled to England, Macdonald pursued the Prussians to Ems, and Pitt's dream of a Triple Alliance—England, Prussia, and Holland—faded into limbo. A secret of victory was the terror of defeat. In three years of war, 1792–1795, 373 French generals resigned or were cashiered. Some were guillotined. New names previously unknown were rising from the ranks. Fresh on the horizon, they would reach their zenith with Napoleon.

These victories in the north were crystallized by the Treaty of Basel, April 5, wherein not only was the Rhine recognized as a "natural" frontier, but France retained Cleves and Obergeldern on the east bank. Also, peace was made with Saxony, Mainz, the Bavarian Palatinate, and the two Hesses. In return for acceptance of the Rhine frontier, a secret article engaged France to aid Prussia on the right or eastern bank. A line was drawn separating neutral states in North Germany from South German states fighting for the Austrians. The North was to be immune. Austria was the enemy. With her war must continue.[4]

In July, Spain, in order to regain territory that had been overrun by the Revolutionary armies, surrendered to France her portion of the island of Santo Domingo. In the opinion of a well known historian, this recognition of the Revolution by a Bourbon king was of more than territorial significance.[5]

Another victory was tallied when a considerable body of émigrés, aided by the British fleet, was defeated July 22 at Quiberon in Brittany. Several hundred nobles were shot immediately in cold blood.[6] It may be said that reliance upon foreign aid was a continuous handicap to the counter-revolution. It was rendered doubly unpopular thereby. The brothers of the late King were by no means growing daily in wisdom and grace.

The Convention, then, victorious at home and abroad—Belgium was officially incorporated into France on October 1—after four years of hypertension in the most exhausting work and fear imaginable, was more than willing to surrender its responsibilities to the new Councils and the Directory. About this new executive a word may be in order. Lazare Carnot was actually its ablest member; but its driving force, the Vicomte de Barras, a member of the old nobility, seized leadership in terms of sheer unscrupulousness. He is described by contemporaries as utterly a rotter. But he remained on the Directory throughout its term, and is remembered chiefly as the discoverer and in some sense the patron of Napoleon.

In a word, by 1795 the Revolution's ninth year if one includes the summons to the Notables in 1787, the Revolution had run the gamut of its constructive and destructive phases. It had become a factor in Western European thought. That man was shifting and unstable who did not regard it from some basic point of view. For Washington that view originally was one of optimism tinged with necessary caution. Enthusiasm was reserved for the earlier and more constructive stages. But even with the mounting Terror, his position of responsibility, his leadership of a nation grateful for French aid, his own judicial qualities, saved him from any rash denunciation even of the Revolution's worst excesses and kept him neutral in a conflict where his own instincts were in part divided.

As a man of property and an aristocrat in the best sense of that word, there was little in the levelling efforts of the period to charm the sensibilities of Washington. On the other hand, as a revolutionist of world fame, as a friend of freedom everywhere, there was little in the *ancien régime* to win his admiration. And making due allowance for inevitable convulsion in so profound a change, one would not have anticipated on his part any surrender to that hysteria which blinded the perspective of old ladies of both sexes. Nor did he so surrender. The intellectual attitude of Washington toward the French Revolution remained detached and calm. His political reaction to it was the careful preservation of neutrality.

To preserve a balance so judicial in the face of some of his friend Morris' more caustic comments was an intellectual feat. Thus from Hamburg, in a communication of December 30, 1794, which could not readily have reached him before late February of 1795, Washington was reminded that

in France they have been lured by one idle hope after another, until they are plunged in the depth of misery and servitude—servitude so much the more degrading as they cannot but despise their masters. I have long, you know, predicted a single despotism, and you have seen how near they have come to that catastrophe. Chance, or rather the want of mettle in the usurper, has alone saved them to the present moment; but I am still convinced that they must end their Voyage in that port, and they would probably reach it, should they make peace with all their foreign enemies, through the channels of civil war.[7]

Also from Hamburg on January 2, Morris attributed the lull in executions following the death of Robespierre not to any revulsion against blood or to any sudden mellowing of the hearts of rulers, but to the widespread complicity of the Convention in all the previous atrocities. Morris still had hopes, however, that the principal associates of the deposed tyrant would meet their just deserts:

A day of final reckoning must come and as the French people enjoy more pleasure at the execution of a Conventionalist than from any other festival it is to be hoped that they will at length be offered up as expiatory sacrifices to justice and humanity.[8]

Monroe, more optimistic, reported the final receipt by Mme de Lafayette of the $2,000 advanced to her by Washington almost a year preceding. She was released, possibly as a token of France's regard for Monroe, and departed, it appeared, in a spirit of much gratitude to Washington and to America, presumably to join her husband, who was still in prison.[9] Monroe meanwhile kept it constantly in mind to aid M. de Lafayette in any way he could.[10]

An elaborate report of the thirteenth set forth the entire situation as Monroe perceived it. There was, to begin with, the good news of a restoration of commerce with America upon favorable terms. Then followed more than a hint that Jay's negotiations were hampering Monroe's and arousing the suspicions of the French Government. As for France herself, a desire was manifest to heal old wounds and avoid the senseless spilling of more blood. To this desire the associates of Robespierre still owed their lives. Unwisely for themselves, however, some of the chief of these associates, Billaud de Varennes, Collot-d'Herbois, and Barrère, were focusing attention on themselves in the Convention and one might not too assuredly predict the future. As for the war, further progress was attending French arms in Spain and there were good prospects against England. Several of the Allies wished ardently for peace.[11]

On February 1, Monroe confirmed the further progress of

French arms. Amsterdam was occupied and the seven United Provinces were apparently about to follow. A change of government would probably ensue. With successes so brilliant and so cumulative, the Rhine frontier was become a popular campaign cry. Boissy d'Anglas had proposed in the Convention that the Republic should hereafter be bounded "by the ocean, the mountains and the great rivers." [12] Ambition grew by what it fed upon. Foundations were already well laid for the Napoleonic superstructure.

On the twelfth, Monroe replied to the strictures in Randolph's recent reprimand. It was an able statement of his case. The contrast between what he found on his arrival and what he had already made of things was very striking. Had he been our only minister and France the only country to consider, his position would have been incontrovertible. Having seen the Revolution so frequently through Morris' eyes, it is fair enough for us to inquire what Monroe thought of his aristocratic predecessor:

> Upon my arrival here, I found our affairs, as it was known they were before I sailed, in the worst possible situation. The treaty between the two Republics was violated. Our commerce was harrassed in every quarter, and in every article, even that of tobacco not excepted. Our seamen taken on board our vessels were often abused, generally imprisoned and treated in other respects like the subjects of the powers at war with them: Our former minister was not only without the confidence of the government, but an object of particular jealousy and distrust: In addition to which it was suspected, that we were about to abandon them for a connection with England, and for which purpose *principally*, it was believed that Mr. Jay had been sent there. The popular prepossession too in our favor had abated, and was in some measure at a stand; for the officers of the fleets from America had brought unfavorable accounts of our disposition towards them. Thus the connection between the two countries hung, as it were, upon a thread; and I am convinced, that if some person possessing their confidence had not been sent, it would have been broken.

Facing such a situation, could the minister be blamed for efforts to undo previous mischief? Particularly since he believed that a strengthening of the cords with France would fortify Jay's mission, as the British would recognize that America did not stand alone. Such reasoning was reinforced by the military success of France. Its further confirmation was British objection to the mission, in a desire to discredit him entirely. Notwithstanding these opposing influences, Monroe had recovered for his countrymen the waning friendship of the French.[13]

Randolph's second letter, with its renewed permission to cultivate the French, greatly pleased Monroe. He promised to obey instructions so completely in accord with his own philosophy.[14] When Randolph repeated these instructions in a formal note of February 15, 1795, the minister perceived in it a repudiation of his reprimand, and approval of his former action. The Government of the United States deprecated the recall of M. Fauchet because of his connection with the Jacobins. "However," as Randolph conceded, "the only thing, which essentially concerns us is, that the Representative of the French Republic in the United States, should lay aside all intrigue, and imitate ourselves in a course of plain and fair dealing." As for Mr. Jay, Monroe need not fear that the interests of his mission or of France as our ally would be jeopardized by any gains at London.[15]

Since so large a portion of the present study is devoted to instructions to and despatches from American ministers in Europe, it may not be amiss to include a despatch from Philadelphia, viewing America through French eyes. M. Jean Antoine Joseph Fauchet was addressing the Committee of Public Safety. He gave the date as 8 Ventôse in the Year III of the Republic, or in other words, February 26, 1795. His comments on George Washington are fair enough, but the chief interest of the despatch lies in the minister's general evaluation of how America treats her heroes. No doubt true at the time, the modern citizen may find these comments relevant to our present day:

> Citizens: The anniversary of General Washington's birthday has been celebrated on the 23rd of February [sic] according to nation wide usage; at Philadelphia as in other years it has been a day for public audience. The Foreign Ministers, Civil and Military officials, members of both Houses of Congress in a body and a large number of influential citizens have been to felicitate him. Every where the popularity of this man veritably the fortunate one of his century, increases, it grows from day to day, and triumphs over the shadows which at first seemed to gather over it. In reading the various Toasts lifted at the festivities held on this day, Toast of which the custom has been to express sincerely

the sentiments of all participating; and taking into consideration that at these festivities all who are influential because of their position, their fortune, and their talents usually take part and recognizing the unity which prevails in the indications of the public opinion which decides or includes the rest, one reaches the conclusion that barring the unforeseen, nothing will effectively attack the influence of Washington nor impress the Government which his name protects even more than the prosperity which has followed its creation. The President has assisted at a ball which a select society of this city gives annually in his honor; he appeared in the simplicity of an ordinary citizen, he was without a special place, mingled with his wife in the crowd, and recognized only by the proximity of some foreign envoys eager to surround him.

The National recognition has been made the order of the day since this epoch. General Washington has united all suffrages. The ministers, Messrs. Knox and Hamilton, whose resignations have been accepted, have received some indications which must be flattering. The latter has received some most distinguished declarations. He recently left for Albany, New York, where his property lies. On departing from Philadelphia and arriving at New York he was honored at a public dinner given by the leading merchants of the two towns. You will see in the translation of the toasts drunk at Philadelphia the spirit which prevailed on the occasion. In retiring from office Mr. Hamilton has had the satisfaction to witness the adoption by Congress of the plan completing his system on the national debt. Nothing can flatter more signally his amour propre than to triumph in so striking a manner over the clamors he has aroused and to retire only having given the final guaranty to his financial concepts.

What is the first idea which comes from observing these movements of public opinion in the United States and the reading of the many panegyrics which are published in favor of men who have been useful in cabinet or war? An idea which confirms the feebleness of men and the fickleness of their judgments. Always in the record of their passions some are deified or proscribed; services are rewarded by Apotheosis or punished by ostracism; one man receiving the laurels of the many! The original heroes of America who still survive, vegetate in an old age forgotten. They wend their way to an obscure grave, while one or two of their more fortunate companions go forward along the road of distinctions and popular honors, towards monuments and altars. And who knows whether having thus arrived, their names so revered to-day will not be handed over to oblivion and to the indifference which surrounds those of their less fortunate competitors?

It is necessary to avow that if the American People has a penchant toward extreme veneration for its illustrious men, it seems less than any other nation led to the contrary excess. In its midst are many men

229

great otherwise who do not receive their due deserts. It counts no one who can complain of extreme injustice or of excessive hardship. The apathy of Americans guards them from great passions and insures their return to equilibrium. Their milieu lies between apotheosis and infamy. They can remove from the Capitol without hurling from the Tarpeian Rock.[16]

Returning to our immediate theme as it concerned the mission of Monroe to France, if the Administration was thus in a relenting mood toward a representative whose popular success was undeniable and who had made decided progress toward the commercial objectives of his mission, the same could not be said for Jay, who renewed his objection to the methods of his rival:

> What passed at Paris on Mr. Munroe's arrival, I am persuaded made a strong and disagreable [sic] impression; and had not your private character prevented those Transactions from being imputable in any Degree to your orders, I do believe that the system of conciliation would have been instantly abandoned— What would have succeeded it, cannot be easily conjectured—certainly no Treaty so favorable to us as the present would then have been attainable—whatever the American opinion of it may prove to be; the Administration here think it very friendly to us; and that it could not, in the present moment have been made more so, without exciting great Discontents & uneasiness in this country.—

Recurring to his theme of the general wickedness of France, Jay added in true Federalist terms, but with a touch of generosity,

> The french Jacobins have greatly injured the cause of rational Liberty. The detestable Massacres Impieties and abominations imputable to them, excited in the people here [England] the most decided Hatred and abhorrence; and the Government by that circumstance rendered the war popular. But the system of moderation and Justice lately adopted in France, the Suppression of the Jacobins and the strict discipline observed in their armies, will doubtless have an Influence on the Sentiments of this Nation—I think I see Traces of this Influence already, on much not suspected of it.[17]

Monroe, on the other hand, who was more sympathetic to the Revolution than Jay or Morris or any other Federalist could be, turned an entirely new light upon these same Jacobins, and in general upon the French nation, than Washington had been accustomed to receive. He attributed responsibility for the atrocities of the Revolution not to the masses of the people, but to small coteries of leaders. Particularly was this true of the massacres of September 2 and 3, 1792, and the invasion of the Convention on May 31, 1793, for the arrest of the Girondists. Of the former, Monroe asserted that "the great mass of the people of Paris were ignorant of what was perpetrating at the time of the transaction, and that those who knew of it were struck with the same horror that we were when we heard of it on the other side of the Atlantic." Of the latter, he declared that while it must be conceded the arrest was accomplished by military power and with mass participation, nevertheless the citizens were obeying duly constituted leaders only very few of whom, Robespierre, Danton, and others, knew the purposes involved. In this case, said Monroe, the people were marshalled in dumb show, to strike terror into the hearts of any who opposed the Mountain. But it was no movement of mass murder; rather a well-organized conspiracy.[18]

Not long afterward, having noted the termination of the war in the Vendée, and the unlikelihood for the present of any further counter-revolutionary movement, Monroe replied to Jay, not directly but through their joint superior, in protest against Jay's refusal to submit a full copy of the treaty recently negotiated. Monroe's despatch was skillfully composed. It revealed that Jay had already forwarded individual articles of the treaty on two occasions, each time with a promise to send him next the whole—a promise now renounced.

To follow Monroe's argument in detail would exceed our present limits, but he made a good case for himself.[19] Sympathy is unavoidable for a minister whose talents were condemned beforehand to futility. For anything approaching the success which his zeal and enterprise deserved would cement the old alliance and would weaken the neutrality to which Washington stood pledged.

Before the protest of Monroe's was uttered, but well timed to soothe any ruffled feelings, Edmund Randolph thanked Monroe for his attention to commercial interests and for his very able exposition of the Jacobins and the history of their party. Parts of his despatch were deemed to be of an interest so general that

231

they had been given to the press under the caption of "Letters of a Gentleman in Paris to his Friend in this City."

These compliments afforded a tactful introduction to news that Jay's Treaty had been received at the Department on March 7, that it would be held in abeyance until June 8, that Mr. Fauchet was uneasy about the Treaty, why could not be guessed:

> The posts, and the spoliations of commerce will never surely be mentioned as requiring war instead of negotiation; and if they do require war, we and no other nation are the judges. Our trade may also be regulated by any treaties which we please; and no other government can find cause of offence, unless we derogate from its rights. You are acquainted with the restrictions on Mr. Jay, against the weakening of our engagements with France; and as far as cursory perusal of the treaty will enable me to speak, I have not discovered any reasonable ground for dissatisfaction in the French Republic. For it cannot be supposed, that the French nation would be displeased that our dispute with other nations should be concluded.[20]

This was precisely the French objection to the treaty. It did mean peace. It did render America independent of a French alliance. It was in fact a declaration of independence of the United States from France. Finally it was the assertion in treaty form of America's neutrality. Unpopular as the treaty proved to be in the United States, and weak as some of its provisions doubtless were, viewed in this larger sense it was a triumph for American diplomacy and the policies of Washington.

If in it all Monroe appeared a cat's-paw, that was his misfortune. Could he only view it so, it was a high offering upon the altar of patriotism.

Meanwhile, the Department did not rely upon him alone for the passing scene in France. John Quincy Adams, at this time American Minister to the Netherlands, manifested now an increased interest in French affairs, though he never developed a solicitude comparable to that of William Short. From the age of eleven, Adams had been associated with his father in diplomatic travels and experience to which his graduation from Harvard in 1787 was a minor interruption, as was admission to the bar in 1790. In and after 1791, under various pseudonyms—Publicola, Marcellus, Columbus, and Barneveld—he attacked Thomas Paine's "Rights of Man," defended American neutrality as proclaimed by Washington, and dealt with Citizen Genêt. These writings obtained wide recognition at home and abroad and elicited the admiration, one might add the gratitude, of George Washington. To them Adams owed his appointment in 1794 to the Netherlands, and that to Prussia in 1797 through Washington's intercession with his father.

Mingling from early youth in the highest circles, his conscientious and voluminous diary, one of the best known in all history, recorded the most trenchant observations. Thus on July 7, 1794, with four days yet to pass before he reached the age of twenty seven, he recorded a meeting in New York with Talleyrand and another refugee: "It is natural to look with reverence, at least with curiosity, upon men who have been so highly and so recently conspicuous upon the most splendid theatre of human affairs. If indeed success is the criterion of political excellence, not one individual that has been hitherto actively engaged in the progress of the French Revolution has been equal to the situation in which he has been placed. The parties have successively destroyed one another and in the general wreck it is not easy to distinguish between those whose fall has been the effect of their own incapacity, and those who have been only unfortunate." [21]

Few young men have received so high a tribute as that paid by Washington in urging John Adams, the incoming President, not to deprive "by over delicacy on your part your country's benefit from the services of your son." [22] Washington's good will was not diminished, one feels assured, by the younger Adams' efforts on behalf of Lafayette.[23]

For some time Adams had been expounding certain aspects of the Revolution as they affected the Netherlands, and on April 14, 1795, he uttered a pronouncement of more general importance. Noting a renewal of disturbances at Paris instigated by the Jacobins and based on the high cost of provisions, Adams reported that a Parisian mob had stormed the doors of the Convention, had interrupted by cries for bread every speaker who addressed them, and had withdrawn only upon hearing that troops were marching to the relief of the Convention.

Once freed from this alarm, the Convention declared the city in a state of siege, and gave command of the local forces to General Pichegru, who was in Paris at the moment on his way to join the Army of the Rhine and the Moselle.

Contrary to the expectations of so violent an era, continued Adams, the prosecution of the Jacobins was leading no longer to the guillotine but to exile only. The bloodiest stages of the Revolution apparently were past. Attempting to explain the most recent outburst, Adams believed it was a struggle between Jacobins and Royalists. The former desired a return to power of the popular societies; the latter desired a restoration of the monarchy in the person of Louis XVII.[24]

If condensation is a mark of intellectual power, an interesting comparison might be made between this despatch from Adams and Monroe's of the same date. Adams contrived to say as much in far less space. But such comparison is possibly unfair, for Monroe, so much nearer to the scene of the disturbances, felt bound to give minute details. Moreover, his despatch contained renewed complaints against the disingenuous tactics of John Jay. These tactics may have constituted good diplomacy from the standpoint of Jay and the Administration; to Monroe they appeared wanting in ordinary candor. He drove home his point with lawyer-like precision.[25]

From the pen of Edmund Randolph there now appeared one of the most searching self-analyses yet made of American foreign policy. It was the crux of an instruction to Monroe of April 7, 1795. ". . . But I must be permitted to remark," the Secretary wrote,

> that the *invariable* policy of the President, is to be as independent *as possible,* of every nation upon earth; and this policy is not assumed now for the first time, when perhaps it may be insidiously preached by some, who lean to Great Britain to prevent a tendency to France; but it is wise at all times, and if steadily pursued, will protect our country from the effects of commotion in Europe. France is at this day in the eye of the President, as she has always been, cordially embraced; and no event could be more afflicting to him, than a suspicion of the purity of our motives in regard to that Republic. But without a steady adherence to *principles* no Government can defend itself against the animadversions of the world, nor procure a permanent benefit to its own citizens.[26]

Here was an utterance of very special interest. It might almost have been dictated by Washington. There was even a personal allusion to his thought upon the Revolution and its resultant problems. Certainly it was an admirable exposition of neutrality, not as a mere expedient but as a fixed principle of the nation's conduct.

To one possessing theories of government so clearly defined as Washington's, and a practice so patiently consistent with those theories, there must have been peculiar interest in the Revolutionary fate of the heir of France's great political philosopher, Montesquieu, whose principles of government were influential with the framers of the Constitution of the United States. A communication on this subject was forwarded to Washington by Joseph Fenwick, an American consular agent in Bordeaux:

> I have the honor to inclose you a letter from Mr. Secondat the only son of the celebrated Montesquieu. He is now about 80 years old and infirm; his moral & social virtues, not less conspicuous than the Talents of his predecessor, have protected him thro' the storm of the Revolution, notwithstanding the prejudice that prevaild against the class of men of which he was born a member.
>
> At his special request I take the liberty to cover you the inclosed— The justly meritted reputation of this Family, at present under some affliction, by the vicissitude of Events, in the seperation from their only son, leaves no room to me to ask anything in their favor.[27]

No record now appears of Washington's reply. That it was considerate one must suppose.

On May 17, Monroe chided his superiors for their delay in submitting to Congress the Jay Treaty. By holding it to June 8, the suspicions of the French, at best but dormant, were further roused and kept at a high pitch. Characteristically, Monroe saw only his side of the case. He failed to perceive that there might be grave domestic reasons for the Government's decision.

On issues less personal to himself, Monroe reported that the relief for Santo Domingo, a subject of earlier dispute, was to be settled amicably, with full credit on the debt of the United States to France. France herself was in need of crop relief. The bread shortage was alarming; people were on the meagrest rations and the uprising of the twelfth of Germinal, now happily subsided, was really based on hunger, though of course politically manipulated. Assignats were still declining. On the frontier the conflict, only just now opening, held signs of promise.[28]

John Quincy Adams again displayed his interest in French affairs. His comments, however, occasionally savored of contemporary gossip, for he propounded in rather quick succession the most contradictory opinions. On May 19 he wrote,

> In the conversations I had with the french Representatives soon after their first arrival here, they all assured me of their entire satisfaction in the *neutrality* of the United States, one of them (Richard) expressly said that the french Government had been fully content with the assurance they had received from Mr. Monroe, that the treaty signed by Mr. Jay in november contained nothing inconsistent with the engagements of the United States, with France. It is not to be dissimulated that the language held by the Citizen Sieyes in the interview I had with him here, and of which an account has already been given is of a different complection. At the present moment the treaty itself may be more a cause of objection than the contents.[29]

Three days later Adams wrote his father a personal letter of much fullness as to French affairs. This letter is known to have been submitted to Washington's perusal and elicited from him a high compliment on the eminent fitness of its author for a career of public service.[30] From his coign of vantage at The Hague, Adams viewed the diplomatic scene with more detachment than either Jay or Monroe, but his conclusions favored Jay. He beheld in the policy of France a fixed hostility to American neutrality and a strong desire to push us into a war that should seem our own, not hers. Genêt's mission aimed at this. The failure of the mission was profoundly disappointing. The project had not been abandoned, and opposition to Jay's Treaty was its latest manifestation.[31]

Officially on the thirtieth, Adams reported a fresh attack upon the Convention, profound dissatisfaction in many quarters with the existing Constitution, and a party movement within the Convention to overthrow the leaders. Adams anticipated eventual success for such a move unless the authorities adopted more severity toward disaffected elements. He advanced one thought of pertinence to government in any time or place:

236

From experience they are entirely satisfied that a Government where all the powers of legislation and execution are in the same hands, must if strong be a tyranny, and if weak an anarchy.[32]

The superior importance of French affairs to happenings at his own post of duty led Adams, as it had earlier led Short, to added news from Paris. On the twelfth of June, he reported a revolt at Toulon some three weeks earlier:

This insurrection, conducted by the party of the Jacobins or Terrorists and professedly directed with peculiar fury against the emigrants, is affirmed to have been concerted and promoted by British agency. The immediate purpose answered and supposed to be intended by the manoeuvre was to prevent the sailing of the fleet at Toulon, which was destined to prevent the junction of the British fleet in the Mediterranean with the reinforcement that has been sent to it.

With some reference to further troubles in the Vendée, Adams proceeded to a temperate statement concerning the death of Louis XVII:

June 18. The son of the last King of France died in the temple on the 8th inst[t]. In consequence say the public accounts of a swelling in the knee, and in one of the wrists. The surgeon who had attended him at the commencement of his illness, mentioned in the french prints as the ablest man of his profession in Europe, died a few days before his patient.

It would be surprizing if under all the circumstances occurring at the time of this child's decease suspicions should not be current relative to the cause of his Death. But they are not supported by an rational foundation. The fact alone is given as proof of its having been prepared and rumour itself has not indicated any person upon whom to fix the design.[33]

Only a hint, here, of a mystery that will not down, and that has teased posterity even down to the present.

As soon as information reached The Hague, Adams set forth the leading features of the proposed new French Constitution with an executive Directory of five members, a Council of the Elders to the number of 250, and a Council of Five Hundred for originating laws over which the Elders had a veto only. The Constitution was reported out by Boissy d'Anglas, a highly popular figure at the moment, and was favorably received.[34]

While Adams at The Hague was taking this pro-Administration view of French affairs, and while Monroe at Paris still was striving to preserve the amenities of Franco-American relations against the Morris influence on Washington and the unusual stresses created by Jay's Treaty, the French chargé at Philadelphia, P. A. Adet, was addressing the Committee of Public Safety a communication approaching the hysterical. If Washington comprehended the intensity of French feeling, his policy remained unchanged. Neutrality was a lodestar to which all else must yield. Let Adet set forth his meaning. In his agitation even his French lacked clarity:

> But how conceive the monstrous alliance which recalls England to its former rights over the United States, if one had not had occasion to believe that it is the secret price of protection promised by the English to the actual agents of the Government and that these Agents thereby assured themselves a double means to destroy our interest here, which they consider harmful to their interests. In short, whether France will preserve the Status Quo with the United States, or whether it will break with them. In the first hypothesis, the English having acquired complete preponderance by their Treaty, we are reduced to playing a passive role, and the Government, supported by England, will be able to accomplish anything it shall dare to attempt; if France, on the contrary, breaks with the United States, the Government in that case finds itself freed of inconvenient allies. The American People, deceived by adroit and perfidious suggestions, will not perceive that war is the work of its own Government; it will accuse France of having broken the bonds of amity which united the two countries, and will throw itself senselessly into the arms of the Executive, who will lead it as he pleases toward the abyss where he wishes to conduct it. Who could assert that in making the treaty with England the President had not that intention? Who could prove that this Treaty does not destroy that of 1778. The more attentively one examines them the more difficult one finds the means of executing Article XXII of our Treaty if the English, granted the same advantages by Article XXV of their Treaty, do not wish to permit it. It would be inevitable, then, that compelled by circumstances the American Government, placed between two rival nations, would incline the balance favorably toward one of them, and I question how we can hope to overbalance the English, when the Executive has already declared in their favor in an unequivocal manner. Perhaps external happenings will alter these dispositions. But in the actual circumstances, I believe that it is disposed to profit by the least important circumstances to destroy the friendship which the American

People feels toward us and to worry it concerning our intentions. Consequently, I am careful about demanding communication of the Treaty. I am certain it would be refused me, and possibly in a manner to leave me no alternative in my conduct. [Apparently he meant that resignation would be inevitable.]

Here Adet complains of inadequate instructions in these very delicate circumstances. "I must act, but be assured, Citizens Representative, that I shall be most circumspect in the steps which I shall take to prevent the definitive ratification of the Treaty." A sentence or two further on, Adet, without specifying any individual, denounced the Government in its entirety. "The intrigues which have been resorted to so as to win Senate approval of the Treaty leave me no hope for a corrupted government which seeks naught save wealth and power. You will be astounded to learn that gold, promises, and fear have dictated the votes of Senators."

From the general, Adet moves to the particular. Senator Reed of Carolina, reported Adet, sold his vote for £1,500. Senator Gunn of Georgia took his pay in the form of a treaty to be concluded with the Indians. Ten Senators only have voted against the Treaty. France is more beloved by certain monarchs than by this Republican Government. The people have been led around by Jay and Hamilton. In the House of Representatives the story would be different. The Patriots still favor France. This may lead to a cleavage between the House of Representatives and the Executive. In such event the balance would turn in France's favor. Meanwhile, let there be no doubt that Adet will serve his country faithfully.[35]

From Philadelphia, meanwhile, there was issued on June 1, one of the most elaborate instructions of the entire Revolutionary epoch. It was the Administration's defense to its own minister and to an offended ally of its conduct in the Jay negotiation. "There never was a moment," insisted Randolph,

when the President hesitated upon these truths: that the antient despotism of France was degrading to human nature; that the people were the sole master of their own fortune, free to overturn their old establishments and to substitute new: and that any other nation, which should presume to dictate a letter in their Constitution was an usurper. . . .

With the fate of the King we could have no political concern, farther

239

than as it might amount to an indication of the will of the French People. That will, it was interesting to us to understand; because being once *fixed*, whether for the Constitution of 1791, or one more democratic, it would have given us the assurance, of which we are bound by public duty to be in quest,—a settled and stable order of things.

In this sense Louis the 16th attracted our notice. In him was beholden a Prince fallen from the Throne of his Ancestors, receiving with apparent cordiality, in lieu of absolute power, the Title of restorer of Liberty—but distrusted by every man. His flight cut all confidence asunder; and it was impossible, that true reconciliation should ever grow again. The revolution of the 10th. August 1792, was the unavoidable sequel of what had preceded, and proclaimed abroad that the Constitution was short lived.

Here followed a lengthy résumé of the disordered state of France following the trial and execution of the King, with due attention to the rise of the Jacobins, the spread of foreign war, and the folly of which the United States would have been guilty had they assumed other than a neutral attitude. "The proclamation of neutrality, therefore, which was our first important act after the eruption of the war, deserved to be the model of our subsequent conduct."

Monroe's attention was next directed to the numerous irritations incident to the mission of Genêt, and to the care with which, notwithstanding, the President kept alive the main provisions of the Treaty of 1778, never once yielding to the argument of casuistry that the Treaty was made with King and not with nation and might, therefore, be abrogated.

The Government of the United States must meanwhile bear in mind continually the rapid shift in power in France. Parties were ephemeral; negotiations correspondingly uncertain:

We knew, from letters, that, as far back as August 1792, the movers of the revolution on the 10th of that month, were sooner or later destined to be victims—that in January 1793, they were conscious of the downfall which awaited them: that in March 1793, an insurrection was brewing for the destruction of the Gironde: and that the revolutionary tribunal, vast and unbounded in its domination, had been erected. Was this then, a season for "modifying the *political* connection," when we might have drawn hostility upon our heads, by betraying a spirit, not impartial, and by taking measures, which amid the fluctuations in the leaders of the French politics might not have been sanctioned? And what did actually happen?

The Secretary noted at this point that Robespierre and his minions were even more destructive to American commerce and good will than their Girondist predecessors, particularly in their decree of October 1793, which made of all commerce a government monopoly. With Fauchet, accordingly, the emissary of Robespierre, no progress was possible toward a commercial treaty. Through it all no policy was feasible other than the neutrality espoused by the Administration.

Reference followed to Monroe's conciliatory instructions in embarking on his mission. These were reaffirmed, with the exhortation further against permitting the Jay Treaty to become a threat to Franco-American good will. Surely a settlement of commercial difficulties with Great Britain, having due regard at all times to the claims of France to most-favored-nation treatment, was no cause for ill will:

> If we are told that we ought not to draw our connection closer with Great Britain, and that France will be jealous; the answer is, that, if we can multiply the markets for our great staples; if we can purchase our foreign goods cheaper, by having many manufacturing nations to resort to; or if even in the maintenance of neutral privileges, we can, by a stipulation, not derogatory from the rights of others, avert vexations; this is a connection unassailable by any reasonable opposition. The romantic extent, to which contrary ideas may be carried, would abolish our trade with every nation, in whose institutions appeared false government, false religion, false morals, false policy, or any other political defect.

Finally, Monroe might tell his hosts that the United States would not cease its friendly attitude toward the French Republic, no matter what its agent in America should do. That he would be mischievous seemed probable enough. Nevertheless,

> if injuries are complained of, let us reason together, like cordial allies; and compensate, where either may have been in fault. But let it be the last blot in the annals of the world, that the United States and France cease to be, what they ought to be,—friends, who will endure no separation.[36]

Here was one of the great state papers of Washington's Administration, bound intimately alike with the Jay Treaty and with the old cordiality toward France. It is not likely that Randolph contributed to it much more than his signature. There was nothing in his career that would enable him to compose so powerful a document. The sentiment was Washington's throughout. It was his own statement to date of his reaction to the French Revolution. Standing quite alone, it would justify his position as a statesman. As a summary of the French Revolution and of its inevitable recoil upon America, it is nothing less than brilliant.

The minister to whom this instruction was addressed needed no spur in the promotion of amicable relations. As an anti-Federalist, he was pro-French on a priori grounds. As a minister, his success depended on the maintenance of cordial contacts. Already he had achieved somewhat, and Jay's Treaty notwithstanding, he would not admit defeat.

On the fourteenth of June, he explained with much minuteness the most recent shifts in politics. The Jacobins had made a final bid for power on the twentieth of the preceding month, and had almost achieved success and a renewal of the Terror. The mob which they assembled was drawn chiefly from the Faubourgs St. Antoine and St. Marceau. The citizens here, according to Monroe, were chiefly industrious artisans, thoroughly loyal to the Revolution, many of them Germans naturalized by the Constitution of 1793, and wholly against monarchy. The leniency of the Convention following Robespierre's downfall, not only to his associates but to Royalists as well, had roused the suspicion of mechanics, at best not too politically minded, and they became the willing tool of schemers from the Mountain. The scenes in the Convention, which they stormed, were of a terror and atrocity seldom equalled in the Revolution. But the extraordinary courage and composure of the delegates and of their presiding officer, Boissy d'Anglas, coupled with the timely arrival of the troops, saved the bloody riot from becoming more than that, a revolution.[37]

Such is the gist of a long-winded despatch, which if contrasted with that of John Quincy Adams cited previously would not be favorable to Monroe. He was a bit prolix, but not deficient in judgment, save when he hinted that British injuries to the commerce of Americans had reached a point where peace was a doubtful virtue.[38]

This communication was followed by one of considerable

commercial and some diplomatic interest, supplemented by a reference to the ill-fated Quiberon Expedition. In this expedition, Great Britain landed on the French coast near Nantes a force of 6,000 émigrés, who with local recruits formed an army of 10,000 men which aimed to renew the troubles in Vendée. Monroe believed the expedition sought to relieve the British from the expense and care of unwelcome guests. Such, at any rate, was French opinion:

> All parties unite here in the sentiment that they are sacrificed, and consider the act of landing them, as an act of barbarity, excelled only by those which were formerly perpetrated in the same neighbourhood by the infatuated Carrier.[39]

Interest in Jay's Treaty throughout this period of tension was greater on our side of the Atlantic than it was in France. Suspense was great. On July 2, the Secretary wrote, "I need not repeat to you how much we have at heart a pure friendship with France uninterrupted and perpetual." [40] But the minister might be assured that Washington would reach his final decision on the matter "unconnected with any considerations, but the interest and duties of the United States." [41] Randolph knew his master.

That master was the recipient, as of July 28, 1795, of "a complete, & exact model of the Bastille, made from the very materials of this once celebrated fortress." [42] It was the gift of an English admirer, and supplemented admirably the key which Lafayette had sent. Men still remembered Washington as a friend of liberty. And why not? His present conduct was unerringly directed toward safeguarding the interests of his own free people.

From France the Quiberon Expedition continued to provide painful news. It was an entire fiasco and resulted in appalling casualties. Coincident with this disaster was a mild resurgence of Royalism when some young men preferred the "Reveil du Peuple," a monarchist song, to "The Marseillaise." The Convention treated it as a boyish prank rather than a serious political phenomenon.[43]

In this unaccustomed atmosphere of calm, the Constitution assumed its final form. Monroe promised a copy as soon as one should be available. Meanwhile, anticipating likely French objections, he condemned the second paragraph of Article XVIII of Jay's Treaty as far too vague on contraband. " 'Tis painful for me to give you a detail of this kind; but being an interesting fact, I do not see with what propriety it can be withheld." [44]

From Gouverneur Morris, also, the President received a timely comment. Deploring the Quiberon Expedition, he overrated the importance of the Royalists, but there was a flash of insight in his conviction that out of all the troubles of the Revolution, "London will become the great Emporium of Trade in Europe." Only a revolution of her own would be likely to prevent this, something not to be anticipated against the present monarch.[45]

On August 19, in one of the major personal tragedies in our history, Edmund Randolph resigned his office under dark suspicions of bribery and corruption, precipitated by a despatch from Joseph Fauchet to the Commissioner of Foreign Relations at Paris, dated September 5, 1794. The despatch was intercepted by the British and later forwarded by them to Philadelphia, where Randolph's enemies immediately brought it to Washington's attention. Fauchet's indiscretion ended the career of a man who had, until then, been one of America's most distinguished statesmen. Educated at the College of William and Mary, Randolph had participated in the American Revolution, sat in the Continental Congress in 1779, and been elected Governor of Virginia in 1786. It was he who had proposed the Virginia Plan in the Constitutional Convention, and, subject to some hesitation, he had worked for the adoption of the Constitution. Before accepting the State portfolio, he had been his country's first Attorney General.[46]

The question of Randolph's guilt or innocence is actively disputed even now, and no verdict is necessary here. But an examination of relevant material reveals some of the problems which beset Washington at this critical period in his Administration.[47]

Following Randolph's resignation, the Department of State fell to a new incumbent, Timothy Pickering,† who was transferred to it from the War Department. A plain, blunt man, Pickering possessed neither the genius of Jefferson nor the finesse of Randolph. Perhaps the lack of these more brilliant qualities was compensated by others equally desirable.

It was Pickering, then, although his appointment was not yet known in France, who henceforth received the despatches of Monroe.[48] For September, there was but one, a rather rambling discourse on the need for holding French good will as a check upon the encroachments of Great Britain; accompanied by some general comments on the new Constitution, a copy of which the minister enclosed. Unlike the self-denying ordinance of the first National Assembly, the present Convention ordained that two thirds of its existing membership be transferred to the legislative branches to be organized under the new Government. Here was a definite advance in common sense. The proposal was unpopular in Paris, where many elements opposed the Convention, but it was believed to be acceptable in the rural departments.[49]

Adams, from his distant post, explained more clearly than did Monroe why the Parisians objected to this legislative provision. He declared that opposition rested chiefly on the limits to suffrage. To elect two thirds of the existing Convention was to narrow the choice of members. Besides, it was argued, not two thirds of the present membership still retained the confidence of the electorate. Against this reasoning, the Convention contended that the times were still too perilous to risk an assemblage of inexperienced men:

> That an assembly resulting from an entire election would be composed of such heterogeneous materials that it would be a new source of violent factions, of extreme discord, and probably of civil war. That the experience of their former Constitution, and the evil consequences which followed the abandonment by the constituent Assembly of their own system, proves the necessity of the present measure and that, like many other circumstances of the Revolution, its irregularity is legitimated by the irresistible urgency of the times.

Pompous language, but the point was clear enough. The minister reported additional French victories and improved prospects for peace. The Vendée was still unpacified.[50] On the twenty-ninth he announced the formal proclamation six days earlier that the Constitution was already in effect, with the Legislature slated to assemble on November 6.[51]

In the midst of news thus mildly cheering, there was interjected for Washington himself a most discordant note. The old, unhappy days of Robespierre were vividly recalled by an insulting missive from the pen of Thomas Paine, now released from prison but furious at his former sufferings:

Paris Sept. 20, 1795

Sir

I had written you a letter by Mr. Lelombe french Consul but at the request of Mr. Monroe I withdrew it and the letter is still by me   I was the more easily prevailed upon to do this as it was then my intention to have returned to America the latter end of this year (1795) but the illness I now suffer prevents me. In case I had come I should have applied to you for copies of such parts of your official letters (and of your private ones if you had chosen to give them) as contained any instructions or directions either to Mr. Morris or to Mr. Monroe or to any other person respecting me; for after you were informed of my imprisonment it was incumbent upon you to have made enquiry into the cause, as you might very well conclude that I had not the opportunity of informing you of it. I cannot understand your silence upon that head upon any other ground than as *connivance* at my imprisonment; and this is the manner it is understood here and will be understood in America unless you give me authority for contradicting it. I therefore write you this letter to propose to you to send me Copies of any letters you may have written that may remove that Suspicion.—In the preface to the second part of the Age of Reason I have given a Memorandum from the handwriting of Robespierre which he prepared a decree of accusation against me *"for the interest of America as well as of France."* He could have had no cause for putting America into the Case but by interpreting the Silence of the American Government into Connivance and Consent—I was imprisoned on the ground of being born in England, and your Silence in not enquiring into the Cause of that imprisonment and reclaiming me against it was tacitly giving me up. I ought not to have suspected you of Treachery, but whether I recover from the illness I now suffer or not, I must continue to think you treacherous till you give me cause to think otherwise. I am sure you would have found yourself more at your ease if you had acted by me as you ought, for whether your desertion of me was intended to gratify the English Government, or to let me fall into destruction in France that you might exclaim the louder against the French revolution, or whether you hoped by my extinction to meet with less opposition in mounting up the American Government, either of these will involve you in reproach you will not easily shake off—

Thomas Paine

George Washington.[52]

246

A sick and drunken man, Paine still possessed low cunning and a pen of vitriol. There was, moreover, an element of truth in what he charged, egomaniac though he was. Altogether, his was not a brief to cheer the heart of its recipient.

Of far more general interest and importance than the lucubrations of a character so thoroughly unpleasant was the diagnosis by John Quincy Adams of the reception accorded the new French Constitution. Passing from some unfavorable judgments on a second emigrant expedition from England under the reputed leadership of the unpopular and discredited Comte d'Artois, Adams estimated the recent vote upon the Constitution at about 40,000 negative in a total of one million. Also the decrees requiring election of seated members to the newly appointed Councils of Five Hundred and of the Elders won by a four-fifths majority if tacit consent was taken as a positive acceptance. Paris, however, remained bitterly opposed and a decided rift was evident between the city and the Convention. Indications were strong that "measures of severity will perhaps become necessary on one side to prevent a popular explosion on the other." [53]

The explosion followed quickly, and on the eighteenth Adams reported a violent eruption which had meanwhile been suppressed. The decrees had been actively approved by 160,000 votes; they had been rejected by 90,000. The assumption that they were favored by non-voters might or might not be true. At any rate Paris was disposed to try the issue. On its side, the Convention was equally insistent. In the ensuing street clashes covering a period of about twelve hours, thousands fell, estimates running all the way from two or three thousand to more than eight, with probability strongly favoring the minimum.

In analyzing the defeated movement, Adams found that it was widely attributed to Royalist plotting, even to the extent of being officered by the Royalist army. Whether this was true or not, the centers of the opposition had previously been staunch adherents of the Convention. In the fresh crisis, the Convention owed its safety to troops brought from a distance. Only upon the army could the Government rely. The army in its turn was decidedly republican and attached to the Convention.[54]

Soon after this report, Adams went to London to settle final forms and signatures for the Jay Treaty. Already he was rising in the service toward those distinctions which Washington forecast when he informed John Adams that his son was the most promising young man in America.

If Adams had omitted anything respecting the uprising, Monroe supplied it. He discussed it at extraordinary length. He minimized the casualty list to as low as five hundred, and emphasized the revival of the Royalists in France in proportion as the Terror was diminished. A new type of terrorism was springing up, a petty terrorism waged here and there by Royalists. So far the nation appeared tranquil on the subject of Jay's Treaty—it had much else to think about, including a reverse beyond the Rhine—but announcement of the treaty's acceptance by the Senate would certainly excite a storm of disapproval. So warned the minister.[55]

Early in November, he announced the dissolution of the former Government on October 27, and the immediate installation of the new. Everything went off serenely, as if it had occurred in the United States, and augured happily for the future. The country was fortunate, too, in the personnel of the Directory. Of the original five members, Sieyès alone declined the office. Carnot replaced him. With the return of Fauchet to France in a mood of much disgust with the Jay Treaty, the opposition to that instrument gained a powerful recruit.[56]

Of Sieyès the minister reported only facts. Adams presented the interpretation. He was writing to his father, privately, but this letter like others in its series was probably made known to Washington. Describing Sieyès as "the main spring of the French external policy," and an enemy of the United States, Adams continued:

> In the present instance he avoids a station of show [the Directorate] as he has always uniformly done; he remains in the Council of five hundred, and will be satisfied with having the great portion of executive management really in his hands. He is so much of a metaphysician that he values the substance more than the appearance of power, and he secures to himself the advantage of protection from the most imminent hazards that may attend new Revolutions.[57]

Meanwhile, Washington was struggling with a personal dilemma as baffling in its way as how to handle Thomas Paine. The

248

heir of Lafayette, accompanied by his tutor, had arrived in the United States. He afforded the most clearcut test to date of the embarrassments of welcoming (or of neglecting, either way) distinguished victims of the Revolution. As in so many other of his more serious predicaments, Washington referred the case to Hamilton, with a full statement of the arguments. To welcome Lafayette might offend the French; to refuse to welcome him would certainly offend Americans.[58] It would violate, moreover, the sentiments of Washington's own heart. The outcome was a compromise. The young heir was sent to Harvard for a time at Washington's expense, after which he was cordially welcomed at Mount Vernon.

A more agreeable reminder of French friends in the American Revolution was a request from August de Grasse, son of the late Comte de Grasse, for a portrait of George Washington. His argument was that Rochambeau possessed one and that his father had equally as good a claim. Such rivalry was complimentary, to say the least.[59]

Equally agreeable, pointing possibly to a fortunate ending for the Revolution, was Monroe's encomium on the renewed energy and efficiency in public life which the new French Constitution was infusing.[60] This was natural, one might suppose, in an organic law which supplied an executive body that had so long been wanting.

Beyond a further despatch from Monroe, of rather minor interest, a personal letter from Gouverneur Morris rounded out communications for the year. Morris had much to say of general politics, military movements, peace possibilities or their reverse, but what linked most immediately with an American, or more especially a Washingtonian view of the Revolution, was a dialogue between Monroe and a Frenchman, soon after the minister's arrival, which was promptly carried to Morris as a choice bit of gossip. "Only think," said his informant,

> of a man's throwing himself into the Arms of the first Persons he met with on his Arrival, and telling them he had no Doubt but that (if they would do what was proper here) he and his Friends in America would turn out Washington. If he meant to deceive us the Artifice was too gross; and if he was in earnest, that Circumstance proves him to be unworthy of our Confidence. Besides he made this Declaration to Peo-

249

ple who (tho they stand high at present) must soon loose [sic] Ground for Reasons I have already communicated.

The informant admittedly did not hear the statement, but got it second hand, and immediately reported it to Morris. Nevertheless, it bears internal evidence of truth. As for Washington, he would have been a colder politician than he was had this gossip not affected his opinion. One may suspect that these barbed quotations from his predecessor were not without their influence in the recall of Monroe.[61]

The year 1795 had proved to be a "lion chained," to use an ancient metaphor. The mighty fears as it began subsided before distinctly moderating tendencies. Jay obtained his treaty; France preserved the peace. Neutrality was a condition, not a theory. The major policy of 1793 was vindicated. The objectives of Washington's diplomacy were in a fair way of fulfillment, though troubles were not over.

CHAPTER
TEN

1796

Napoleon, victorious over the English at Toulon in 1793, saviour of the Convention by street fighting in 1795, had won his spurs. But he was not to soar on eagle's wings until the campaign of Italy in 1796. Explanations vary as to how opportunity knocked, since more than one of the French Directorate claimed credit for this amazing find. The most sordid explanation was advanced by the notorious Barras. Command of the Army of Italy was to be Napoleon's reward for relieving the Director of the Vicomtesse Josephine de Beauharnais, a mistress of whom he had grown tired. This canard is refuted by Napoleon's very ardent passion for Josephine and by the testimony of Carnot and others that he was their choice as a soldier.

The retiring commander, Schérer, a second or third rater, left his successor an ill clad, ill shod, hungry and wholly dispirited mob of some 37,000 men who had forgotten the meaning of either purpose or accomplishment. But such was the magic of Napoleon's leadership that within a few days the entire spirit had changed to eager confidence. His task was to separate the Sardinians covering Piedmont and its capital, Turin, from the Austrians, whose main concern was Lombardy and the dominating city of Milan.

The Sardinians, being nearer, were the immediate object of attack. The Armistice of Cherasco, April 28, 1796, removed them from the war. Napoleon could then address his troops in words as memorable as any that Livy ever attributed to Hannibal or Scipio:

> Soldiers, in fifteen days you have won six victories, taken twenty-one stands of colors, fifty-five pieces of cannon and several fortresses, and conquered the richest part of Piedmont. You have done nothing, since there remains something for you to do. You still have battles to fight, towns to take, rivers to cross.[1]

The final phrase in this powerful adjuration had as much significance for Napoleon as for his men, for it was at the Adda River, a northern tributary of the Po, that on May 10 occurred the famous battle of the Bridge of Lodi. In their pursuit of the Austrians, victory depended upon possession of the bridge. But advancing troops here encountered appalling gun-fire and equally appalling losses. They recoiled; retreat seemed inevitable. It was then that Napoleon entered personally into battle. He turned its tide. Six days later he entered Milan in triumph. It was at Lodi that the troops bestowed upon him the affectionate title, "The Little Corporal." Years later on St. Helena he admitted that it was from that evening that he first came to regard himself as a superior person. George Washington at Fort Duquesne had undergone a similar experience. The providential interpretation of history is not accepted universally but it is not absurd.

Such spectacular accomplishments far exceeded the expectations, possibly even the desires, of the Directory. A general of such surpassing caliber might get out of hand—the more so as his fellows in the North were winning no comparable successes. Prudence suggested the appointment of Kellermann and a division of the Army of Italy between the older and the younger man. With a due show of respect, Napoleon admitted that Kellermann had great ability and far more experience, that given sole command he might do the better job, but rather than accept a divided command, which he contended would be fatal, he offered to resign. There the matter dropped. Napoleon remained master on the local scene. It would be some years before he was ready to overthrow the authorities in Paris.

When Sardinia fell, there still was work to do. After Milan, the story was the same. Continuing his drive against the Austrians, Napoleon came perilously close to defeat November 15 to 17, at Arcola near the River Adige in the territories of the Venetian Doge. At Arcola as at Lodi the conflict centered on a bridge, but there resemblance ended. There was no sudden, overwhelming push, no drive to immediate victory. This time it was the troops who rescued their leader. In this give and take, loyalties were deepened. Master and men were welded into an invincible unity. Victory did come but only after the most persistent courage.

Napoleon was unique—one of earth's most towering figures. But among the lesser breed, history was measurably repeating itself. After his early victories in Belgium, Dumouriez had turned traitor. After similar and neighboring successes, Pichegru likewise was plunging deeper into a treason as yet so little guessed that he was offered the embassy to Sweden.[2] In a treason so incomprehensible to his countrymen that it could scarcely be believed, he had transferred his loyalty from France herself to her dynastic claimant. Not France but Louis XVIII henceforth possessed his sword. In all charity it may be said that amid such rapid shifts in government, treason to one or another is perhaps a natural phenomenon.

Partially offsetting Napoleon's victories and further contributing to his eminence were the military operations north of the Alps. Moreau and Jourdan pushed their armies far beyond the Rhine and almost effected an extremely threatening junction looking toward a fresh offensive. Their victories resulted instead in armistices concluded by Moreau with the Duke of Wurtemberg and the Margrave of Baden, followed soon by peace with their respective countries signed at Paris on August 7 and 22.[3]

In the Archduke Charles, however, the Austrians had found

a very able general who soon brought the French leaders to defeat. After defeats at Amberg, August 20; Wurzberg, September 3; and Altenkirchen, September 19, Jourdan recrossed the Rhine on September 20. Moreau, now isolated, prudently retreated across the Black Forest. Desaix resisted vigorously until January 9, 1797, and Ferino till February 5. By then the French no longer had even bridgeheads beyond the Rhine.[4]

On August 19 in this eventful year, Spain at San Ildefonso entered into an alliance which was to carry fateful implications for the future. France must guarantee all Spain's possessions. She must conclude no peace with England save as restitution or compensation was assured to Spain. Again a Bourbon king extended his hand to France in Revolution. An immediate consequence of the alliance was such an access of Franco-Spanish naval power in the Mediterranean that the British abandoned the Middle Sea for the next two years. Lavisse goes so far as to say that "the victories of Bonaparte in Italy are due, in some degree, to the disappearance of the English, and consequently to the Spanish alliance."

A minor incident in all the vastness of the Revolution was trouble in Santo Domingo wherein Toussaint L'Ouverture saved the island for the French. One day that story would be different.[5]

The realm of economic theory also afforded interest in this memorable year. Fouché, later to be a millionaire, in 1793 had toyed with the idea of nationalizing the factories. In 1795, it was François Noel Babeuf's turn to advocate public ownership of all land and the equal distribution of its products. He gained a few adherents, was arrested in 1796 and executed in 1797. Thus he became one of the originators if not the father of World Communism.[6]

Of wider economic interest was the mounting issuance of assignats, the increasing severity of inflation, and the total inability of the Directory to grapple with economic problems which had defied solution since 1787 and the summons of the Notables. The plunder of Italy was merely a palliative. It was no solution. A starving people might yield to parks of artillery strategically placed. But it would welcome the overthrow of a Government incapable of solving its problems by any method short of foreign war. The victor in that war would find a country ready for a *coup d'état*. Before that time seemed ripe to the future First Consul and Emperor, the Directory would try its own hand at the game.

While Napoleon's ever widening fame was a major factor in the expansion of the Revolution, the more immediate concern of Washington and his Administration was to preserve neutrality. Indeed, the year 1796 was to witness a further test of neutrality, as France awoke with increased disgust to what she designated as betrayal by her old ally. With growing tension on this issue, accompanied by various reprimands from an offended Government, Monroe was destined for recall, a victim of his mistaken concept of his mission; in some sense, also, a victim of the larger aspects of Washington's policy. Angered by harsh treatment of so popular a minister, France manifested her disgust by refusing to welcome Charles Cotesworth Pinckney as his successor, and drifted more or less unconsciously and imperceptibly into the XYZ Affair and the unofficial war that followed. Thus the remoter consequences of Jay's Treaty and of Monroe's mission would link the Administrations of Washington and of John Adams in a continuity of policy, and postpone the final verdict of success or failure for Federalist diplomacy. Open war would spell defeat for the larger program of neutrality. Yet open war might be averted. The issue was still upon the looms of Fate. Time alone would yield the answer.

Meanwhile for Washington, reaction to the French Revolution would continue in terms of its immediate issues, his larger principles of toleration yet vigilance being long ago defined.

The President was favored early in the new year with informal communications from Gouverneur Morris, invariably acute and penetrating. On the fifth of January, Morris opposed the doctrine, already popular in America, that "free ships make free goods," contending that it was doctrinaire, a notion of philosophers, more fitted for the closet than the world.[7] On the eleventh, he offered a dissertation on the assignats and their steadily declining prices, together with a résumé of the fluctuations in their price from their date of issue to the present. Since Morris left France they had attained a ratio of 100 to 1 with the end not yet

255

in sight. With stern reliance upon figures, and a curious ignorance of how powerless figures are in deterring nations bent on
war, the erstwhile minister portrayed a prostrate land that could
not possibly finance a war. The reasoning was good, but facts
defied it.

If Morris here was pardonably in error, he was daringly acute
in an observation or perhaps a prophecy as to what the war with
France would eventually accomplish for Great Britain. "All the
World," said he, "except the Members of Parliament who are in
the Opposition, see that Britain is gaining more by the present
War than she ever did in any equal Space of Time during her
History." [8]

As was not infrequently the case, unofficial comments proved
more illuminating than official. Certainly Morris on finance and
war was more sparkling than Monroe on a *fête* to celebrate the
Revolution conducted under Governmental auspices in the
Champ de Mars, and timed for January 21 to celebrate the anniversary of the late King's execution.[9]

Unofficial, but not the less illuminating, was a communication
from Rochambeau—the first in several years, if the existing files
are to be trusted—explaining to a third person, who promptly
forwarded it to Washington, why France displayed a growing
coolness toward America. Five main reasons could be adduced
for this. First, the Government of the United States was becoming more sympathetic toward Great Britain. Secondly, the
French Republic was not pleased with either the Jay Treaty or
the dismissal of Edmund Randolph. Thirdly, a vast speculation
in the assignats had its origins in the United States. Fourthly,
France suspected misrepresentation and fraud on the part of
Americans in selling lands to Frenchmen. And fifthly, numerous
refugees had been defrauded of what property they retained
from the wreck of their estates in France.[10] Serious accusations
the last three! Yet few Americans today would question the truth
of them. Fraud is not a vice peculiar to our time.

Among those individually accused of infamy, there might
readily be differing views on the guilt of Edmund Randolph.
His self-vindication, for example, aroused only the most contemptuous ridicule in the mind of John Quincy Adams. "I con-

fess," he wrote his father, "I should never have thought that even the delirium of guilt could publish *such* a production, and imagine it would injure the reputation of the President, or defend that of the writer." [11]

Whatever the merits or demerits of the French position on American delinquencies, it was reported with all bluntness by Monroe on February 16 that the Minister of Foreign Affairs had declared the Alliance of 1778 terminated the moment Jay's Treaty was ratified. Of this the Government of the United States would soon be notified in form. No indication was afforded as to whether or not diplomatic relations would be continued. Their maintenance seemed dubious, however, in view of the Minister's assertion that the treaty threw the weight of the United States upon the side of the Allies.[12]

In the Foreign Minister's explosion, Monroe sensed instantly the breakdown of his efforts. He lost no time in presenting to the Minister all the arguments at his command against the proposal of sending an envoy extraordinary to the United States to declare the alliance terminated. He emphasized the pleasure that a rupture in Franco-American relations would afford the enemies of either country, and similarly the horror with which their friends would view it. He apparently made some impression on his interlocutor. But indignation was too deep for the indulgence of any promises. Thus the issue hung suspended in Monroe's report of February 20.[13]

Whatever the larger policies animating either nation, the personal efforts of Monroe were entitled to a better outcome than seemed at all in prospect. In his mission there was something of the tragic as the ancient Greeks perceived it. Man, however high his aspirations, however splendid his endeavors, was caught in a web not of his own weaving. The hero was the plaything of the fates. For the present Monroe had his way, for on his urgent representations, the Foreign Minister decided against sending the proposed mission. Internal troubles were sufficient for the moment. A forced loan was proving unproductive and discontent was rife among the people. War preparations nevertheless continued active.[14]

Later Monroe reported his appearance before the Directory

to protest the special mission. He had achieved considerable success in disarming their resentment, and he relieved their minds on another moot issue by explaining that Americans received all Frenchmen kindly, émigrés included, because of gratitude for previous services. But with some of the most distinguished, the American President denied them an official welcome so as to avoid political offense.[15]

In the total absence of material for April in the customary files, it may not be amiss to summarize the views of John Quincy Adams on French reaction to Jay's Treaty. He was writing to his father, but quite possibly this letter, like the others, came to Washington's attention. With patriotic indignation, Adams raised the since familiar bogey of Americans in Paris who deliberately or ignorantly misled their hosts concerning public feeling in America. In the present case, they stimulated French resentment at Jay's Treaty by information that America had become in very fact the ally of Britain. Among these mischief makers, Thomas Paine must be included. It was a partisan manoeuvre, and an injection of Anti-Federalism into politics on both sides of the Atlantic.

The basic cause of French hostility, wrote Adams, was a conviction that the treaty meant peace between the United States and Great Britain. This seriously blocked French hopes of bringing America into the war as an ally. Disappointment led to blustering which further vitiated good relations and induced some hope even yet for the overthrow of the American Constitution. A Directory should supersede the President. But the Executive should not command the army.

The scheme was too ambitious; those who entertained it aimed too high, and set their goal too soon. Adams was convinced that these subversive principles would come to naught. This did not mean, however, that he was all for England. Her supremacy at sea menaced all commercial powers.[16]

Plodding along toward his inevitable recall, Monroe was meanwhile occupied with attempts to mollify the wrath of the Directory. The details need not concern us. His despatch of May 2, 1796 is of more general interest for its mention of the Army of Italy:

The campaign was lately opened on the side of Italy, by a suite of three brilliant victories obtained in the space of a few days, by the French under Buonaparte, over the Austrians, commanded by Beaulieu; and in which the latter lost, in slain, about five thousand men, and in prisoners, between 8 and 10,000! The road is now open to Turin, where it is thought the French are pressing, and perhaps by this time arrived.[17]

With these matchless victories Napoleon was rising to the heights which Morris all along predicted were in store for someone. Mirabeau, Danton, Robespierre, Carnot never quite could wield the thunderbolt of Jove. When that man was found who could, the French Revolution took a new turn. Let all the world take note, America included!

The achievements of Bonaparte were further mentioned on the twenty-fifth. Peace with Sardinia was won. The King surrendered Savoy and Nice and placed himself under French protection. The Pope, fearing an unwelcome visit, was believed to be purchasing immunity by calling off the disaffected in the Vendée. Bonaparte was investing Mantua whither the beleaguered Austrian had retreated. Meanwhile, in Paris a dangerous conspiracy had been unearthed, which aimed politically to overthrow the existing Constitution, and economically to expose the rich to pillage. The danger of the mission for denouncing the Franco-American alliance, which had been a frequent theme of late, was believed now to be past.[18]

While these larger issues of diplomacy confronted his minister, and, of course, himself, Washington faced more personal difficulties in his unceasing efforts for the relief of Lafayette. The theme has been so fully treated elsewhere that only an allusion need here be made. Suffice it that his efforts and solicitude never once relaxed. Paine might complain of some neglect; never Lafayette.[19]

In the broader aspects of diplomacy Washington's intervention was felt decisively, partly in instructions to Monroe on June 13, rebuking him for neglecting to put more clearly before the French Government the actual position of the United States toward the Jay Treaty; [20] partly in inquiries to Pickering and Hamilton on how to make effective protest against French seizures of our vessels.

Washington was particularly incensed by these latter, not only for the offense premeditated, but also because the opposition press in the United States made political capital out of these misfortunes by assuring the public they were the inevitable result of the Jay Treaty. That Washington was correct in his suspicions of Monroe is confirmed by a letter from Monroe himself to Dr. George Logan, of Stenton, near Philadelphia, a leading Anti-Federalist, offering to furnish him political news under the *nom de plume* of "a gentleman in Paris to his friend in Philadelphia." The offense was all the blacker because the paper to receive these precious items was the *Aurora*, edited by Bache, grandson of Franklin and enemy of Washington. Washington soon learned the source of these communications. They undoubtedly reinforced his decision to recall their author.[21]

That worthy refreshed the Department and likewise Washington, if by this time the President was not too angry to read communications from the ill-fated minister, by a most complacent picture of enlightenment and happiness in France and the disposition even of men heretofore unreconciled to rally round the Revolution.[22] Under the growing suspicion of Monroe's fidelity and competence, the communication, whether true or otherwise, was probably unwelcome. The Administration, however friendly it might be to the essential principles of the Revolution, was not attached to the Directory, to its clamors against Jay's Treaty, or to its piracy on our commerce.

To a student of biography, the parallels and eventual intertwinings of the careers of James Monroe and John Quincy Adams provide food for speculation. Because no one who thinks of either can avoid some stand on the climax of the diplomacy of each, namely, the promulgation of the Monroe Doctrine. Which of them deserved the greater credit for this remarkable document? Obviously this theme lies far beyond the confines of the present study. Yet even here a modest contribution can be made. It lies in a comparison of the simultaneous despatches of the two men regarding France in Revolution. Monroe, at the very scene of action, was not only less acute than either Morris or Short, his predecessors; but he was also less acute in observation and less compact in phrasing than his junior at The Hague.

If the written word is a measure of intellectual power, then Adams overshadowed Monroe in 1796; and by any theory of an intelligence quotient that is permanent, he just as completely overshadowed him in 1823.

The despatches of Adams were especially illuminating in July. The unparalleled achievements of Napoleon in Italy provided excellent "copy." And Adams seemed to grasp the huge strategy of a general encircling movement upon Germany with the three converging armies, those of Sambre and Meuse, of Rhine and Moselle, and of Italy, pressing on in unison.[23]

Three weeks later, the campaign having been a swift one, further details were available. Operations on the Rhine were prospering, but the overwhelming victories were in Italy. With complete disregard for the neutrality of the several Italian states, all of Italy save Rome was now subdued, and Napoleon might already be in the Papal capital. His conduct in Tuscany and at Lucca had been particularly flagrant.

At this point, Adams interestingly forecast the later "Continental System." He saw in the conduct of the French at Leghorn a desire to exclude British commerce as far as might be from the Mediterranean, something already hinted at in the treaty with Sardinia and now becoming a fixed policy:

> This mode of warfare against Britain is naturally suggested to the French by the clear and unequivocal naval superiority which she possesses over them, and which becomes every day more decided. They cannot indeed expect rationally to meet her fleets again upon the ocean during the present war, with any prospect of success, but they may in a great degree deprive her commerce of the circulation, which the naval superiority is meant to secure and protect by shutting the doors of the earth against it. Thus the most effectual manner of carrying on their maritime war is by their armies on shore, and their triumphs in Italy will afford them the the principal advantages even of a victory upon the ocean.

The subject was developed further with respect to British commerce with Corsica and Spain; and to the threat of dwindling commerce in this area was attributed the recent sharp decline in British stocks.[24]

While Monroe somewhat pathetically was putting a good face upon the Revolution, and while Adams was brilliantly forecasting the major strategy of the Napoleonic Wars, Washington set himself to cleaning house. Monroe must go. The "recall of our minister to Paris" was broached on July 6 in an inquiry to the Attorney General upon the procedure appropriate to sending a special mission.[25] On the eighth, Pickering was informed of the President's determination to recall Monroe. A successor was already being sought.[26] That same day the post was offered to Charles Cotesworth Pinckney,† with notice that the case was urgent. On the twenty-seventh, Washington privately to Pickering censured Monroe for severe dereliction of duty.[27] And on the same date he further noted dryly that the constant fulminations of the French, and equally Monroe's report of them, were vague. Always they would do terrible things. Just what would be these terrors? [28] Formal notice of recall was transmitted to Monroe on August 22, with instructions to place his papers at the disposal of General Pinckney.[29]

Monroe did not leave, however, without one important service and, as is well known, without a protest. The service consisted in pointing out negotiations in which Spain was to surrender to France her possessions in Louisiana. Thus the United States had advance notice of a transaction that was not consummated till years later. Already Monroe was identified with the Louisiana Purchase.[30]

If Monroe was entering an eclipse, Adams assuredly was not. His comments throughout August on the various possibilities of commercial war were characteristically far-sighted. On the second, he anticipated that any interval of peace between France and Great Britain would be attended by changes in commercial policy certain to affect American trade and navigation.[31] A week later, his forebodings became more categorical. Quoting the Leyden *Gazette,* he noted the determination of the French Government to "act against the vessels of every Country in the same manner *as their Governments shall suffer the English to act towards them.*" It was a scheme to persuade merchants that their own Governments were their worst enemies, whereas France truly loved them and ruined them not from pleasure, but necessity. At all events, it was part and parcel of an immense system which Adams would from time to time elucidate.[32]

Commercial restrictions and their possibilities of success or failure were further analyzed on August 21, when Adams forecast extensive use of this new weapon. Far from minimizing the dangers implicit in these schemes, the minister with singular prescience predicted that northern Europe would provide the greatest difficulties to their employment. "The plan will be most likely to fail, in the Countries upon the Baltic." Veiled of course in detail, but an extraordinary glimpse into a future that would behold the defection of Russia from Napoleon's orbit as the fundamental reason for his downfall. Here was an intellectual *tour de force*.

Nor was it weakened by some generalizations that followed:

> If the design should be carried fully into effect, it still remains a question what the balance of its operations will be. There is no doubt but that it will very much distress the British Commerce but it will distress in like manner all the Commerce of Europe. The consequence must be an universal stagnation, and if it should be continued for any length of time, it must end in a commercial revolution from Lisbon to Archangel, as complete as the political Revolution from which it will arise. It is to be hoped for the general interests of humanity that the threatening appearances of a more extensive war than the present will subside, and that a peace of some sort will be arranged before the commencement of the next season.[33]

Thus through a glass darkly, but a glass which admitted not inconsiderable rays at that, the eyes of Washington might penetrate the future, even to the commercial issues of 1805 to 1812 and the war that finally broke down neutrality.

For the moment, though, the disposal of Monroe was more pressing. On August 10, Washington instructed Pickering that the time had come to apprize Monroe of his recall and of the motives leading to it.[34] To Monroe himself on August 25, he directed a self-vindication, briefly summarizing his attitude toward the entire course of the French Revolution:

> My conduct in public and private life, as it relates to the important struggle in which the latter nation is engaged, has been uniform from the commencement of it, and may be summed up in a few words; that I have always wished well to the French revolution; that I have always given it as my decided opinion that no nation had a right to meddle in the internal concerns of another; that everyone had a right to form

263

and adopt whatever government they liked best to live under themselves; and that, if this country could, consistently with its engagements, maintain a strict neutrality and thereby preserve peace, it was bound to do so by motives of policy, interest, and every other consideration, that ought to actuate a people situated and circumstanced as we are, already deep in debt, and in a convalescent state from the struggle we have been engaged in ourselves.

On these principles I have steadily and uniformly proceeded; bidding defiance to calumnies calculated to sow the seeds of distrust in the French nation, and to excite their belief of an influence, possessed by Great Britain in the councils of this Country; than which nothing is more unfounded and injurious; the object of its pacific conduct being truly delineated above.[35]

The President took care that these principles should be incorporated in the instructions to Pinckney as successor to Monroe. They read in part,

You have felt, and you have witnessed in your fellow citizens, a solicitude for the success of the French Revolution, scarcely surpassed, and hardly to be distinguished from that which was manifested in our own struggle for Independence. This strong sympathy demanded all the prudence and energy of our rulers to restrain it within limits of that neutrality which our duty and safety, and the interests of France herself required us to maintain.[36]

Other instructions more specific were provided the new minister, but nothing could be clearer than the above paragraph as a key to Washington's general attitude.

Monroe, for his part, having received the reprimand of June 13 but unaware of his dismissal, laid the groundwork of his own defense in a temperate and, on the whole, a convincing reply of September 10, in which he demonstrated to his own satisfaction that he had left nothing undone for propitiating French sentiment and that his sins were neither of omission nor commission. A blameless minister, as one might see! [37] Shortly afterward he transmitted a matter-of-fact description of French movements in politics and war, just as if no question of his tenure had arisen.[38]

Nor were the communications of John Quincy Adams of much greater import. Some progress on the battlefield he did record; a further attempt (speedily dispersed) on September 10 against the executive authority, he outlined; recall of Adet at Philadelphia, and his replacement by Mangourit, he intimated were decided on. But interest must be conceded to be moderate in any or all of these occurrences.[39]

For Washington himself the month was distinguished by publication on September 17 of the "Farewell Address to the People of the United States." A summary of this great document would be superfluous here. It embodied the wisdom of a lifetime spent in every species of public service. It crystallized a sum total of experience, of which the French Revolution and his reaction to it were but a part. And yet it is reasonable to believe that the wars of the French Revolution, and the neutrality which Washington proclaimed as America's fixed policy thereto, combined with his personal misadventures at the hands of an opposition party that shaped its policies in terms of European attitudes, were in no small degree responsible for those famous passages on entanglements with foreign nations which many still regard as Washington's supreme contribution to his country's foreign policy.

To this "Address," although it makes no mention of the French Revolution, one looks nevertheless for Washington's supreme reaction to it. Viewed in this way, the French Revolution has exerted for more than a century and a half a profound effect upon American diplomacy. Its influence persists, or did till recently.

To descend from the "Farewell Address" to the routine of dull despatches is, indeed, an anticlimax, but life is not all climactic, nor is it passed solely upon high tablelands. Apexes like the "Address" tower above the commonplace, but the commonplace is a principal ingredient of the landscape, historical or otherwise.

Of such was the only despatch for October respecting French affairs. It was penned by Adams from The Hague. The minister reported a considerable party in the French Government still friendly to the United States. Also, alluding to rumored designs upon Louisiana, he predicted that these would not be consummated. There was too much unfinished business before the meeting, he implied, though his language was by no means so colloquial.[40]

More individual than the news of Louisiana, which could be had from other sources, was a complaint from Adams that the

French Government had sought to use its influence with the Netherlands to obtain cooperation for defeating the Jay Treaty.[41] The event, of course, was past, but reminders of the sort would keep alive George Washington's indignation.

That France intended to pursue such tactics to an open breach, Adams gravely doubted. Finding them of no avail it would speedily abandon them. For the present Talleyrand would bear close watching:

> The character of the french Minister for foreign affairs is probably known to you. His conduct upon an occasion which has been a subject of particular observation in Europe, and his avowed preference of the minority in the American House of Representatives discovers his purposes and what is to be expected from him.[42]

Meanwhile, Pinckney, the first of the triumvirate to cross Talleyrand's path in one of the most humiliating episodes of his career, and theirs as well, arrived at Bordeaux. He favored the Department on November 17, with the earliest of his despatches. The economic situation commanded his attention. Trade was brisk and for hard cash. Old coins were coming into circulation. Provisions were abundant and proportionately cheap. Imports from Great Britain had been recently cut off. Trade conditions must be carefully attended as opportunity presented.[43]

This commercial contest between the chief belligerents provided Rufus King, at London, with a similar far-seeing comment. Indeed, if all the observations on this theme made by John Quincy Adams and his fellow ministers were assembled, the total would constitute a curiously prophetic vision of the struggle yet to come. King was writing privately to Washington:

> France will bend all her energies against that commerce in which England finds such immense Resources to prosecute the war, not by attacking her navy, not by attempting the threatened invasion, but by compelling the neighbouring nations to exclude the commerce of England from the great and profitable markets of Europe—England in turn will endeavour to balance the account, by conquering, or emancipating, the colonies of Spain & France, thereby opening new, and extensive, markets in another quarter of the Globe.[44]

Precisely this occurred in 1808, with British penetration into South America! King, like Adams, was a prophet. To both the ministers, as to Washington, the future was astonishingly limned, although neither was aware of it.

Both ministers possessed the further advantage, painfully denied Monroe, of frequent instructions from their Government. Affairs were critical enough to rouse the Secretary from the strange lethargy against which their predecessors must all too frequently complain. Pinckney in especial was instructed to maintain both courtesy and dignity. In certain cases, possibly, severity would be the proper course.[45]

Pinckney, more than the others, would need precise instructions if his acts were to meet with full approval, for on December 12, the Directory decided it would not receive him. He was thus left stranded—a minister without a mission. Adams, from The Hague, defined the situation accurately. "It seems that France wishes to possess in the United States an authority similar to that which she enjoys here." [46]

Pinckney himself took his isolated position calmly. He attributed his delayed reception to a waiting policy to see how the forthcoming American election would affect French interests. A Federalist would not be welcomed; whereas an Anti-Federalist might find the door ajar. For it was French opinion—certainly if Du Pont de Nemours commanded credence—that Americans were "a people divided by party, the mere creatures of foreign influence, and regardless of our national character and interest." [47]

Against this summary of the concluding year of the Monroe mission, it may be of interest to note a recent French estimate of the difficulties that led to his recall. France had good reason for her viewpoint at the time. Pro-French followers of Thomas Jefferson had solid reasoning to bolster their sentimental attitude. Washington, for his part, had the categorical imperative to preserve American security through the safeguard of neutrality, whatever might have been the language of a treaty negotiated eighteen years before having in view an objective completely different. The modern French conclusion is stated moderately by the eminent historian Ernest Lavisse, whose opinions are not necessarily those of the present author:

Finally, in North America, events turned to the profit of England. France broke off relations with the United States and the two sister republics seemed on the verge of war. The treaty signed at London by the American minister Jay . . . was in effect contrary to the treaty of amity and of commerce concluded between France and the United States, February 6, 1778. The treaty of 1778 consecrated the principle of the freedom of neutrals in time of war: if one of the two contracting powers made war, the other remaining neutral, the belligerent power recognized the right of the neutral to transport its goods everywhere, with the exception of contraband of war. But the English did not admit the freedom of neutrals; they made it a rule to seize American ships destined for France and to confiscate their cargoes. By still further vexations, they had compelled Americans who wished at least to trade peaceably with the British Isles and other countries [than France] to recognize their claims. The Jay Treaty forbade the United States to trade at all with France or its allies, under penalty of seizure. It had not been easily accepted by Americans, because their commerce with France and her colonies in the Antilles was important. Furthermore the Republican Party (i.e. Democratic) of Jefferson preferred France, while the Federalists (Centralizers) then in power were Anglophile. The American minister at Paris, James Monroe, by his integrity, his democratic convictions, and his friendships with Frenchmen, had succeeded in maintaining at least the appearance of the usual relations between the two republics. But when, at Washington's command, he had presented his letters of recall . . . the Directory refused to accept his successor. It decreed on November 22, 1796 that France should treat neutral flags, whether for confiscation or for a visit of warning in the same way that the neutrals permitted England, and on April 10, 1797, declared that passports delivered or visaed by American diplomats had no validity.[48]

Thus in a diplomatic sense, the last full year of Washington's administration was terminating gloomily. The train was set for those difficulties with Talleyrand and the Directory which disgraced relations of the two republics in the XYZ Affair. True, neutrality was by no means shaken. Also true that the Jay Treaty had not actually driven France to war. But Franco-American relations were strained, and personal relations with Monroe were painful and likely to grow worse. Neutrality was purchased at a heavy price. No wonder, then, that as he wearily surrendered power, Washington cautioned his fellow citizens against just such entangling alliances as the one then in process of dissolving.

CHAPTER
ELEVEN

1797

The Year IX of the Revolution beheld the expected and the unexpected. The expected was a continuation of food shortages, depreciation of the assignats to zero, their replacement by mandats-territoriaux soon to be equally valueless, and temporarily, at any rate, a relaxation in favor of émigrés, monarchical and clerical. Weakness of the Directory might be expected to continue. Also it might be assumed that Napoleon's mastery of tactics would not desert him. Less predictable would be the time and place of victories; while hidden in the womb of Fate was the shift of Napoleon's ambitions to the wider ranges of diplomacy and politics.

Considering the exhaustion in France and Austria alike, an armistice was probable enough, but who could have anticipated the magnanimity of the preliminaries at Leoben and the Peace of Campo Formio? Patience with the Directory might continue.

A *coup d'état*—for there was one in 1797—would be the Directory's, not Napoleon's. War with England would presumably continue, though there was actually a moment when peace was averted by a narrow margin. England and France alike desired it, but neither quite enough to pay the other's price.

Among the improbabilities of the opening year, a natural death could not have been anticipated to remove Hoche, the ablest of Napoleon's competitors, for Hoche on many a field had demonstrated a generalship only slightly if at all inferior to Napoleon's.

Among the émigrés certain changes were in evidence. Louis XVIII, for example, "King" since the death of his unhappy nephew, was learning some degree of moderation. On March 10, from exile, he issued a proclamation "in the year of grace 1797 and of our reign the second," wherein he actually admitted that the institution of monarchy was suspectible of improvement. He promised forgetfulness of mistakes, injuries, and crimes, at the same time denying that in order to restore legitimate authority it was necessary to utilize the atrocious means which had been employed to overthrow it. He expected from public opinion "a success which it alone can render solid and durable." [1] A far cry this from the impotent threats of the émigrés accompanying the Duke of Brunswick in his first invasion. Monsieur, Artois, and Condé had contributed vastly to the breach which the Eighteenth of his name now sought to heal.

The Royalists enjoyed considerable support from British funds, a substantial portion being utilized for propaganda. For a time the "King's" agents were tolerated, émigrés returned in numbers, some unhampered, others by use of liberal bribes. Concurrently a really noble religion was unfolding. Called Theophilanthropy, it represented an amiable endeavor to reconcile God and man. La Revellière, a member of the Directory, was a convert, but the whole movement was terminated by Napoleon. In these early days of 1797, Free Masonry, after a lapse, was resuming its activities. Paralleling these conservative developments, deported priests, bishops among them, were returning to the number of twelve or thirteen, possibly twenty, thousand. And such was the degree of toleration that the Minister of the Interior entrusted the education of his daughter to the Ursulines of Saint-Germain-en-Laye. Church bells once more tolled. Nuns helped in hospitals. France was assuming something of her traditional mien.

Amid undiminished poverty, the luxury of the salons under the Directory has remained proverbial, with Mme Récamier and the still irresistible Mme Tallien, formerly Marquise de Fontenoy and subsequently Princesse de Chimay, among their presiding enchantresses. Mme de Staël, daughter of the financier Necker, was among the many hostesses lending brilliance to the *haute monde,* though she did not share all of its opinions. Within the Councils and possibly the Directory itself, moderate if not actually monarchist opinion had won adherents.[2] These near-Royalists were called Clichyens after a favorite rendezvous. An opposing group of republicans soon would put an end to this neo-Royalism, but not until an effort had been made toward actual restoration of the monarchy.

Whatever its extent, the conspiracy encountered a body blow when Napoleon transmitted to the Directory the incriminating papers of the Comte d'Antraigues, which, along with the Count himself, had been seized at Trieste.[3] To the dismay of the Clichy Royalists, these papers provided incontrovertible proof of the treason of their darling Pichegru. This treason was of no concern to the Clichyites, but Pichegru's later conduct disappointed them. His exposure was a bit of Napoleonic politics. The General was prodding the Directory toward two objectives. First, he desired the suppression of the budding Royalists. Second, and more important, he wished the Directory to proceed against the Councils of Five Hundred and the Ancients. In each he was obeyed, and what was more alarming, the Directory relied on troops from the armies at the front—an abdication of power and of constitutional government itself. The way to dictatorship now lay open whenever Napoleon might decide the time was ripe.

On the third of September, the Councils held their usual session. The atmosphere, however, suggested a calm before the storm. It was proposed to replace the five Directors by a Triumvirate. Five thousand troops from the Army of Italy and two thousand from the Rhine and the Moselle were threatening

271

Marseilles, Lyon, and Dijon. Proclamations were distributed setting forth the treason of Pichegru and menacing all who might aid him. That night a dozen of the Deputies took refuge at the Tuileries with Pichegru and Willot, guarded by 800 men. The actual *coup d'état* came next day, September 4, or in Revolutionary chronology, 18 Fructidor. Troops invested the Tuileries and other key points. All was accomplished quietly. Carnot fled; Barthélemy was taken prisoner. The guards offered no opposition, having no intention of emulating the Swiss Guards of the late King.

An appearance of legality was cultivated. Next day the Five Hundred and the Ancients met briefly amid a minimum of civic disorder. The Directory approving, regulations were passed with a semblance of constitutionality. On the fifth of September (19 Fructidor) the Royalist conspiracy was denounced. The recent elections which favored the Royalists were thrown out. Forty-nine departments were affected. Altogether 140 Deputies were disqualified, 95 in the Five Hundred, 45 in the Ancients. Eleven of the Five Hundred and 42 of the Ancients were ordered to be deported and their goods confiscated. Recent legislation friendly to the émigrés was repealed. They must quit France anew in fifteen days. A law passed this same day authorized the Directory to deport priests individually, and constrained all ecclesiastics to an oath "of hatred to royalty and anarchy, of attachment to the Republic and the Constitution of the Year III." Officials who neglected to enforce the law were liable to two years in irons. The press was muzzled. The Directory in addition was empowered to deport "proprietors, entrepreneurs, directors, authors and editors," to sequestrate their goods and to make domiciliary visits. These latter measures were not executed, but the counter-revolutionary press disappeared.[4]

Of the sixty-five condemned to deportation only eighteen were actually transported to Guiana. Seven died there. Two perished in attempted escapes. Six, among them Pichegru, evaded their captors and later made their way to England. Three were pardoned. A milder law of November 9 transferred the deportees to the more general category of émigrés. To escape confiscation of their property some of these latter remained as prisoners on the Isle of Oleron until the Directory was overthrown. The Royalist movement was crushed. Louis XVIII sought refuge with the Czar, who took into his service what remained of the army of Condé. The British minister, Wickham, who had been deeply compromised, was recalled.[5] In short, counter-revolution had completely failed. Without exposing his own hand, Napoleon had accomplished what he much desired.

These were trying days across the Channel. British economic power was low. The pound sterling was in trouble and there were mutinies on land and sea. Negotiations with France, not too promising at best, were languishing. The *coup d'état* had destroyed what hope remained. Lord Malmesbury, the British representative, quit Lille on September 18. The French awaited his return. He did not come.

Meanwhile, what of Napoleon? At Rivoli, on January 13 to 14, in one of his historic victories, he defeated the Austrian General Würmser, who had come south to the relief of Mantua. Turning northward he outmanoeuvred the Archduke Charles, and on April 7 reached the town of Leoben about sixty miles from Vienna. At this point in an amazing bit of hypocrisy, he assured the Archduke, in preliminaries to the armistice signed on April 18, that "if the opening which I have the honor to make you may save the life of a single man, I shall be more proud of the civic crown which I should consider myself to have deserved than of the sorry glory that may come from military success." [6] This precious bit from one of Mars' most eminent disciples ranks with the same author's well known assertion that his first communion marked the happiest day in his life.

These overtures met immediate response. The Austrians listened as to a reprieve. After numerous defeats they were tendered a victorious peace. In several details the extraordinarily magnanimous pledges at Leoben were actually surpassed at the definitive peace of Campo Formio.[7] Austria must yield Belgium but should receive full compensation in Italy. Napoleon was prepared to surrender the left bank of the Rhine—a "natural frontier." The Milanese, a poor substitute for the Rhenish provinces, not contiguous and generally less desirable, were to be retained by France. Venice was to be the prize of the defeated

Austrians. Napoleon did not yet possess it, but with the most brutal cynicism he proceeded to overthrow France's elder sister among republics—a state that had endured for over a thousand years. The city itself, not pledged at Leoben, was included at Campo Formio, October 17. These arrangements were not in the interest of France, but such was the desire for peace that the French were as delighted as their enemies.

On his return from Campo Formio by way of a brief attendance at the Conference at Rastadt,[8] Napoleon received an ecstatic welcome from Parisians. Peace had actually been made; the Conqueror was home among his people. The Directory had no choice but to welcome him. At the same time it sought to remove him by tendering him command in the war against England. This led to a sort of billiard technique of attacking England by way of Egypt. The Pyramids were reserved for 1798, but advance planning was in order.

More immediately, Italy remained the stepping stone to destiny. From various fragments, Napoleon had erected the Cisalpine Republic, the nucleus of modern Italy; and in the murder of some wounded grenadiers he had discovered an excuse for seizing Venice. Command of the Army of England furthered dreams of empire indulged during several weeks of luxurious repose at the Château of Mombello. Dominion over the Mediterranean, Corfu, the Ionian Isles, overthrow of the decadent empire of the Ottomans, triumphs in Greece, Sparta, Athens, Malta [9]—all mingled in the visions of a genius who saw no limits to his future. Of primary interest was Egypt, provided the Directory could comprehend its importance for the war with England. This the Directory was pretty sure to recognize, for master and man had reversed positions. Napoleon might preserve the amenities for another year or so, but the decisions increasingly were his. On the agenda accordingly the major item now was Egypt.

These preliminary chapters to consulate and empire for Napoleon were of earth-shaking import to Western civilization. To Washington, however, they carried less significance than many previous developments. As 1797 opened, there remained to him only two months of power, insufficient to bring France to her senses, but ample for encountering fresh annoyances. The French Revolution, so happily saluted at its first appearance, so patiently accepted as it progressed, was becoming in its later stages a burden unendurable. It would be a vast relief to Washington to lay aside the helm and let others guide the ship.

It was not his way, like Jefferson's, however, to abdicate to all intents and purposes as soon as his successor was announced. To his last day in office, Washington was President. As such, one of his chief concerns in these concluding weeks was the tone of the instructions to our minister in France. It must be such that not only might France comprehend our point of view, but no opportunity would be afforded the domestic opposition to distort our meaning or dispute our facts.[10] Above all it must guard and emphasize neutrality while protecting America's own dignity and sovereignty.[11] As finally transmitted on January 16, these careful and elaborate instructions reveal the courtesy, the strength, the indignation, of George Washington. He influenced them directly.[12]

French depredations on our commerce were passing previous bounds and led on January 19 to a special message to Congress, temperate in its language but bitter in its implications.[13] To Alexander Hamilton he was less restrained:

> The conduct of France towards this country is, according to my ideas of it, outrageous beyond conception; not to be warranted by her treaty with us, by the Law of Nations, by any principle of justice, or even by a regard to decent appearances. From such considerations something might have been expected; but, on her professions of friendship and loving-kindness to us I built no hope; but rather supposed they would last as long and no longer, than it accorded with their interest to bestow them, or found it would not divert us from the observance of that strict neutrality, which we had adopted and was persevering in.[14]

Considerably more there was, to similar effect.

The French farewell to Monroe and the extraordinary speech of Barras on behalf of the Directory were not yet known in the United States. Adams transmitted the account of January 12, along with caustic comments of his own. He expressed his faith that the United States would not be "bullied out of the neutrality which every other artifice has in vain been tried to defeat."

These tactics failing, France might some day return to common sense. For the present the minister admitted that while French concerns lay beyond his jurisdiction,

> I find it impossible as an American to withhold the expression of my feelings, upon witnessing treatment so contumelious to my Country and its Government: while at the same time the conviction is so clear that this terrific pomp of demonstration is intended as a mere experiment to produce what they call a *diversion* against Great Britain.

Adams next depicted the French situation, which was brilliant superficially but with underlying deep anxieties.[15]

This conception was confirmed by Pinckney, especially as regarded the finances, which could support further warfare only in so far as the victors might levy contributions on the vanquished.[16] The speech of Barras also elicited a comment. Pinckney viewed it as a bid to separate the people of the United States from the Government of their own choosing. One thing could be said for it, however, it was Barras' own composition and had not been submitted previously to the Directory.[17]

A further despatch represented Pinckney's endeavor to emulate his predecessors, Short, Morris, and to some extent Monroe, in an elaborate summary of French politics. Apologizing for a lack of confidential information, unobtainable by one whose reception was denied; and complaining incidentally of the failure of instructions to reach him, Pinckney nevertheless believed it his duty to sketch the existing lineup of the parties. There were four. The Jacobins were very enterprising, but not particularly numerous, and their name was still attended by the odium and obloquy which resulted from The Terror. A second party, also small in numbers and looking to the Abbé Sieyès for inspiration, favored a restoration of the monarchy with the Duc de Chartres as King. These were, in short, the Orleanists. More numerous than these, strong especially among the peasantry, were partisans of the *ancien régime*. Their strength lay partly in the idea they had managed to implant, that only the old Government could bring about a peace. Finally, there were the upholders of the Constitution of 1795, genuine friends of a republic. Pinckney believed these were the dominant group and that for the present, at any rate, the Government was safe.[18]

Pinckney might henceforth enlighten the Department of State and a new President, John Adams. In the slow communication of the period, no further despatches could possibly reach Philadelphia while George Washington was still in office.

In retirement at Mount Vernon, Washington would still be eager for French news, but of an unofficial sort. What came would be chiefly from old friends. He must have read with poignant interest the following from an associate in the American Revolution:

Paris 5 Pluviose   5th year
January 24th   old style

My General

General Pinckney to whom I am obliged for information on your excellency's health will be so kind as to forward to you with this packet the hommage of my respect and of my grateful remembrance. I beg of you to accept of this short pamphlet on our military and political situation as a witness of my sentiments. your excellency will acknowledge in it the effect of your lessons and perhaps also the caracter of the true public opinion in France. I beg of you to preserve for the true friends of the common cause of the Liberty of both nations your particular esteem of which they will always endeavor to be worthy. the last news we have received from general Lafayette and his unfortunate companions are not more satisfactory than those we had before. his health is very much impaired as well as that of his virtuous and respectable wife. we are in hope that peace unavoidable even on account of the exhausted state of the belligerent powers will give us both in and out of our own country, means to serve effectually our friends.

General Rochambeau is still at his country seat near Vendome. he enjoys there a tolerable good health considering his great age [71], and reckons as well as his military family amongst his most dear and glorious remembrances that of the time we had the honor to serve under your command.

I have the honor to be with the greatest
respect My general
  Your Most humble
  and obedient servant
  signed M[ieu] dumas.[19]

Likewise of personal interest was a private letter from General Pinckney saying that his nephew Harry was bringing Washington a verbal account of French affairs, but that it would be necessary to make a liberal discount of what he said, for the younger man was too hostile to the Terror to give a fair impression of French politics.[20]

By the time the Pinckney nephew, or further written communications either, might arrive, Washington would be what he had long aspired to be—a private citizen. Nevertheless it was inevitable that he would keep well informed of his successor's policies and difficulties. Government despatches at first came indirectly, although he later saw the entire correspondence on the XYZ Affair. McHenry in the Cabinet was a faithful correspondent, but there was respite from heavier responsibilities.

Washington had long ere this attained his permanent philosophy of the Revolution. His political reaction to it also largely terminated with his own retirement, save for his brief and pathetic recall to military life when war loomed between ourselves and France. From the beginning of the Revolution to the present, he had been intelligent, sympathetic, loyal and consistent in his attitude toward the French, little as some of them appreciated it. In the short span of life remaining, he would not deviate from his former course.

From London, on February 6, Rufus King reported further astonishing victories for the French in Lombardy, and that possibly in consequence of these, the Directory had on January 28 ordered Pinckney to quit Paris. He left accordingly for Amsterdam on the last day of the month.[21] On the fifteenth, Washington's old correspondent, Newenham, reported from Dublin that some malicious publications against him had circulated there but had been answered promptly and effectively. "Cato's Letters" could not find an Irish printer. Portions of Paine's insulting letter did appear but were utterly refuted.[22]

It was approximately at this time, somewhere between six and ten weeks following its publication, that Washington must have learned of the famous Mazzei letter, the Parthian shot of the pro-French-Revolutionary Jefferson at a master whom he had served ably but unenthusiastically, their good will undermined by a deepening chasm of political distaste. The letter was written at Monticello on April 24, 1796, printed in Italian at Florence, January 1, 1797, and later in French and English. Jefferson never denied authorship of this scurrilous epistle whose highlight read as follows: "It would give you a fever were I to name to you the apostates who have gone over to these heresies [British examples] men who were Samsons in the field & Solomons in the council, but who had their heads shorn by the harlot England." [23]

Here one ventures to suspect an abiding malice on the part of the war governor of Virginia, who fled his capital so ignominiously, toward the hero of the American Revolution and the man whose fame so steadily eclipsed his own. Washington, at any rate, took the allusion as personal and broke off all relations with the author.

On March 25, Senator William Bingham of Philadelphia, whose mansion, presided over by his wife, Anne Willing, America's most famous hostess, had been long noted for its hospitality to foreigners, wrote Washington a note of commendation for the Orleans princes, refugees, of course, and visiting in America:

> Dear Sir
>
> Amongst the number that experience the Hospitalities of Mount Vernon, there are non whose personal Merit (independent of their Education, their Rank & Pretensions) more deservedly entitle them to this attention, than my Friends Mons' d'Orleans, Mons' de Montpensier & Mons' de Beaujolais.
>
> Your previous acquaintance with these Gentlemen, renders it unnecessary to recommend them more pointedly to your Notice & Civilities.
>
> They intend, after paying their respects to you & Mrs. Washington, to make a Short Excursion to the Westward.
>
> I have the Honor to be with Respect
> > Sir Your obed hble serv
> > > Wm Bingham
>
> Philadelphia
> March 25th 1797.[24]

To James McHenry, Secretary of War in the Cabinet of Adams, the newly emancipated Washington wearily remarked that "the conduct of the French government is so much beyond calculation, and so unaccountable upon any principle of justice or even of that sort of policy wch. is familiar to plain understanding that I shall not *now* puzzle my brains in attempting to develop their motives to it." [25] He was alluding to the most recent injuries and insults growing out of the refusal to receive Pinckney, and his expulsion from the country.

279

Picking up the thread of former letters, Rufus King reported Great Britain to be weary of the war. Peace was anxiously desired, without immediate expectation of its coming. France was further harassing the commerce of Americans, and the presence of Pinckney at Amsterdam instead of Paris was not an augury of good relations.[26] An elaborate account of Pinckney's treatment at the hands of the Directory was enclosed in a letter from McHenry of May 14. It was not calculated to leave Washington unmoved.[27]

Still less would he bear patiently the efforts of Monroe to vindicate his conduct. A minister stands upon a different footing than does a private citizen. When things go wrong, he needs must grin and bear it. He is not privileged to introduce state secrets into the pattern of his personal defense. To do so is a breach of trust. Information, therefore, from Charles Lee, the Attorney General, that Monroe was demanding from the Secretary of State an explanation for his recall could not be agreeable to Washington or any members of the Government. As Lee observed,

> Mr. Monroe I am told is preparing for the press and complains of the act of Dismissal in the most vehement terms. In a private character I shall not scruple to give him my reasons justifying the act and submit them to him and our country. In doing this I shall find it not amiss to mention some matters that I believe are not extant in the opinion which was sent you.
>
> Whether the mission of conciliation will succeed is very uncertain. There are simptoms in france of returning justice benevolence and peace: If there be not peace our country must & will blame the french faction that within our bowels is working the calamities and miseries of their country.[28]

Washington was inclined to accept this optimistic view of Lee's, although with some reservations, as he observed to Pickering:

> From a variety of accounts as well as from extracts you had the kindness to send me, I have no doubt of a change in the sentiments of the People of France favourable to the interests of this Country; but I can scarcely believe that it will be so great, or so sudden as some imagine. Candour is not a more conspicuous trait in the character of Governments, than it is of Individuals. It is hardly to be expected then, that

the Directory of France will acknowlege its errors; and tread back its steps *immediately*. This would announce, at once, that there has been precipitancy and injustice in the measures they have pursued; or that it was incapable of judging, and had been deceived by false misrepresentations. Pride would be opposed to all these, and I can scarsely think the Directory will relinquish the *hold it has* upon those who, more than probable, have suggested and promoted the measures, they have been pursuing. I rather suppose that it will lower its tone by degrees and (as is usual) place the change to the credit of *French magnanimity*.[29]

A shrewd observation, this, and the fruit of ripe experience! Washington had cut a great figure in the world, and he knew both life and human nature. If man had many limitations, he nevertheless had great potentialities. Only the cynic fails to see these latter, and Washington was too great a man to play the cynic. His faith in human nature, all too often sorely tried, must have been happily reinforced, however, by news of Lafayette's release at last from prison, the result of arrangements made by Napoleon at the Peace of Campo Formio. William Vans Murray relayed the news to him from The Hague on August 26,[30] and on September 6, Rufus King confirmed it from London.[31]

With news like this from home, George Washington Lafayette was intensely eager to join his parents. At the first opportunity, he returned to France, the bearer of a very touching letter from his foster-father, as it were, to his father, only part of which I quote:

He can relate, much better than I can describe, my participation in your sufferings, my solicitude for your relief, the measures I adopted (though ineffectually) to facilitate your liberation from an unjust and cruel imprisonment, and the joy I experienced at the news of its accomplishment. I shall hasten therefore to congratulate you, and be assured that no one can do it with more cordiality, with more sincerity, or with greater affection, on the restoration of that liberty, which every act of your life entitles you to the enjoyment of; and I hope I may add, to the uninterrupted possession of your Estates, and the confidence of your Country. The repossession of these things, though they cannot compensate for the hardships you have endured, may nevertheless soften the painful remembrance of them.

Further explanation followed of the difficulty Washington had experienced in harmonizing his emotions as a friend with his responsibilities as a statesman. Lafayette should have seen this point, if he was ever going to, nor did Washington dwell upon it at much length. The remainder of the epistle was devoted chiefly to compliments for young Fayette, and for his tutor, both of whom had won their host's affection. Washington concluded with the hope that Lafayette might come to America, where his old friend would be more than delighted to welcome him.[32]

The entire epistle expressed the utmost sincerity and grace. Their antithesis, the utmost dislike and contempt, was reserved for the unfortunate Monroe, whose "View of the Conduct of the Executive of the United States," so contrary to the prescribed etiquette for diplomats, aroused Washington's deep scorn. Throughout the major part of 1798, Monroe was an object of Washington's anxiety and even hatred.

It may be supposed—and a relative paucity of correspondence would confirm the belief—that Washington was more completely retired in the year of his return to private life than he was in the two years that followed. True, he was informed of happenings both foreign and domestic; true, he was in touch with leaders at home and abroad. But release from power exhilarated. The closing phase of his relation to the Revolution was yet to come, in the undeclared war with France, 1798–1800. For Washington, speaking relatively of course, there was a brief repose.

CHAPTER
TWELVE

1798

By 1798, the French Revolution had run almost full cycle. From the theoretical absolutism of Louis XVI, it was approaching the genuine absolutism of Napoleon Bonaparte. Constitutional forms persisted and Councils and Directors appeared to govern. But Campo Formio had internal as well as diplomatic repercussions. Old relationships of authority and obedience were crumbling. International relationships were equally in flux. Switzerland was one object of ambition and a portion of her territory was incorporated into France. French imperialism was stretching impious hands toward the Eternal City. As the old year closed, the French ambassador left Rome, and on January 11, the Directory sought Napoleon's opinion on the crisis. Military intervention followed. The Pope was exiled; the cardinals were imprisoned. But French occupation was steadily opposed.

Four successive *coups d'état* in the Cisalpine Republic, a Napoleonic creation, attested its fragility. Conditions were no less difficult in Genoa and Piedmont, and Tuscany gave refuge to the exiled Pontiff. Italy in short was an uneasy conquest. Nor did the slow-moving Congress at Rastadt afford much compensation. Prussia by now was neutral between France and Austria. It was for the Czar Paul of Russia to infuse new energy into the league opposing France. To this Austria was amenable, Prussia far less. But by October it was clear that she would refuse to be allied with France.

Peace on the Continent being increasingly precarious, and the maritime war with England far from ended, France looked to Spain, her ally, to the Batavian Republic, her vassal, and to the United States of America, a neutral but morally indebted to her, as three powers likely to be of assistance amid her multiplying dangers.

Relations with the United States were turning sour. Following Monroe's departure and the failure to receive Pinckney, President Adams named John Marshall † and Elbridge Gerry † to a three man commission, of which Pinckney should be the third and senior member. The purpose of the commission was to negotiate with Talleyrand, French Foreign Minister, with a view to restoring Franco-American relations. Presenting themselves to Talleyrand on October 8, 1797, the commission soon learned that he and the Directory were committed to the principle that merchandise is not protected by a neutral flag. A law of January 1798 declared that the status of ships as neutrals or enemies would be determined by their cargoes. In other words, freedom of goods would not be assured by freedom of the flag. Neutrals must not carry English goods nor land first in England if they wished to trade with France. French privateers might pursue neutrals as readily as enemies.

If American good will was really sought, this was a strange approach. As an added insult, Talleyrand, apparently nursing a personal grudge at never having been received as a French refugee by Washington, and animated further by a greed that became proverbial, kept the three Americans at arm's length for months, while he worked upon them through three of his agents, Messrs. Hottenguer, Bellamy, and Hauteval, whose instructions were to

284

procure a personal bribe for Talleyrand and the other Directors of one million dollars, as well as a subscription by the United States to a large war loan for France. To preserve the amenities, these agents of corruption were referred to in our ministers' despatches as Messrs. X, Y, and Z. To them might properly be added Madame de Villette, widow of a Royalist colonel, who sought especially to soften the patriotism if not the heart of Marshall.

Throughout these protracted and humiliating negotiations, the three Americans could scarcely preserve a united front. Gerry, though personally a friend of Adams, was so strongly pro-French that he saw little to condemn in the disgraceful demands of Talleyrand and his emissaries. Talleyrand had relied all along on Republican opposition to the foreign policy of both Washington and Adams, and he cultivated Gerry as the commission's weakest link. Seduced in part by flattery, but moved more deeply by the pro-French sympathies of his party, Gerry remained behind when Pinckney and Marshall, properly indignant at the insult to their country, left France. Fortunately for his fair fame, this delay was short.

On their return to America, the commission members published proofs of Talleyrand's venality. The scandal, hushed in France, created an enormous stir in America and England. An anonymous toast proposed "Millions for defense, but not one cent for tribute." And the average American, whose sympathies had been counted on by Talleyrand, now saw foreign affairs from a more nationalistic—or in other words, a more patriotic—viewpoint. Talleyrand, meanwhile, was a laughing stock in England and wherever the press enjoyed some freedom.

What followed the XYZ Affair was virtually war, lasting into 1799, when it was terminated by John Adams and Napoleon, by then First Consul.

In France, meanwhile, plans had been drawn earlier for a Dutch descent upon the Clyde and a French descent upon Ireland. These proved abortive, and when Napoleon surveyed the situation and examined the plan of the United Irelanders to make a direct attack on England, he vetoed the project. His opinion, delivered February 23, 1798, surprised the Directory. Their

285

astonishment increased when Napoleon proposed to divert the entire operation to Egypt.

Common sense indicated that in Egypt the risks were greater and the prospects less. Moreover the European situation was adverse. But such was Napoleon's prestige that he obtained the assent of the Directory on March 5, Reubell, one of the most forceful of the Directors, alone dissenting. Even today the causes of this shift remain obscure. The idea was not new. It had been rejected by the last three Kings of France. At the moment French relations with the Sublime Porte were unusually cordial. French commerce with the Levant was presented with exceptional opportunities. Why confuse these favorable prospects by an attack upon the Sultan's most important vassal?

The explanation seems to be that Napoleon was a dreamer and a visionary whose figments of imagination were strangely shared by Talleyrand. Undoubtedly the Foreign Minister gave his approval to the plans for Egypt.[1] Napoleon's grandiose plan for converting the Nile into a Rubicon sprang largely from his ignorance of geography. He knew little of the European continent. Only gradually, and chiefly as a military leader, did he attain such knowledge. He ignored Germany and Prussia as unimportant. He had not yet learned to fear England, which during his Italian campaign was excluded from the Mediterranean. To remain in France was an unprofitable use of glory, which even might be compromised in party conflicts. Better to win fresh laurels. And within the limits of his Mediterranean and Levantine imagination nothing equalled the distant East.

Elaborate preparations delayed the expedition, which when finally assembled was on a magnificent scale. Its best memorial is not war on sea or land but the Egyptian Institute,[2] founded by the scientists who accompanied it under the patronage of Napoleon. By rare good fortune the expedition arrived at Alexandria just one day after Admiral Nelson left, and proceeded promptly to attack the Turks. It was at the Pyramids on July 21 that Napoleon, after a horrible march across the desert and a memorable victory over the Mamelukes, coined one of his best phrases: "Soldiers, from the summit of these pyramids forty centuries look down upon you."

286

But Nelson could not be eluded permanently. On August 1, at Aboukir Bay, he destroyed the French fleet. Nelson became the Baron of the Nile, while the conqueror of Egypt became the prisoner of his conquest. From such a magnificent demonstration of British sea power, consequences flowed in widening circles. Details may be omitted here as there is slight if any evidence that they were known to Washington. Suffice it that by the end of 1798, a whole series of alliances was featured, constituting in effect a second coalition. Some strange partnerships included Russia and Turkey; Russia and England; Russia and Naples; Turkey and England; Turkey and Naples. Through her ambassador at St. Petersburg, England proposed a program for the eventual peace settlement, flexible to be sure, which sixteen years later bore fruit in the treaties that followed the downfall of Napoleon.

From a military victory nullified by a defeat at sea, Napoleon sought a moral victory among his new subjects by professing himself a Muslim, devoted to Mohammed and a constant reader of the Koran. This provided no insurance against a bloody revolt in Cairo, which was violently suppressed. A further step was to extend the war to Upper Egypt. The particulars may be reserved for 1799.

That year, it may be added, would see the end of the French Revolution as such, and with the emergence of Napoleon Bonaparte as First Consul, the commencement of the dictatorship toward which the Revolution long had tended.

This sketch of France and her warrior in 1798 serves only as a background for the France of which George Washington was cognizant. That was the France of the XYZ Affair and of near war between Allies so recent. Here Washington's emotions found full vent. "Coolness" was no longer his predominating trait. Inevitably he associated Monroe with the calamity and he was not prepared to question Timothy Pickering when the Secretary wrote from Philadelphia that

Monroe's publication, like Randolph's vindication, is considered by every one whom I have heard speak of it, as his own condemnation, or as some have expressed themselves his death warrant. A writer in Fenno's paper, under the signature of *Scipio,* has undertaken the exami-

287

nation of it, and clearly convicted Monroe from his own written documents. I believe the writer of Scipio is Mr. Tracy. The pieces are written with uncommon perspicuity. If you do not get Fenno's paper, and will permit me, I will send you the whole series. Eleven numbers have already appeared, and I suppose the writer is near the conclusion.[3]

Replying to the above, and to a communication of a week later, Washington bitterly condemned the political tactics of the French and of their American adherents. A case in point was a sentence by Fauchet to the following effect: "It is the general opinion that Mr. Talon † came to Philadelphia on a confidential mission from the 'Pretender' to Genl. Washington. He was admitted to a very particular audience with the President before the arrival of Mr. Genet at Philadelphia." Admitting that he might casually have met the gentleman at a levee, Washington unequivocally denied acquaintance with him or anything suggestive of an interview. The episode was fabricated so as to place a sinister construction on the reception of Genêt.[4]

But with Monroe, his fellow countryman and one-time friend, he was more severe than with Fauchet. Monroe's use of confidential material in presenting his "View" was in the last degree contemptible. It elicited a biting comment:

> As to the propriety of exposing to public view his private Instructions, and correspondence with his own Government, nothing needs be said; for I should suppose, that the measure must be reprobated by the well-informed and intelligent of *all Nations,* and not less by his abettors in this Country, if they were not blinded by Party views, and determined at all hazards to catch at any thing, that, in their opinion will promote them. The mischievous, and dangerous tendency of such a practice is too glaring to require a comment.[5]

Whoever doubts the depth of feeling Monroe aroused in Washington should examine the pungency of his comments on Monroe's unfortunate production. They are bitter, dry, disillusioned, and intensely keen.[6] Few men ever antagonized George Washington so deeply as did Monroe, yet underneath it all, one cannot quite believe that Monroe himself had a fair deal. Some perception of this truth may have intensified Washington's anger in the premises.

With Monroe returned in such high dudgeon; with Pinckney scorned by France and ignominiously despatched to Amsterdam;

the Administration determined on a commission to replace him, of which, however, Pinckney should be a member. Hence the addition of Elbridge Gerry and John Marshall, and their tragic dealings with a corrupt and discredited Directory. John Marshall, fellow Virginian, just at the outset of his great career even as Washington was at the closing of his, courteously corresponded with the aging statesman at Mount Vernon. His letter derives its chief importance from the recipient; perhaps also from the sender. A passage or two will show its general tenor:

> An army which arriving safe would sink England may itself be encountered & sunk in the channel. The effect of such a disaster on a nation already tir'd of the war & groaning under the pressure of an enormous taxation, which might discern in it the seeds of another coalition, & which perhaps may not be universally attachd to the existing arrangements, might be extremely serious to those who hold the reins of government.
>
> It is therefore believed by many who do not want intelligence that these formidable military preparations cover & favor secret negotiations for peace.[7]

Here was no passive acceptance of surface indications but a disposition to seek the bedrock of reality. The great jurist of the future was already speaking.

But it need not be supposed that Washington in retirement received only such crumbs of information as courtesy might allow a forlorn old man who once had held the center of the stage. Quite otherwise. He was very near the center of it still; too near, in fact, for the comfort of John Adams. On April 16, 1798, for example, Washington thanked the Secretary of State for all the correspondence, both instructions and despatches, relating to "the Envoys of the United States at Paris."[8] As the XYZ Affair unfolded, Washington was at the very fount of information. Had he been still in office, his sources could have been no more authoritative.

It is both relevant and irrelevant to the present study to trace the growing indignation of Washington as the XYZ Affair progressed, even to his willingness to draw the sword as a final service to his country. I say both, because, after all, it was the French Revolution, now pretty fully gone to seed, which drove him to this action. Furthermore, the entire affair, whether experienced

289

by contemporaries or interpreted by historians of either nation, can be traced directly to the Proclamation of Neutrality as implemented further by Jay's Treaty. Thus the XYZ Affair was definitely a part of Washington's Administration, an important consequence of his reaction to the French Revolution. The mere circumstance that John Adams was chief of state at the time of its occurrence should not blind one to the fact that the affair was an unpleasant accompaniment to the foreign policy of Washington.

On the other hand, emergence from retirement, Washington's last costly offering to his country, was inevitable if his career was to remain consistent. But our study has fixed limits. It is not a biography. It is not concerned with the disappointments and annoyances of this last of Washington's adventures as a soldier. Suffice it that he saw his duty, then did it at whatever cost.

To Alexander Hamilton, on May 27, he exceeded his previous complaints of France when he declared that

> dark as matters appear at present, and expedient as it is to be prepared at all points for the worst that can happen, (and no one is more disposed to this measure than I am,) I cannot make up my mind *yet* for the expectation of *open war*, or, in other words for a formidable invasion by France. I cannot believe, although I think them capable [of] any thing bad, that they will attempt to do more than they have done; or that, when they perceive the spirit and policy of this country rising into resistance, and that they have falsely calculated upon support from a large part of the *people* thereof to promote their views and influence in it, that they will desist even from those practices, unless unexpected events in Europe, and their possession of Louisiana and the Floridas, should induce them to continue the measure.

France might continue to rely for moral support upon Anti-Federalist leaders. But the rank and file were leaving them. Should, however, the crisis be compelling, Washington would not refuse, however reluctant he might be, to emerge from his retirement.[9]

A month later to a day, Washington permitted himself, in the mounting tide toward war with France, to accuse the French, from an early moment in their Revolution, of aiming at their present object, infringement on the sovereignty of the United States.[10] Political and military passion was at its height. Washington was deeply stirred. But this assertion may be discounted from his own utterance and action throughout the ten years past. Undoubtedly he believed what he was saying, exasperated as he was by cumulative irritations. But this peevish utterance does not convey his true attitude toward the French Revolution.

Equally hostile, but nobler in expression, was his attack on France in a formal letter to John Adams accepting the office of Lieutenant-General and Commander-in-Chief of the armies of the United States:

> The conduct of the Directory of France towards our Country; their insidious hostility to its Government; their various practices to withdraw the affections of the People from it; the evident tendency of their Arts and those of their Agents to countenance and invigorate opposition; their disregard of solemn treaties and the laws of Nations; their war upon our defenceless Commerce; their treatment of our Minister of Peace, and their demands amounting to tribute, could not fail to excite in me corresponding sentiments with those my countrymen have so generally expressed in their affectionate Addresses to you.[11]

It is unnecessary to cite every extant expression of the indignation felt by Washington at this period of menace. His anger was in part political. The imminence of war meant a complete breakdown of his cherished neutrality. So completely was the Administration of John Adams a continuation of his own, even to the carry-over of the Cabinet, that his personal credit was intimately involved with the credit of the President. Reasons were not lacking, then, why Washington in 1798 should utterly condemn the current phase of the French Revolution. To his thinking it had fallen upon the sere and yellow leaf.

Moreover, the whole French situation was inextricably involved, in Washington's opinion, with the pettifogging tactics of a miscreant opposition in America, and his feelings derived additional intensity from this conviction. When the French Revolution became a chief ingredient of Anti-Federalist propaganda, Washington could no longer view the movement with that "coolness" which Gouverneur Morris had earlier admired.

While Washington was surrendering to this warlike mood, the French Directory, embarrassed by the disclosures of its corruption, and far from wishing war, made preliminary overtures for peace through the American poet Joel Barlow, author of *The Columbiad*, then resident in Paris. On October 2, Barlow put forth a feeler in a letter still preserved in the files of Washington. A brief quotation will reveal its temper:

> The dispute at this moment may be characterised simply & literally a *misunderstanding*. I cannot persuade myself to give it a harsher name as it applies to either government. It is clear that neither of them has an interest in going to war with the other, and I am fully convinced that neither has the inclination, that is I believe the balance of inclination, as well as interest, on both sides, is in favor of peace. But each government though sensible of this truth with respect to itself, is ignorant of it with respect to the other. Each believes the other determined on war, and ascribes all its conduct to a deep rooted hostility. The least they can do therefore under this impression is to prepare for an event which they both believe inevitable, while they both wish to avoid it.—The point that I wish to establish in your mind is that the French Directory is at the present sincerely desirous of restoring harmony between this country & the United States on terms honorable & advantageous to both parties. I wish to convince you of this, & through you the American Government, because that government, being desirous of the same thing, would not fail to take such steps as would lead immediately to the object.[12]

Barlow was more readily the spokesman for the Directory, notwithstanding his status as an American, than Lafayette could hope to be. Yet Lafayette in his private character was equally insistent upon peace. Out of deference to the sentiments of his friend, on the birthday of the Prince of Peace, Washington expressed himself as pacifically as warlike circumstances would permit, giving a résumé of the injuries and insults which had brought grateful friends and sincere allies to the brink of war. The tone was considerably tempered for a recipient who boasted of his dual citizenship and professed a love for each of his two countries.[13]

Almost at the close of this painful year of 1798, Washington alluded briefly to the well known mission of Dr. George Logan to France, bringing the Directory assurance of the undiminished homage of leading Anti-Federalists in the United States, himself among them; and returning with empty assurances from the perfidious Directory. Altogether a discreditable intervention was Logan's in the diplomacy of his country; one punished shortly afterward by Congress in the so-called Logan Act of 1799, which forbade such private enterprise in future.

Washington took personal account of Logan's mission in a letter to William Vans Murray, who was Minister Resident for the United States at The Hague.[14] He spoke with undisguised contempt of the mission, its purposes and results. A saving sense of realism preserved Washington from all such fly-by-night adventures. The forerunner of the *Peace Ship* of Henry Ford was no hero to George Washington.

After all, 1798 was the war year, such as it was. With no opening declaration, and equally no formal peace while Washington yet lived, the season of the highest ferment was already past. Barlow's letter would alone prove this. Even Logan's mission bore some added testimony. The gravest climax of the French Revolution passed without formal war. Other crises would arise, but the worst would not occur while Washington was alive.

His faith, therefore, in the French Revolution, severely tried and driven to the point of vanishing, never was subjected to the acid test of war. With the gradual subsidence of fever heat, Washington in the last year of his life would find surcease from bitterness in resuming a correspondence with his beloved Lafayette. Fortunate it was for his serenity that this correspondence was resumed in the spring of 1798 and continued for above a year. Lafayette retained copies of what would otherwise have perished. The power of personal friendship mitigated in some measure the asperities of international disputes.

In April 1798, Lafayette contemplated a journey to the United States. From this he was dissuaded. Of greater interest was the vision he retained of the worldwide spread of Revolutionary principles. It would be to the whole world's advantage if North and South America should gradually adopt the principles on which the independence and freedom of the United States were founded. Similarly he trusted that the principles of the French Revolution would spread throughout Europe, hastening emancipation for the subjects of despots. By Revolutionary principles Lafayette meant, of course, the bourgeois and individualistic principles of the French Revolution's early stages—the principles which he himself avowed. The excesses of the later Revolution he attributed in no small part to the schemes of neighboring despots, anxious to discredit the movement as a whole.

Those same despots now were trembling before the irresistible power of France. This afforded Lafayette a text for a political survey, less important than his vision of a world succumbing to the march of new ideas. The vision naturally embraced the destiny of Bonaparte to which apparently no limits could be set. Even "the destiny of Asia will be much concerned in the outcome of his operations."

Lafayette was certain that Washington could appreciate the conflict in his heart over the dissensions of his two fatherlands. He was far from blaming the United States for asserting their national dignity and sovereignty. With honor satisfied, however, he hoped the feud might terminate:

> If party spirit, personal prejudices, resentment and vanity unite to compound the difficulties, my consolation is to believe that the elevation of your character and situation give you the power, as you have, I am sure the will, to terminate this deplorable quarrel between two nations whose troops were happily united under your command.

Lafayette had been urged to go to America on a mission of reconciliation. He had refused to do so unless assured in his own mind that the Directory was prepared to right the previous wrongs. But Washington was there already, "independent of parties, venerated by all." Lafayette knew that Washington would do his utmost to prevent the breach from widening and to assure a noble and permanent reconciliation.[15]

To Alexander Hamilton, Lafayette addressed, on August 12, a communication of interest almost equal to the preceding. And in view of the intimacy between Hamilton and Washington throughout this period of war excitement, it is probable enough that Washington was permitted to see the letter or at least to know its contents. It amounted to a brief constitutional summary of the French Revolution, and was compact and thoughtful.[16] But no analysis is needed here, Washington being already familiar with the matter covered. It would seem, however, that long incarceration had deepened Lafayette's philosophy of the Revolution. I do not mean that previously he had lacked such guidance. Indeed the Declaration of the Rights of Man, prepared by Lafayette for the first Constitution, would give him rating as a political philosopher. But imprisonment confirmed a pre-existing tendency. After Olmütz, Lafayette deserved a high place among the philosophical interpreters of the French Revolution. Friends in America were the natural beneficiaries of his wisdom.

For Washington, on the contrary, the fragmentary evidence for 1798 as here set forth is not a little tragic. A career that merited a Cincinnatus-like retirement was still beset with cares. That these were personal as well goes without saying. America's great statesman must serve his country till the end.

CHAPTER
THIRTEEN

1799

Even as Washington's star was setting in 1799, that of Napoleon was rising. The Revolution having moved to its eclipse, Napoleon quit Egypt the better to receive his patrimony. The estate came to probate in the *coup d'état* of 18 Brumaire, that is, November 8 to 9, 1799. The First Republic now was history, a dictatorship its successor. The hero of Lodi, Arcola, the Pyramids and Aboukir (the land battle, not the naval) was girding to dominate the world.

Early events were not too encouraging in Europe, Africa or the Near East. The bitter results of the Battle of the Nile were still unfolding. But at Aboukir on July 25, Napoleon notched one of his major victories. He slaughtered 3,000 Turks, wounded 6,000, and captured 2,000 more. This overwhelming victory was his *congé* for France. Leaving Kléber in charge of a triumphant but captive army, Napoleon left Egypt on August 22. By great good luck he avoided Nelson and on October 9 arrived in France.

In France, meanwhile, anxiety was mounting. The presence of Russian troops on Imperial territory was menacing. The Directory was alarmed by the proximity of the "barbarians." To avert war it was prepared to make concessions and to negotiate with England and Turkey for peace at sea. Negotiations came to naught. Accordingly, after various preliminaries the Councils declared the Republic to be at war with the Emperor, King of Hungary and Bohemia, and the Grand-Duke of Tuscany. The French entered Florence on March 25. Pius VI, the exiled Pope, was removed once more. He died in France on August 29, 1799.

Elsewhere in Italy the Russian General Souvaroff entered Milan on April 28. But the Austrians so manoeuvred that the fierce and able Russian was soon transferred to Switzerland, though not before he had defeated the French at Novi, August 15, in a battle which resulted in the temporary loss of Italy.

On the brighter side, a brilliant victory for the French at Zurich, September 23 to October 1, averted any junction of the Austrians with the two Russians, Souvaroff pushing north from Italy and Korsakoff bringing reinforcements from Russia. Thus the situation was by no means desperate when the Corsican adventurer came slinking from the army of Egypt which he had ingloriously abandoned. Also in fairness to the Councils and the Directory, it should be noted that prosperity was returning just as the régime expired. Financial reorganization dated from the Directory and not, as sometimes has been assumed, from the Constituent Assembly or the Consulate.

Conspiracy was in the air before Napoleon could bring to it his fine Italian hand. Counter-revolution was the aim. Traces of monarchism were reappearing. An opposition press dared rear its head, and Jacobinism was demanding fresh blood. Two laws were alienating the best disposed. The law of hostages threatened to punish the innocent for the real or imagined crimes of absent kindred. And a huge forced loan antagonized the capitalists who had befriended the Revolution. Royalism in the south was descending to banditry and petty crime, inviting stern reprisals. There was incipient insurrection in the west. Altogether the picture presented opportunities when Napoleon decided that his destiny was come.

Bonaparte reached Paris on October 16. Some days were spent in official visits and in meeting possible accomplices. On the twenty-second he dined with Gohiér of the Directory, Moreau, Sieyès and others. The conspiracy may have dated from that meeting. It was hoped that the projected *coup* could be limited not merely to Paris, but to small groups within the city, entailing a minimum of excitement elsewhere.

Key figures must be reconciled, outwitted or removed. Barras, for example, was bribed or coerced into resignation. Fouché, Chief of Police, remained neutral as long as possible, ready to aid or to suppress the plotters. The Institute of France was taken into partial confidence. Some overtures were made to the Royalists, while capitalists were offered a pledge to terminate the forced loan. Among the generals, Napoleon found varying degrees of support. His brother Lucien, as President of the Council of Five Hundred, was in a key position to assist.

On November 7, Bonaparte joined three of his fellow generals, Bernadotte, Jourdan, and Moreau at dinner. The *coup d'état* was staged within the next two days. It was accompanied by a major show but slight utilization of force. For the army, which alone insured success to the conspiracy, long remained in joyous ignorance of what really happened.

Plans for the eighth were detailed and minute. Those for the ninth were haphazard and almost ended in disaster. The Ancients, with loyal names omitted, were summoned for the unusual hour of eight. Upon assembling at the Tuileries, they perceived from neighboring troop placements that their deliberations would be scrutinized by veterans of many battles. The sessions being opened, a pretended Jacobin plot was exposed. Faced with this imaginary peril, it was decided that the Councils should adjourn to Saint Cloud to meet at noon next day. Bonaparte was charged with their protection.

Executive authority still lay with the Directory. Hence the nomination of Bonaparte by the Ancients was unconstitutional. To avert discussion on this point the President of the Ancients declared the decree adopted and closed the session. Meanwhile at the Luxembourg, three of the Directors, constituting a majority, held a meeting. It was here that Barras performed his part of the conspiracy. By an inspired passivity and inaction, he completely paralyzed the executive power and thus the Government.

Not so with Bonaparte. With his chief of staff he hastened to the Tuileries, where he took the oath in a continued endeavor to preserve the semblance of legality. Nevertheless his tone was that of master. He had by-passed the Constitution. Next joining Sieyès and Ducos,† soon to emerge with him as consuls in the new order, he issued his first commands, associating Moreau with himself as an accomplice. He then addressed the troops in a violent tirade against the Directory, from which at this precise juncture Barras conveniently resigned.

While these events were occurring at the Tuileries and the Luxembourg, Lucien Bonaparte informed the Council of the Five Hundred, sitting at the Palais-Bourbon, of the decree of the Ancients, and immediately dismissed the session. Notices were posted pledging that Napoleon would never be a Caesar or a Cromwell. As the conspirators had hoped, all this was accompanied by a minimum of excitement. But at Saint Cloud next day Napoleon arranged a maximum troop deployment.

On the equally crucial ninth, failure was narrowly averted. The two Councils were told to meet at noon but due to incomplete arrangements there was considerable delay. The session of the Five Hundred opened tumultuously with cries of "Down with Dictatorship. Long live the Oath," that is, of hatred for tyranny. With the Ancients, deputies not summoned to the previous session were loud in their complaints. Confusion in both chambers continued until four o'clock when Napoleon in uniform personally intervened. Unaccustomed to address civilians his speech fell flat. A later speech to the troops was more in character. Lucien helped. He told the soldiers that liberty was in grave danger. Traitors in both Councils had betrayed their native land for British gold. The soldiers saw their duty. By five-thirty the halls were cleared. Sieyès, Ducos, and Napoleon proclaimed themselves the three Consuls of a new régime. Two days later, November 11, the Consuls took the oath before the two Assemblies. The soldiers returned to Paris, rejoicing that liberty was saved.

Thus ended the French Revolution; or is it more correct to say that the Revolution goes marching on?

These late developments were not known to George Washington, who at distant Mount Vernon had little more than a month to live. Notwithstanding Washington's emergence from retirement as commander of the army in the undeclared war with France, the last year of his life was more concerned with politics than with an army which John Adams, in complete disobedience of Congress, never troubled to assemble. Thus the Barlow letter of October 2, 1798, might be interpreted as unfinished business for the new year. There is no evidence that Barlow was accepted as a credible witness or as other than the agent for a corrupt Directory. Through Barlow the Directory put forth an *essai de ballon*. It was free to accept him or reject him as circumstances seemed to warrant. Similarly Washington and the Government of Adams might accept him *cum grano salis,* or reject him, as the general European situation might direct. Thus the Barlow letter was invested with the aura of intrigue.

Nor was Washington left long in doubt of this. A letter written by Major Mountflorence at The Hague on March 12, 1799, and forwarded by Pinckney on June 25, set forth the case in language unmistakable:

> In my letter to the Secry of State of the 9th instant [March], I communicated the positive intelligence I had from Paris, that the Consul there & Mr. Barlow, had individually written to the French Directory, praising their wise & prudent conduct towards the U States & recommending that a Minister be immediately sent to America to adjust matters, & thereby to be beforehand with the President— They recommend particularly, that this person should have manifested even before the French Revolution, if possible, Republican principles, & done some great service to America.
>
> I smell in this, a double intrigue of crafty Talleyrand, & I believe you will be of my opinion, when I inform you that Lafayette, has been in this country for some weeks, with an intention of going to America. That he has letters from Talleyrand advising him strongly to it, & buoying him up with his canting flattery; that a man of his talents respectability &c. could be of infinite service in settling matters between the two nations, & sounding his disposition to that effect.[1]

At approximately the same time, John Trumbull, the artist, son of the war governor of Connecticut who long had been an intimate of Washington's, wrote from London in such a way as to neutralize any pacific utterance by Barlow or Lafayette or any intriguing manoeuvre of Talleyrand. A single sentence will convey the letter's tone. "I certainly do not exaggerate when I say that Europe is rotten to the Heart—and that, in Europe, America has not one friend, on whose support she can rely." This long political epistle expressed some fear that France might take Louisiana and menace the United States with fifteen million Jacobins.[2]

In this last year of Washington's life, only two letters from Lafayette to Washington have been preserved. They were dated April 19 and May 9. The former deplored the acts of tyranny and brigandage which had disgusted all mankind with the failure of the armies to uphold the ideals of the Revolution. Only a return to principles of freedom, and even that with difficulty, could reconcile humanity to the new order. And yet popular institutions and equality before the law offered advantages so superior to the aristocracies now being overthrown; the counsels of the kings and emperors, Pitt alone excepted, were so absurd; the leaders of the counter-revolution were so mad; the French army was so substantial in numbers, so well disciplined and courageous, that to Lafayette it seemed the next campaign would surely be favorable to France provided she returned to the principles of freedom and justice on which the Revolution was originally based.[3]

The concluding letter in the series bore affectionate testimony to Washington's influence upon Lafayette's whole career. The inspiration of Washington and of the principles of American liberty had been with him especially in the years when to some extent he directed the French Revolution. Lafayette specifically affirmed this point and it undoubtedly was true. It was only when the Revolution had swept far beyond these principles that Lafayette sought refuge elsewhere and found instead a prison. From 1787 to 1792, the French Revolution had been something of which Washington could heartily approve. Even in its later stages his friendship for it had cooled but slowly. And it was only when it ran amok that his patriotism as an American drove him into opposition. The affectionate words of Lafayette are unimpeachable testimony that Washington did influence not only Lafayette himself but the French Revolution as a movement:

> I have served in Europe the cause and the friends of liberty; penetrated by your lessons, my dear General, and those of your friends, I have proclaimed with boldness and not without public approval sustained during three years, on the great and stormy theatre of the French Revolution, those principles for which you have fought so gloriously and have guided us so fortunately.

The French Revolution as Lafayette conceived it and approved it was, like that of Washington, a bourgeois revolution. It became, of course, something altogether different. As it moved farther and farther to the left, as moderns would express it, it was divorced more and more completely from Lafayette's and Washington's ideals. That Washington retained for the Revolution some spark, at least, of his original good will speaks volumes for his openness of mind.

Continuing his theme, Lafayette admitted the timeliness of the caution by Washington and other friends against coming to the United States in the midst of the existing crisis. It would be unwise, he admitted, and yet there was a strong temptation to do his utmost in the cause of Franco-American good will. He was still convinced of the Directory's desire for peace with the United States. The conviction was born not of faith in the Directory, but of common sense and the undoubted will of the French people. "I hope, then, that a good understanding is to prevail between the republics."

England, the old enemy, had been expending enormous sums for corrupting newly liberated France. "It is the old method of Machiavellianism. How completely it runs counter to the noble doctrine of liberty! Who knows it better than you, my dear General? and, I have the right to add, who knows it better than I?" [4]

Lafayette had better communicate these views from a safe distance. His presence in America would be most disturbing. Washington sealed his verdict on the case on October 26, 1799, in one of his last comments on the French Revolution or anything thereto related. He was writing to William Vans Murray, successor to the victims of the XYZ Affair, whose appointment was, on the one hand, an olive-branch to France, and on the other a bombshell to Alexander Hamilton and the coterie of Federalists who thought they could ignore John Adams on vital issues of Administration policy. To Murray, then, as Washington expressed his views,

> I most devoutly wish, that the cogent, indeed unanswerable arguments you urged to dissuade our friend, from visiting the United States in the present crisis of our Affairs may have prevailed. The measure would be injudicious in *every* point of view (so says my judgment) in which it can be placed; Embarrassing to himself; Embarrassing to his friends, and possibly embarrassing to the Government in the result. His final decision however must have been made 'ere this, I shall add no more on this head, nor indeed, for the reasons already assigned, on any other subject.[5]

A decision to send three commissioners to France in a definitive peace move called forth from Washington possibly his last recorded utterance on the French Revolution and its consequences to America. "I have, for some time past," he wrote the Secretary of War,

> viewed the political concerns of the United States with an anxious, and painful eye. They appear to me, to be moving by hasty strides to some awful crisis; but in what they will result, that Being, who sees, foresees, and directs all things, alone can tell. The Vessel is afloat, or very nearly so, and considering myself as a Passenger only, I shall trust to the Mariners whose duty it is to watch, to steer into a safe Port.[6]

In the preceding pages, George Washington has spoken for himself. At the risk of burdening the reader, quotations have been amassed from numerous communications both to and from Washington. Among the various items cited, Washington's opinions are probably most completely summarized in the preliminary instructions to Pickering and the final instructions to the ministers, Monroe and more especially Pinckney, just at the period when the rift between the French Directory and the United States was widening into war. These instructions, while they upheld the national dignity with much strength and firmness, emphasized nevertheless the essential friendliness of the United States and of George Washington personally to the French Revolution.

Our study has covered a period of almost thirteen years of intense Revolutionary activity. It would have been incredible had Washington's reaction throughout the period been uniform and undeviating. Actually, as we have seen, it underwent three phases—enthusiasm, acceptance, and increasing opposition. Throughout each of them, the prevailing mood was steady. At no time was Washington hysterical. The "coolness" which Morris so admired not often left him. To few other men was so complete a vision of the Revolution tendered. He saw it virtually whole. Much of it he inevitably admired; some of it with equal inevitability he disliked. Yet never till the Revolution threatened the dignity and independence of his native land did Washington indulge in criticism. Even then he was not captious.

A study of Washington's reaction to the French Revolution leaves one with increased appreciation of his intelligence, his tolerance, his faith. Also from it he emerges as one of the great students and observers of the Revolution. Abundant information acted upon a judicial temperament to create a faithful picture. Distance gave perspective. Few Frenchmen could have understood their Revolution with such completeness. After all the lapse of years, Washington's observations carry weight. In the French Revolution he beheld the fulfillment and at the same time the negation of his own career. Such dualism could not leave him cold.

From the opening of his active life on the frontiers of Virginia to its termination as Lieutenant-General and Commander-in-Chief of the armies of the United States, France and her affairs were a vital factor in Washington's life. Her Revolution coincided with the apex of his own career, and the disheartening Directory coincided with his final burst of patriotic effort. Assuredly the French Revolution was a vital element in Washington's experience.

EPILOGUE

The preceding pages represent to the best of his ability the author's concept of the French Revolution in its impact upon Washington. Perhaps its impact on the author, too, is more or less unconsciously revealed. Frankly he looks upon Washington as the first and greatest of Americans. But there were eminent contemporaries who could not see wholly eye to eye with Washington, the foremost being Jefferson, and in the lapse of time since 1799, it is possible to recognize their claims to ability and patriotism even where their views diverged.

In the emergence of a two party system, foreign policy represented the major cleavage between Federalists and Anti-Federalists. For Washington to guide diplomacy along a path conciliatory to England and infuriating to the French may have been the ultimate in wisdom; but it is scarcely fair to lavish praise upon the exceedingly unneutral Morris at the expense of the equally unneutral Monroe, merely because Morris accepted neutrality as a policy that favored his beloved England, while Monroe opposed neutrality as essentially a threat to his beloved France. Between such diametrical positions friction was inevitable. One may agree that the will of Washington must and should prevail, without discounting the loyalty of Monroe or that of the average citizen, who almost certainly favored France.

Similarly one may grant the brilliance of Gouverneur Morris, which nearly everyone has done both then and since, while marveling that Washington retained him at his post so long in obvious defiance of the will of France, for Morris made no concealment of his dislike for the French Revolution and its successive governments, and made scarcely any pretense of obeying Washington's strict admonitions to avoid offense.

A minor point in general history, but a major in personal relations, was the antagonism which Thomas Paine came to feel toward Washington. A mere chronology reveals that he was in a French prison as long as Gouverneur Morris had power to keep him there and that his release was prompt when Monroe advanced the valid argument that Paine was unquestionably an American citizen. Morris displayed pure spite in accusing Paine of amusing himself with a pamphlet attacking Jesus Christ. That was sheer fabrication. Nor was Morris other than spiteful and vindictive in his hope that Citizen Genêt would be returned to France and the awaiting guillotine.

It will be recalled that Paine expected no release while Robespierre remained in power. He even blamed his detention on Robespierre's wish to please George Washington. That Paine was wrong in this has been demonstrated by his very sympathetic biographer and editor, Moncure Daniel Conway, who shows that while Washington did nothing for the prisoner, he was not, at any rate, responsible for his incarceration. But while Paine was mistaken in his curious linking of Robespierre and Washington, he was right as to the strange community of interest between Gouverneur Morris and the French Committee of Public Safety, a most astounding partnership. In angry phrasing, which imprisonment had not deprived of eloquence, Paine wrote Monroe as follows:

> However discordant the late American Minister Gouverneur Morris and the late French Committee of Public Safety were, it suited the pur-

pose of both that I should be continued in arrestation. The former wished to prevent my return to America that I should not expose his misconduct; and the latter, lest I should publish to the world the history of its wickedness. Whilst that Minister and the Committee continued I had no expectation of liberty. I speak here of the Committee of which Robespierre was a member.[1]

Washington was inconsiderate, too, in overriding the just claims of William Short in favor of Gouverneur Morris, an extremist. And his anger at Monroe during his French mission and particularly in its aftermath, while perfectly intelligible, does not arouse in a citizen of today any marked enthusiasm. In his special function of conciliating France, Monroe was brilliantly successful. He served his country, and incidentally the over-all policy of Washington, most helpfully, and a modern must regret the enmity which followed, however unavoidable it was.

If these asperities are not exactly pleasing, they are counterbalanced by the vast patience which Washington displayed over a protracted season toward the unreasonable demands of the self-centered and imperceptive wife of Lafayette. This friendship for the Marquis, the richest that Washington experienced, exacted heavy toll, which Washington paid without demur. In prosperity he had been the perfect friend; in adversity there was no deviation.

When all is said and the balance totted, there remains a wise and prudent record. The backwash of the mightiest of Revolutions could not leave America untouched. With Washington at the tiller, the ship of state held its course amid tempestuous seas.

BIOGRAPHICAL
APPENDIX

Numerous references to Frenchmen and Americans of the Revolutionary period are of course inevitable in a work such as this. And inasmuch as many of these personages may not be well known to the average reader, it has seemed advisable to place them historically, in a few cases by footnotes, but for several of them in an appendix. The very scholarly and complete *La Grande Encyclopédie* has been an unfailing source of information concerning these notables. Frequently it is followed *calamo currente*, but not in direct quotation.

These brief biographical sketches are arranged alphabetically by the names most frequently used in the text.

Charles Philippe, Comte d'Artois, Monsieur, and King of France, was born at Versailles, October 9, 1757, and died at Goritz, Austria, November 6, 1836. A charming child, he was badly educated and early spoiled. He never served but helped to ruin the monarchy. He had no military interests, but was present for eight days in a war with Spain in August 1782, where his chief contribution was to give indigestion to certain officer captives. His private life included mistresses from the various social classes. An accusation of intimacy with his sister-in-law, Marie-Antoinette, is not believed. He had one rather harmless duel with a kinsman, the Duc de Bourbon, over his familiarity with the latter's wife.

A leader of the gilded youth, Charles' enormous expenditures were encouraged by Calonne, even to a debt of fifty-six million livres which was paid by the State. His whole experience led him to defend arbitrary government and privilege. He was even more an extremist than Louis XVIII, his brother.

In 1789, as a leader in the Second Estate, the Count opposed doubling the membership of the Third. Together with the Queen he was the center of counter-revolution with its disastrous consequences, among the earliest of which were the Oath of the Tennis Court and the storming of the Bastille. Becoming apprehensive for his personal safety, he emigrated with his family to Turin on July 17, 1789. His self-appointed task thenceforth was to arouse the European sovereigns against his native land.

In 1791, he had at Mantua a celebrated interview with the Emperor Leopold II, to urge Imperial intervention in French affairs. Shortly afterward he joined the Comte de Provence in Belgium, where the two brothers arrogated unto themselves the right to speak for the Government, Louis XVI being a captive.

Artois provoked the Declaration of Pillnitz, August 27, 1791, which really precipitated the war between Revolutionary France and monarchical Europe. Both he and Monsieur disobeyed the King's order to return to France, going instead to Italy. His income now was cut off by law. Next he betook himself to the Duke of Brunswick's army and its inglorious defeat.

After the death of Louis XVI, Artois went to Russia, where Catherine II welcomed him ironically as a conquering hero and gave him a diamond encrusted sword. This he never used, but later sold. He intrigued vainly in 1793–94; and after the Quiberon debâcle in July 1795, a British admiral escorted him toward Brittany, but the "Lieutenant General of the Kingdom" stopped short of personal danger. His criminal incompetence was in no small degree responsible for the failure of the Royalist movement in the Vendée.

Upon the death of Louis XVII at The Temple, June 8, 1795, Artois became Monsieur, but resided at London on a British pension of 24,000 livres sterling. Next he went to Edinburgh, where he lived for some time at Holyrood Palace. In 1799, he thought to quit England for Condé's army, but when the tides of battle were adverse he returned to London. In 1800, he interceded with Louis XVIII on behalf of the Duc d'Orleans and his younger brothers. His subsequent career could be of no interest to Washington, who had died in 1799.

Antoine Pierre Joseph Marie BARNAVE was born at Grenoble, October 22, 1761. As a Protestant he was deprived of the usual schooling, but was reared by a distinguished mother and a learned father who trained him for the law. He shared Montesquieu's belief in the division of powers, though without plagiarizing from that eminent authority. His *Esprit des édits Enregistrés militairement à Grenoble le 20 mai 1788* enjoyed great popularity. He was active in local events preceding the summons of the States General, to which he was a delegate. He was one of the conciliating commissioners named by the Third Estate and edited its first address to the King. His feelings in 1789 were strongly favorable to the Revolution. More democratic than many, he nevertheless opposed republican ideas. This was the original position of the Jacobin Club, whose first manifesto he edited and of which he was a director until 1791.

The murders attending the fall of the Bastille disgusted Barnave, whereas his spontaneous oratory won him a hearing on all constitutional questions. In August 1790, he won acclaim by a duel. But his apogee was the debate with Mirabeau, May 16–23, on the law of war and peace.

The King's flight to Varennes taught him to abhor the Revolution, which he believed had gone too far. Whether he furthered the intrigues of the counter-revolution is in some doubt. He was suspected of transmitting dangerous information to the King. On the discovery of compromising documents, he was imprisoned first at Grenoble, later at the Conciergerie in Paris. Tried on November 28, 1793, he was executed on the following day —a brilliant victim of dangerous cross currents.

Louis Charles Auguste Le Tonnelier, Baron de Preuilly, called Baron de BRETEUIL, was born at the Château d'Azay-le-Feron, March 7, 1730, and died at Paris, November 2, 1807. He came from a judicial family with some political influence. After a tour of military duty he entered the diplomatic service, where his penetration, audacity, and activity early won him recognition and important posts. He sought to stem the Revolution. When Calonne proposed in 1787 some concessions to the Third Estate, Breteuil was bitterly opposed. He lost his position as minister but continued to live at Versailles, where he was active in the feudal and absolutist coterie surrounding Marie-Antoinette. After the Oath of the Tennis Court, he was commissioned June 28, 1789, to prepare a *coup d'état* which might stop the onrushing Revolution. When Necker was dismissed, Breteuil was briefly his successor. The Parisians countered by storming the Bastille. Breteuil then emigrated to Switzerland and later to the absolutist courts, where he served as secret agent for Louis XVI. Failing to agree with Calonne and the Princes, he found his powers revoked. For a time in and after 1792 Breteuil's movements are not recorded. He lived at Hamburg until 1802, when he returned to France. He played no part under the Consulate or the Empire.

Jacques Pierre BRISSOT, who later added the name de Warville, from some lands of his father, was born at Chartres, January 15, 1754, and guillotined at Paris, October 31, 1793. Following some minor writings, toward 1778 he composed a major work admired in manuscript by Voltaire and published in 1781. For a time he followed literary pursuits in London, but on his return to Paris in 1784, he was sent to the Bastille for a brochure, entitled *le Diable dans un bénitier,* deemed seditious. He was liberated after four months through the efforts of his wife, who was concerned with the education of Mlle de Chartres and enjoyed the patronage of the House of Orleans. The next year he became Lieutenant-General of the Chancellerie of the Duke, a sinecure with a small income. Broad human sympathies won him in 1790 and 1791 the presidency of the *Société des Amis du noirs.*

By Americans he is best remembered for the *Examen du voyage du marquis de Chastellux,* 1786, and more especially for *de la France et des États-Unis,* 1787. In 1788, he traveled in Holland and America, where he would have remained had not the Revolution beckoned. He was its earliest journalist, launching on April 1, 1789, before the States General had assembled, a bold prospectus of the *Patriote français.* Though immediately suppressed, it became a daily on July 28 of that year and continued till June 2, 1793, as the organ of the Girondists. Brissot opposed all counter-revolution. He angered the Court after the flight to Varennes, and petitioned for a republic on the occasion of the festival at the Champ de Mars.

At the end of 1792 and the beginning of 1793, Brissot's counsel to the Jacobins and to the Assembly advising an offensive war against monarchical Europe led to a breach with Robespierre. Absorbed in diplomacy, he no longer appeared at the Jacobin Club, where Robespierre sapped his popularity. A notable speech of July 26, 1792, opposing the dethronement of Louis XVI, cost him popularity in Paris.

As a deputy to the National Convention, he actively promoted war abroad and decentralization of power at home. What did the King matter? Brissot's concern was to oppose Robespierre, Danton, and dictatorship. He voted for the King's death, not to take place, however, until the Constitution should have been ratified. In a little book published in March 1793, he dared to advocate the closing of the Jacobin Club. The Club struck back. Camille Desmoulins smeared his honor. His arrest was decreed June 2, 1793. He fled, was seized at Moulins, returned to Paris, and tried with his friends before the Revolutionary Tribunal. His defense is said to have been eloquent, but was garbled in the official report. Sentenced to death, he refused the consolation of a priest, preferring to die a *philosophe.* His widow later was pensioned and a son inherited his staunch republican principles.

Karl Wilhelm Ferdinand, reigning Duke of BRUNSWICK after 1780, was born October 9, 1735, and died at Ottensen, near Altona, November 10, 1806. He was the eldest son of Duke Charles (1713–80). He devoted himself early to a military career, and made a good record in the Seven Years' War under the name of Prince Héritrier. As General of Infantry in the

Prussian Army, he received in 1792 command of the Austro-Prussian forces levied to terminate the French Revolution. On July 25, 1792, he published the celebrated Coblentz Manifesto, seized Longwy and Verdun, but was stopped at Valmy. In 1793, he recaptured Mainz, and with General Würmser won the battle of Pirmasens. In 1806 he was placed once more in command of Prussian forces. He lost both eyes at the battle of Auerstädt on October 14 and was expelled from Brunswick. Before death, he learned that Napoleon was about to declare, "The House of Brunswick has ceased to reign."

Jean Baptiste CARRIER was possibly the most odious man the Revolution spawned. He was born at Yolet in 1756 and was guillotined at Paris, November 16, 1794. From the beginning of the Revolution, he was an extremist, voting death for the King, and advocating the creation of the Revolutionary Tribunal, the arrest of the Duc d'Orleans, the expulsion of all former nobles from the army, and other extreme measures, particularly against the Girondists and Federalists. He impressed the Cordeliers and Jacobins as a man of action. Sent to Nantes in October 1793 to counteract the Vendéen insurrection, he employed sadistic terror, even drowning in the Loire numerous refractory priests. A horrible legend grew about him, fully justified by his butcheries. He was shortly recalled by Robespierre and the Committee of Public Safety, after which he pursued Robespierre with "Death to the Tyrant." His arrest was decreed on November 11, 1794, with only two opposed, and he was incarcerated with some ninety-four Nantes terrorists who rejoiced that he would share their fate.

Charles Eugene Gabriel, Marquis de CASTRIES, was born in 1727 and died January 11, 1801. Following a distinguished military career in the Low Countries and a command in Corsica, he served throughout the Seven Years' War. He became a Marshal of France on June 13, 1783. From 1780 to 1787, he was Minister of Marine. Following a governorship of Flanders and Hainaut, he emigrated in 1790, first to Lausanne, then to Germany. In 1792, he commanded part of the Royalist army in Champagne, signed the Declaration of Louis XVIII on January 23, 1793, and, with the Comte de Saint-Priest, was co-director of Louis' cabinet at Blankenburg. A mausoleum for him was erected at Brunswick.

Marie Jean Antoine Nicolas Caritat, Marquis de CONDORCET, was born September 17, 1743, at Ribemont in Picardy, and died at Bourg-la-Reine, March 29, 1794. He was a scholar, man of letters, philosopher, economist, and politician. Of precocious intellect, at sixteen it was predicted by eminent examiners that he would be a member of the Academy of Sciences. This he became a decade later. His first published work, an *Essai sur le calcul*, 1765, was deemed remarkable, though his noble kinsmen despised his devotion to scholarship. His entry to the French Academy came in 1782. Among his almost innumerable writings, *De l'Influence de la révolution d'Amérique sur l'Europe* is of particular interest to Americans.

Friendship with Turgot and Voltaire influenced Condorcet's natural bent toward liberalism, and his voluminous writings included lives of both. His assistance to Turgot's reforms begat powerful enmities. On Turgot's dismissal as Minister of Finance, he resigned his post, but his resignation was declined until 1791. At forty-four he contracted a happy marriage. A daughter was born, and his contentment was at its peak; but politics were soon to intervene. The philosopher, on most issues a Girondist, participated in the Revolution, but as a moderating influence. Already he was recorded as a foe of slavery and a promoter of civil rights for Protestants. After the King's flight to Varennes, he, like Brissot de Warville, advocated a republic. He opposed the declaration of war in 1792, and strove to reconcile the Gironde and the Mountain—an impossible feat. On the downfall of the Girondists he was proscribed, but for several months was unmolested. Finally, he was obliged to flee. After brief wanderings in disguise, followed by imprisonment, this towering genius ended his own life by poison, thereby cheating the otherwise inevitable guillotine.

George Jacques DANTON was born at Arcis-sur-Aube, October 28, 1759, and was guillotined at Paris, April 5, 1794. He belonged to the respectable middle class. To his mother he owed a vigorous constitution, physical and moral. He resented discipline. Early intellectual interests were directed to antiquity, and he became widely read. While convalescing from an illness he is said to have read the entire *Encyclopédie*. Law became his profession, and in it he won distinguished clients and an ample income. Marriage, too, was fortunate.

His early associates believed in moderate revolution from above. By 1787, he perceived the oncoming avalanche. His sympathies were aroused. After October 8, 1791, he devoted his whole energy to a complete overthrow of the social order. The *ancien régime* must be destroyed at home and abroad. A founder of the Cordeliers Club, he was active in all the chief developments of the Revolution. The King's flight to Varennes intensified his zeal. Lafayette sought to capture him, but he fled to England briefly. On September 30, 1791, he was granted amnesty. To follow him from then until the guillotine devoured him is to summarize the Revolution. More, perhaps, than any other man, he overthrew the King, armed the capital for defense, and girded France to meet the invading monarchies. Blotting his fair fame at this time was his failure or refusal to avert the September massacres of 1792, coinciding with the proclamation of the Republic on September 21. He mounted the scaffold not as a spotless lamb, we may regret, but assuredly as a lion among men.

Lucie Simplice Camille Benoist DESMOULINS, journalist and politician, friend of Danton and Robespierre, was an influential member of the Cordeliers Club and distinctly in the avant-garde of the Revolution from 1789 to 1792. He was born at Guise, March 2, 1760, of an influential family, and was a classmate of Robespierre in the College Louis le Grand. By 1784, he was a republican and passionately interested in antiquity. He was unsuccessful at the bar, and the two pamphlets he wrote in the incipient stages of the Revolution were of slight impact. But in 1789, during the excitement over Necker's dismissal, his power as an orator brought him to the fore. To an assembly of six thousand he cried, "To arms! to arms! Let us all wear green cockades, color of hope." The movement thus incited led to the fall of the Bastille. Three or four days later he called for a republic. The first issue of his celebrated newspaper, *les Révolutions de France et de Brabant,* appeared on November 28 and continued through eighty-six numbers till the end of July 1791. It remains as one of the most remarkable in the literature of French politics. In April 1792, together with Fréron, he started *la Tribune des patriotes,* which achieved only four numbers. He attacked Brissot de Warville, violently and unjustly, and lived to regret an attack upon the more moderate Girondists. He was later secretary to Danton and a deputy of Paris to the National Convention, where he sat on the left with the Mountain. After 1792, however, his influence declined. In the growing rivalry between Robespierre and Danton, he favored the latter. This terminated his career, for at the command of Robespierre, he was arrested on March 31, 1794, and executed six days later with Danton and other Dantonists. Eight days later his wife suffered the same fate.

Pierre Roger DUCOS was born at Montfort, France, July 23, 1747. He was an attorney at Dax, and President of the Criminal Court at Landes. By this department he was elected to the National Convention. He voted death for Louis XVI. As a member of the Council of the Ancients, he supported all republican measures. He presided over the Assembly on the eighteenth of Fructidor. In the year V of the Republic, he served once more in his former capacity at Landes. After 30 Prairial in the year VII, he replaced Merlin as one of the Five Directors. He countenanced the *coup d'état* of 18 Brumaire, and was provisionally one of the Three Consuls. He entered the Senate on December 13, 1799, and in 1808 was made a Count of the Empire. Peer of France in the One Hundred Days of Napoleon's return, he was proscribed as a regicide in 1816 and fled to Ulm, where his death on March 16 was due to a carriage accident.

Charles François DUMOURIEZ was born at Cambrai, January 25, 1739, and died at Turville Park, England, March 14, 1823. He it was who pushed Louis XVI into the European War. As *La Grande Encyclopédie* remarks,

"What mattered to Dumouriez the dangers of this war provided his ambition had free play?" With many previous honors to his credit, his real importance lay in the early stages of the great wars of the French Revolution. He won crucial battles at Valmy and Jemappes but was defeated at Neerwinden. He was an unprincipled opportunist in very stormy times, and his career is a study in duplicity. He betrayed his wife, his king, his country. But as Thiers once said, "If he abandoned us, he has saved us." John Quincy Adams, whose acquaintance with Dumouriez was only literary, remarked of his *Mémoires,* "If you look through his book for a moral principle as the guide to his actions, you will find abundant proof that he had none," a fact which was glaringly evident from Dumouriez's pretended admiration for Lafayette, Roland and others, coupled with his endeavor on almost every page to smear them. (C.F. Adams, ed., *Memoirs of John Quincy Adams,* I, 33.)

Adrien Jean François DuPort was born at Paris, February 5, 1759, and died at Appenzell, Switzerland, August 15, 1798. He was a staunch opponent of ministerial despotism and, foreseeing the Revolution, was hospitable to several leftist leaders. He was a deputy of the nobility of Paris to the States General and was one of forty-six nobles who joined the Third Estate, where he sat on the extreme left benches with Barnave and Lameth. His concern with the unfolding Revolution was largely as a jurist. He was one of three commissioned to receive the King's explanations on his return from Varennes. Thenceforth, he became more friendly to the monarchy, anticipating as he did many later developments of the Revolution. He opposed the death penalty as uncivilized, with the state itself setting the example of murder. On August 10, 1792, he fled from Paris and was arrested near Nemours. Despite the efforts of Marat, he was liberated at Melun, September 17, 1792, by the humane and able efforts of Danton. His subsequent career was undistinguished.

Elbridge Gerry was born July 17, 1744, and died November 23, 1814. His father was an English sea captain who had settled at Marblehead and married the daughter of an old Massachusetts family. He graduated from Harvard in 1762, and for some years was in business with his father. In 1772, he came under the influence of Samuel Adams, was a member of the Committee of Correspondence and active in the moves preliminary to Lexington and Concord. In 1776, he went with John Adams as a delegate to the Second Continental Congress, where he rendered useful service as a member of the Treasury Board.

As a true New Englander he felt a strong interest in the fisheries. He disliked standing armies and militarism, and shared Jefferson's antipathy to the Order of the Cincinnati. Politically, he was antagonistic to one of his fellow signers of the Declaration of Independence, John Hancock. He declined to attend the Annapolis Convention of 1786, but was elected to

Congress in 1789. At times he seemed a Federalist, but basically he was a Democrat. On June 20, 1797, he was appointed along with Marshall and Pinckney to compose affairs with France. In what is generally known as the XYZ Affair, he was sufficiently the dupe of Talleyrand to remain in France after the departure of his colleagues, an unwise but not ignoble decision. His later career included election in 1810 as Governor of Massachusetts, and the Vice-Presidency of the United States in 1813 under James Madison. His name is immortalized in the political device called gerrymandering, which was instituted in his term as governor.

Alexandre Théodore Victor, Comte de LAMETH, was born at Paris, October 20, 1760, and died there on March 19, 1829. He served in America under Rochambeau, was a colonel in 1789, and was elected by the nobility of Péronne to the States General, where he was ardent for the new ideas and played a considerable role in the Constitutional Assembly. He was a member of important committees—constitution, colonies, finance, and military. In this latter capacity, he drafted a distinguished report on promotion in the army. With Barnave and Adrien DuPort, he was a triumvir to whom thirty to forty leftist members of the National Assembly looked for guidance. The triumvirate was suspicious of Mirabeau's relations with the Court and opposed his moderation. On February 28, 1791, Lameth disconcerted Mirabeau by a vigorous attack. Camille Desmoulins called it the most effective speech he ever heard. To find a parallel, said Desmoulins, one would need to turn to Cicero and Catiline. In an orator of, for the most part, secondary talent, hate created here the impetus. But after Louis' flight to Varennes, Lameth moderated his antagonism to the Court.

Named *maréchal de camp* when war with Austria was declared, he joined fortunes with Lafayette, was a subject of accusation behind the lines, and on August 15, 1792, resorted to flight. Following a harsh imprisonment in Austria, he was exchanged. After some years in Hamburg and England he returned to France when Napoleon was Consul. Thereafter, shifting between Napoleon and the Bourbons, he prospered. From 1820 to 1824, and again in 1827, he sat in the Chamber of Deputies as an opposition Liberal. His poorly written *Histoire de l'Assemblée constituante* is important largely because of its authoritativeness.

Chrétien Guillaume de Lamoignon de MALESHERBES was born at Paris, December 21, 1721, and executed there April 22, 1794. Son of Chancellor Guillaume de Lamoignon, he was destined for the law, first as counsellor to the Parliament, then as successor to his father as President of the Court of Aides. Simultaneously he was named Director of the Library, where he protected the *philosophes* and men of letters and personally facilitated publication of the *Encyclopédie*. On February 18, 1771, he addressed to the King his famous remonstrances on the imposition of new taxes and in opposition to creation of the so-called Parlément Maupeou. For this he was banished from Paris. When Louis recalled the parliaments, he named Malesherbes Minister of the Royal House and of Paris—a peculiarly thankless assignment. While in office, Malesherbes renounced all use of *lettres de cachet* but could not secure their formal abolition. In vain he opposed the prodigalities of the courtiers. Finding opposition fruitless, he resigned in advance of Turgot.

For some years he traveled in France, Holland, and Switzerland. In 1785, he published a *Mémoire sur le mariage des protestants,* and did much to secure their civil rights. Minister of State, 1787, he resigned the following year. He emigrated during the Revolution, but with the mounting gravity of events, he returned to his post in July 1792, because "the King might have need of him." On December 13, the Convention permitted him to act as counsel to the King, whom he served until the end. Eight months later he himself was arrested as a suspect and was condemned to death by the Revolutionary Tribunal. His memory still is honored.

Jean Paul MARAT was born at Boudry, Switzerland, May 24, 1743, and was assassinated at Paris, July 14, 1793. He studied numerous languages, intended to follow his father as a painter, but became instead a physician, with a degree from St. Andrews, Scotland, June 30, 1775. His first book, *A Philosophical Essay on Man,* had appeared two years previously and had been ridiculed by Voltaire. His early practice was as physician to the body guard of the Comte d'Artois. Also he specialized in pulmonary troubles. His scientific interests led to publications on fire, electricity, light, and optics. Against Newton he proclaimed that there are but three primary colors, yellow, blue, and red.

Embracing the new ideas, Marat devoted himself to journalism from 1789. His best known publication was *l'Ami du peuple ou le Publiciste parisien.* He himself chose to be called *l'Ami du peuple.* Publication was interrupted from time to time by arrests and by brief exiles in London. He was a member of the Cordeliers and an antagonist of Lafayette. Events attending the arrest of Louis XVI at Varennes directed his anger toward the Girondist party. He found time, besides, to flay in print illustrious members of the French Academy. He, too, found accusers in the National Assembly. When his printing press was seized, he turned to research.

Danton introduced him to the administration of the Commune of Paris. He became a deputy from Paris to the Convention, where he singled out for attack Roland, Dumouriez and Pétion. In October 1792, warming to the attack on the Girondists and Roland in particular, he declared that to insure tranquillity 270,000 more heads should fall. He was correctly denounced as a monster, but the Convention pressed no charges. He insisted that voting for the execution of the King should be by name. The treason of Dumouriez appeared to justify some of his apprehensions. The Girondists regarded him as the chief architect of their misfortunes. While in his bath on Bastille Day, 1793, he was assassinated by the heroine Charlotte

Corday. He replaced Mirabeau in the Panthéon, but like Mirabeau he found it not a permanent haven.

As a physician he is still regarded as a genius. As a monster he has been the object of psychiatric study.

John MARSHALL was born September 14, 1755, and died July 6, 1835. His youth was spent on the Virginia frontier in what is now Fauquier County. His father's family was capable but not especially distinguished. His mother's family, through the Randolphs, was part of the Virginia aristocracy; and through the Keiths, was equally prominent in Scotland. As a close companion of his father and the eldest of fifteen children, he developed early a sense of responsibility. Books were few but choice. Political discussion preceding the American Revolution awakened his eager interest. He fought at Brandywine, Germantown, and Monmouth, shared the rigors of Valley Forge, and aided in the capture of Stony Point. He studied law only briefly under the celebrated George Wythe at the College of William and Mary. Marriage to Mary Ambler in 1783 was followed by a lucrative law practice.

Politically, Marshall disliked the loose federalism under the Articles of Confederation, and was ripe to aid adoption by Virginia of the Constitution. In his state he was a leading upholder of the measures of Washington and Hamilton, and a vigorous defender of Jay's Treaty. In 1798, he declined a position as Associate Justice of the Supreme Court, but in 1801 did accept the post of Chief Justice, having meanwhile served, at John Adams' insistence, as Secretary of State following the dismissal of Timothy Pickering. In 1797 he was a member of the three-man mission to France that resulted in the XYZ Affair. He was also a biographer of Washington. His great imprint upon his country, for like Washington he was always first an American and only secondly a Virginian, came in his chief justiceship, from 1801 until his death.

Gabriel Honoré de Riqueti, Comte de MIRABEAU, was born at Bignon, France, March 9, 1749, and died at Paris, April 2, 1791. The foremost orator of the French Revolution, he was possibly its most powerful intellect. His earliest years were precocious. At sixteen, he wrote a memorable comparison between the Prince of Condé and Scipio Africanus. Partly because of parental discord, and also because of personal incompatibility, he early incurred his father's displeasure. This followed him through a youth of rare distinction, military, literary, even athletic, which alternated between phenomenal success and condign punishment. For some years he was forbidden to use the family name. His love life developed early and was subject to terrific stress. He was even sentenced to death for an alleged rape at the instigation of an angry husband—a sentence which was ultimately rescinded. Happy years were passed with a tranquil Dutch woman. His only son in the marriage bed died early.

321

From the outbreak of the Revolution, Mirabeau was active in the Assembly of the Notables and in the National Assembly. He was the complete antithesis of Lafayette. Their mutual and intense antagonism injured the monarchy, which never really trusted either man, though each in his very different way was loyal to the throne. Indeed, one of Mirabeau's best known phrases, written to his uncle, the Bailli, on October 25, 1789, runs as follows: "I have always thought, like you, my dear Uncle, and now much more than ever, that royalty is the sole anchor of safety which can preserve us from shipwreck."

Eventually, upon the royal payment of his debts, Mirabeau became a servant of the monarchy. He gave frequent advice to the King, its wisdom seldom heeded. He foresaw in extraordinary detail the later stages of the Revolution, whose horrors, had he lived, he might have modified in some degree. His death brought nationwide sorrow and he was buried in the Panthéon with majestic honors. Later, when his financial dealings with the King were revealed, his body was removed. Posterity honors him as one of the titans of mankind.

MONTMORIN de Saint Hérem was a branch of a family originating in Auvergne numbering several distinguished members. Of chief interest to Americans was Armand-Marc, Comte de Montmorin Saint Hérem, who was born in 1745 and slain at Paris, September 2, 1792. Previously ambassador at Madrid, he succeeded the Comte de Vergennes in 1787 as Minister of Foreign Affairs, a post which he held until October 1791. In 1789, he appeared to agree with Necker. He became an intermediary between the Court and Mirabeau and was inscribed as a member of the Society of the Friends of the Constitution.

He had no part in the King's flight to Varennes, but he transmitted to the legislative body the replies purportedly received by Louis XVI after he had given notice to the neighboring powers of his acceptance of the Constitution of 1791. These replies, in which the King's freedom of action was doubted, hinted of drastic projects wherein the ministers were deemed responsible. Montmorin, after a defense before the bar of the Assembly, resigned his portfolio but continued secretly as an adviser to the King in what was called not ineptly the Austrian Committee. Denounced in 1792, he was proscribed after the tenth of August. Imprisoned in the Abbaye, he was one of the many victims of the September massacres. With Jefferson and other eminent Americans his relations were invariably cordial. His death grieved many.

Timothy PICKERING (July 17, 1745–January 29, 1829), New Englander though he was, found Washington, the Virginian, rather more to his liking than his compatriot, John Adams. Member of a well-to-do family of Salem, a Harvard graduate in 1763, he had an undistinguished practice at the bar until the American Revolution somehow released his talents. In 1775, he published "An Easy Plan of Discipline for a Militia," which was superseded only by the standard manual of Steuben. Before the Revolution ended, he had endured with Washington at Valley Forge and had become successively Adjutant General and Quartermaster General.

Following the Revolution, Pickering's attitude toward Loyalists was kindly rather than vindictive. Having moved with his large family to the Wyoming Valley, he represented Luzerne County in the Constitutional Convention. After a successful mission to the Senecas, he was named in 1791, Postmaster General in the Washington Administration, later Secretary of War, and was largely responsible for the dismissal of Randolph.

As the French Revolution degenerated into violent radicalism, Pickering came to view the British navy as America's best defense against a group of madmen. He supported war with France in 1798, and for twenty years never deviated from a hostility which became so extreme as to injure him politically. Alexander Hamilton was his hero. His disloyalty to John Adams weakened the Federalist Party, and led on May 10, 1800, to his dismissal from an office in which Adams had continued him unwisely as a sort of legacy from Washington. Pickering is not a gracious figure in our history, but strength he did possess.

Charles Cotesworth PINCKNEY (February 25, 1746–August 16, 1825) was born at Charleston, South Carolina and in 1753 went to England, where his father was agent for the Colony. He studied at the Westminster School, and Christ Church College, Oxford, and on being admitted to the bar, rode one circuit for experience, later traveling extensively on the Continent. He was admitted to the bar of South Carolina in January 1770, and enjoyed an extensive practice, interrupted only by war and politics. In the American Revolution he saw active service, and rose from Captain to Brigadier General. Before this military phase of his career was ended, he had been elected to the lower house of the South Carolina legislature. A person of great charm as well as of distinction, he was appreciated by Washington. He was offered, but declined, command of the Army of the West, the Secretaryship of War and the Secretaryship of State, but in July 1796, he did accept the mission to France which terminated in the XYZ Affair. His attitude toward the Revolution had been friendly from 1789 to 1793, but cooled thereafter. In the undeclared war with France, 1798–1800, he was named commander of the United States forces south of Maryland with the rank of Major-General. He was nominated in both 1804 and 1808 for President on the Federalist ticket. He was what might be termed a States-rights Federalist, by no means an extreme position.

Louis XVIII was born at Versailles, November 17, 1755, and died at Paris, September 16, 1824. He was baptized Louis Stanislas Xavier, and received the title Comte de PROVENCE. It was not until his elder brother ascended the throne as Louis XVI in 1774 that he assumed the title

Monsieur. He was a thoroughly unpleasant character, a calumniator of Marie-Antoinette, and by his intrigues a menace to the throne. Upon the execution of his brother he was the nominal regent for his nephew, and later in his own right of succession was leader of the monarchists. With advancing years he became distastefully obese.

Maximilien François Marie Isidore de ROBESPIERRE was born at Arras, May 6, 1758, and was executed at Paris, July 28, 1794. At the age of nine he lost his mother. Sponsored by his Bishop and aided by his own precocity, he won a scholarship at the College Louis le Grand, with Desmoulins and Fréron as fellow students. Bilious, contrary, vindictive, he won no friends. Poverty isolated him. But his precocity was recognized. He became an advocate in Arras, where he particularly defended the weak and the poor. In November 1783, thanks to varied cultural interests, he was elected to membership in the Academy of Arras. At this time his ideas were a blend of monarchical, Catholic, and revolutionary. At the provincial assembly of Artois in 1788, he attacked privilege, whether noble or ecclesiastical. He was chosen to the States General by the Third Estate of his province. Mirabeau soon said of him, "He will go far, he believes what he says." His speaking power and influence grew steadily.

Henceforth Robespierre's career was the epitome of the Revolution, only a few highlights of which can be noted here. The taking of the Bastille he defended. Freedom of opinion he championed. He denied the right of the executive to name the ministers. He approved public honors for Mirabeau. He feared the National Guard as a potential military caste (how like Thomas Jefferson and the Order of the Cincinnati!). Military decorations he disliked. He embodied the spirit of proletarian and Jacobin Paris as opposed to Girondist commercialism in the provinces, his opinions shared, at least in part, by Danton. He laid a foundation for the Republic. Desmoulins hailed him as "our Aristides," and Marat called him "the Incorruptible," a title seized upon so avidly by Carlyle.

Strangely, this man linked with so much bloodshed favored on May 30, 1791, abolition of the death penalty. But after Varennes, he proposed civic crowns for all who helped arrest the King. After April 1792, with war declared, he inflamed mass spirit. He voted for the death of Louis, and attacked the Girondists unmercifully as accomplices of Pitt and the traitor, Dumouriez. In the Committee of Public Safety he was virtually a triumvir, with Couthon and Saint-Just as colleagues, to whom he consigned administrative functions while he exercised a high and vague, rather priestly control. As such he fought Hébert and his fellow atheists, overthrew the Goddess of Reason, and restored belief in the existence of God and the immortality of the soul. Danton, also, he destroyed.

Robespierre's position excited both jealousies and fears. Complicated manoeuvres sped his downfall. He was depicted, not quite truly, as tyrant

324

and dictator. Horribly wounded one day, he was guillotined the next. Yet in private life he in no way resembled the monster of legend. He killed neither vindictively nor for wealth, of which he left virtually none. It has been said of Napoleon that he was "Robespierre on horseback." As a rather friendly biographer, H. Monin, writing in *La Grande Encyclopédie*, remarks, "To him [Robespierre] have been imputed all the crimes committed by Hébert, Collot d'Herbois and others. They were men more frightful and more bloody than he whom they destroyed; they have blamed all on him."

Jean Baptiste Donatien de Vimeur, Comte de ROCHAMBEAU, was born in 1725. Though destined for the Church, he entered the army upon the death of an elder brother. He served with distinction in numerous campaigns from 1742. After the Yorktown campaign, in which, as Lieutenant General under Washington, he commanded 6,000 French troops, Rochambeau was further honored by the King and given command in Picardy. In 1788, he sat in the second Assembly of the Notables, went to Alsace, and in 1790 accepted command of the Army of the North. On December 28, 1791, Louis XVI commissioned him a Marshal of France. In the following year he advised a defensive strategy against Germany. Dumouriez disapproved and ordered him to fight. Wounded by this disregard he resigned his command and withdrew to his estates near Vendôme. The Terror sought him and imprisoned him in the Conciergerie, but released him. In 1803, he was presented to Napoleon, who awarded him a marshal's pension. He died May 10, 1807.

Philippe Henri, Marquis de SÉGUR, was born in 1724 and died at Paris on October 3, 1801. He fought in the major battles of his time, was wounded at Raucoux and lost an arm at Laufeld. He was a commander in Corsica, 1756–1757, and fought in Germany in the Seven Years' War. He commanded Franche-Comté in 1775, became Minister of War in 1780, and in 1783 received the baton of Marshal of France. He quit the War Ministry in 1787, and in 1792 was imprisoned for some months. Mme de Ségur was a lady-in-waiting to the Duchesse d'Orleans and was on cordial terms with Gouverneur Morris.

Emmanuel Joseph, Abbé (later Comte) SIEYÈS, was born at Frejus, May 3, 1748, and died at Paris, June 20, 1836. He entered Holy Orders and became Canon of Tréguier in 1775, following his bishop, M. de Lubersac, to the Cathedral of Chartres as Vicar-General. He became counsel-commissioner to the Chamber of the Clergy when the Assembly of Notables met in 1787. A man of great erudition, he advanced reform ideas in the Provincial Assembly of Orleans. In 1788 and 1789, he published his *Essai sur les privileges*, still noted for its passage asking, "What is the Third

Estate? Everything. What has it been up to the present in the political order? Nothing. What does it demand? To become something." Some 30,000 copies were distributed.

A scholar in the Church, Sieyès avoided the customary duties of his profession. He was chosen to the States General in 1789, not by his order, but by the Third Estate of Paris. An able tactician, he early achieved prominence, subscribed to the Oath of the Tennis Court, and affirmed emphatically the sovereignty of the National Assembly. He helped to found the Breton Club, precursor of the Jacobins. But the Revolution soon outdistanced him. "They wish to be free," he complained, "but know not how to be just." From 1795 on, his power was very great, being a member of the Committee of Public Safety and the Council of Five Hundred. In 1798 he was French Ambassador at Berlin. As a member of the Directory he cooperated with Napoleon in the *coup d'état* of 18 Brumaire, but contrary to his expectation, Napoleon, not he, became First Consul. He did enter the Senate and in 1809 became a Count of the Empire. During the Hundred Days he sat in the Chamber of Peers. He was proscribed as a regicide by Louis XVIII, but on the exile of Charles X, he returned from Brussells to Paris. He died in 1836, a man of talent who nevertheless missed true greatness.

Antoine-Omer TALON IV was descended from an Irish family. Of the several distinguished members of the family, he alone is of Revolutionary interest. Descended from a branch settled in Champagne, he was born January 20, 1760, at Paris. Attorney, then King's advocate at the Châtelet in 1777, he became in 1781 *conseiller aux enquêtes*. In 1789, he was advanced to Civil Lieutenant at the Châtelet. He presided over the inquiry into the Affair of October 5 and 6, and over the trial of Favras. Entered before the Assembly as a suppliant, he was accused by Desmoulins and another and was condemned. He was imprisoned during the flight of the King and emigrated to America. Returning to Tournau in the district of Seine and Marne, he served as a correspondent for the Bourbons. Again arrested in 1804, he was confined in the Ile Sainte-Marguerite. From this imprisonment he emerged in 1807 with intellect greatly enfeebled and died at Gretz, Austria, on August 18, 1811.

Jean de TERNANT was born in 1740 and died in 1816. He served in the American Revolution as inspector under Steuben, and as Lieutenant Colonel and Inspector of Troops in the South. The Marquis de Chastellux describes him as a young man of great wit and talent, with a perfect knowledge of English. As chargé d'affaires and then minister to the United States, his appointment was acceptable to Washington and Jefferson. The President received him cordially. "You and I," he said in opening the conversation, "are old friends and it is a great pleasure for myself and Mrs. Washington to see you once more with us." This in an informal meeting previous to the presentation of credentials. By October 24, 1791, two and one half months after his arrival, there was a certain coolness. While acknowledging Washington's hospitality at Mount Vernon, Ternant deplored some reserve on his part as well as that of Jefferson, a fellow guest.

Ternant, now become Citizen Ternant, was relieved of his duties on May 16, 1793. His mission was hampered by confusion and inefficiency in the French Foreign Office as well as by the complications of American policy.

NOTES

INTRODUCTION

1. Henry Vallotton, *Marie-Antoinette et Fersen,* p. 160.
2. *Ibid.,* p. 52.

CHAPTER ONE

1. Paul Leicester Ford, ed., *The Works of Thomas Jefferson,* I, 153–155.
2. It will be remembered that this lady was the first and only love of the historian Edward Gibbon.
3. A contrary opinion, that the Court was weakened by an absence of true grandeur, is advanced by the Duc de Lévis-Mirepoix in *Aventures d'une famille française,* p. 27.
4. Newenham's interest in either Washington or the French Revolution is not mentioned in the *Dictionary of National Biography.* He was, in modern terms, a moderate "liberal."
5. The lady visited Mount Vernon in 1785 and was one of the most intellectual of Washington's women friends.
6. A. Esmein, *Gouverneur Morris, un Témoin Américain de la Révolution Française,* p. 3.
7. *Mémoires, Correspondance et Manuscrits du Général Lafayette,* III, 218. The translation is my own.
8. *Ibid.,* III, 222–223.
9. *Ibid.,* III, 224–228. See also Lafayette to Jefferson, Paris, June 6, 1787, in the Jefferson Papers, Library of Congress.
10. Written by a secretary in English but signed by Rochambeau. In the Washington Papers, Library of Congress.

11. Lafayette to Washington, Paris, August 3, 1787, in *Mémoires du Lafayette*, III, 233–236.
12. Jefferson to Washington, August 14, 1787, in Jefferson Papers.
13. Washington to Lafayette, Philadelphia, August 15, 1787, in "Letters of Washington and Lafayette," *Old South Leaflets*, IV (1886), 76–100.
14. Lafayette to Washington, October 9, 1787, in *Mémoires du Lafayette*, III, 237–248.
15. Washington to Jefferson, Mount Vernon, January 1, 1788, in John C. Fitzpatrick, ed., *The Writings of George Washington*, XXIX, 350.

CHAPTER TWO

1. This monetary relief was due apparently to a fresh loan of 420 millions which Loménie de Brienne had caused Parliament to register on November 19, 1787. Charles Gomel, *Les Causes Financières de la Révolution Française*, II, x–xi, is notably hostile to Loménie de Brienne, stating that he precipitated the fall of Calonne with no real plans of his own for reform. Having procured a loan of sixty millions, with no diminution of the privileges of the upper orders, he dissolved the Notables.
2. Lafayette to Washington, Paris, January 1, 1788, in *Mémoires du Lafayette*, III, 249–252.
3. Lafayette to Washington, Paris, January 2, 1788, in *Mémoires du Lafayette*, III, 252–254.
4. Rochambeau to Washington, Paris, January 18, 1788, in Washington Papers.
5. Washington to Rochambeau, April 28, 1788, in Fitzpatrick, *Writings of Washington*, XXIX, 474.
6. Washington to Rochambeau, January 8, 1788, in Fitzpatrick, *Writings of Washington*, XXIX, 359.
7. Lafayette to Washington, Paris, February 4, 1788, in *Mémoires du Lafayette*, III, 254–257.
8. William Short to Carrington, Paris, February 4, 1788, in the William Short Papers, Library of Congress.
9. Jefferson to Jay, Paris, February 5, 1788, in Jefferson Papers.
10. Lafayette to Washington, March 18, 1788, in *Mémoires du Lafayette*, III, 257–260.
11. Jefferson to Washington, Paris, May 2, 1788, in Washington Papers.
12. *La Grande Encyclopédie*, XXIII, 1054.
13. The Keeper of the Seals, a Court functionary.
14. Lafayette to Washington, Paris, May 25, 1788, in *Mémoires du Lafayette*, III, 261–267. The translation is my own.
15. After various moves between Paris and the United States, Short spent the remainder of his ninety years in Philadelphia in the enjoyment of a great fortune tempered by the memory of numerous frustrations. His death on December 5, 1849, coincided with the anniversary of the founding of Phi Beta Kappa.
16. Lafayette to Washington, May 25, 1788, in *Mémoires du Lafayette*, III, 261–267.
17. Short to Crevecoeur (French consul at New York), Paris, July 5, 1788, in Short Papers.
18. *La Grande Encyclopédie*, XXVIII, 1002.

19. Rochambeau to Washington, June 15, 1788, in Washington Papers.
20. Washington to Lafayette, Mount Vernon, June 18, 1788, in Louis Martin Sears, *George Washington*, p. 373.
21. Washington to Jefferson, Mount Vernon, August 31, 1788, in Fitzpatrick, *Writings of Washington*, XXX, 81.
22. Jefferson to Monroe, Paris, August 9, 1788, in Jefferson Papers.
23. Jefferson to Jay, Paris, August 20, 1788, in Jefferson Papers.
24. Short to Carrington, Paris, September 6, 1788, in Short Papers.
25. Jefferson to Jay, Paris, September 24, 1788, in Jefferson Papers.
26. Jefferson to Washington, Paris, December 4, 1788, in Washington Papers.

CHAPTER THREE

1. Henry Vallotton, *Marie-Antoinette et Fersen*, p. 180. "Cousin" may have been merely a courteous expression. King and Count were, however, very distant kinsmen.
2. Jefferson to Jay, February 4, 1789, in Jefferson Papers.
3. Later he emigrated formally and continued to oppose the Revolution until the Royalists returned in 1814. His family remained prominent throughout the Nineteenth Century.
4. Jefferson to Madison, Paris, October 8, 1787, in Ford, *Works of Jefferson*, V, 356.
5. Jefferson to de Moustier, Paris, May 17, 1788, and similarly to William Carmichael, Paris, June 3, 1788, both in Ford, *Works of Jefferson*, V, 392.
6. Jefferson to Short, in Ford, *Works of Jefferson*, VI, 117.
7. Rochambeau to Washington, January 31, 1789, in Washington Papers.
8. Rochambeau to Washington, Paris, February 17, 1789, in Washington Papers.
9. *Ibid.*
10. French chargé d'affaires to the Minister of Foreign Affairs, March 10, 1792, in Archives of the State Department, Paris, *États Unis*, XXXV, 301.
11. Gouverneur Morris to Washington, February 23, 1789, in Washington Papers.
12. Rochambeau to Washington, Calais, April 3, 1789, in Washington Papers.
13. Morris to Washington, Paris, April 29, 1789, in Washington Papers.
14. Morris to Washington, Dieppe, July 31, 1789, in Washington Papers.
15. A further source of information concerning these dramatic changes was C. W. F. Dumas, a native Hollander who acted for the United States at The Hague. See Dumas to Jay, The Hague, July 20, 1789, in the Dumas Papers, Library of Congress.
16. Here Morris displayed less than his usual acumen when he blamed the Court rather than the Duc d'Orleans for the planned shortage of bread.
17. Jefferson to Jay, Paris, September 23, 1789, in Jefferson Papers.
18. Short to Jay, Paris, September 30, 1789, in U.S. Department of State, Diplomatic Despatches, France. This series of documents contains all official communications to the Department from our ministers to France during the period covered by this book which are of record. All such communications cited here, unless otherwise indicated, are drawn from this source.
19. Short Papers.
20. Short to Jay, Paris, October 9, 1789.
21. Short to Jay, Paris, October, 11, 1789, in Short Papers. The possible connection between the Duc d'Orleans and the October crisis is set forth rather

fully in Short to Jay, Paris, October 20, 1789. See also Short to Jay, October 25, 1789, much of it in cipher.

22. The material in brackets was inserted in Worthington C. Ford, ed., *The Writings of George Washington*, XI, 441–443.
23. Washington to Morris, New York, October 13, 1789, in Fitzpatrick, *Writings of Washington*, XXX, 440–445.
24. Short to Secretary of State, Paris, October 28, 1789.
25. Short to Secretary of State, Paris, November 7, 1789.
26. Short to Secretary of State, Paris, November 19, 1789.
27. Short to Secretary of State, Paris, November 30, 1789, and December 15, 1789.
28. Jefferson to Washington, December 15, 1789, in Jefferson Papers.
29. Short to Secretary of State, Paris, December 22, 1789, and December 26, 1789.

CHAPTER FOUR

1. Louis Madelin, *The French Revolution*, p. 120.
2. *Ibid.*, p. 124.
3. Ernest Lavisse, ed., *Histoire de France Contemporaine*, I, 153–154.
4. *Ibid.*, I, 162.
5. He had assumed the title Monsieur in 1774 when his brother became King.
6. La Rouërie to Washington, January 2, 1790, in Washington Papers.
7. Comte de Moustier to Washington, Paris, January 16, 1790, in Washington Papers.
8. Lafayette to Washington, Paris, January 12, 1790, in *Mémoires du Lafayette*, IV, 237–238.
9. Luzerne to Washington, London, January 17, 1790, in Washington Papers.
10. Short to Secretary of State, Paris, January 2, 1790. See also Charles Oscar Hardy, *The Negro Question in the French Revolution*.
11. Short to Secretary of State, Paris, January 6, 1790.
12. Short to Secretary of State, Paris, January 12, 1790.
13. Short to Secretary of State, Paris, January 23, 1790, and January 31, 1790.
14. Morris to Washington, Paris, January 22, 1790, in Washington Papers. Quoted also in *American State Papers, Foreign Relations*, I, 382.
15. Morris to Washington, January 24, 1790, in Washington Papers. Morris, who was a very successful man of business, in this same letter held that Necker's was an inflated reputation, and that he was "a very poor financier." *American State Papers, Foreign Relations*, I, 383.
16. Short to Secretary of State, Paris, February 10, 1790.
17. Short to Secretary of State, Paris, March 3, 1790.
18. Short to Secretary of State, Paris, March 9, 1790.
19. Short to Secretary of State, Paris, March 17, 1790.
20. Short to Secretary of State, Paris, March 25, 1790.
21. Short to Secretary of State, Paris, March 29, 1790.
22. Lafayette to Washington, Paris, March 17, 1790, in *Mémoires du Lafayette*, IV, 245–247. The translation is my own. Cynics have noted, however, that many duplicates were made, of which the key at Mt. Vernon may be one.
23. Short to Secretary of State, Paris, April 4, 1790.
24. Jefferson to Short, New York, April 6, 1790, in U.S. Department of State, Foreign Letters, Vol. CXXI. Hereafter cited as State Department, Foreign Letters.
25. Short to Jefferson, Paris, April 12, 1790.

26. Short to Jefferson, Paris, April 23, 1790.
27. Rochambeau to Washington, April 11, 1790, in Washington Papers.
28. Short to Jefferson, Paris, May 1, 1790.
29. Short to Jefferson, Paris, May 9, 1790.
30. Short to Jefferson, Paris, May 16, 1790.
31. Short to Jefferson, Paris, May 23, 1790.
32. Paine to Washington, London, May 1, 1790, in Washington Papers.
33. Paine to Washington, London, May 31, 1790, in Washington Papers.
34. De Moustier to Washington, Paris, May 11, 1790, in Washington Papers.
35. Washington to Luzerne, New York, April 29, 1790, in Fitzpatrick, *Writings of Washington*, XXXI, 40.
36. Washington to Lafayette, New York, June 3, 1790, in Fitzpatrick, *Writings of Washington*, XXXI, 44.
37. Short to Jefferson, June 3, 1790, in Short Papers.
38. Short to Jefferson, June 14, 1790, in Short Papers.
39. Short to Jefferson, Paris, June 25, 1790.
40. Short to Jefferson, Paris, June 29, 1790.
41. Short to Jefferson, July 7, 1790, in Short Papers.
42. Short to Jefferson, Paris, July 7, 1790.
43. Short to Jefferson (private), Paris, July 11, 1790, in Short Papers.
44. Short to Jefferson (private), Paris, July 14, 1790, in Short Papers.
45. Short to Jefferson (private), Paris, July 16, 1790, in Short Papers.
46. Short to Jefferson, Paris, July 22, 1790.
47. De Moustier to Washington, Paris, July 12, 1790, in Washington Papers.
48. Short to Jefferson, Paris, August 4, 1790.
49. Short to Paine, Paris, August 8, 1790, in Short Papers.
50. The Fitzpatrick edition (XXXI, 86) in obvious error substitutes "benefits" for "tempests."
51. Washington to Lafayette, New York, August 11, 1790, in Ford, *Writings of Washington*, XI, 494.
52. Short to Jefferson (private), Paris, August 15, 1790, in Short Papers.
53. Short to Jefferson, Paris, August 22, 1790.
54. Short to Jefferson, Paris, August 27, 1790.
55. Morris to Washington, London, August 30, 1790, in Washington Papers.
56. Hamilton to Washington, in Washington Papers. Answers to queries of Washington on the Nootka Sound Affair, which centered around a dispute between Great Britain and Spain regarding the ownership of the present Pacific Northwest. With war threatening, Great Britain asked permission for her troops to cross U.S. territory from Detroit to the Mississippi. After much consideration this permission was refused.
57. La Rouërie to Washington, August 20, 1790, in Washington Papers.
58. Lafayette to Washington, August 28, 1790, in *Mémoires du Lafayette*, V, 168–172. The translation is my own.
59. Short to Secretary of State, Paris, September 5, 1790. Reference was to the bloodthirsty Marat.
60. Short to Secretary of State, September 9, 1790.
61. Short to Secretary of State, Paris, October 3, 1790.
62. Short to Secretary of State, Paris, October 21, 1790.
63. Short to Secretary of State, Paris, November 6, 1790. See also Short to Secretary of State, Amsterdam, December 2, 1790.

64. Short to Secretary of State, Amsterdam, November 26, 1790.
65. Morris to Washington, Paris, November 22, 1790, in Washington Papers. Quoted also, with much more, in *American State Papers, Foreign Relations*, I, 384–385. The sovereign had been "humbled to the level of a beggar's pity."
66. Morris to Washington, Paris, December 1, 1790, in Washington Papers.
67. Short to Secretary of State, Amsterdam, December 23 and 30, 1790.

CHAPTER FIVE

1. Madelin, *French Revolution*, p. 184.
2. Vallotton, *Marie-Antoinette*, p. 239.
3. *Ibid.*, p. 206.
4. *Ibid.*, pp. 239, 240.
5. Narbonne was said to be both a son and grandson of Louis XV through incest with a daughter, Madame Elisabeth, Duchess of Parma, though one finds this incest sometimes attributed to Madame Adelaide.
6. Short to Secretary of State, January 16, 1791.
7. Short to Jefferson (private), Amsterdam, January 17, 1791, in Short Papers.
8. Short to Secretary of State, Amsterdam, January 24, 1791.
9. The reference is to *L'Ile des Pinguins*, by Anatole France.
10. Short to Jefferson (with enclosure), Amsterdam, January 28, 1791.
11. Lafayette to Washington, Paris, January 25, 1791, in *Mémoires du Lafayette*, V, 193.
12. Newenham to Washington, January 31, 1791, in Washington Papers.
13. *Dictionary of National Biography*, XIV, 333–334.
14. Short to Secretary of State, Amsterdam, February 7, 1791. See also Short to Secretary of State, February 22, 1791.
15. Short to Secretary of State, Amsterdam, February 18, 1791.
16. This was true politically, though they displayed feminine spite toward Marie Antoinette.
17. Short to Secretary of State, Amsterdam, February 25, 1791.
18. Short to Secretary of State, Amsterdam, March 4, 1791.
19. Short to Secretary of State, Amsterdam, March 11, 1791.
20. The *Société de 1789*, founded by Lafayette and the Mayor of Paris in May 1790, shortly to become the Feuillants Club in July 1791.
21. Short to Secretary of State, Amsterdam, March 12, 1791, and enclosure from Short's secretary as of Paris, March 7, 1791.
22. Short to Secretary of State, Paris, March 30, 1791, in Short Despatches.
23. Lafayette to Washington, Paris, March 7, 1791, in *Mémoires du Lafayette*, V, 204–207.
24. Morris to Washington, Paris, March 9, 1791, in Washington Papers.
25. Newenham to Washington, March 10, 1791, in Washington Papers.
26. La Rouërie to Washington, "La Rouërie," March 22, 1791, in Washington Papers.
27. Department of State to the President of the National Assembly of France, Philadelphia, March 8, 1791, in U.S. Department of State, Instructions, United States Ministers, I. Hereafter cited as State Department, Instructions.
28. Washington to Lafayette, March 19, 1791, in Fitzpatrick, *Writings of Washington*, XXXI, 248–249.

29. Short to Secretary of State, Paris, April 8, 1791. Subsequent discovery that Mirabeau for some time before his death had been in the King's pay reversed contemporary judgment, but not that of posterity.
30. Short to Secretary of State, Paris, April 25, 1791. An exceptionally long and interesting despatch.
31. De Moustier to Washington, Berlin, April 26, 1791, in translation in Washington Papers.
32. Short to Secretary of State, Paris, May 3, 1791.
33. Short to Secretary of State, Paris, May 8, 1791.
34. Lafayette to Washington, Paris, May 3, 1791, in *Mémoires du Lafayette*, V, 212–215.
35. Luzerne to Washington, London, May 15, 1791, in Washington Papers.
36. Short to Secretary of State, Paris, June 6, 1791.
37. *Ibid.*
38. Short to Secretary of State, Paris, June 10, 1791.
39. Short to Secretary of State, Paris, June 22, 1791.
40. Short to Secretary of State, Paris, June 26, 1791.
41. Short to Secretary of State, Paris, June 29, 1791. The one man most responsible for the flight, but by no means for its failure, was Count Axel Fersen, a favorite of the Queen, who had seen service in the American Revolution.
42. Lafayette to Washington, Paris, June 6, 1791, in *Mémoires du Lafayette*, V, 217–221. Perhaps Lafayette sensed Short's approaching transfer to another mission and was endeavoring to protect him.
43. Short to Secretary of State, Paris, July 8, 1791. The work of Necker's referred to is *sur l'Administration de M. Necker, par lui-même* (1791).
44. Short to Secretary of State, Paris, July 20 and 21, 1791.
45. Paine to Washington, London, July 21, 1791, in Washington Papers.
46. Short to Secretary of State, Paris, July 24, 1791.
47. Short to Secretary of State, Paris, July 27, 1791.
48. Washington to Lafayette, Philadelphia, July 28, 1791, in *Mémoires du Lafayette*, V, 221–225.
49. Fitzpatrick, *Writings of Washington*, XXXI, 325.
50. Washington to Morris, July 28, 1791, in *American State Papers, Foreign Relations*, I, 387. Washington had been on a tour of the Southern states.
51. Short to Jefferson, Paris, August 9, 1791.
52. Short to Jefferson, Paris, August 24, 1791.
53. Short to Jefferson, Paris, August 30 and 31, 1791.
54. Short to Jefferson, Paris, September 4, 1791.
55. Short to Jefferson, Paris, September 5, 1791.
56. Short to Jefferson, Paris, September 14, 1791. Lafayette resigned on October 8, and on the seventeenth he returned to his château at Chavaniac after a triumphal tour. The interlude of domesticity was brief.
57. Short to Jefferson, Paris, September 22, 1791.
58. Short to Jefferson, September 25, 1791.
59. Morris to Washington, Paris, September 30, 1791, in Washington Papers. Morris was right; Moustier did not accept.
60. Washington to Lafayette, Philadelphia, September 10, 1791, in Fitzpatrick, *Writings of Washington*, XXXI, 362–363.

61. Washington to Lafayette, Philadelphia, September 21, 1791, in *Mémoires du Lafayette*, V, 222–227, especially 227.
62. Tobias Lear to Washington, Philadelphia, October 2, 1791, in Washington Papers. Ternant was minister at this time.
63. Short to Secretary of State, Paris, October 2, 1791.
64. Short to Secretary of State, Paris, October 9, 1791. Short did not like this new Assembly. Cf. a private letter to Jefferson, October 22, 1791, in Short Papers.
65. Short to Secretary of State, Paris, October 14, 1791.
66. Short to Jefferson, La Roche Guyon, October 22, 1791, in Short Papers. The translation is my own.
67. Short to Secretary of State, Paris, November 8, 1791.
68. Short to Secretary of State, Paris, November 21, 1791.
69. Washington to Lafayette, November 22, 1791, in Fitzpatrick, *Writings of Washington*, XXXI, 426.
70. Newenham to Washington, December 22, 1791, in Washington Papers.
71. Morris to Washington, Paris, December 27, 1791, in Washington Papers.
72. Short to Secretary of State, Amsterdam, December 30, 1791.

CHAPTER SIX

1. Madelin, *French Revolution*, p. 252.
2. The Pillnitz Declaration (August 27, 1791) was the result of a meeting between the Comte d'Artois and the Emperor Leopold. The Emperor had not invited Artois and had no desire for war. The King of Prussia, on the other hand, did want war. Following lively discussions, Artois obtained the following rather unemphatic declaration:

> The Emperor and the King of Prussia look upon the situation in which the King of France finds himself as a matter of common interest to all the sovereigns of Europe. They hope that these will not refuse to employ along with them the most effective means corresponding to their forces, to place the King of France in a position to confirm, in complete freedom, the foundations of monarchical government equally adapted to the rights of the sovereigns and to the prosperity of the French people. Then, and in such event, the Emperor and the King of Prussia are resolved to act promptly, in mutual agreement, with the strength needed to obtain the common end proposed.

Basically displeased, Monsieur and Artois made great propaganda of this innocuous declaration and indulged in menaces against French factions. Patriots were alarmed, but Louis and his Queen perceived that they could not count upon the Emperor. The Queen warned that four millions of armed Frenchmen menaced every throne in Europe. But Leopold was unmoved.

Of the Brunswick Manifesto (August 1, 1792), Ernest Lavisse writes, "On August 1 Paris learned of the manifesto of the Duke of Brunswick, commander of the Prussian army. It was, to be sure, the work of an émigré, of Limon, and of the former Secretary of Mirabeau, passed to the pay of the Court, Pellenc, who, to save the Queen, wished to terrorize the patriots; but it expressed the sentiments of the Prussians and the Austrians."

> The allied powers declare:
> 1. Engaged in the present war by irresistible circumstances, the two allied Courts have the welfare of France as their sole object without pretending to enrich themselves by conquests.

2. They do not propose to meddle in the internal government of France, but they seek only to deliver the King, the Queen, and the Royal Family from their captivity. . . .

3. The city of Paris and all its inhabitants without exception are ordered to surrender immediately and without delay to the King, and to put that Prince at full and complete liberty.

Further their said Majesties declare on their faith and word as Emperor and King, that if the château of the Tuileries is attacked or insulted, if the least violence, the least outrage is done to their Majesties the King, the Queen, and the Royal Family, if provision is not made instantly for their safety, their protection and their freedom, they will exact a vengeance exemplary and forever to be remembered, in delivering the city of Paris over to military execution and complete destruction.

3. Short's regret at the transfer was increased in the following year by his failure to win in marriage the Duchesse de la Rochefoucauld, widow of one of the most liberal nobles in France. The Duke took an eager part in the early movements for genuine reform, but was stoned to death in September 1792 in the presence of his wife and mother when over a minor issue he incurred the mob's displeasure.

4. For the cold and emphatic instructions of Thomas Jefferson to the new minister, see Jefferson to Morris, Philadelphia, January 23, 1792, in State Department, Instructions, I.

5. Washington to Morris, Philadelphia, January 28, 1792, in Fitzpatrick, *Writings of Washington*, XXXI, 468–470.

6. Newenham to Washington, January 9, 1792, in Washington Papers.

7. They were in complete disobedience of the King. The Queen even viewed their activities as intentionally subversive of their brother's authority and aimed at his overthrow.

8. Lafayette to Washington, Metz, January 22, 1792, in *Mémoires du Lafayette*, VI, 184–187.

9. Short to Jefferson, Paris, January 25, 1792.

10. This was the contemporary opinion of the aristocracy. History has modified it considerably.

11. Morris and Talleyrand were rivals for the Comtesse de Flahaut, who bore a son to Talleyrand and later became the mistress of Morris.

12. Morris to Washington, London, February 4, 1792, in Washington Papers.

13. Newenham to Washington, February 12, 1792, in Washington Papers.

14. Short to Secretary of State, Paris, February 29, 1792.

15. Short to Secretary of State, Paris, March 11, 1792.

16. Morris to Washington, London, March 17, 1792, in Washington Papers.

17. Morris to Washington, London, March 21, 1792, in Washington Papers.

18. Short to Secretary of State, Paris, March 25, 1792.

19. Lafayette to Washington, Paris, March 15, 1792, in *Mémoires du Lafayette*, VI, 189–193. The translations are my own.

20. Morris to Washington, London, April 6, 1792, in Washington Papers. Gustavus III had gone to Aix-la-Chapelle the previous summer to work out an agreement with the partisans of Louis XVI. The project, difficult in any case, was nullified by a conspiracy of the Swedish nobles, one of whom stabbed the King at a masked ball on March 16, 1792. His quarrel with the aristocracy was the more singular in proportion as the King's personal views bent strongly in that direction. He had, in fact, forbidden Count Axel Fersen to join the Order of the Cincinnati on the ground that it was too democratic.

21. Short to Secretary of State, Paris, April 22, 1792. See also Jefferson to Morris, Philadelphia, April 28, 1792, in State Department, Instructions, I.
22. Short to Secretary of State, Paris, May 2 and 15, 1792.
23. Morris to Washington, Paris, June 10, 1792, in Washington Papers.
24. Morris to Jefferson, Paris, June 10, 1792, in U.S. Department of State, Diplomatic Despatches, France. See above, Chapter Three, note 18.
25. Morris to Jefferson, Paris, June 17, 1792.
26. Short to Jefferson, The Hague, June 29, 1792.
27. Washington to Morris, Philadelphia, June 21, 1792, in Fitzpatrick, *Writings of Washington*, XXXII, 60–61, 131–132.
28. Morris to Secretary of State, Paris, July 10, 1792.
29. Short to Jefferson, The Hague, July 20, 1792.
30. Short to Jefferson, The Hague, July 27, 1792.
31. Short to Jefferson, The Hague, July 31, 1792.
32. Morris to Jefferson, Paris, August 5, 1792.
33. A. Aulard, *Histoire Politique de la Révolution Française*, p. 5, note 2. The translation is my own.
34. Morris to Jefferson, Paris, August 11, 1792.
35. Short to Secretary of State, The Hague, August 15, 1792, in U.S. Department of State, Despatches, The Hague and Spain. Hereafter cited as State Department, Hague and Spain.
36. Morris to Secretary of State, Paris, August 16, 1792.
37. The catalogue of his prisons, each apparently more harsh than the preceding, is a dreary one. On August 25, he was transferred to Namur; on September 3, to Luxemburg; on September 15, to Coblentz, where he was confined in the fortress of Wesel. On December 31, he was imprisoned at Magdeburg, where he remained until his transfer to Neisse on January 16, 1794. In May of that year he was given by the Prussians to the Austrians. It was not until mid-October 1795 that Mme de Lafayette was permitted to join him.
38. Gilbert Chinard, *Letters of Lafayette and Jefferson*, p. 157. Quoting especially a letter from Lafayette to the Duc de la Rochefoucauld.
39. Morris to Jefferson, Paris, August 22, 1792. Morris, it may be added, was the only minister of a foreign power to remain in France throughout the Terror.
40. Short to Secretary of State, The Hague, August 24, 1792, in State Department, Hague and Spain.
41. Short to Secretary of State, The Hague, August 31, 1792, in State Department, Hague and Spain.
42. Morris to Jefferson, Paris, August 30, 1792.
43. Morris to Jefferson, Paris, September 10, 1792.
44. Short to Jefferson, The Hague, September 18, 1792, in State Department, Hague and Spain. See also Short to Jefferson, September 28, 1792, in State Department, Hague and Spain.
45. Morris to Jefferson (with enclosures), Paris, September 19, 1792.
46. Morris to Jefferson, Paris, September 27, 1792.
47. Tobias Lear to Washington, Philadelphia, October 7, 1792, in Washington Papers.
48. At the end of December, she was granted provisional freedom.

49. Mme de Lafayette to Washington, Chavaniac near Brionde, France, October 8, 1792, in Washington Papers.
50. He placed a large credit at the disposal of Mme de Lafayette, invited her son and his tutor to Mt. Vernon and paid his way at Harvard College.
51. Short to Secretary of State, The Hague, October 12, 1792, in State Department, Hague and Spain.
52. Jefferson to Morris, Philadelphia, October 15, 1792, in State Department, Instructions, I.
53. Short to Secretary of State, The Hague, October 19, 1792, in State Department, Hague and Spain.
54. Morris to Washington, October 23, 1792, in Washington Papers.
55. Morris to Jefferson, Paris, October 23, 1792.
56. Washington to Morris, Philadelphia, October 20, 1792, in Fitzpatrick, *Writings of Washington*, XXXII, 188–189. See also *American State Papers, Foreign Relations*, I, 395.
57. Jefferson to Morris, Philadelphia, November 7, 1792, in State Department, Instructions, I.
58. Short to Secretary of State, The Hague, November 2, 1792, in State Department, Hague and Spain.
59. Short to Secretary of State, The Hague, Despatch No. 118, in State Department, Hague and Spain.
60. Short to Secretary of State, The Hague, November 16, 1792, in State Department, Hague and Spain.
61. Short to Secretary of State, The Hague, November 30, 1792, in State Department, Hague and Spain.
62. Short to Secretary of State, The Hague, December 8, 1792, in State Department, Hague and Spain.
63. His blood lust was for birds and animals, which he slew in numbers almost unbelievable.
64. He did repent, however, just before he himself reached the scaffold.
65. Morris to Jefferson, Paris, December 21, 1792.
66. Morris to Washington, Paris, December 28, 1792, in Washington Papers. See also *American State Papers, Foreign Relations*, I, 395.

CHAPTER SEVEN

1. Paine, as a revolutionist of world renown, was invited officially to France to assist in forming her government. His voice was much heard and he sat and voted in the Convention that deliberated on the King.
2. Madelin, *French Revolution*, p. 367.
3. These are quoted most effectively in Albert J. Beveridge, *The Life of John Marshall*, II, 94–96.
4. Jefferson to Short, Philadelphia, January 3, 1793, in Ford, *Works of Jefferson*, VII, 202–206.
5. Morris to Jefferson, Paris, January 1, 1793. Most of these communications may be found also printed in *American State Papers, Foreign Relations*, Vol. I (1789–1797).
6. Morris to Jefferson, January 6, 1793.
7. Morris to Washington, Paris, January 6, 1793, in Washington Papers.
8. Morris to Washington, Paris, January 10, 1793, in Washington Papers.

9. Morris to Jefferson, Paris, January 25, 1793. See also on the death of Louis, Dumas to Secretary of State, The Hague, January 29, 1793, in U.S. Department of State, Miscellaneous Letters. Hereafter cited as State Department, Miscellaneous.

10. Washington to Mme de Lafayette, Philadelphia, January 31, 1793, in Fitzpatrick, *Writings of Washington*, XXXII, 322. See also for the aid to Lafayette, Morris to Jefferson (with enclosures), Paris, January 27, 1793.

11. Morris to Jefferson, Paris, February 13, 1793.

12. Morris to Washington, Paris, February 14, 1793, in Washington Papers.

13. Morris to Secretary of State, Paris, March 7, 1793.

14. Newenham to Washington, Dublin, March 8, 1793, in Washington Papers.

15. Morris to Secretary of State, Paris, March 8 and March 9, 1793.

16. Morris to Secretary of State, Paris, March 13, 1793.

17. Morris to Secretary of State, Paris, March 26, 1793.

18. Gilbert Chinard, *Lafayette and Jefferson*, pp. 158, 159.

19. Jefferson to Morris, Philadelphia, March 12, 1793, in State Department, Instructions, I.

20. Jefferson to Morris, Philadelphia, March 15, 1793, in State Department, Instructions, I.

21. Washington to Mme de Lafayette, Philadelphia, March 15, 1793, in Chinard, *Lafayette and Jefferson*.

22. Mme de Lafayette to Washington, Chavaniac, France, March 12, 1793, in Washington Papers.

23. *American State Papers, Foreign Relations*, I, 396–397.

24. Morris to Jefferson, Paris, April 4, 1793.

25. Morris to Jefferson, Paris, April 5, 1793.

26. Short to Jefferson, Aranjuez, Spain, April 5, 1793, in Short Papers.

27. Rodolph Vall-Travers to Secretary of State, Rotterdam, April 9, 1793, in State Department, Miscellaneous.

28. Morris to Jefferson, Paris, April 19, 1793.

29. Jefferson to Morris, Philadelphia, April 20, 1793, in State Department, Instructions, I.

30. Fitzpatrick, *Writings of Washington*, XXXII, 430–431. See also as a preliminary, Washington to Jefferson, April 12, 1793, in Fitzpatrick, *Writings of Washington*, XXXII, 415–416.

31. Jefferson to the President of the United States, Philadelphia, April 28, 1793, manuscript in the Department of State.

32. See Ford, *Writings of Washington*, XII, 280–281 and footnotes.

33. Washington to Hamilton, May 5, 1793, in Fitzpatrick, *Writings of Washington*.

34. David Humphreys to Washington, Lisbon, May 5, 1793, in Washington Papers.

35. Morris to Jefferson, Sain Port near Paris, May 20, 1793.

36. Newenham to Washington, June 7, 1793, in Washington Papers.

37. Morris to Jefferson, Sain Port, June 12, 1793.

38. Jefferson to Morris, Philadelphia, June 13, 1793, in State Department, Instructions, I.

39. Jefferson to Morris, Philadelphia, June 15, 1793, in State Department, Instructions, I.

40. Morris to Secretary of State, Sain Port, June 25, 1793.

41. Morris to Washington, June 25, 1793, in Washington Papers.
42. Lafayette to C. C. Pinckney, Magdeburg, July 4, 1793, in Jules Thomas, *Correspondance Inédite de Lafayette, 1793–1801*, pp. 206–210. See also *Mémoires du Lafayette*, VII, 292–297.
43. Jefferson to Monroe, May 5, 1793, and Jefferson to Madison, May 19, 1793, in Ford, *Works of Jefferson*, VIII, 309.
44. Washington to Henry Lee, Philadelphia, July 21, 1793, in Fitzpatrick, *Writings of Washington*, XXXIII, 22, 23–24, 28–29.
45. Morris to Jefferson, Sain Port, August 7, 1793.
46. Morris to Jefferson, Sain Port, August 13, 1793.
47. Jefferson to Morris, Philadelphia, August 16, 1793, in State Department, Instructions, I.
48. Newenham to Washington, Dublin, September 12, 1793, in Washington Papers.
49. David Humphreys to Washington, Lisbon, September 13, 1793, in Washington Papers.
50. Morris to Jefferson, Sain Port, September 22, 1793.
51. Jefferson to Morris, October 3, 1793, in State Department, Instructions, II.
52. Morris to Deforgues, Minister of Foreign Affairs, Paris, October 8, 1793, enclosed in Morris to Jefferson, Paris, October 10, 1793.
53. Morris to Jefferson, Paris, October 10, 1793.
54. Morris to Jefferson, October 19, 1793.
55. Morris to Jefferson, October 20, 1793.
56. Morris to Washington, Paris, October 18, 1793, in Washington Papers.
57. Morris to Washington, Paris, October 19, 1793, in Washington Papers.
58. Lafayette to Mme de Lafayette, Magdeburg, October 2, 1793, in Thomas, *Correspondance de Lafayette*, p. 227. The translation is my own.
59. Henry Mosnier, *Le Château de Chavaniac-Lafayette*, p. 37.
60. Morris to Washington, Paris, November 12, 1793, in Washington Papers.
61. Morris to Jefferson, Sain Port, November 16, 1793.
62. Morris to Jefferson, Sain Port, November 16, 1793, in *American State Papers, Foreign Relations*, I, 399.
63. Morris to Jefferson, Paris, November 26, 1793. He met with dignity a deserved death.
64. Jefferson to Mrs. Church, Germantown, November 27, 1793, in Chinard, *Lafayette and Jefferson*, p. 176.
65. Lafayette to M. La Colombe, Magdeburg, December 10, 1793, in Thomas, *Correspondance de Lafayette*, pp. 241–242.
66. Lafayette to C. C. Pinckney, Magdeburg, December 14, 1793, in Thomas, *Correspondance de Lafayette*, pp. 243–246.
67. Morris to Secretary of State, Paris, December 12, 1793.

CHAPTER EIGHT

1. For a somewhat milder interpretation, see Hilaire Belloc, *Robespierre, 1758–1794*.
2. Quoted in J. Holland Rose, *The Revolutionary and Napoleonic Era, 1789–1815*, p. 89.
3. *Ibid.*, p. 89.
4. Charles Downer Hazen, *The French Revolution*, II, 811–812.

5. Washington to King of Prussia, Philadelphia, January 15, 1794, in J. Pierpont Morgan Library, New York. Copy retained by Washington in his notebook. Copy inserted in State Department, Instructions, II.

6. Morris to Secretary of State, Paris, January 21, 1794.

7. Tobias Lear to Washington, London, January 26, 1794, in Washington Papers.

8. Newenham to Washington, Dublin, February 11, 1794, in Washington Papers.

9. Baron de La Morre de Villaubois to Jefferson, in State Department, Miscellaneous, file of February 15, 1794.

10. Morris to Secretary of State, Sain Port, March 6, 1794.

11. Morris to Washington, Sain Port, March 12, 1794, in Washington Papers.

12. Morris to Edmund Randolph, Sain Port, April 15, 1794.

13. Morris to Randolph, Sain Port, April 18, 1794.

14. Morris to Washington, Sain Port, April 18, 1794, in Washington Papers.

15. Randolph to Morris, Philadelphia, April 29, 1794, and June 10, 1794, in State Department, Instructions, II.

16. Washington to Morris, Philadelphia, June 19, 1794, in Ford, *Writings of Washington*, XII, 433–436, and Fitzpatrick, *Writings of Washington*, XXXIII, 409–410.

17. Morris to Randolph, Paris, May 6, 1794.

18. Morris to Randolph, Paris, May 31, 1794.

19. Morris to Randolph, Sain Port, May 31, 1794.

20. Randolph to Washington, Philadelphia, May 15, 1794, in Washington Papers.

21. It may be observed that the heir to the Marquess was, like Morris, in love with Talleyrand's mistress, the Comtesse de Flahaut.

22. Washington to Alexander Hamilton, May 6, 1794, in Fitzpatrick, *Writings of Washington*, XXXIII, 352–353.

23. Randolph to Monroe, Philadelphia, June 30, 1794, in State Department, Instructions, II.

24. John Jay to Washington, London, June 23, 1794, in Washington Papers.

25. Morris to Randolph, Sain Port, July 22, 1794.

26. Morris to Randolph, Sain Port, July 23, 1794. Here Morris, while complimenting Jefferson's "masterly performance" in stating the U.S. case against Great Britain and hoping "his abilities will not be lost to the public," congratulated the country on Randolph's accession. It would promote unity in the national counsels.

27. Morris to Washington, Sain Port, July 25, 1794, in Washington Papers. It will be recalled that the lady had been arrested the previous November 12. On June 7, 1794, she was transferred from Brionde to Paris.

28. Morris to Randolph, Paris, August 18, 1794.

29. Morris to Randolph, Paris, August 31, 1794.

30. Monroe to Randolph, Paris, August 15, 1794, in U.S. Department of State, Diplomatic Despatches, France. See above, Chapter Three, note 18.

31. Monroe to Randolph, Paris, August 25, 1794.

32. Jay to Washington, London, September 13, 1794, in Washington Papers.

33. Monroe to Randolph, Paris, September 15, 1794.

34. Morris to Randolph, Paris, September 18, 1794.

35. Randolph to Monroe, Philadelphia, September 25, 1794, in State Department, Instructions, II.

36. Comte de la Belinaye to Washington, London, September 30, 1794, in State Department, Miscellaneous.

37. Monroe to Randolph, Paris, October 16, 1794.
38. Monroe to Randolph, Paris, November 7, 1794.
39. Monroe to Washington, Paris, November 19, 1794, in Stanislaus Murray Hamilton, ed., *The Writings of James Monroe*, II, 112–117.
40. Monroe to Randolph, Paris, November 20, 1794, in Hamilton, *Writings of Monroe*, II, 117–124.
41. Randolph to Monroe, Philadelphia, November 17, 1794, in State Department, Instructions, II.
42. Randolph to Monroe, Philadelphia, December 2, 1794, in State Department, Instructions, II.
43. Randolph to Monroe, Philadelphia, December 5, 1794, in State Department, Instructions, II.
44. Monroe to Randolph, Paris, December 2, 1794.
45. Morris to Washington, Hamburg, December 30, 1794, in Ann Cary Morris, ed., *The Diary and Letters of Gouverneur Morris*, II, 77–80.

CHAPTER NINE

1. Hazen, *French Revolution*, II, 818.
2. Madelin, *French Revolution*, pp. 482–483. Quoted by permission of the publishers, G. P. Putnam's Sons.
3. Lavisse, *Histoire de France*, II, 300–301. Pichegru embarked upon his treason by abandoning Mannheim, November 21, 1795, leaving Jourdan isolated amid the Austrians. An unfavorable armistice followed on December 21, 1795.
4. Rose, *Revolutionary and Napoleonic Era*, pp. 89–91.
5. Hazen, *French Revolution*, II, 828. Lavisse, *Histoire de France*, II, 272. Curiously this treaty gave Manuel Godoy his title, "Prince of the Peace."
6. Rose (p. 94) says 700; Hazen (pp. 828–829) is content with 400. Lavisse (II, 261) compromises: 748 were killed, of whom 428 were gentlemen émigrés.
7. Morris to Washington, Hamburg, December 30, 1794, in *American State Papers, Foreign Relations*, I, 412.
8. Morris to Randolph, Hamburg, January 2, 1795.
9. She reached Olmütz on October 15, 1795, where she and her two daughters shared her husband's imprisonment. Later she returned to France, where she had never been proscribed as an émigrée, to retrieve in some measure the family estates. She is credited with much diplomatic skill in fencing with the disagreeable Thugut, who as Imperial Minister controlled her husband's fate. Regardless of the author's prejudice against Madame de Lafayette because of her imperceptive and unappreciative attitude toward Washington, it must be admitted that she merited Rochambeau's quaint epithet "respectable." For respect she earned by her protection of the local curé, and by her guardianship of her children and of her own and her husband's property. She was a worthy mistress of the château and estate of Chavaniac. (See Mosnier, *Le Château de Chavaniac-Lafayette*, especially pp. 32–40.)
10. Monroe to Washington, Paris, January 3, 1795, in Hamilton, *Writings of Monroe*, II, 164–167.
11. Monroe to Randolph, Paris, January 13, 1795, in Hamilton, *Writings of Monroe*, II, 167–179.
12. Monroe to Randolph, Paris, February 1, 1795, in Hamilton, *Writings of Monroe*, II, 186–193.

13. Monroe to Randolph, Paris, February 12, 1795, in Hamilton, *Writings of Monroe*, II, 193–206.

14. Monroe to Randolph, Paris, February 18, 1795, in Hamilton, *Writings of Monroe*, II, 212–213.

15. Randolph to Monroe, February 15, 1795, in State Department, Instructions, II.

16. *The Correspondence of French Ministers to the United States, 1791–1797*, Vol. II of *The American Historical Association Annual Report for 1903*, pp. 584–586.

17. Jay to Washington, London, March 6, 1795, in Washington Papers.

18. Monroe to Randolph, Paris, March 6, 1795, in Hamilton, *Writings of Monroe*, II, 217–229.

19. Monroe to Randolph, Paris, March 17, 1795, in Hamilton, *Writings of Monroe*, II, 229–236.

20. Randolph to Monroe, March 8, 1795, in State Department, Instructions, II. See also in similar vein, Randolph to Monroe, April 7, 1795, in State Department, Instructions, II.

21. Charles Francis Adams, ed., *Memoirs of John Quincy Adams*, I, 33.

22. February 20, 1797, in *ibid.*, I, 193–194.

23. October 29, 1797, in *ibid.*, I, 201.

24. J. Q. Adams to Secretary of State, The Hague, April 14, 1795, in Worthington C. Ford, ed., *The Writings of John Quincy Adams*, I, 326–328.

25. Monroe to Secretary of State, Paris, April 14, 1795, in Hamilton, *Writings of Monroe*, II, 238–255.

26. Randolph to Monroe, April 7, 1795, in State Department, Instructions, II.

27. Joseph Fenwick to Washington, Bordeaux, May 10, 1795, in Washington Papers.

28. Monroe to Randolph, Paris, May 17, 1795, in Hamilton, *Writings of Monroe*, II, 255–264.

29. J. Q. Adams to Randolph, The Hague, May 19, 1795, in U.S. Department of State, Despatches, Netherlands, I. Hereafter cited as State Department, Netherlands. See also Ford, *Writings of J. Q. Adams*, I, 352–353, with punctuation modernized.

30. Ford, *Writings of J. Q. Adams*, I, 409, footnote.

31. J. Q. Adams to John Adams, The Hague, May 22, 1795, in Ford, *Writings of J. Q. Adams*, I, 353–363.

32. J. Q. Adams to Secretary of State, The Hague, May 30, 1796, in State Department, Netherlands, I.

33. J. Q. Adams to Secretary of State, The Hague, June 12 and 18, 1795, in State Department, Netherlands, I.

34. J. Q. Adams to Secretary of State, The Hague, June 25, 1795, in State Department, Netherlands, I.

35. P. A. Adet to the Committee of Public Safety, June 25, 1795, in *Correspondence of French Ministers*, pp. 734–739.

36. Randolph to Monroe, June 1, 1795, in State Department, Instructions, II. For a more routine instruction concerning the losses of Stephen Girard, see Randolph to Monroe, June 8, 1795, in State Department, Instructions, II.

37. Monroe to Randolph, Paris, June 14, 1795, in Hamilton, *Writings of Monroe*, II, 272–288.

38. Monroe to Randolph, Paris, June 26, 1795, in Hamilton, *Writings of Monroe*, II, 309.

39. Monroe to Randolph, Paris, July 6, 1795, in Hamilton, *Writings of Monroe*, II, 317–330. For the sad fate of these unfortunates, see J. Q. Adams to Randolph, The Hague, July 25, 1795, in State Department, Netherlands, I.

40. Randolph to Monroe, July 2, 1795, in State Department, Instructions, III.

41. Randolph to Monroe, July 21, 1795, in State Department, Instructions, III.

42. Sam Bayard to B. Dandridge, Secretary to Washington, London, July 28, 1795, in Washington Papers.

43. Monroe to Secretary of State, Paris, August 1, 1795, in Hamilton, *Writings of Monroe*, II, 331–339.

44. Monroe to Secretary of State, Paris, August 17, 1795, in Hamilton, *Writings of Monroe*, II, 339–343.

45. Morris to Washington, Wimbledon, August 23, 1795, in Washington Papers.

46. After his resignation, his career was anticlimactic. He wrote a vindication which pleased his friends but failed to silence opposition. He found some consolation in an important law practice in which he served as senior counsel for the defense of Aaron Burr in the treason trial at Richmond. His home life was affectionate and before his death in 1813 he came to feel that Washington, while wrong in removing him, had acted as the circumstances demanded, and he died with no bitterness in his heart.

47. Much evidence relative to Randolph's guilt is contained in *The Correspondence of French Ministers to the United States, 1791–1797* (Vol. II of *The American Historical Association Annual Report for 1903*), from which the following quotations are taken.

    In his incriminating despatch of September 5, 1794, Fauchet, addressing the Commissioner of Foreign Relations, had been discussing internal confusion within the United States, then flaring into the Whiskey Rebellion in western Pennsylvania. He generalized effectively. It was when he mentioned Randolph that the trap was sprung. In Fauchet's words:

    > Hardly was the Explosion known when the Secretary of State came to me, his face grief stricken, to request an intimate interview. Civil war, said he, is about to ravage our unhappy country. Four men by their talent, their influence and their energy could save it, But they are in debt to [English] merchants, and their slightest activity would cost their freedom. Could you offer them temporarily sufficient funds to free them from English persecution? This request astonished me greatly; it was impossible to make a satisfactory response. You are aware of my lack of authority and of my deficiency of funds. I withdrew from the affair with some generalities and cast myself on the pure and unalterable principles of the Republic. Since then I have heard nothing more of a proposition of this nature. A reflection which has affected me sadly and which this circumstance has recalled is that the English have had the skill by the commercial opportunities which they have bestowed to enchain a large part of a People designed for liberty. They have extended a great credit to this nation and that credit is increasing annually. The Americans will never escape from this mercantile enslavement save by war. If originally our Government which understood its purposes in Commerce as in Liberty, had aided them and put them in condition to compete with the English merchants, our commerce would have crushed that of this nation, whose empire in other respects will be destroyed when we wish it. [pp. 411–418]

    In another despatch of a few weeks later (October 31), Fauchet again mentioned Randolph, quoting him to the effect that

    > *under pretext of giving energy to the Government it was planned to introduce absolute power and to guide the President on mistaken courses*

345

which would lead him to unpopularity. . . . It seems, then, that these men [the Governor of Pennsylvania and others], with others whom I do not mention, all of them without doubt having Randolph at their head were balanced as to deciding on a party. Two or three days before the proclamation was published and with the Cabinet in consequence arrested in its measures, Mr. Randolph came to see me with a very earnest manner, and made to me the overtures which I have set forth in my No. 6. Thus with some thousands of dollars the Republic would have decided here on Civil War or on Peace. Thus the consciences of the pretended Patriots in America already have a price tag. [pp. 444–445]

Numerous details lengthen the despatch. From the total viewpoint the Randolph interview was merely incidental. But it set in train more actual events than most exchanges in diplomacy. For when the ship conveying the despatch was captured by the English, the incriminating comments of the Secretary were relayed to Philadelphia. There was glee among the ultra-Federalists when Washington hastened to the scene and accepted the most sinister interpretation of Randolph's indiscretion.

Whatever may have been the arrière pensée in Fauchet's despatch so ruinous to Randolph, to his successor, P. A. Adet, it was clear that removal from the Department of State of a Secretary who was essentially a friend of France, in favor of Timothy Pickering, who was not in any sense a friend, was the ultimate in folly. Adet's despatch of August 26, 1795, shows that by the time he quit our shores, Fauchet himself was prepared to aid the fallen Secretary:

The Despatch No. 10. of the 10th Brumaire of the Year II, postmarked Secret Correspondence of the Minister, addressed by my predecessor to the Commissioner of Foreign Affairs, has fallen into the hands of the President. . . . It did not fail to excite the suspicion of the President respecting Mr. Randolph. He has sent for him and addressed him with harsh reproaches. Angered by this Mr. Randolph immediately tendered his resignation. It has been accepted. Mr. Randolph came to me at five in the morning the day following that in which the President informed him that he held in his hands this despatch of my predecessor. Between chagrin at finding himself suspected, and the fear of losing his credit and his reputation, he has begged my assistance and has seemed to open his heart without reserve. He told me that the serious annoyance he experienced was stirred by the English, whose intrigues he was constantly obliged to circumvent; that in every circumstance he had endeavored to open the President's eyes to the machinations of Hamilton and his creatures Wolcot and Pickering, Secretaries in fact of the Treasury and of War, that he was opposed to ratifying the treaty with Great Britain, and that it was to punish him for this resistance to the will of England that his removal was sought. Fortunately for him he could prove that if the President had followed these counsels the United States would not be to-day under the British yoke. . . .

Having made me these confidences and having confirmed me in the opinion that the President detested France and her Revolution, he has added that not only was it of the first importance for himself, but also for our interests that he be able to overcome suspicions that were current as to himself and those who were most attached to France; that if he could not succeed in this, these men, angered at seeing themselves compromised would cease to defend our interests, or that the English party would succeed by the help of these suspicions in rendering them unpopular and depriving them of their influence. I recognized the importance of Mr. Randolph's reflection and I have considered that our interest and the consideration due to a man who has been sacrificed at this time would not allow me to abandon him in this situation. Mr. Randolph, being determined to approach my predecessor to obtain a statement which would remove these suspicions, I have given him a letter for him. . . . Besides the reasons I have alleged, there is another which has motivated me in this circumstance. It is that Mr. Randolph has assured me that if we furnish the means for his vindication, the House of Representatives would oppose the execution of the treaty. [pp. 774–776]

Randolph's efforts on his own behalf culminated in his interview with Fauchet on the eve of the latter's departure for France. Adet reported it as a matter of official business in his communication of September 30, 1795, to the Committee of Public Safety, stating,

Mr. Edmund Randolph, according to his plan, has gone to Newport, has seen Citizen Fauchet on the eve of his departure and has put in his hands a model of the declaration which he wished him to have. Citizen Fauchet made the affidavit almost in the form suggested and sent it to me so that I could deliver a copy to Mr. Randolph. I have obeyed his wishes and have joined to the declaration a copy of passages relative to Mr Edmund Randolph in Nos. 3, and 16.

I have not thought it right to neglect anything toward putting Mr Edmund Randolph in a way to exculpate himself.

Other portions of this despatch are of equal interest in a consideration of George Washington and the French Revolution, as, for example, the following comments on the President:

A conflict is arising within the English party, and its outcome, I believe, will favor us. Already the conduct of the President is vigorously attacked in the public prints. His servile attachment to England is condemned; the treaty which he has concluded with that Power. The People reads without resentment articles attacking Washington, and people who a year ago would have demolished a printing establishment rash enough to attack the American idol, to-day applaud tracts launched against him. One may conclude from that, and perhaps justifiably, that the Reign of Washington is over, because it is a known truth that anyone who has been lifted by popular enthusiasm to supreme power is ready for his fall when that enthusiasm cools. If this to-day is reconfirmed we can only applaud; for Washington is not our friend. . . . If events are such as I anticipate, there is room to believe that the timing of his resignation is not distant. Spirits everywhere are heated greatly. The towns and especially the rural districts object to the treaty, and the work which Mr. Edmund Randolph now is writing for his vindication will aid in enlightening everyone on the conduct of the President. One may presume that when he shall see the majority of his fellow citizens in opposition to him, he will quit the Presidency, and that a new choice conforming to the popular view will assure peace and the ruin of the English party. (It is probable that Jefferson will be the choice), but also we shall be witnesses of great events if Washington and his friends decide to bare their heads to the storm, for in that event, either some States will separate from the Union or war will break out between the two parties which divide America. I cannot answer you for the turn which affairs will take, but it appears that as things are now, discontent will not be limited as on numerous occasions to complaints and murmurs. I know for certain that six thousand firearms have been bought and distributed in the country sides. Others are on order, and not to defend the English cause and that of the President. At the same time the subjoined copy of a petition is being circulated. It has been signed already by a great number of persons, and it is hoped that it will be covered with a million signatures. [pp. 783–785]

These notes on Randolph's resignation convey French reaction to an event of their own precipitation. What began as malicious defamation of prominent Americans, with Randolph included at least by implication, was speedily perceived to have reacted to French disadvantage. Adet deserves credit for recognizing this so promptly, the more so as next to Genêt he was probably the least friendly to our country of French agents of this period. Whether moved by politics or generosity (the latter quite unlikely) he placed in clear focus French interest in the Randolph case.

48. Also he, of course, now sent instructions, as witness an elaborate explanation of Jay's Treaty and the viewpoint of the Government in Pickering to Monroe, September 12, 1795, in State Department, Instructions, III.

49. Monroe to Secretary of State, Paris, September 10, 1795, in Hamilton, *Writings of Monroe*, II, 359–366.

50. J. Q. Adams to Secretary of State, The Hague, September 14, 1795, in State Department, Netherlands, I.

51. J. Q. Adams to Secretary of State, The Hague, September 29, 1795, in State Department, Netherlands, I.

52. Paine to Washington, Paris, September 20, 1795, in Washington Papers.

53. J. Q. Adams to Secretary of State, The Hague, October 5, 1795, in State Department, Netherlands, I.

54. J. Q. Adams to Secretary of State, October 18, 1795, in State Department, Netherlands, I.

55. Monroe to Secretary of State, Paris, October 20, and Post Script, October 25, 1795, in Hamilton, *Writings of Monroe*, II, 379–407.

56. Monroe to Secretary of State, Paris, November 5, 1795, in Hamilton, *Writings of Monroe*.

57. J. Q. Adams to John Adams, London, November 17, 1795, in Ford, *Writings of J. Q. Adams*, I, 433.

58. Washington to Hamilton, Philadelphia, November 23, 1795, in Fitzpatrick, *Writings of Washington*, XXXIV, 374–376.

59. August De Grasse to Washington, Charleston, S.C., December 7, 1795, in Washington Papers.

60. Monroe to Secretary of State, Paris, December 6, 1795, in Hamilton, *Writings of Monroe*, II, 422–427.

61. Morris to Washington, London, December 19, 1795, in Washington Papers.

CHAPTER TEN

1. Quoted in Hazen, *French Revolution*, II, 891.

2. Lavisse, *Histoire de France*, II, 302.

3. *Ibid.*, II, 320.

4. *Ibid.*, II, 320–321.

5. *Ibid.*, II, 321–323.

6. *Ibid.*, II, 313–314. Lavisse does not credit Babeuf with communistic originality. He holds that the division of land might have been democratic. But he does admit the transmission of his ideas to Nineteenth Century radicals.

7. Morris to Washington, London, January 5, 1796, in Washington Papers.

8. Morris to Washington, London, January 11, 1796, in Washington Papers.

9. Monroe to Secretary of State, Paris, January 26, 1796, in Hamilton, *Writings of Monroe*, II, 447–454.

10. Coxe to Washington with enclosure, Paris, February 6, 1796, in Washington Papers.

11. J. Q. Adams to John Adams, London, February 10, 1796, in Ford, *Writings of J. Q. Adams*, I, 476–478.

12. Monroe to Secretary of State, Paris, February 16, 1796, in Hamilton, *Writings of Monroe*, II, 454–456.
13. Monroe to Secretary of State, Paris, February 20, 1796, in Hamilton, *Writings of Monroe*, II, 456–460.
14. Monroe to Secretary of State, Paris, March 10, 1796, in Hamilton, *Writings of Monroe*, II, 463–466. Failure of the loan was confirmed by Gouverneur Morris, London, March 4, 1796, in Washington Papers.
15. Monroe to Secretary of State, Paris, March 25, 1796, in Hamilton, *Writings of Monroe*, II, 484–488.
16. J. Q. Adams to John Adams, London, April 4, 1796, in Ford, *Writings of J. Q. Adams*, I, 481–488.
17. Monroe to Secretary of State, Paris, May 2, 1796, in Hamilton, *Writings of Monroe*, II, 489–494.
18. Monroe to Secretary of State, Paris, May 25, 1796, in Hamilton, *Writings of Monroe*, III, 1–4. For the campaign in Italy see also J. Q. Adams to Secretary of State, June 4, 1796, in State Department, Netherlands, I.
19. Thomas Pinckney to Washington, London, May 7 and July 31, 1796, in Washington Papers. See also Washington to Thomas Pinckney, February 20 and May 22, 1796, in Ford, *Writings of Washington*, XIII, 169–172, 208–210.
20. Pickering to Monroe, June 13, 1796, in State Department, Instructions, III.
21. Monroe to Dr. Logan, Paris, June 24, 1796, in Washington Papers. Copy in the files of Washington. See also Hamilton, *Writings of Monroe*, III, 6–7. Cf. Washington to Pickering, June 24, 1796, and Washington to Hamilton, June 26, 1796, in Ford, *Writings of Washington*, XIII, 214–216, 217–221.
22. Monroe to Pickering, Paris, July 24, 1796.
23. J. Q. Adams to Secretary of State, The Hague, July 8, 1796, in State Department, Netherlands, I.
24. J. Q. Adams to Secretary of State, The Hague, July 28, 1796, in State Department, Netherlands, I.
25. Fitzpatrick, *Writings of Washington*, XXXV, 122–124.
26. *Ibid.*, XXXV, 126–127.
27. *Ibid.*, XXXV, 127–128, 129–131.
28. *Ibid.*, XXXV, 156–157.
29. Pickering to Monroe, August 22, 1796, in State Department, Instructions, III. *American State Papers, Foreign Relations*, I, 741–742.
30. Monroe to Secretary of State, Paris, August 4, 1796, in Hamilton, *Writings of Monroe*, III, 48–51. In this letter and a second of August 15, Monroe recited his strong objections to the appointment of M. Mangourit as chargé d'affaires to succeed Adet. That was one lesson taught by the Genêt affair.
31. J. Q. Adams to Pickering, The Hague, August 2, 1796, in State Department, Netherlands, I.
32. J. Q. Adams to Pickering, The Hague, August 9, 1796, in State Department, Netherlands, I.
33. J. Q. Adams to Pickering, The Hague, August 21, 1796, in State Department, Netherlands, I.
34. Washington to Pickering, Mount Vernon, August 10, 1796, in Fitzpatrick, *Writings of Washington*, XXXV, 174–175.
35. Washington to Monroe, August 25, 1796, in Fitzpatrick, *Writings of Washington*, XXXV, 187–190.

36. Pickering to C. C. Pinckney, Philadelphia, September 24, 1796, in State Department, Instructions, III.
37. Monroe to Pickering, Paris, September 10, 1796, in Hamilton, *Writings of Monroe*, III, 54–62.
38. Monroe to Pickering, Paris, September 21, 1796.
39. J. Q. Adams to Pickering, September 19 and 25, 1796, in State Department, Netherlands, I.
40. J. Q. Adams to Pickering, The Hague, October 16, 1796, in State Department, Netherlands, I.
41. J. Q. Adams to Pickering, The Hague, November 4, 1796, in Ford, *Writings of J. Q. Adams*, II, 35–40.
42. J. Q. Adams to Secretary of State, The Hague, November 16, 1796, in State Department, Netherlands, II.
43. C. C. Pinckney to Pickering, Bordeaux, November 17, 1796, in U.S. Department of State, Diplomatic Despatches, France. See above, Chapter Three, note 18.
44. Rufus King to Washington, London, November 12, 1796, in Washington Papers.
45. Pickering to C. C. Pinckney, November 5 and November 26, 1796, in State Department, Instructions, III.
46. J. Q. Adams to Secretary of State, The Hague, December 20 and December 28, 1796, in State Department, Netherlands, II.
47. C. C. Pinckney to Pickering, Paris, December 20, 1796.
48. Lavisse, *Histoire de France*, II, 324. Quoted by permission of the publishers, Librairie Hachette. The translation is my own. Monroe's address to the Directory on presenting his letter of recall is of considerable interest, although too lengthy for inclusion in the text:

> I have the honor to present you with my letter of recall from the President of the United States of America, which closes my political functions with the French republic; and I have likewise the honor to add, that I am instructed by the President to avail myself of this occasion to renew to you, on his part, an assurance of the solicitude which the United States feel for the happiness of the French republic.
> In performing this act, many other considerations crowd themselves upon my mind. I was a witness to a Revolution in my own country. I was deeply penetrated with its principles, which are the same with those of your Revolution. I saw, too, its difficulties; and remembering these, and the important services rendered us by France upon that occasion, I have partaken with you in all the perilous and trying situations in which you have been placed.
> It was my fortune to arrive among you in a moment of complicated danger from within and from without; and it is with the most heartfelt satisfaction that, in taking my leave, I behold victory and the dawn of prosperity upon the point of realizing, under the auspices of a wise and excellent constitution, all the great objects for which, in council and the field, you have so long and so nobly contended. The information which I shall carry to America of this state of your affairs will be received by my countrymen with the same joy and solicitude for its continuance, that I now feel and declare for myself.
> There is no object which I have always had more uniformly and sincerely at heart, than the continuance of a close union and perfect harmony between our two nations. I accepted my mission with a view to use my utmost efforts to increase and promote this object, and I now derive consolation in a review of my conduct, from the knowledge that I have never deviated from it. Permit me, therefore, in withdraw-

ing, to express an earnest wish that this harmony may be perpetual.

I beg leave to make to you, citizen directors, my particular acknowl-edgments for the confidence and attention with which you have honored my mission during its continuance, and at the same time to assure you that, as I shall always take a deep and sincere interest in whatever con-cerns the prosperity and welfare of the French republic, so I shall never cease, in my retirement, to pay you, in return for the attention you have shown me, the only acceptable recompense to generous minds, the tribute of a grateful remembrance.

To this evidently heartfelt tribute, the President of the Directory, Barras, replied in terms most courteous to Monroe, if not to the United States:

Mr. Minister Plenipotentiary of the United States of America:

By presenting this day to the executive directory your letters of recall, you offer a very strange spectacle to Europe. France, rich in her freedom, surrounded by the train of her victories, and strong in the esteem of her allies, will not stoop to calculate the consequences of her condescension of the American Government to the wishes of its ancient tyrants. The French republic expects, however, that the successors of Columbus, Raleigh, and Penn, always proud of their liberty, will never forget that they owe it to France. They will weigh in their wisdom the magnanimous friendship of the French people, with the crafty caresses of perfidious men, who meditate to bring them again under their former yoke. Assure the good people of America, Mr. minister, that, like them we adore liberty; that they will always possess our esteem, and find in the French people that republican generosity which knows how to grant peace, as well as to cause its sovereignty to be respected.

As for you, Mr. minister plenipotentiary, you have combated for prin-ciples; you have known the true interests of your country—depart with our regrets. We restore, in you, a representative to America; and we preserve the remembrance of the citizen whose personal qualities did honor to that title. [*American State Papers, Foreign Relations,* I, 747.]

CHAPTER ELEVEN

1. Lavisse, *Histoire de France,* II, 329.
2. *Ibid.,* II, 338, 340 and *passim.* The Marquis de Barthélemy may well have been a monarchist.
3. Lavisse, *Histoire de France,* II, 341. Madelin, *French Revolution,* p. 533, says Verona. Antraigues was a confidential agent of the "King."
4. This account follows closely Lavisse, *Histoire de France,* II, 345–348.
5. *Ibid.,* II, 350.
6. Hazen, *French Revolution,* II, 903.
7. For comprehensive details of the Peace, see Lavisse, *Histoire de France,* II, 368–370.
8. Hazen, *French Revolution,* II, 917.
9. Lavisse, *Histoire de France,* II, 368.
10. Washington to Pickering, Philadelphia, January 4, 1797, in Fitzpatrick, *Writings of Washington,* XXXV, 351–352.
11. Washington to Pickering, January 9, 1797, in Fitzpatrick, *Writings of Washington,* XXXV, 360–361.
12. Pickering to C. C. Pinckney, January 16, 1797, in State Department, In-structions, III.
13. January 19, 1797, in Fitzpatrick, *Writings of Washington,* XXXV, 368–369.
14. Washington to Hamilton, Philadelphia, January 22, 1797, in Fitzpatrick, *Writings of Washington,* XXXV, 369–371.

15. J. Q. Adams to Secretary of State, The Hague, January 12, 1797, in State Department, Netherlands, II.
16. Pinckney to Pickering, Paris, January 15 and 17, 1797.
17. Pinckney to Pickering, Paris, January 16, 1797.
18. Pinckney to Pickering, Paris, January 24, 1797.
19. Dumas to Washington, Paris, January 24, 1797, in Washington Papers.
20. Pinckney to Washington, Paris, January 25, 1797, in Washington Papers.
21. Rufus King to Washington, London, February 6, 1797, in Washington Papers.
22. Newenham to Washington, Dublin, February 15, 1797, in Washington Papers.
23. Ford, *Works of Jefferson*, VIII, 235–241, especially 240–241. Some of Jefferson's admirers regret the *Anas Papers* as certainly too frank and perhaps imperfectly recalled. The present writer is not of these. To him their occasional acrimony is proof of their sincerity. On August 2, 1793, for example, the author describes Washington in one of his rare fits of temper. It was in cabinet. There had been discussion of the policies of Citizen Genêt on the one hand and of Monsieur and the Comte d'Artois on the other. The President made some remarks. Then

> Knox in a foolish incoherent sort of a speech introduced the *Pasquinade* lately printed, called the funeral of George W——n, and James W——n [Wilson was an Associate Justice of the United States Supreme Court]; King & judge &c. where the President was placed on a guillotine. The President was much inflamed, got into one of those passions when he cannot command himself, ran on much on the personal abuse which had been bestowed on him, defied any man on earth to produce one single act of his since he had been in the govmt which was not done on the purest motives, that he had never repented but once the having slipped the moment of resigning his office, & that was every moment since, that *by god* he had rather be in his grave than in his present situation. That he had rather be on his farm than to be made *emperor of the world* and yet that they were charging him with wanting to be a king. That the *rascal* Freneau sent him 3 of his papers every day, as if he thought he would become the distributor of his papers, that he could see in this nothing but an impudent design to insult him. He ended in this high tone. [*Works of Jefferson*, I, 306–308. August 2, 1793.]

This was doubtless accurate reporting, but may one not detect a certain glee, perhaps a little malice?
24. William Bingham to Washington, Philadelphia, March 25, 1797, in Washington Papers.
25. Washington to James McHenry, Mount Vernon, April 3, 1797, in Fitzpatrick, *Writings of Washington*, XXXV, 430–431.
26. Rufus King to Washington, London, April 26, 1797, in Washington Papers.
27. James McHenry to Washington, May 14, 1797, in Washington Papers.
28. Charles Lee to Washington, Philadelphia, July 24, 1797, in Washington Papers.
29. Washington to Pickering, Mount Vernon, August 29, 1797, in Fitzpatrick, *Writings of Washington*, XXXVI, 18–20.
30. William Vans Murray to Washington, The Hague, August 26, 1797, in Washington Papers. Photostat copy from the collection of Dr. Abraham S. Wolf Rosenbach.
31. Rufus King to Washington, London, September 6, 1797, in Washington Papers.
32. Washington to Lafayette, Mount Vernon, October 8, 1797, in Fitzpatrick, *Writings of Washington*, XXXVI, 40–43.

CHAPTER TWELVE

1. This highly condensed account of Europe in 1798 and the preliminaries to the Egyptian campaign is based on Lavisse, *Histoire de France*, II, 371–385.
2. The Rosetta Stone was one of the most important discoveries of this expedition.
3. Pickering to Washington, Philadelphia, January 20, 1798, in Washington Papers.
4. Washington to Pickering, Mount Vernon, February 6, 1798, in Fitzpatrick, *Writings of Washington*, XXXVI, 155–157.
5. Washington to John Nicholas, Mount Vernon, March 8, 1798, in Fitzpatrick, *Writings of Washington*, XXXVI, 182–184.
6. Fitzpatrick, *Writings of Washington*, 194–237.
7. John Marshall to Washington, Paris, March 8, 1798, in Washington Papers.
8. Washington to Pickering, Mount Vernon, April 16, 1798, in Fitzpatrick, *Writings of Washington*, XXXVI, 248–249.
9. Washington to Hamilton, Mount Vernon, May 27, 1798, in Fitzpatrick, *Writings of Washington*, XXXVI, 271–274.
10. Washington to James Lloyd, Mount Vernon, June 27, 1798, in Fitzpatrick, *Writings of Washington*, XXXVI, 303.
11. Washington to John Adams, Mount Vernon, July 13, 1798, in Fitzpatrick, *Writings of Washington*, XXXVI, 327–329.
12. Joel Barlow to Washington, Paris, October 2, 1798, in Washington Papers.
13. Washington to Lafayette, Mount Vernon, December 25, 1798, in Fitzpatrick, *Writings of Washington*, XXXVII, 64–70.
14. Washington to William Vans Murray, Mount Vernon, December 26, 1798, in Fitzpatrick, *Writings of Washington*, XXXVII, 71–72.
15. Lafayette to Washington, Wittmold, April 20, 1798, in *Mémoires du Lafayette*, VIII, 150–157. The translations are my own.
16. Lafayette to Hamilton, Wittmold, August 12, 1798, in *Mémoires du Lafayette*, VIII, 144–150.

CHAPTER THIRTEEN

1. Pinckney to Washington, June 25, 1799 (enclosing a letter from Major Mountflorence, The Hague, March 12, 1799), in Washington Papers.
2. John Trumbull to Washington, London, March 24, 1799, in Washington Papers.
3. Lafayette to Washington, Vianen, April 19, 1799, in *Mémoires du Lafayette*, VIII, 187–190.
4. Lafayette to Washington, Vianen, May 9, 1799, in *Mémoires du Lafayette*, VIII, 202–207. The translation is my own.
5. Washington to William Vans Murray, Mount Vernon, October 26, 1799, in Fitzpatrick, *Writings of Washington*, XXXVII, 399–400.
6. Washington to James McHenry, Mount Vernon, November 17, 1799, in Fitzpatrick, *Writings of Washington*, XXXVII, 428–429.

EPILOGUE

1. Paine to Monroe, in Moncure Daniel Conway, ed., *The Writings of Thomas Paine*, II, xiii.

BIBLIOGRAPHY

This unpretentious bibliography is far from comprehensive as to the French Revolution, which could be a book in itself. What it does reveal is a liberal use of source materials, direct or reprinted. A further limitation is the slight use of strictly Federalist materials, which usually were pro-English or anti-French, partisanship being bitter. Alexander Hamilton, for example, is ignored. At no time has Washington been lost to sight as the central figure in this story.

Adams, Charles Francis, Editor. *Memoirs of John Quincy Adams, Comprising Portions of his Diary from 1795 to 1848.* 12 vols. Philadelphia: J. B. Lippincott and Co., 1874–1877. Especially Vol. I.

———. *The Works of John Adams, with a Life of the Author.* 10 vols. Boston: Little, Brown and Co., 1856.

American State Papers. Foreign Relations (1789–1828). 6 vols. Washington: Government Printing Office, 1832–1859.

Archives of the State Department of France. États Unis. Vol. XXXV.

Aulard, A. [François Victor Alphonse] *Histoire Politique de la Révolution Française.* Paris: A. Colin, 1901. Translated by Bernard Miall and published under the title *The French Revolution, a Political History, 1789–1804.* London: T. Fisher Unwin, 1910.

Belloc, Hilaire. *Robespierre, 1758–1794.* New York and London: G. P. Putnam's Sons, 1928.

Bemis, Samuel Flagg, Editor. *The American Secretaries of State and their Diplomacy.* 10 vols. New York: A. A. Knopf, 1927–1929. Vol. II covers the incumbencies of Jefferson, Randolph, Pickering and Marshall.

———. *The Jay Treaty: A Study in Commerce and Diplomacy.* New York: The Macmillan Co., 1923.

Beveridge, Albert J. *Life of John Marshall.* 4 vols. Boston and New York: Houghton, Mifflin Co., 1916–1919.

Bond, Beverly W. *The Monroe Mission to France, 1794–1796.* Baltimore: The Johns Hopkins Press, 1907. Bond says (p. 97) that Monroe tried to facilitate C. C. Pinckney's reception in France.

Chinard, Gilbert. *Letters of Lafayette and Jefferson.* Baltimore: The Johns Hopkins Press, 1909; also Paris, 1929.

Conway, Moncure Daniel. *The Life of Thomas Paine; with a history of his literary, political and religious career in America, France and England. To which is added a sketch of Paine by Cobbett.* 2 vols. New York and London: G. P. Putnam's Sons, 1892.

———. *Omitted Chapters of History Disclosed in the life and papers of Edmund Randolph, Governor of Virginia, first attorney-general of the United States, secretary of state.* New York and London: G. P. Putnam's Sons, 1888.

———. *Thomas Paine et la révolution dans les deux mondes.* Paris: Plon-Nourrit and Co., 1900.

"Correspondence of the Comte de Moustier with the Comte de Montmorin, 1787–1789." *American Historical Review,* VIII (1902–1903), 709–733, IX (1903–1904), 86–96.

The Correspondence of French Ministers to the United States, 1791–1797. Vol. II of *The American Historical Association Annual Report for 1903.* Washington, D.C.

Dictionary of National Biography. Edited by Leslie Stephen. 63 vols. New York: Macmillan and Co.; London: Smith, Elder, and Co., 1885–1900.

The Charles William Frederick Dumas Papers. Library of Congress. Dumas was United States secret agent in the Netherlands.

Esmein, A. [Adhémar] *Gouverneur Morris, un Témoin Americain de la Révolution Française.* Paris: Hachette and Co., 1906. Esmein shows Morris' high rating in monarchical society previous to assuming his mission in 1792. Influential friends considered him, though an American, just as eligible for membership in the King's Cabinet as Necker, a Swiss.

Fauchet, Joseph. "Mémoire sur les États Unis d'Amerique." Edited by Carl Ludwig Lokke. *American Historical Association Annual Report for 1936.* Washington, D.C. I, 83–123.

Fay, Bernard. *L'Esprit Révolutionnaire en France et aux États-Unis à la fin du XVIIIe siècle.* Paris: E. Champion, 1925.

Fitzpatrick, John C., Editor. *The Writings of George Washington.* 39 vols. Washington: Government Printing Office, 1931–1944.

Ford, Paul Leicester, Editor. *The Works of Thomas Jefferson.* Federal Edition. 12 vols. New York: G. P. Putnam's Sons, 1904–1905.

Ford, Worthington Chauncey, Editor. *The Writings of George Washington.* 14 vols. New York: G. P. Putnam's Sons, 1889–1893.

————, Editor. *The Writings of John Quincy Adams.* 7 vols. New York: The Macmillan Co., 1913–1917.

Gomel, Charles. *Les Causes Financières de la Révolution Française.* 2 vols. Paris: Guillaumin and Co., 1892–1893.

Gottschalk, Louis R. *The Era of the French Revolution (1715–1815).* Boston: Houghton, Mifflin Co., 1929.

La Grande Encyclopédie. 31 vols. Paris: H. Lamirault and Co., 1886–1902.

Hallgarten, George W. F. *Imperialismus vor 1914.* 2 vols. Munich: C. H. Beck, 1951. A section entitled "Die Französische Revolution und Ihre aussenpolitischen Folgen" (I, 80–84) contrasts the rural background of the Gironde with the industrial fabric of the Mountain. Washington may or may not have recognized this.

Hamilton, Stanislaus Murray, Editor. *The Writings of James Monroe.* 7 vols. New York: G. P. Putnam's Sons, 1898–1903.

Hardy, Charles Oscar. *The Negro Question in the French Revolution.* Menasha, Wisconsin: George Banta Publishing Co., 1919. This University of Chicago doctoral dissertation explores a bypath of the Revolution near America's shores and of undoubted concern to the President, but contains no specific reference to Washington.

Harper, Robert Goodloe. *Observations on the Dispute between the United States and France. Addressed to his Constituents, in May, 1797.* Philadelphia (publisher not indicated) and London: Philanthropic Press, 1797. In the Duane Pamphlets, Vol. CXXXV, Peter Force Collection, Library of Congress, Rare Books Division. This is a lucid and vigorous account of the United States' grievances against France from Genêt to the time of writing.

Hazen, Charles Downer. *Contemporary Opinion of the French Revolution.* Baltimore: The Johns Hopkins Press, 1897. Part Two, "Opinions of Americans at Home," demonstrates the hysteric intensity of sympathy for France among large sections of the populace right down to 1797 and the undeclared war with France.

————. *The French Revolution.* 2 vols. New York: Henry Holt and Co., 1932.

The Jefferson Papers. Library of Congress.

Kimball, Marie G. "William Short, Jefferson's Only 'Son.'" *North American Review,* CCXXIII (September, October, November, 1926), 471–486.

King, Charles R., Editor. *Life and Correspondence of Rufus King.* 6 vols. New York: G. P. Putnam's Sons, 1894–1900. These volumes, especially I and II, contain much material on American reaction to the French Revolution, with only an occasional reference to Washington.

Lavisse, Ernest, Editor. *Histoire de France Contemporaine depuis la Révolution jusqu'à La Paix de 1919.* 10 vols. Paris: Hachette, 1920–1922. A classic. Volumes I and II cover the Revolutionary period. The present study makes extensive reference to them.

357

"Letters of Washington and Lafayette." *Old South Leaflets*, IV (1886), 76–100 (No. 98, p. 14).

Lévis-Mirepoix, Duc de. *Aventures d'une famille française*. Paris and Geneva: La Palatine, 1955. The history of France as experienced by a single family.

Madelin, Louis. *The French Revolution*. (Translated from the French.) New York: G. P. Putnam's Sons, 1916.

Mathews, Shailer. *The French Revolution, 1789–1815*. New York, London, Bombay: Longmans, Green and Co., 1901. This is an exceptionally well balanced study.

Mémoires, Correspondance et Manuscrits du Général Lafayette. 6 vols. Brussels: The Lafayette family, 1837–1838. There are other editions.

Monroe, James. *A View of the Conduct of the Executive in the Foreign Affairs of the United States, as connected with the Mission to the French Republic, During the Years 1794, 5, and 6*. Philadelphia: Benjamin Franklin Bache in *The Aurora*, 1797; also London, 1798. Abridged edition in the Duane Pamphlets, Vol. CXXXV, Peter Force Collection, Library of Congress, Rare Books Division. A refutation of Charles Goodloe Harper's address, above. Monroe's vindication is particularly hostile to Gouverneur Morris as a friend of monarchy, and to the Washington Administration, which retained him in France notwithstanding the known wishes of the Republic. Several documents are appended.

Morison, S. E. *The Oxford History of the United States, 1783–1917*. 2 vols. Oxford: Oxford University Press; London: Henry Milford, 1927.

Morris, Ann Cary, Editor. *The Diary and Letters of Gouverneur Morris*. 2 vols. New York: Charles Scribner's Sons, 1888.

Morris, Gouverneur. *A Diary of the French Revolution*. Edited by Beatrix Cary Davenport. 2 vols. Boston: Houghton, Mifflin Co., 1939.

Mosnier, [J. B. F.] Henry. *Le Château de Chavaniac-Lafayette*. Le Puy, Imprimerie Marchessou Fils, 1883.

Otto, Louis Guillaume, Comte de Mosloy. *Considérations sur la Conduite du Gouvernement Americain envers la France, depuis le commencement de la Révolution jusqu'en 1797*. With an introduction by Gilbert Chinard. Princeton: Princeton University Press, 1945.

Randolph, Edmund. *A Vindication of Mr. Randolph's Resignation*. Philadelphia: Samuel H. Smith, 1795.

———. *Political Truth or Animadversions on the Past and Present State of Public Affairs with an Inquiry into the Truth of the Charges Preferred against Mr. Randolph*. Philadelphia: Samuel H. Smith, 1796.

Rose, J. Holland. *The Revolutionary and Napoleonic Era, 1789–1815*. Cambridge, England: Cambridge University Press, 1898.

Sears, Louis Martin. *George Washington*. New York: Thomas Y. Crowell Co., 1932.

The William Short Papers. Library of Congress.

Thomas, Jules, Editor. *Correspondance Inédite de la Fayette, 1793–1801*. Paris: Delagrave, 1903. Part Two, "Lettres de Prison—Lettres d'Exil."

Trescot, William Henry. *Diplomatic History of the Administrations of Washington and Adams, 1789–1801.* Boston: Little, Brown and Co., 1857. Based largely upon primary source material, this work has been utilized often by later authors. It is unfriendly alike to Gouverneur Morris and Citizen Genêt.

Turner, Frederick Jackson. "The Policy of France toward the Mississippi Valley in the Period of Washington and Adams." *American Historical Review,* X (1904–1905), 249–279. This article tells of persistent French interest in Louisiana from De Moustier to Napoleon, and treats of a phase of the French Revolution of immediate concern to Washington, and in part influencing portions of the Farewell Address.

United States Department of State. Diplomatic Despatches, France.

————. Diplomatic Despatches, The Hague and Spain. 1792–1795.

————. Diplomatic Despatches. Netherlands. Vols. I and II.

————. Foreign Letters. Vol. CXXI.

————. Instructions, United States Ministers. Vols. I–III.

————. Miscellaneous Letters. July to September, 1794.

Vallotton, Henry. *Marie-Antoinette et Fersen.* Paris and Geneva: La Palatine, 1952.

The Washington Papers. Library of Congress.

Winsor, Justin. *Narrative and Critical History of America.* 8 vols. Boston and New York: Houghton, Mifflin and Co., 1884–1889. Not extensively used in the present study.

359

INDEX

Edited by GEORGIANA WARD STRICKLAND
Designed by RAYMOND L. COLBY
Set in Linotype Baskerville and Caslon
display faces
Printed on Warren's Olde Style
Antique Wove
Bound in Bancrofts Lynnene cloth
Manufactured in the
United States of America